This optimized ReadHowYouWant edition contains the complete, unabridged text of the original publisher's edition. Other aspects of the book may vary from the original edition.

Set in 16 pt. Verdana

ReadHowYouWant partners with publishers to provide books for ALL Kinds of Readers. For more information about Becoming A RHYW Registered Reader and to find more titles in your preferred format, visit:
www.readhowyouwant.com

TABLE OF CONTENTS

References for the Rest of Us!™

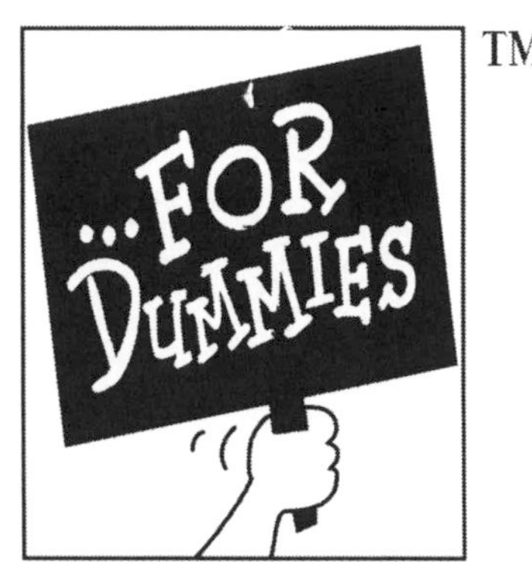

BESTSELLING BOOK SERIES

Do you find that traditional reference books are overloaded with technical details and advice you'll never use? Do you postpone important life decisions because you just don't want to deal with them? Then our ... *For Dummies* ® business and general reference book series is for you.

...For Dummies business and general reference books are written for those frustrated and hardworking souls who know they aren't dumb, but find that the myriad of personal and business issues and the accompanying horror stories make them feel helpless.... *For Dummies* books use a lighthearted approach, a down-to-earth style, and even cartoons and humorous icons to dispel fears and build confidence. Lighthearted but not lightweight, these books are

perfect survival guides to solve your everyday personal and business problems.

"More than a publishing phenomenon, 'Dummies' is a sign of the times."
—The New York Times

"...you won't go wrong buying them."
—Walter Mossberg, Wall Street Journal, on IDG Books' ...For Dummies books

"A world of detailed and authoritative information is packed into them..."
—U.S. News and World Report

Already, millions of satisfied readers agree. They have made ... ***For Dummies*** **the #1 introductory level computer book series and a best-selling business book series. They have written asking for more. So, if you're looking for the best and easiest way to learn about business and other general reference topics, look to ...** ***For Dummies*** **to give you a helping hand.**

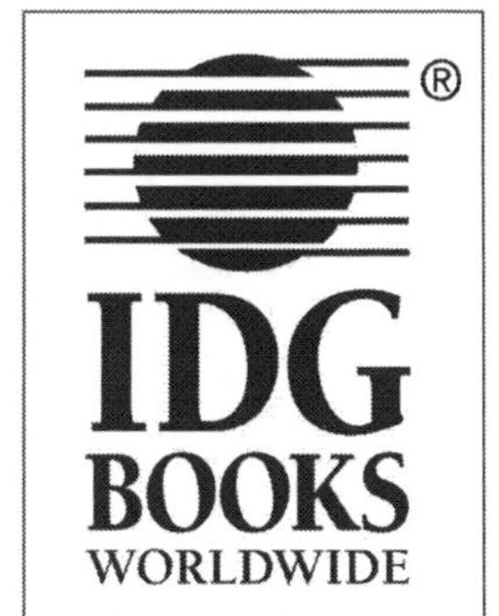
IDG
BOOKS
WORLDWIDE

About the Authors

James M. Rippe, M.D., is a board-certified, cardiologist who graduated from Harvard Medical School with postgraduate training at Massachusetts General Hospital and the University of Massachusetts Medical School. He currently serves on the faculty as an Associate Professor of Medicine (Cardiology) at Tufts University School of Medicine. He is the Founder and Director of the Rippe Lifestyle Institute and Founder and Director of the Rippe Health Assessment at Celebration Health.

Early in his career, Dr. Rippe specialized in heart catheterization, one of the most complicated and technically difficult procedures in cardiology, used in the diagnosis of severe heart disease. After performing thousands of these procedures, Dr. Rippe was frustrated that individuals required heart catheterization—and often two or three of them—usually because they took such poor care of themselves. He believed that a better way of taking care of the heart had to exist, so he founded the Rippe Lifestyle Institute, which has grown into the largest exercise, nutrition, weight management, and lifestyle research laboratory in the world. Every day, Dr. Rippe and his team study individuals who are striving to improve their health in general and their cardiovascular health in particular.

In addition to being a cardiologist, Dr. Rippe is also a restaurant-trained French chef. He served as the pastry chef in a French restaurant in Boston before going to medical school. Recently, he served for three years as the medical editor of the Food Network in New York.

Amy Myrdal, M.S., R.D., is a registered dietitian with a Master of Science degree in Nutrition Communication from Tufts University School of Nutrition Science and Policy in Boston and a Bachelor of Science degree in Dietetics from the University of California Davis.

Having had insulin-dependent (Type 1) diabetes since the age of 7, Amy developed an early respect and understanding of the critical relationship between food choices and health, as well as an early interest in and passion for cooking. At the age of 9, she opened the Sunshine Diner in her parents home, where she prepared and served brunches for her family and relatives. Today Amy's cooking focuses on creating and preparing healthful meals from a variety of cuisines for herself, her family, and her friends.

Formerly a Senior Research Dietitian at the Rippe Lifestyle Institute, today Amy is the Director of Marketing and Communication for the organization. As a research dietitian, Amy focused on the relationship between food choices and health, and, in particular, on food choices that decrease risk of heart disease. As the Director of Marketing and

Communication for the Rippe Lifestyle Institute, Amy is now focused on communicating research results to the medical community and the public at large.

Amy is a member of the American Institute of Wine and Food, as well as the Food and Culinary Professionals, an American Dietetic Association Dietetic Practice Group composed of dietitians who focus on teaching patients and clients about healthful food choices and culinary skills that can enhance the quality of life and health.

Angela Harley Kirkpatrick, R.D., is a registered dietitian who received her Bachelor of Science degree in Food and Nutrition from the University of Maine (Orono) and completed her dietetic internship at New York Institute of Technology in Old Westbury, New York.

After her father's death at the age of 43 from heart disease, Angela devoted great attention to studying and teaching about the importance of healthful lifestyle habits for patients and clients of all ages and backgrounds.

As a medical professional, Angela provides patients and clients with the support they need to develop healthful, lifelong eating and activity habits. Angela and her husband, Jeremy, enjoy spending time creating nutritionally balanced menus and great tasting recipes that have pleased so many clients.

Angela is currently self-employed as a nutrition consultant to a variety of companies and fitness clubs in the Greater Boston area.

Mary Abbott Waite, Ph.D., is an Atlanta-based writer and editorial consultant with a Ph.D. in English from Duke University. She specializes in health, fitness, and consumer issues, and collaborated with Dr. Rippe on one of his previous books, *Fit Over Forty.* With two parents who have had bypass surgery, Mary Abbott also enjoys cooking and creating heart-healthy recipes to entertain family and friends at "Chez M.A.," a.k.a., her kitchen.

ABOUT IDG BOOKS WORLD WIDE

Welcome to the world of IDG Books Worldwide.

IDG Books Worldwide, Inc., is a subsidiary of International Data Group, the world's largest publisher of computer-related information and the leading global provider of information services on information technology. IDG was founded more than 30 years ago by Patrick J. McGovern and now employs more than 9,000 people worldwide. IDG publishes more than 290 computer publications in over 75 countries. More than 90 million people read one or more IDG publications each month.

Launched in 1990, IDG Books Worldwide is today the #1 publisher of best-selling computer books in the United States. We are proud to have received eight awards from the Computer Press Association in recognition of editorial excellence and three from Computer Currents' First Annual Readers' Choice Awards. Our bestselling ... *For Dummies*® series has more than 50 million copies in print with translations in 31 languages. IDG Books Worldwide, through a joint venture with IDG's Hi-Tech Beijing, became the first U.S. publisher to publish a computer book in the People's Republic of China. In record time, IDG Books Worldwide has become the first choice for millions of readers around the world who want to learn how to better manage their businesses.

Our mission is simple: Every one of our books is designed to bring extra value and skill-building instructions to the reader. Our books are written by experts who understand and care about our readers. The knowledge base of our editorial staff comes from years of experience in publishing, education, and journalism—experience we use to produce books to carry us into the new millennium. In short, we care about books, so we attract the best people. We devote special attention to details such as audience, interior design, use of icons, and illustrations. And because we use an efficient process of authoring, editing, and desktop publishing our books electronically, we can spend more time ensuring superior content and less time on the technicalities of making books.

You can count on our commitment to deliver high-quality books at competitive prices on topics you want to read about. At IDG Books Worldwide, we continue in the IDG tradition of delivering quality for more than 30 years. You'll find no better book on a subject than one from IDG Books Worldwide.

John Kilcullen
Chairman and CEO
IDG Books Worldwide, Inc.

Image A

IDG is the world's leading IT media, research and exposition company. Founded in 1964, IDG had 1997 revenues of $2.05 billion and has more than 9,000 employees worldwide. IDG offers the widest range of media options that reach IT buyers in 75 countries representing 95% of worldwide IT spending. IDG's diverse product and services portfolio spans six key areas including print publishing, online publishing, expositions and conferences, market research, education and training, and global marketing services. More than 90 million people read one or more of IDG's 290 magazines and newspapers, including IDG's leading global brands—Computerworld, PC World, Network

World, Macworld and the Channel World family of publications. IDG Books Worldwide is one of the fastest-growing computer book publishers in the world, with more than 700 titles in 36 languages. The "...For Dummies®" series alone has more than 50 million copies in print. IDG offers online users the largest network of technology-specific Web sites around the world through IDG.net(http://www.idg.net), which comprises more than 225 targeted Web sites in 55 countries worldwide. International Data Corporation (IDC) is the world's largest provider of information technology data, analysis and consulting, with research centers in over 41 countries and more than 400 research analysts worldwide. IDG World Expo is a leading producer of more than 168 globally branded conferences and expositions in 35 countries including E3 (Electronic Entertainment Expo), Macworld Expo, ComNet, Windows World Expo, ICE (Internet Commerce Expo), Agenda, DEMO, and Spotlight. IDG's training subsidiary, ExecuTrain, is the world's largest computer training company, with more than 230 locations worldwide and 785 training courses. IDG Marketing Services helps industry-leading IT companies build international brand recognition by developing global integrated marketing programs via IDG's print, online and exposition products worldwide. Further information about the company can be found at www.idg.co m.

1/26/00

Dedication

To Stephanie, Hart, Jaelin, and Devon—you are safe in my heart.

Dr. Rippe's Acknowledgments

Many individuals provided valuable advice and support during the time it took to complete this book. Several deserve special recognition for particularly significant contributions.

First, my main collaborator, Mary Abbott Waite, makes undertaking complex writing projects not only possible, but sometimes even pleasurable. This is the third book (following *Fit Over Forty* and *The Healthy Heart For Dummies*) on which Mary Abbott and I have collaborated. Mary Abbott is every writer's dream collaborator. She not only has the ability to take complex medical and nutritional topics and make them understandable, user-friendly, and practical, but she also has a knack for catching the nuances and cadences of various writers' voices (in this case my own, Amy Myrdal's, and Angela Kirkpatrick's) and blending them into a seamless whole. In the midst of this complexity, she manages to always keep her cool and work with great diligence, competence, and grace.

Second, my coauthors Amy Myrdal and Angela Kirkpatrick, are not only superb clinical and research nutritionists, but also wonderful writers. They contributed not only very important information but also outstanding writing skills. Amy Myrdal is also blessed with incredible editorial and organizational skills, and, along with Mary Abbott, did a magnificent job blending sound clinical nutrition with a deft and lively writing touch and a skillful and adventuresome approach to food.

Third, my Editorial Director and good friend, Beth Porcaro, always keeps a watchful eye on every editorial project that emerges from our organization. She manages to keep the whole process on track with superb editorial skills, good humor, and grace under pressure.

Of course, this book would not have been possible without the passionate commitment of top chefs from around the United States who agreed to contribute recipes that are included throughout this book. These individuals took seriously the challenge of blending lively, adventuresome cuisine with heart-healthy nutrition. Contributing chefs include:

Paul Agnelli, Greg Atkinson, René Bajeux, Hans Bergmann, Thierry Bregeon, Ignatius Change, Garrett Cho, Marcel-Henri Cochet, Alfonso Constriciani, Felicien Cueff, Michael Degenhart, Jody Denton, Rocco DiSpirito, Gary Donlick, Jonathan Eismann, Michael Foley, Edward Gannon, Todd Gray, David Gross, Dale Gussett, Gordon Hamersley, Sandra Holland, Brian Houlihan, Kevin T. Jones, Saleh Joudah, Bernard Kantak, Constantin Kerageorgiou, Ris Lacoste, Fredéric Lange, Laura Maioglio, Joe Mannke, Frank McClelland, James McDevitt, Stacey McDevitt, Michael Mina, Carrie Nahabedian, Patrick O'Connell, Bradley Ogden, Alvaro Ojeda, Douglas Organ, Marius Pavlak, Walter Pisano, Sylvain Portay, Nora Pouillon, Jacky Robert, Toni Robertson, Jeffrey Russell, J.P. Samuelson, Marcus Samuelsson, Mary Ann Saporito-Boothroyd, Michael Schwartz, Kimberly Shaker, Hans Spirig, RoxSand Suarez, Allen Susser, Mark Tarbell, Chris Toole, David Waltuck, and last but not least, Peter Zampaglione.

Chefs' titles, restaurant names, and restaurant locations can be found with each of their recipes.

In addition to the contributing chefs, we would like to acknowledge the various assistants and public relations professionals who worked with us to get recipes from the chefs. In many instances, these professionals were the gatekeepers, and we sincerely appreciate their assistance in helping us meet our deadlines and answering our numerous questions on ingredients and techniques.

The initial concept for this book as a companion to my previous IDG book, *The Healthy Heart For Dummies,* was developed by my friend and former Executive Editor at IDG Books, Tami Booth, in conjunction with my literary agent, Reid Boates. Tami and Reid are good friends and bright and hard-working professionals. Subsequent editors at IDG including Elizabeth Kuball, Emily Nolan, and Linda Ingroia brought great passion and expertise to this process.

The talented research staff at my laboratory, the Rippe Lifestyle Institute, in Shrewsbury, Massachusetts, kept a busy research outfit moving forward while making time for Amy, Angela, Mary Abbott, and me to maintain the arduous process of writing and editing this book.

In addition, my clinical facility, the Rippe Health Assessment at Celebration Health, offered a venue to test many of these nutritional principles in a clinical setting. My superb staff there includes Rick Wassel, Director of Sales and Marketing; Chris Young, R.N., Clinic Manager; Sara McCoy, my executive assistant; Kim Hamilton, RHA Ambassador extraordinaire; Carol Benson, our marketing assistant; and Tara Geise, M.S., R.D., our Director of Nutrition. All have provided important insights and clinical corroboration of many of the concepts discussed in this book.

My own background as a part-time chef and lover of fine food has been motivated and informed by many individuals. Odette Bery, founder and owner of Another Season was my first mentor in the kitchen. My colleagues at the Food Network when I worked there as Medical Editor, Donna Hanover and David Rosengarten, were always quick to help me with nutritional advice as well as insights about how to communicate it to the public. Every cookbook that Julia Child has written is a gem, and the few opportunities that I have had to interact with her over the years have always left me inspired to believe that fine cooking and good health can go hand in hand.

My responsibilities and commitments as a cardiologist, researcher, teacher, consultant, husband, father, and writer require meticulous attention to details and schedules. My executive assistant, Carol Moreau, does a phenomenal job keeping all of these important aspects of my life moving forward.

Finally, but certainly not least, my darling wife, Stephanie Hart Rippe, has provided the love, safety, and security to keep a strenuous work schedule going with the firm knowledge that I am wrapped in the love of an incredible family. She sets a phenomenal example, not only as a mother, but also as a superb chef who emphasizes the joy of fresh foods and subtle and delicate flavors to our entire family. While serving as a full-time television news anchor through three pregnancies, she has given me three beautiful daughters—Hart Elizabeth Rippe, Jaelin Davis Rippe, and Devon Marshall Rippe—who have convinced me that I am the most loved man in the universe. Our capable assistant and oldest daughter, Natasha Kocberg provides a wonderful example as an older sister to our daughters and keeps our household moving forward, all the while balancing full-time studies as a college student. These five individuals comprise the "Rippe Women" and make it all worth-while.

I am grateful to all of these individuals and many others who have helped along the way. I hope that this cookbook reflects the expertise and passion for good nutrition, great food, and cardiac health that unites us in this effort. I hope that this book helps individuals who are engaged in the ongoing battle against our nation's number one killer—heart disease—to prevent it or manage it by providing useful facts and information. Above all, I hope this book creates the indelible impression that good-tasting food and cardiac health can go hand in hand!

Amy Myrdal's Acknowledgments

I would like to thank Dr. Rippe for the opportunity to participate in such a meaningful and pleasurable experience. My love of cooking and food is only surpassed by my love for writing, so this project was a joy for me to be involved with so intimately, from conception to publication.

I would also like to thank my best friend and partner, Jefferson, whose love, patience, support, and encouragement helped me get through the most tedious and stressful days during the past year. Jefferson also eagerly taste-tested and critiqued recipes I created for this book. His honesty and taste buds encouraged me to create better and better recipes.

I would also like to thank my fearless assistant and intern, Melanie Mulcahy, whose assistance and enthusiasm for this project helped keep this book on track. From identifying top chefs to analyzing recipes to researching unique ingredients and equipment to creating recipes for this book and even coauthoring The Part of Tens chapter, Melanie was a pleasure to work with during the entire project.

Finally, I would like to thank Gail Pettit for her administrative assistance with this project. Gail's professionalism, expertise, and uncanny sense of humor helped make the numerous mailings we did seem like a breeze.

Angela Kirkpatrick's Acknowledgments

In addition to individuals who were mentioned by the other authors, I would like to thank my husband and best friend, Jeremy Kirkpatrick, whose support, encouragement, and culinary expertise kept me going when inspiration was lacking but a deadline was looming.

Mary Abbott Waite's Acknowledgments

I join the other authors in thanking the members of the Cookbook Team and the professionals at the Rippe Lifestyle Institute for going the extra mile to make this book accurate, timely, useful, and fun for our readers.

Publisher's Acknowledgments

We're proud of this book; please register your comments through our IDG Books Worldwide Online Registration Form located at http://my2cents.dummies.com.

Some of the people who helped bring this book to market include the following:

Acquisitions, Editorial, and Media Development

Project Editor: Elizabeth Netedu Kuball
Executive Editor: Tammerly Booth
Acquisitions Editors: Emily Nolan, Linda Ingroia
Acquisitions Coordinator: Karen Young
Technical Editor: Lea Ann Holzmeister, R.D.
Recipe Tester: Laura Pensiero
Editorial Director: Kristin A. Cocks
Editorial Administrator: Michelle L. Hacker

Production

Project Coordinator: Regina Snyder
Layout and Graphics: Amy Adrian, Joe Bucki, Tracy K. Oliver, Jill Piscitelli, Brent Savage, Kathie Schutte, Brian Torwelle, Erin Zeltner
Special Art: Elizabeth Kurtzman
Proofreaders: Laura Albert, Corey Bowen, Nancy L. Reinhardt, Charles Spencer

Indexer: Sharon Hilgenberg

Special Help

Melissa Bluhm

***

General and Administrative

IDG Books Worldwide, Inc.: John Kilcullen, CEO

IDG Books Technology Publishing Group: Richard Swadley, Senior Vice President and Publisher; Walter R. Bruce III, Vice President and Publisher; Joseph Wikert, Vice President and Publisher; Mary Bednarek, Vice President and Director, Product Development; Andy Cummings, Publishing Director, General User Group; Mary C. Corder, Editorial Director; Barry Pruett, Publishing Director

IDG Books Consumer Publishing Group: Roland Elgey, Senior Vice President and Publisher; Kathleen A. Welton, Vice President and Publisher; Kevin Thornton, Acquisitions Manager; Kristin A. Cocks, Editorial Director

IDG Books Internet Publishing Group: Brenda McLaughlin, Senior Vice President and Publisher; Sofia Marchant, Online Marketing Manager

IDG Books Production for Branded Press: Debbie Stailey, Director of Production; Cindy L. Phipps, Manager of Project Coordination, Production Proofreading, and Indexing; Tony Augsburger, Manager of Prepress, Reprints, and Systems; Laura Carpenter, Production Control Manager; Shelley Lea, Supervisor of Graphics and Design; Debbie J. Gates, Production Systems Specialist; Robert Springer, Supervisor of Proofreading; Kathie Schutte, Production Supervisor

Packaging and Book Design: Patty Page, Manager, Promotions Marketing

***

The publisher would like to give special thanks to Patrick J. McGovern, without whom this book would not have been possible.

***

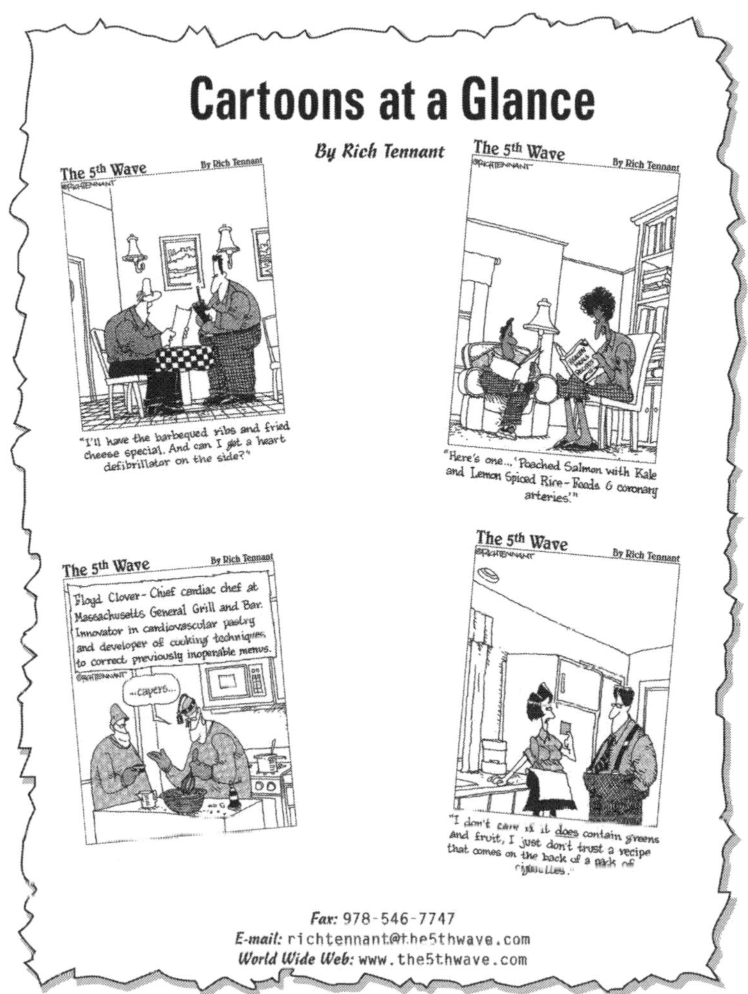

Cartoons at a Glance
By Rich Tennant
The 5th Wave
By Rich Tennant
"I'll have the barbequed ribs and fried cheese special. And can I get a heart defibrillator on the side?"
The 5th Wave
By Rich Tennant
"Here's one...'Poached Salmon with Kale and Lemon Spiced Rice - Feeds 6 coronary arteries.'"
The 5th Wave
By Rich Tennant
Floyd Clover - Chief cardiac chef at Massachusetts General Grill and Bar. Innovator in cardiovascular pastry and developer of cooking techniques to correct previously inoperable menus.
...capers...
The 5th Wave
By Rich Tennant
"I don't care if it does contain greens and fruit, I just don't trust a recipe that comes on the back of a pack of cigarettes."
Fax: 978-546-7747
E-mail: richtennant@the5thwave.com
World Wide Web: www.the5thwave.com

Image B

Recipes at a Glance

Appetizers and Snacks

Chilled Hapa Shrimp Rolls with Thai Citrus Dipping Sauce

Diver-Caught Maine Sea Scallops with Grapefruit

Garlic, Sun-Dried Tomato, and Herb Cheese Spread

Homemade Dill and Celery Seed Hummus

Jicama Chips with Fresh Salsa

Lafayette's Chesapeake Oysters with Asian Scallion Sauce

Rice Vermicelli and Salad Rolls with Peanut Sauce

Smoked Salmon Tartare

Spicy White Bean Dip

Taylor Bay Scallops with Uni and Mustard Oil

Warm Oysters in Kumquat and Verjus Sauce

Yellow Tomato and Fennel Gazpacho

Beverages

Blackberry Lemonade

Chocolate Banana Soy Shake

Citrus Tea

Dana's Sangria

Fruit and Yogurt Smoothie

Breakfasts and Brunches

Apple-Blackberry Soufflé
Eggs Benedict with Asparagus and Low-Fat Hollandaise Sauce
Homemade Granola
Mark's Low-Fat Oat Bran Muffins with Fresh Peaches
Pacific Time's Broiled Pink Florida Grapefruit with Wild Flower Honey
Pan-Roasted Alaskan Halibut with Red and Yellow Pepper Coulis
Peach Scones
Popeye's Favorite Breakfast
Pumpkin Cheesecake Muffins
Sweet Potato Hash Browns

Desserts

Caramelized Peach Cake Roll
Chilled Melon Soup with Anise Hyssop
Chilled Strawberry Soup with Champagne
Chocolate Meringue Mousse
Cranberry Macadamia Nut Biscotti
Dark Fudge Brownies
Nutty Cran-Apple Crisp
Peanut Butter Banana Cookies
Phyllo-Crusted Berry Cobbler
Poached Pears with Orange Yogurt Sauce
Red Fruits Soup
Schaum Torte with Fruit Compote

Poultry and Meat

Salads

Salsas and Sauces

Seafood

Husk-Wrapped Salmon with Toasted Israeli Couscous and Grilled Corn Relish

Grilled Copper River Salmon with Rhubarb and Ginger Chutney

Lavender-Grappa Glazed Tuna

Lime-Marinated Shrimp

Maine Halibut with Basil Mustard Crust Served with Sherry Onions and Portobello Mushrooms with Baby Spinach

Red Snapper with Braised Fennel and Spinach

San Francisco Crab and Wild Fennel Cioppino

Sautéed Halibut with Roasted Fennel and Swiss Chard

Seared Ahi Tuna with Tomatoes, Lime, and Basil

Seared Scallops in Grilled Eggplant (Lasagna-Style) with Mango Salsa

Spinach-Wrapped Halibut with Yellow Tomato Sauce and Creamy Asparagus Polenta

Steamed Trout Stuffed with Root Vegetables and Truffle Vinaigrette

Stuffed Cylinder Potatoes with Duxelle Mushrooms and Vegetable Jus

Yellowfin Tuna with Green Gazpacho Sauce

Side dishes

Braise of Spring Vegetables

Cinnamon-Roasted New Potatoes

Maple-Syrup-Roasted Acorn Squash with Fresh Herbs

Organic Root Vegetable Risotto

Soups

Vegetarian Entrées

THE INFORMATION IN THIS REFERENCE IS NOT INTENDED TO SUBSTITUTE FOR EXPERT MEDICAL ADVICE OR TREATMENT; IT IS DESIGNED TO HELP YOU MAKE INFORMED CHOICES. BECAUSE EACH INDIVIDUAL IS UNIQUE, A PHYSICIAN MUST DIAGNOSE CONDITIONS AND SUPERVISE TREATMENTS FOR EACH INDIVIDUAL HEALTH PROBLEM. IF AN INDIVIDUAL IS UNDER A DOCTOR'S CARE AND RECEIVES ADVICE CONTRARY TO INFORMATION PROVIDED IN THIS REFERENCE, THE DOCTOR'S ADVICE SHOULD BE FOLLOWED, AS IT IS BASED ON THE UNIQUE CHARACTERISTICS OF THAT INDIVIDUAL.

Introduction

Julia Child in her classic book, *The Way to Cook* (published by Knopf), writes of her concern that low-fat cooking may rob us of "the pleasures of the table." I couldn't agree more! There is no reason for low-fat, low-cholesterol, heart-healthy cooking to rob us of the pleasures of food. Eating is one of the great joys of life. And food doesn't have to be grim and punishing in order for it to be healthy for your heart. In this book, with the assistance of over 50 top chefs, I show you how to make heart-healthy cooking one of the great "pleasures of the table." You'll be surprised at how simple measures can help you cut the fat without cutting the taste. The recipes in this book are not your run-of-the-mill low-fat recipes. Here, you'll find *gourmet* recipes that are easy to make and taste great.

Although I care passionately about the links between nutrition and the healthy heart, I am not a food cop. My background as both a cardiologist and a chef make me uniquely suited not only to care for your heart but also to provide you with meals that won't leave you feeling deprived. I recognize that in order for people to change their habits, they must be given food options that are tasty and exciting. The nutrition aspects of food must meld with pleasure and taste. So *The Healthy Heart Cookbook For Dummies* is about great tasting, heart-healthy nutrition. I want to make you the heart-healthiest, most satisfied eater—and reader—ever to walk this planet.

The Bad News

The *Surgeon General's Report on Nutrition* reports that eight out of the ten leading causes of death in the United States have a nutrition or alcohol component. Leading the list is ... you guessed it, heart disease! Failing to pay attention to proper nutrition significantly increases your risk of coronary heart disease, hypertension, elevated cholesterol, and obesity and puts you at an unacceptably high risk for dying from any one of these conditions or a combination of them.

Consider these two facts about everyday life in the United States:

- **Food permeates virtually every aspect of our lives.** We need food in order to maintain life, of course, but we rely on food for much more than that. Food is part of our celebrations and our sense of community. We serve food at virtually every gathering, whether we are celebrating a joyous event or mourning a sad one. Food provides nourishment, comfort, and pleasure. And, for most Americans, food is abundant. In fact, every day, the food industry produces 3,700 calories for each American man, woman, and child—far more than we need. (On average, adult women need 1,800 calories daily; adult men, 2,400.) Unlike many people in other parts of the world and some in our own country, most of us simply have access to *too much* food.

- **We Americans are locked in a ferocious battle with a very powerful enemy: heart disease.** This enemy causes more deaths each year than any other disease in the United States—over one million. In fact, together, heart disease and stroke, two related conditions, are responsible for more deaths each year than *all other diseases combined!* Just take a look at the following statistics, and you'll understand the seriousness of this disease:
    - Heart disease kills one American every 33 seconds.
    - Heart disease does not discriminate based on gender or race. It's the number one killer of men and women of all races.
    - The risk factors for heart disease—including high blood pressure, high cholesterol, physical inactivity, obesity, and smoking—leave no family in America untouched.

The Good News

If you already have heart disease or a related condition such as high blood pressure, elevated cholesterol, or diabetes, what you eat and how you eat it can either assist in the treatment of these conditions or severely undermine the effectiveness of any treatment. This link between nutrition and coronary heart disease (CHD) is so profound that every scientific and medical panel of experts studying the issues in the last decade or more has recommended proper nutrition as *the* key lifestyle measure in combating all of these significant problems and in lowering your risk of developing them in the first place.

The good news is that it's not hard to learn what you need to know and to take the simple steps, including cooking with great healthy-heart recipes, that will help you lower your risk of developing heart disease or manage its manifestations if you already have it.

About This Book

When my staff and I at the Rippe Lifestyle Institute decided to write a *gourmet* heart-healthy cookbook, we knew that we would need the assistance of the top culinary minds in America. Fortunately, I am blessed with staff research dietitians who are as passionate about food and cooking as they are about cardiac health and nutrition. After identifying the top chefs in the top markets in the United States, we asked them to participate in this unique health and culinary journey. The response was overwhelming. Chefs wrote back sharing their favorite recipes along with stories and anecdotes not only about their restaurants and cooking, but also about their own cardiac health. The result is a book unlike any other on the market—and one we hope you'll enjoy!

This book is about healthy eating. Just as important, it's about great tasting, pleasurable eating. But in order for you to understand the importance of food in maintaining overall health, and cardiac health in particular, we provide a solid background into heart health up front.

Combating the ongoing epidemic of heart disease is the greatest health issue in the United States today. And food plays a primary role in your fight against this proven enemy. In fact, food can be your first line of defense and your greatest ally, or it can be your greatest source of weakness and vulnerability. The choice is yours. The fact that you've picked up this book is proof that you're at least interested in figuring out what it takes to cook heart-healthy meals. And you've come to the right place!

The Healthy Heart Cookbook For Dummies can help you enlist good nutrition and good cooking—no, make that *great* cooking—in your quest for health and pleasure. It's a collaboration between myself (a board-certified cardiologist with a background as a chef), the superb nutrition staff at the Rippe Lifestyle Institute (which I direct), and over 50 top chefs in the United States. Together, we set the challenge to do something that had never been done before: produce a book on heart-healthy cooking that features *gourmet* heart-healthy recipes.

Our goal is not only to provide you with the facts about heart-healthy nutrition, but also to give you some practical and simple tips on how to incorporate these changes into your daily lifestyle. To please your palate, top chefs from across the United States have provided over 100 reasons to eat "heart-smart"—recipes that are not only gourmet but also heart-healthy. But the chefs and I haven't worked alone. Amy Myrdal, M.S., R.D., and Angela H. Kirkpatrick, R.D., research dietitians at my laboratory, have contributed recipes and dozens of tips to make it easy to incorporate the foods and techniques featured in the recipes into your healthy-heart kitchen and cooking. With such a fantastic team working for you, you can't go wrong!

The Healthy Heart For Dummies: A shameless plug

You may be aware that I have written another book that bears a similar title to this one. That book, *The Healthy Heart For Dummies,* was published several months before this book. While *The Healthy Heart Cookbook For Dummies* is intended to, and certainly can, stand alone, I believe that it is optimum to own both books. This is particularly true if you, or a member of your family, has significant heart disease. In *The Healthy Heart For Dummies* I provide an "owner's manual" on how to manage virtually every significant heart disease. Thus, while this book will focus on nutrition and great recipes, my previous book emphasized more specific cardiac conditions and factors in daily life that make an enormous difference in whether you ever develop those conditions and how they are treated if you or a family member does have them. So, if you will allow me a shameless plug, I recommend that if you are approaching this topic for the first time, you use both books together!

Foolish Assumptions

Because you've picked up this book—or had it thrust upon you by a loving family member or friend—I'm assuming that you are, first and foremost, interested in taking care of your heart. But coming in a close second in your list of priorities is making sure you don't have to give up taste. You want a book that will give you the nutritional and medical information you need, along with some great-tasting recipes that don't skimp on the pleasure factor of food.

In addition, you may be scared by a recent diagnosis of heart disease in yourself or a loved one. Or you may be trying to lower your risk of developing heart disease, perhaps because your doctor cautioned you or heart disease runs in your family. Either way, you're taking positive steps to figure out what *you* can do to take care of yourself *and* enjoy your life.

Finally, I *don't* assume that you're a gourmet chef. So I've made sure that each and every recipe in this book, while created by gourmet chefs, is one you'll be able to prepare in your own kitchen. Remember, though, that if you want even more information on cooking techniques, you can check out *Cooking For*

Dummies, 2nd Edition, or *Gourmet Cooking For Dummies* (both published by IDG Books Worldwide, Inc.), and satisfy your appetite.

Conventions Used in This Book

To make the healthy-heart recipes easy to prepare in your kitchen, we provide all the information that you will need to prepare each recipe or tell you where to find it. A few recipes may look difficult because they include several components or perhaps a sub-recipe. Actually, none of the recipes in this book requires any difficult techniques. Whether you're a kitchen pro or just learning your way around the kitchen, we've used several conventions in presenting the recipes to make it easy for you to achieve great results. Your first step in preparing any recipe is to read it all the way through, making notes of what you need at each step.

At the beginning of each recipe you will find listed any tools you need, the preparation and cooking times required, and how many servings the recipe makes.

Next comes the list of ingredients needed. If a recipe requires several components or steps—and gourmet recipes often do—the ingredients for each component are presented separately.

Because this is a healthy-heart cookbook, we try to be very specific about ingredients. But just to be safe, if you see the following ingredients or instructions listed in the recipes, keep in mind that, unless specifically stated otherwise, we mean the following:

- All milk is skim milk.
- All eggs are large.
- All olive oil is extra-virgin.
- All pepper is freshly ground.
- All flour is all-purpose.
- Added salt in a dish is treated as optional.
- All temperatures are given in degrees Fahrenheit.
- The nutritional analysis is always based on the recipe *without* optional added salt or other optional ingredients.

You'll find a list of all recipes in a chapter on the chapter's first page. For those of you who are eating vegetarian—all the time, or just occasionally, to reap the health benefits—we mark all vegetarian recipes with Boldface letter **(V)**.

How This Book Is Organized

This book has been, from its inception, a hybrid—a guide to heart-healthy nutrition *and* a cookbook. Therefore, I had to blend heart-healthy, great tasting recipes with those key practical strategies for how to prepare nutritious heart-healthy foods. What shortcuts work? What utensils will be required? How can you find necessary ingredients? How can you fit heart-healthy cooking into a busy life? What should you do when you are on the road? All of these questions require answers, and you can find them throughout this book.

In essence, the structure of the book reflects my response to meeting the challenge of blending health and good cooking.

Part I: Building a Healthy Heart

Part I presents the keys to building a healthy heart. I start in Chapter 1 with an overview of those daily habits and practices that form the essence of a heart-smart lifestyle. Then, in Chapter 2, I specifically link sound nutrition to cardiac health. Chapter 3 delves into the practical issues so critical to heart-healthy cooking, giving you information on important topics like substitutions and modifications, as well as providing you with some heart-friendly cooking techniques. Chapter 4 takes you on a quick trip to the grocery store as that final step that prepares you to explore the heart-healthy recipes. Chapter 5 helps you plan a heart-healthy meal.

Part II: Laying the Foundation: The Main Course

Part II presents the heart-healthy main courses in all their glory. You'll find recipes in this part for all kinds of meals and occasions—from the everyday to the special occasion. This part includes recipes for any main course—from breakfast to dinner. I include special chapters for poultry, meat, and seafood, as well as vegetarian entrées.

As a special bonus, I even provide recipes for meals for special occasions. These aren't dishes you'll want to eat every day (because they're a little higher in fat than we recommend for your daily eating). But for special occasions, they're perfect—proving that moderation is key in a heart-healthy diet. In this chapter, we also provide suggestions for ways to feature the recipe in a menu that meets nutritional guidelines or to reduce the fat in your other meals on the days you splurge, so that you come out on track in the end.

Part III: Adding the Extras: Recipes for Before and After the Main Meal

This part provides recipes ranging all the way from beverages to healthy desserts, with stops along the way at soups and salads, appetizers and snacks, and side dishes. By the end of this journey, you will have your imagination, creativity, and palate stimulated. Most important you will be convinced that heart-healthy cooking is neither boring nor tasteless.

Part IV: The Part of Tens

The book concludes with The Part of Tens so familiar to readers of *... For Dummies* books. In this section, I provide tips on improving your diet, making recipe substitutions, and lowering your cholesterol. I also cover strategies for teaching your children heart-healthy nutrition, and I list ten essential kitchen tools for heart-healthy cooking.

Appendix: Resources

I end the book with an entrée (pardon the pun) into the vast and rapidly emerging field of Internet nutrition, including Web sites and other nutritional resources in the world of cyberspace and beyond. I even throw in the names and contact information of organizations that can help with heart-smart eating and guide you to places to do some further reading.

Icons Used in This Book

What would a *...For Dummies* book be without icons? Icons are those funny little symbols that crop up in the margins to remind you of a particularly important point. In this book, we use eight different icons:

This icon highlights general tips to help make living a heart-healthy lifestyle easier.

What would a book by a cardiologist be without a few warnings in it? Flashing this icon issues you a friendly and simple alert about issues of cardiac health, things not to do in the kitchen, dishes to avoid at a restaurant, or foods to avoid at a the grocery store, and so on.

This icon marks important nutrition facts made easy.

There is nothing that a cardiologist (or a top chef for that matter) likes to do more than bust myths—particularly the many that abound about food and nutrition. This icon tells you when "it ain't so."

When I provide technical information on heart health, I spell it out in terms that are easy to understand, and I flag it with this icon.

When a particular practice can help you prevent heart disease or help you keep your heart healthy, this icon points it out for you.

Every person who helped with the creation of this book has worked his or her way around the kitchen. Along the way, they learned a few things that help make heart-smart cooking easier to accomplish. And I present this wealth of knowledge for you in paragraphs marked by this icon.

This icon points out simple substitutions or alterations you can make to the recipes in this book. The paragraphs marked by this icon help you get creative in the kitchen and try your hand at new ways of preparing things.

Part I

Building a Healthy Heart

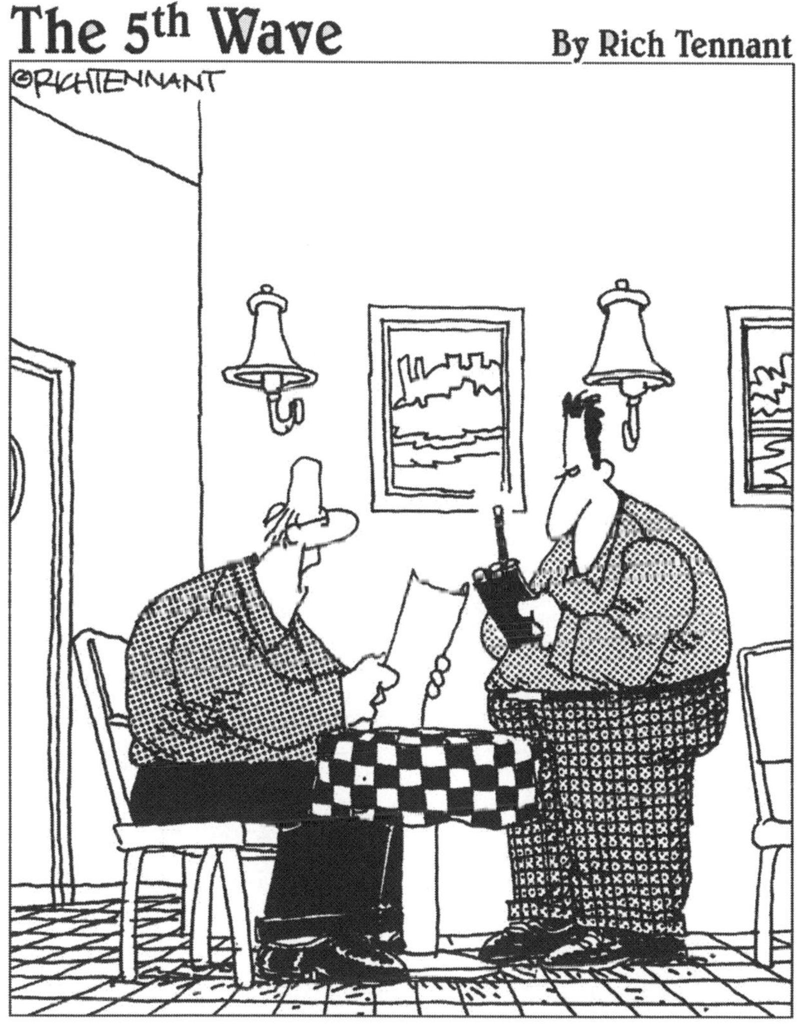

Image 1.1: "I'll have the barbequed ribs and fried cheese special. And can I get a heart defibrillator on the side?"

In this part...

This part starts you off with five great chapters that lay the foundation of knowledge you need to be able to live a heart-healthy lifestyle. Here you'll find background information on heart health and the ways in which your diet impacts you ... and your heart. We guide you through the process of cooking heart-healthy, including helping you steer your cart through the aisles of your neighborhood grocery store in search of healthy foods. We conclude the part with Meal Planning 101, a great resource for those of you who reach 6:00p.m. after a long day of work and can't stand that question, "What's for dinner?"

Chapter 1

Choosing a Healthy-Heart Lifestyle

In This Chapter

- Understanding the miraculous muscle that we call the heart
- Dispelling common myths about heart disease
- Knowing the risk factors for heart disease—and determining whether you're at risk
- Defending yourself from heart disease
- Taking stock of your lifestyle and making changes where you can
- Getting motivated to make changes in your life, for the sake of your heart

In his poem "The Road Not Taken," the American poet Robert Frost wrote, "Two roads diverged in a wood and I—/I took the one less traveled by,/and that has made all the difference." Unfortunately, when it comes to making lifestyle choices that affect the heart, many people are taking the modern superhighway right to the grave. They do that with a diet laden in fat, a caloric speed limit set way too high, and physical inactivity. Check your speedometer. Are you one of the speeders? If so, it's time to put on the brakes and look for the road less traveled. You can use this book as your good eating roadmap, and, believe me, it *will* make "all the difference."

Your daily nutritional habits and practices have a profound effect on your overall health, but especially on your cardiovascular health. Consider this:

• If your cholesterol is high (greater than 240mg/dl), you double your risk of heart disease.

• If you have high blood pressure or are at risk of developing it, eating salt-laden, processed foods can adversely affect your blood pressure, thereby creating stress for your heart and all your major arteries.

• Over-consumption of calories (yes, calories still count!) contributes significantly to our national epidemic of obesity. And obese people do not die because they are too fat; they die of heart disease.

• Add physical inactivity to the mix, and you double your risk of heart disease again.

The good news is that common sense and a little attention to some basic "traffic rules" for good eating and other lifestyle practices can not only make the journey safer but more comfortable, enjoyable, and memorable.

In this chapter, I look at the key habits and practices that constitute a healthy-heart lifestyle. Although this is a cookbook, how and what you eat is not the *only* healthy-heart lifestyle practice that you need to think about. To launch this adventure in terrific healthy-heart cooking along the road less traveled, I start by giving you a bird's-eye view of the whole territory of heart health. The tour starts with the heart itself—the magnificent vehicle of life's journey—and how it functions both in health and disease.

One Heart, One Life

Each of us, at birth, is given a magnificent organ—a heart. Although this organ is only the size of an adult fist, it accomplishes truly miraculous feats over the course of a lifetime:

- Every year, this phenomenal, four-chambered pump beats 40 million times.
- Quietly and efficiently, it pumps over 1 gallon of blood per minute at rest and up to 8 gallons per minute during vigorous exercise.
- The pressure required to pump all this blood through our blood vessels during one year

would be enough to elevate our bodies 100 miles into the atmosphere.

The human heart: Poetry in motion

Seventy times per minute, electrical activity starts in a group of cells high up in the heart and courses down a specialized conducting system to alert every cardiac muscle cell that it is time to contract. Then, in synchronicity, the muscles contract to eject three quarters of the blood from two heart chambers called *ventricles* either into the lungs for re-oxygenation or into the body to carry oxygen and nourishment to every working cell. In concert, four cardiac valves snap open or closed to direct blood flow where it needs to go. And so the beat goes on—rhythmically, reliably—at least 100,000 times a day, every day.

The human heart: Necessary for life

It is not surprising that poets write about the heart, heroes are said to possess "great heart," our loved ones are said to "live inside our hearts," or, when we are sad or disappointed, we refer to ourselves as "heartbroken." We have a tremendous emotional attachment to our hearts—and with good reason. A dependable heart means life itself, and when the heart is damaged or injured, life can hang in the balance. When the heart stops, life ends.

Each magnificent heart is intended to, and should, last a lifetime. Yet, because the healthy heart does its work so effortlessly and efficiently, we sometimes forget that this finely tuned pump is also fragile. Many people behave as though their hearts can take any kind of abuse and continue working as though their owners had treated them with care. How else can we possibly explain cigarette smoking, an inactive lifestyle, obesity, high-fat eating, or any one of the myriad other insults that people give to their hearts?

Our hearts are the magnificent vehicles that carry our lives. Think of them as elegant machines—like super Ferraris—that can go for hundreds of thousands of miles without requiring a tune-up. If you had such an amazing car in your garage, you'd certainly pay attention to how you drove it and how you maintained it, wouldn't you? In fact, I'm willing to bet that, like most of us, you already pay more attention to the dingmobile that's actually sitting in your driveway than you do to your heart. Why do so many of us do this? Perhaps because we don't realize how vital our hearts' health is until we've lost it.

Heart Disease: Public Health Enemy #1

When I was growing up, I turned on my favorite television program, *Dragnet,* simply to hear Sergeant Joe Friday say, "Just the facts, ma'am," as he cut right to the chase in his no-nonsense monotone. So, in the spirit of Joe Friday, let's cut to the important facts about heart disease.

The bad news

Even though we have had dramatic reductions in the prevalence of heart disease in the United States over the last 25 years, it is still, by far, the leading cause of death in our country. Affecting over 58 million Americans, coronary heart disease results in more than 40 percent of all deaths in the United States every year, claiming more lives than the next *seven* leading causes of death combined. Even worse, when cardiovascular disease and stroke are combined, these two related conditions cause more deaths each year than *all other diseases* in the United States combined.

The good news

Although bad news about heart disease abounds, plenty of good news is out there, too. For example, a positive, healthful, enjoyable lifestyle can help prevent heart disease in the first place and can help you fight it if you already have it. Take a look at a few of these good news facts:

- Individuals who are physically active cut their risk of heart disease in half.
- Overweight individuals who lose 5 to 10 percent of their body weight can substantially lower their risk of heart disease as well as dramatically re duce their blood pressure and cholesterol level, and keep their diabetes under control.
- Individuals who successfully stop smoking cigarettes reduce their risk of heart disease and stroke to almost normal levels within five years of quitting.
- Simple changes in what you eat can dramatically lower blood cholesterol, a major risk factor for heart disease.

Heart Disease: An Equal Opportunity Menace

If I asked the question "Who has the most risk of having heart disease?" of a random group of Americans, many of them would answer, "Middle-aged or older white men." And those people would be wrong. Heart disease is the leading cause of death for both men and women of all ethnic groups. Even children and young adults need to think about heart disease, because the conditions and habits that contribute to heart disease start in our youth. In the following sections, I dispel a few common myths and misconceptions about heart disease.

Heart disease and women

Of all the misconceptions about heart disease in the United States, perhaps the most dangerous one is that it is a disease that affects men more than women. The sad truth is that, every year, more women die of heart disease than men.

Women may not fear heart disease as much because men tend to get heart disease, on average, a decade earlier than women do; but after menopause, women rapidly catch up. Instead, women, in general, fear breast cancer more than they fear heart disease. In fact, even though breast cancer is unquestionably a dangerous and difficult disease, only 1 woman out 27 (just under 4 percent of women) will ultimately die of breast cancer, whereas 1 in 2 (50 percent) will die of heart disease. In addition, a woman is significantly more likely to die within the year following a heart attack than a man (42 percent mortality in women versus 24 percent in men).

Heart disease and African Americans

Heart disease is the leading cause of death for African Americans, just as it is for Americans of European descent. In some ways, heart disease is more dangerous for African Americans than it is for European Americans. Consider these examples of conditions that put African Americans at greater risk for heart disease:

- African Americans tend to develop high blood pressure at a younger age than white Americans. Plus, they tend to suffer more complications from their high blood pressure than white Americans do.
- African Americans are more than twice as likely to die from stroke than white Americans.
- African Americans are twice as likely to suffer from Type 2 diabetes than are white Americans.

Heart disease and children

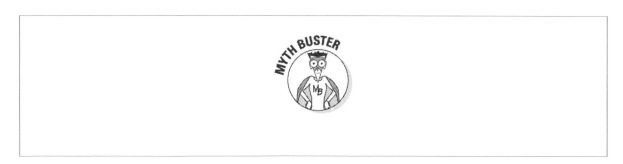

Many people have the misconception that heart disease is a disease of middle and older age. Nothing could be farther from the truth. Even though the manifestations of heart disease typically do not occur until middle or older age, the roots of heart disease lie in childhood.

Children and youth can have *atherosclerosis,* the fatty buildup in the coronary arteries that indicates coronary artery disease. This condition has been demonstrated by a number of autopsy studies of young soldiers killed in wars. A surprisingly high percentage of these young soldiers already had significant atherosclerosis in one or more coronary arteries before the age of 20.

Furthermore, the eating habits and level of weight control established during childhood and teenage years are highly likely to track into adulthood and either promote good cardiovascular health or become the setup for disaster. So the bad news is that everyone is confronting a very powerful enemy. The good news is that whatever your individual heritage and conditions, the same healthy-heart lifestyle can help everyone effectively fight this dangerous disease, regardless of age.

Examining the Risk Factors for Heart Disease

To understand the power of a healthy-heart lifestyle, you need to have a basic understanding of cardiac risk factors and how they affect your likelihood of developing heart disease. A *cardiac risk factor* is, as the name implies, a condition or behavior that either increases or decreases your risk of heart disease. Most risk factors are linked to lifestyle choices while others may be genetically determined.

Much of the scientific knowledge of risk factors comes from studies of very large groups of people (known as population or epidemiological studies) that have been conducted over the last 30 to 40 years in the United States and throughout the world. In the United States, such studies as the Framingham Heart Study, the Nurses Cooperative Trial, and the U.S. Physician's Health Study have shown how daily habits and practices contribute to the likelihood of developing heart disease.

Based on these studies, the American Heart Association, in the 1970s, developed the first list of risk factors, identifying some as "major" risk factors, because the presence of these conditions at least doubled the risk of heart disease. As research increased knowledge, the number of identified risk factors has grown. Table 1-1 lists the cardiac risk factors now commonly accepted in the medical community.

Table 1-1 Risk Factors for Heart Disease

Major Risk Factors	Other Risk Factors
High blood pressure (Hypertension)	Diabetes
Elevated cholesterol	Family history of premature heart disease (a parent or sibling who has suffered from heart disease before the age of 60)
Cigarette smoking	Age
Inactive lifestyle	Stress
Obesity	Male gender

Table 1-1

It's important to note, in looking at the risk factors in Table 1-1, that men are at a greater risk for developing heart disease at a younger age than women. But the overall risk for men and women is the same.

All five major risk factors listed in the table are largely controllable through lifestyle choices and practices. In fact, two (elevated blood cholesterol and obesity) are particularly affected by daily nutritional habits and practices. Lifestyle measures can help control many of the other significant risk factors as well.

Unfortunately, risk factors tend to multiply each other rather than add. So if you have one major risk factor for heart disease, your risk doubles. And if you have two of the major risk factors, your risk quadruples. Finally, if you have three major risk factors, your risk of heart disease increases between 8 and 20 times compared to someone who has no risk factors at all. Taking charge of the risk factors you *can* control Is all the more important.

In medicine, we have tended to underestimate the likelihood of risk factors occurring together. We now know that risk factors tend to cluster. For example, if you're significantly overweight, you are more like to have high blood pressure and high cholesterol. If you are overweight, you are also at greater risk of developing diabetes, which makes you more likely to have abnormal lipid levels. This clustering of risk factors dramatically increases the risk of heart disease and is particularly prevalent in individuals who are overweight or obese. Just one more reason to eat smart.

A Healthy-Heart Lifestyle: Your First Line of Defense against Heart Disease

Although proper nutrition leads my list of healthy-heart lifestyle habits, it is not a cure-all. A number of other positive cardiac lifestyle choices are important to minimize the risk of heart disease. If a wish-granting genie ever emerges from that oil lamp that I've been diligently rubbing my entire professional life, I have my top three healthy-lifestyle wishes for every American ready to go:

1. Every adult (and every child over the age of two) would follow a low-fat, low-cholesterol diet consistent with the guidelines published by the American Heart Association and the American Dietetic Association.
2. Every adult (and also every child) would accumulate at least 30 minutes of moderate physical activity on most, if not all days.

3. Every adult (and every child over the age of two) would maintain a proper weight by balancing the calories that he or she consumed with the calories that he or she expended.

Do you remember the image of three monkeys who sit together, one with its hands over its eyes, the next with its hands over its ears, and the last with its hands over its mouth? This image reminds us of the simple wisdom to "See no evil, hear no evil, and speak no evil." If you pay attention to proper nutrition, physical activity, and weight management, your heart will most likely respond just as nicely—seeing and hearing no evil from your lifestyle, it won't talk back to you by getting sick. In the following sections, I take a look at each of these three factors that form the keys to a heart-smart lifestyle.

Nutrition for a healthy heart: Are you what you eat?

To a very large degree, yes—you are what you eat. A healthful diet is a key factor in lowering cholesterol, maintaining proper weight, and lowering the risk of coronary heart disease. Unfortunately, a lot of misinformation is floating around about nutrition, so much so that it seems you're told not to eat a certain food one week, and then told it's okay to eat that food the next. In the rest of this book, I not only give you the tools and recipes to make great-tasting, healthy-heart foods, I also dispel some of the myths about nutritional practices and heart health.

Throughout this book, you will see that we follow guidelines that have been carefully developed by the American Heart Association, the American Dietetic Association, and the United States Federal Government. Based on the cumulative evidence of extensive research, these guidelines have been developed by leading experts in nutritional and medical science to steer you toward the simple, proven practices that decrease the risk of cardiac disease and other maladies and increase your overall health. Many recommendations, such as these examples, will be familiar to you:

- **Limit the total fat in your diet to less than 30 percent of total calories and saturated fat to less than 10 percent of total calories.**
- **Consume far less salt or sodium.** The average American consumes three times as much sodium as the 2,400 milligrams daily recommended by the American Heart Association. If your blood pressure is high, cutting back on salt/sodium may help lower your blood pressure and help re duce your risk of heart disease.
- **Eat at least five servings of fruits and vegetables daily.** Only 10 percent of Americans consume the recommended five servings of fruits and vegetables per day.
- **Consume no more calories than required to maintain your best body** weight. Chapter 2 pro-

vides a checklist to help you choose the right foods in the right amounts for you.

Although many of these recommendations just seem like good common sense, the approach many people take to nutrition often finds common sense in short supply. Too many folks, for instance, look for that magic pill that will let them eat all the fat they want and still lose weight. Or they shell out hard-earned cash for the latest magic diet or gizmo that will help them reach weight management goals in two weeks, if not yesterday. The Pied Piper of the Impossible is alive ... and leads many people to disappointment and failure.

What works is simple: If you stick to the basic guidelines that have been thoroughly researched and proven in practice over many years, you will take a giant step toward eating your way toward a healthy heart. That premise is the foundation of this book. Healthy-heart cooking and eating is about choosing a wide variety of foods prepared in healthful ways and eaten in healthful amounts. Thumb quickly through the recipes in this book if you think healthy-heart eating isn't more appealing than trendy fad diets.

Physical activity: Medicine's modern magic bullet

There is no true "magic bullet" in medicine. When it comes to your health, however, regular physical activity is the closest thing to it. Physical activity has almost no negatives, but hundreds of positives. Let me boil down to its essence the information from hundreds of studies:

An active lifestyle is a healthy lifestyle. Inactivity is hazardous to your health.

To me, the most dramatic statement of the problem of inactivity comes from a major summary study of physical activity and cardiovascular health performed by the Centers for Disease Control and Prevention (CDC). Their analysis and synthesis of 43 previous studies showed that inactive people doubled their risk of heart disease. Unfortunately, by CDC criteria, 60 percent of the United States population are classified as sedentary.

Think about that fact for a moment. By lounging in front of our TVs and computers or tethering ourselves to our work desks, over half of American adults have chosen a lifestyle that doubles the likelihood that they'll develop heart disease. To put this in perspective, *inactivity increases the risk of developing heart disease as much as if you smoked a pack of cigarettes per day.* And inactive adults now outnumber pack-a-day smokers six to one!

So what should you do if you want to be more active? You can choose among literally hundreds of options, but I always recommend fitness walking. Why?

- **Almost everyone can walk.** It's a skill we've had since we were children and, if we use it regularly, a skill most of us will maintain until we die.
- **Walking is easy on the body.** Injuries in walking are fewer than in jogging and other activities.
- **You don't have to walk very long to get the benefits.** Even walking at a moderately brisk pace 30 minutes a day can significantly lower your risk of heart disease.
- **You can spread it out throughout your day.** You don't have to get your 30 minutes in one continuous session. You can accumulate walking and physical activity over the course of the day.

But if you don't like walking, your best choice of a good physical activity is *any activity* you will do on a regular basis. If you're looking for guidance in the area of physical activity, don't hesitate to ask your physician about it.

While you are cooking your way to culinary nirvana with *The Healthy Heart Cookbook For Dummies,* you may also want to check out the individualized walking and other physical activity programs found in my companion book, *The Healthy Heart For Dummies.* Or check out *Fitness For Dummies* or *Workouts For Dummies* for additional tips.

Weight management: How to kill three threats with one action

From your heart's point of view, there's no such thing as pleasingly plump. Being overweight by just a few pounds can substantially increase your risk of heart disease. Being 20 percent over your ideal weight (the medical definition of *obese*) doubles your risk of heart disease.

Scientific research has long shown that obesity increases an individual's risk of heart disease through its well-known interaction with hypertension, lipid problems, and diabetes. More recent and growing research has now proven that obesity alone—even without any additional risk factors—increases the risk of heart disease.

To find out whether your weight places you in this category of significantly increased risk for heart disease, use Figure 1-1 to determine your body mass index (BMI). *Body mass index* is a more sophisticated way of comparing your weight to your height than the height/weight tables with which you may be familiar.

To use the body mass index table, shown in Figure 1-1, find your height on the vertical axis and then run your finger across the horizontal table until you reach your weight. Then look up to the top of the column to determine your body mass index number. If this number is between 25 and 29 you are overweight; if your BMI is 30 or greater, you can be assured that you have a substantially increased risk of heart disease. A BMI between 19 and 24 is healthy. (Figure 1-1)

Body Mass Index Chart

	19	20	21	22	23	24	25	26	27	28	29	30	31	32	33	34	35
Height (inches)							**Body Weight (pounds)**										
58	91	96	100	105	110	115	119	124	129	134	138	143	148	153	158	162	167
59	94	99	104	109	114	119	124	128	133	138	143	148	153	158	163	168	173
60	97	102	107	112	118	123	128	133	138	143	148	153	158	163	168	174	179
61	100	106	111	116	122	127	132	137	143	148	153	158	164	169	174	180	185
62	104	109	115	120	126	131	136	142	147	153	158	164	169	175	180	186	191
63	107	113	118	124	130	135	141	146	152	158	163	169	175	180	186	191	197
64	110	116	122	128	134	140	145	151	157	163	169	174	180	186	192	197	204
65	114	120	126	132	138	144	150	156	162	168	174	180	186	192	198	204	210
66	118	124	130	136	142	148	155	161	167	173	179	186	192	198	204	210	216
67	121	127	134	140	146	153	159	166	172	178	185	191	198	204	211	217	223
68	125	131	138	144	151	158	164	171	177	184	190	197	203	210	216	223	230
69	128	135	142	149	155	162	169	176	182	189	196	203	209	216	223	230	236
70	132	139	146	153	160	167	174	181	188	195	202	209	216	222	229	236	243
71	136	143	150	157	165	172	179	186	193	200	208	215	222	229	236	243	250
72	140	147	154	162	169	177	184	191	199	206	213	221	228	235	242	250	258
73	144	151	159	166	174	182	189	197	204	212	219	227	235	242	250	257	265
74	148	155	163	171	179	186	194	202	210	218	225	233	241	249	256	264	272
75	152	160	168	176	184	192	200	208	216	224	232	240	248	256	264	272	279
76	156	164	172	180	189	197	205	213	221	230	238	246	254	263	271	279	287

Figure 1-1: Body mass index table.

If you are overweight and are reading this book because you want to improve your eating habits and lose weight, you've come to the right place. Losing weight is one of the best things you can do to lower your risk of heart disease. In fact, because risk factors such as obesity, high cholesterol, and high blood pressure tend to cluster or occur together when you're overweight, when you reach and maintain a healthy weight, you reduce at least three cardiovascular threats:

- **Coronary artery disease.** Maintaining an appropriate weight reduces the risk of developing coronary artery disease and helps control its progression if you already have it. Losing weight also helps lower cholesterol and other lipid abnormalities in the blood. Eliminating adult obesity in the United States would eliminate over 50 percent of all lipid abnormalities.
- **Diabetes.** Although not all obese people are diabetic, over 80 percent of individuals with adult-onset diabetes (also called *Type 2 diabetes*) are obese. In fact, if we could eliminate adult obesity in the United States, we could eliminate almost all of these cases of diabetes.
- **High blood pressure.** Eliminating adult obesity would eliminate between 40 and 70 percent of all cases of high blood pressure (also known as *hypertension*).

Fine-Tuning a Positive Lifestyle

In addition to proper nutrition, regular physical activity, and weight loss/management, you need to consider some other very important lifestyle habits that you may be able to eliminate. These areas are so important that each of them has been treated as a separate topic in my companion book *The Healthy Heart For Dummies.*

Smoking

If you are a cigarette smoker, ceasing this deadly habit is the best health decision you will ever make. Quitting smoking is even more important than my big three lifestyle changes (proper nutrition, physical activity, and weight management). Smoking is dangerous to your heart and to your overall health, not to mention the fact that it reduces your ability to taste the foods you love.

Stress reduction

Although stress reduction may be more beneficial for some people than for others when it comes to lowering the risk of heart disease, it is always valuable in this fast-paced world to think about how much stress you are under and, if it is an excessive amount, to seek some measures to lower it. Exercise, adequate rest, and meditation may all help lower stress levels.

Mind/body connections

Finally, I would be remiss if I didn't speak about the power of love and of connecting with other people to help lower the risk of heart disease. Multiple studies have now shown that individuals who are able to "open up their hearts" in response to other people lower their risk of heart disease and tend to do better following major life-changing events, such as a heart attack.

Ready, set ... change!

Everyone gets stuck in old ways. Change is hard. But change *is* possible. In my career as a cardiologist and as a lifestyle researcher, I have seen literally thousands of patients and research subjects take charge of their lives by paying attention to their daily habits and practices. Here are some pointers I can share from their experiences of success:

- **Don't try to turn your life upside down all at once.** Because old habits are hard to change, you are much more likely to adopt permanent changes if you ease into new practices a few at a time.

• **Permanent change is exactly what you are seeking.** Never forget that.

• **Even small changes will make an immediate positive difference.**

• **Expect the minor disruptions and frustrations.** Don't use them as an excuse to quit.

• **Remember: This race is always won by the tortoise and not the hare.** The greatest rewards of improved health and well-being come to those who stick with new healthy practices until they become long-term healthy habits.

Healthy-Heart Living: The Force Is within You

You know the *Star Wars* movies, right? If you do, you know that the movies' heroes, the Jedi Knights, are protected from danger and empowered to do extraordinary feats by the Force. At one point, one of the wise old knights is asked by his young apprentice where to find the Force. He replies, "The Force is within you."

When it comes to leading a healthy-heart lifestyle, truer words could never have been spoken. The force for living a healthy-heart lifestyle is within each of us. It's the force that motivates us to live up to our potential for full, happy, and healthy lives. You can tap that force for well-being by adopting daily habits and practices that will aid you in the fight against public health enemy number one, heart disease. Use this book as a battle plan—no, make that a life plan—for accomplishing those goals that relate to how you eat well, in every way!

Chapter 2

You Are What You Eat: The Link between Your Diet and Your Heart

In This Chapter

- Identifying the eight key factors that contribute to your overall heart health
- Determining how many calories you need each day
- Lowering your total fat, saturated fat, and cholesterol intake
- Reducing the sodium in your diet
- Getting more antioxidants in the foods you eat
- Assessing the healthfulness of your diet

Not long ago, at my research laboratory, a man who had just finished an 18-week dietary intervention study sat down with a research dietitian to review his cholesterol results. The purpose of the study he participated in was to see if following a healthful, low-saturated-fat diet, which included a whole-grain, oat, ready-to-eat cereal, could lower cholesterol levels in adults. The man's cholesterol results revealed a distinct correlation between the amount of saturated fat in his diet and the level of his LDL cholesterol (see "Controlling Your Fat and Cholesterol Intake," later in this chapter for more information on the different forms of cholesterol). When he ate the most saturated fat during the study, his LDL cholesterol was at its highest, and when he ate the least saturated fat during the study, his LDL cholesterol was at its lowest. When the dietitian pointed this out to him, he excitedly said, "You mean what I eat makes a difference in my cholesterol level?"

You bet it does! What you eat makes a big difference not only in your cholesterol levels but also in other risk factors for heart disease, including obesity, high blood pressure, and diabetes. Your diet can also help you promote healthy coronary arteries. In this chapter, I give you the information you need in order to make the link between these scientific facts and the issues you encounter every day, particularly selecting and preparing heart-healthy foods.

Understanding the Eight Key Eating Habits

Hundreds of scientific studies have established that your eating habits and food choices can either increase or decrease your risk of heart disease. In the following list, I highlight the eight key factors these studies point to, all of which affect your risk of heart disease:

- The number of calories you consume
- The amount of total fat you consume

- The amount of saturated fat you consume
- The amount of monounsaturated and polyunsaturated fat you consume
- The amount of cholesterol you consume
- The amount of fiber you consume
- The amount of sodium you consume
- The amount of antioxidant-rich foods you consume

Figure 2-1 illustrates the way these key eating habits or food choices influence individual risk factors and your overall risk of heart disease.

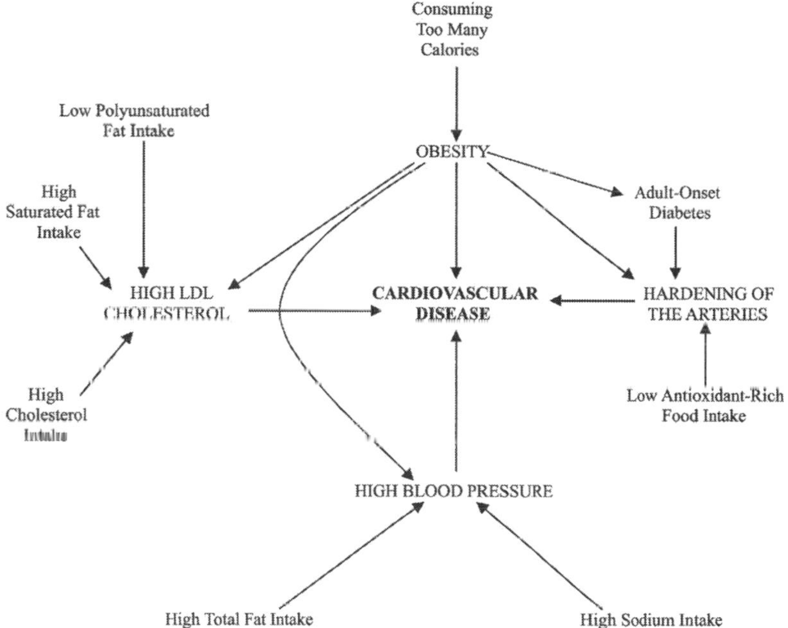

Figure 2-1: Diet-related factors that influence your risk for cardio-vascular disease.

These eight key eating practices don't refer to specific foods; instead, they refer to nutrients that are found in a wide variety foods. My research dietitians are fond of reminding me that "People eat food, not nutrients." So rather than focusing heavily on nutrients, I try, in this book, to keep the information practical and easy to use. But this chapter establishes an important foundation for the practical shopping strategies, cooking techniques, and great recipes you can find in the rest of the book. In order to provide you with this foundation, I give you a brief look at how nutrients such as saturated fat, cholesterol, and sodium contribute to obesity, elevated blood cholesterol, and high blood pressure—all of which are risk factors for heart disease. I also discuss nutrients (such as antioxidants, phytochemicals, and fiber) that you should eat more of in order to *decrease* your risk of cardiovascular disease.

Calories Count

Although healthy-heart cooking doesn't ask you to count calories, calories do count in helping you achieve and/or maintain a healthy weight. And the nutrient value in the calories you consume is important to heart health, too.

A *calorie* is a way of measuring the amount of energy that is available in the foods you eat, which your body uses to fuel all its functions. Calories come from four major nutrient groups: fat, protein, carbohydrates, and alcohol. All calories are equal in energy, but not in their nutritive value for the human body. For example, a bag of potato chips and a banana may have the same number of calories (about 150). But where the potato chips provide mainly fat calories, which, in excess, contribute to elevated cholesterol and high blood pressure, the banana provides carbohydrate calories, the foundation of good nutrition, as well as essential vitamins and minerals. That's why you want to select wisely when preparing or selecting a meal or snack. You want to get the most bang for your nutrition buck, so choose foods that not only provide calories you need for energy but also nutrients you need for good health. All the recipes in this book can fit within a heart-healthy way of eating. In addition, I provide a nutritional analysis with each recipe so you can tell what you're getting and plan accordingly.

Everyone needs a certain number of calories (a certain amount of energy) each day to maintain his or her body weight. (Of course, your daily calorie intake varies, but it is your *average calorie intake* over time that matters.) The number of calories you consume has a direct effect on your body weight:

- **When you consistently eat *more* calories than you need, your body weight increases.** Just 50 extra calories each day (the amount in two Hershey's Kisses), over the span of one year, would lead to a 5-pound weight gain. Over time, weight gain may lead to obesity, one of the major risk factors for heart disease.
- **When you consistently eat *fewer* calories than you need, your body weight decreases.** Your body weight may also decrease if you eat the same number of calories as you have in the past but increase your level of exercise. Increasing activity

increases the need for energy (which means you burn more calories).

Figuring out how many calories you need

Your daily caloric need is based on a number of factors, including gender, age, height, weight, body composition, health status, and physical activity level. But the two biggest determinants of calorie needs are *current body weight* and physical activity level.

Table 2-1 gives you a quick and easy way to determine how many calories you need based on your activity level and your current body weight. Find your current activity level in the table, and locate the number that corresponds with your gender. Then multiply that number, called a *metabolic multiple,* by your current weight in pounds. The resulting number gives an estimate of your current calorie needs.

Table 2-1 Average Metabolic Multiples for Adults

Women	Men	Activity Level
10	12	Sedentary lifestyle (no regular physical activity)
12	15	Sedentary to average lifestyle (mild aerobic exercise less than 2 hours per week)
15	17	Average to active lifestyle (2 to 4 hours of regular aerobic exercise per week)

Women	Men	Activity Level
17	20	Active lifestyle (daily regular aerobic exercise more than 4 hours per week)

Table 2-1

For example, Mary takes three 45-minute aerobics classes each week, which means she exercises for a total of 2 hours and 15 minutes, which translates to an average to active lifestyle. Her metabolic multiple is 15. Mary weighs 150 pounds. Multiplying her metabolic multiple by her current body weight indicates she needs about 2250 calories per day to maintain her weight. Compare this to Sue who also weighs 150 pounds but who never engages in physical activity. Sue's metabolic multiple is 10. Multiplying her metabolic multiple by her current body weight indicates that Sue only needs 1500 calories per day to maintain her weight. As you can see, the more you exercise, the more food you can eat and still maintain your weight.

Why can men eat more than women?

Why does a man have a higher metabolic multiple than a woman if they both engage in the same amount of physical activity? Because men tend to have more muscle mass than women do (male hormones, specifically testosterone, account for this difference in body composition). Muscle is more metabolically active than fat, bone, and other non-muscle components of the body. So, pound for pound, men simply burn more calories than women do.

Looking at the connection between your caloric intake and your heart's health

Even small amounts of weight gain substantially increase your risk of heart disease. By the time that you are 20 percent overweight (the medical definition of *obese*), you have doubled your risk of heart disease. Obesity also interacts strongly and negatively with other risk factors for heart disease such as cholesterol and lipid problems, high blood pressure, and diabetes.

If your current pattern of eating is maintaining your body weight within an optimal range for health, as indicated by your body mass index (BMI), then you are on the right track. You can assess your current body weight by using the BMI chart included in Chapter 1. A BMI between 19 and 24 is optimal; a BMI between 25 and 29 indicates you're overweight, and a BMI of 30 or higher indicates obesity. If you are overweight or obese, the best thing you can do to reduce your risk of heart disease is lose weight.

Losing weight

If you need to lose a few pounds (or more) to improve your health, remember that the payoff for modest weight loss is huge. Losing weight, even 5 percent of your current body weight, can help reduce your cholesterol level, reduce your blood pressure, and reduce the risk of adult-onset diabetes, all of which are risk factors for heart disease.

To lose those pounds, you can cut calories, burn more calories, or do both. To cut your caloric intake, you need to cut back on the amount of food you eat. I recommend cutting back on empty-calorie and high-fat foods, such as sodas, candy, and fried foods. I don't recommend cutting out entire foods groups, such as dairy or grain products; doing so may give you an inadequate supply of nutrients. To burn more calories, you need to get more physical activity and exercise. If you eat less and increase your physical activity, you'll have the best plan for successful weight loss and weight management.

If you want to track your calories the easy way, you don't need to make tedious lists of what you eat. All you have to do is weigh yourself frequently. If you weigh yourself three days in a row each week for several weeks and your weight does not vary by more than a couple pounds, you're eating the right number of calories to maintain your weight. If you notice a trend over a couple of weeks in which your weight is increasing, that's a good indication you should cut back on your food intake and increase your physical activity level until your weight stops increasing.

If you're trying to lose weight, don't weigh yourself more than once a week. A healthy rate of weight loss is 1 to 2 pounds per week. Small drops in weight don't register on the common household scale, and not noticing a change in weight can be discouraging. Pick one day each week to weigh yourself and only step on the scale that day until you've reached your goal. After you've reached your goal, start weighing yourself more frequently to make sure you're maintaining that goal weight.

If you want to explore the topic of weight management more thoroughly, refer to *Dieting For Dummies* or seek assistance from a medical professional, such as a registered dietitian who specializes in weight management.

Controlling Your Fat and Cholesterol Intake

Fat and cholesterol are both vital nutrients, used by your body to perform specific functions. However, when you consume too much fat or cholesterol, they can be damaging to your body instead of helping it. Most importantly, eating too much fat or cholesterol increases the level of cholesterol in your blood and contributes to the development of heart disease. In the following sections, I explain cholesterol and fat in terms that are easy to understand, and I let you know how you can watch your fat and cholesterol intake to maintain a healthy heart.

The cholesterol connection

The amount and type of fat you consume and the amount of dietary cholesterol you consume have an important connection to a major risk factor for heart disease: They influence the amount of cholesterol and other lipids (fats) in your blood.

Cholesterol is a naturally occurring waxy substance present in human beings and all other animals. It is an important component of the body's cell walls. The body also requires cholesterol to produce many hormones (including sex hormones) as well as the bile acids that help to digest food. Humans get cholesterol from two sources: Our livers produce cholesterol and we consume it in animal products (particularly meat, eggs, and dairy).

How high cholesterol contributes to heart disease

When cholesterol levels in the blood are too high, excess cholesterol is deposited on the inside walls of the arteries, where special cells latch on to these deposits. The process creates a cholesterol-rich "bump" in the wall that is then covered with scar tissue that creates a hard, shell-like covering. This buildup of matter, called *plaque,* causes the arteries to narrow. The result is the condition called *atherosclerosis,* which can lead to coronary heart disease, angina, and heart attacks.

The higher your level of blood cholesterol, the greater your risk of coronary artery disease. If your cholesterol is above 200mg/dl, your risk of heart disease increases dramatically. If your cholesterol is above 240mg/dl, your risk of dying from heart disease is *more than two times* greater than the risk faced by individuals whose cholesterol level is below 200mg/dl. Generally speaking, the lower your cholesterol level is below 200mg/dl, the better.

The good news is that lowering your overall blood cholesterol level even a smidgen can make a positive difference. And the more you lower it, the greater the benefit. It is estimated that for every *one point* that your cholesterol drops, your risk of heart disease drops by *2 percent.* Thus, a drop in your overall cholesterol of 10 points can decrease your risk of heart disease by 20 percent. Except for a few people who have inherited a predisposition to high cholesterol, the amount and type of fat and the amount of cholesterol in food you consume play the most important role in keeping your blood cholesterol levels low or in lowering them if they are too high.

"Bad" versus "good" cholesterol

Cholesterol as a whole, however, is made up of different types of substances, some of which are bad for your heart health and some of which are good. Cholesterol travels around the blood stream on complex structures called *lipoproteins,* which are made up of cholesterol or other fats (lipids) and proteins (now you know how they got the fancy name). Lipoproteins can be separated and measured according to their weight and density. They range all the way from very-low-density lipoproteins (VLDL) to high-density lipoproteins

(HDL). Some lipoproteins are dangerous to your heart and some are helpful.

One particularly dangerous form of cholesterol is called *low density lipoprotein* (LDL). LDL cholesterol is dangerous because it contains more fat and less protein, making it fairly unstable. Because LDL cholesterol is unstable, it's prone to fall apart, making it easy for the LDL cholesterol to adhere to artery walls.

On the other hand, a beneficial type of lipoprotein called *high density lipoprotein* (HDL) can actually help protect your heart from heart disease. HDL cholesterol is stable, so it does not adhere to artery walls the way LDL cholesterol does. Instead, it actually helps carry cholesterol *away* from the artery walls, which is particularly important for the coronary arteries.

Controlling the total amount of fat, the kinds of fat, and the cholesterol you consume in your daily diet can do a lot to help you lower your overall cholesterol, as well as lower the bad LDLs and increase the good HDLs. The following sections look at how.

Fat: The good, the bad, and the sludgy

Fat has gotten a bad rap as an evil substance that raises cholesterol, makes people fat, and increases their risk of cancer. The truth is that there are many types of fat, some harmful and some helpful. Fat comes in three basic forms:

- **Saturated fat.** This kind of fat is typically found in animal sources, although some fats from plants such as cocoa butter, palm oil, and coconut oil are also saturated. *Trans fats* (unsaturated fats that are turned into solid form, such as margarine, through the process of *hydrogenation*) function like saturated fats. Typically, saturated fats and trans fats are solid at room temperature. Eating saturated fat promotes increased LDL cholesterol (the "bad" cholesterol) levels; that's why cutting back on saturated fat intake can help reduce your LDL cholesterol level.
- **Monounsaturated fat.** Derived from vegetable sources, such as olive, canola, and peanut oil, monounsaturated fat is typically liquid at room temperature. Recent evidence has suggested that consuming monounsaturated fats (particularly when part of a Mediterranean diet featuring olive oil) can significantly lower the risk of heart disease by raising HDL cholesterol (the good cholesterol that helps remove the bad LDL cholesterol from your blood) without raising total cholesterol.
- **Polyunsaturated fat.** Like monounsaturated fat, polyunsaturated fat also comes primarily from vegetable sources and is typically liquid at room temperature. Corn oil and most other salad oils are examples of polyun-saturated fats. Although saturated fats may raise your LDL cholesterol (the "bad" cholesterol) level and monounsaturated fats may raise your HDL cholesterol (the "good"

cholesterol) level, polyunsaturated fats may reduce your VLDL cholesterol (another type of harmful blood cholesterol) levels. Polyunsaturated fat from cold-water fish (referred to as *omega-3 fatty acids*) provide other heart health benefits. More information on these benefits come later in this chapter.

DASH to lower your blood pressure

Do you know that you can DASH to lower your blood pressure by increasing your consumption of fruits and vegetables and cutting your fat intake back?

DASH refers to a large clinical study called *Dietary Approaches to Stop Hypertension.* This study examined the effects of the DASH Eating Plan on blood pressure. The DASH Eating Plan emphasizes whole-grain foods and encourages a high consumption of fruits and vegetables (8 to 10 daily servings). It also encourages people to eat 4 to 5 servings of nuts, seeds, and legumes every week as well as 2 to 3 servings of low-fat and nonfat dairy products every day. Finally, it suggests cutting fat intake back to less than 30 percent of your total caloric intake.

The results of the DASH study were very impressive. The DASH diet was just as effective in lowering blood pressure as blood pressure medication in many participants with moderate hypertension.

Here are four things you can do to adopt the DASH Eating Plan:

• **Increase your intake of fruits and vegetables to at least eight servings each day.**

• **Increase your intake of low-fat or nonfat calcium-rich dairy products to at least two servings each day.** For adequate calcium intake, many people (especially postmenopausal women not taking hormone-replacement therapy) need 3 to 4 servings of calcium-rich foods each day.

• **Center your meals around beans, rice, pasta, and vegetables instead of meat to reduce your fat intake and increase your nutrient intake.** The recipes in this book feature lots of these very healthful foods.

• **Keep your fat intake low.** Keep in mind that you can't eat a few more servings of fruits and vegetables while still eating a high-fat diet and expect your blood pressure to drop dramatically.

For more information on the DASH Eating Plan, request information from:

The National Heart, Lung, and Blood Institute Information Center

P.O. Box 30105

Bethesda, MD 20824-0105

Read more about the DASH Eating Plan online at dash.bwh.harvard.edu or on the Web site of The National Heart, Lung, and Blood Institute at www.nhlbi.nih.gov.

All fat-rich foods contain a combination of the three basic types of fat, but the proportions of the three types of fat vary greatly. For example, only 6 percent of the fat in canola oil is saturated, whereas 87 percent of the fat in coconut oil is saturated. Experts recommend choosing dietary fats with the *least* amount of saturated fat and the *greatest* amount of monounsaturated fat. The following sections provide specific suggestions on limiting your intake of fat.

Limiting the total fat in your diet

Because of the negative role excess fat can play in health, experts such as the American Heart Association and the American Dietetic Association recommend that you limit the total amount of fat in your diet to *less than 30 percent of your total calorie intake.*

Recent studies suggest that reducing dietary fat intake to *less than 25 percent of your total calorie intake* may help you lower your blood pressure and cholesterol level, as well as helping you to lose weight. Cutting back on calories from dietary fat also leaves room for calories from non-fat foods such as fruits and vegetables, which contain nutrients such as magnesium and potassium that lower blood pressure.

Lowering your intake of saturated fat

The biggest myth about the dietary management of cholesterol is that limiting the cholesterol in food is most important. Actually, limiting your intake of saturated fat is even *more* important. Why? Because only about 20 percent of the cholesterol in your bloodstream comes from the cholesterol in the foods you eat. That means that 80 percent of the cholesterol in your bloodstream comes from what the liver produces, and saturated fat plays a major role in this process.

Limiting your intake of saturated fat to *less than 10 percent of total calories* is the best way to reduce both your LDL cholesterol and your overall cholesterol level. These five tips can help:

- Use lean meats such as poultry, all seafood, lean cuts of beef (eye of round and top round, for example), lean cuts of pork (pork tenderloin, for example), and 95 percent lean ground beef.
- Switch to skim or nonfat milk.
- Eat low-fat and nonfat cheeses and dairy products.
- Use soft tub margarine instead of butter.

- Avoid packaged cookies, crackers, and other foods that contain tropical oils such as coconut, palm, or palm kernel oil.

If a product has very little total fat, it will also have very little saturated fat. Chapter 4 provides more tips on choosing products with the least amount of saturated fat. Chapter 19 also offers more tips on reducing your cholesterol level.

Emphasizing monounsaturated and polyunsaturated fats

Although saturated fat is detrimental to your heart health, monounsaturated and polyunsaturated fats may both have beneficial effects on your heart health.

Monounsaturated fat, when used in place of saturated fat, helps raise levels of HDL cholesterol. The following are good sources of monounsaturated fat:

- **Olive oil.** A whopping 74 percent of the fat in olive oil is monounsaturated.
- **Canola oil.** Ranking second, 62 percent of the fat in canola oil is monounsaturated.
- **Other sources:** Peanuts, natural peanut butter, olives, and avocados are also good sources of monounsaturated fat.

Polyunsaturated fats are found in a variety of foods, but the best known for their effects on heart health are the omega-3 fatty acids. *Omega-3 fatty acids* are a type of polyunsaturated fat found in cold water fish. Research indicates that the regular consumption of fish rich in omega-3s reduces the risk of heart disease. Omega-3s appear to reduce the risk of heart disease by reducing VLDL cholesterol levels (another type of bad cholesterol), lowering blood pressure, and reducing the stickiness of platelets. Eating fish just two to three times each week may reduce your risk of heart disease.

Cutting your cholesterol intake

Plants do not produce cholesterol—only animals can make cholesterol, so the cholesterol in foods you eat comes from animal products such as dairy products with fat, egg yolks, meat, seafood, and poultry. The American Heart Association recommends limiting dietary cholesterol intake to 300 milligrams per day. You can limit your intake of cholesterol in three easy ways:

- **Choose nonfat or low-fat dairy products.** If a dairy product doesn't contain any fat, it won't contain any cholesterol either.
- **Limit your total intake of meat to less than 6 ounces per day.** Unlike dairy products, lean meat doesn't always have a low cholesterol content, because cholesterol is present in flesh as well as in fat and skin. The amount of cholesterol in a very high-fat meat, such as salami, is actually less than the amount of cholesterol in an equal amount of skin-less chicken! One ounce of salami has 17 milligrams of cholesterol, whereas 1 ounce of chicken has 25 milligrams of cholesterol. By limiting your total meat intake each day, you can limit your cholesterol intake as well.

- **Use liquid oil or soft tub margarine instead of butter or lard.** Although 1 tablespoon of olive oil, 1 tablespoon of soft margarine, and 1 table-spoon of butter all have 110 to 130 calories and 12 to 14 grams of total fat, butter and other animal fats have cholesterol (vegetable fats don't) and more saturated fat. So vegetables fats are always preferable.

Fighting cholesterol with fiber

Consuming more fiber can help you fight the good fight against cholesterol and other health threats such as certain cancers. Fiber only comes from plant-based foods. No matter how hard you look you will never find any fiber in animal-based foods such as milk, meat, fish, or cheese. Fiber contains no calories but is considered an essential dietary component. Guidelines for healthy eating recommend that you consume 25 to 30 grams of fiber each day. Most Americans get only half that amount.

Butter versus margarine: The trans fatty acid wars

After years of hearing "butter is bad" consumers then started hearing "margarine is worse." The confusion arose over the issue of *trans fatty acids,* which are created when oils are hydrogenated, a process that makes the oils solid at room temperature, more stable, and more flavorful. Trans fatty acids have the same effect on our bodies as saturated fat: They raise blood cholesterol levels.

So what's a health conscious-consumer supposed to do? Margarine is still the better choice for day-to-day use. Look for soft tub margarines that list a liquid vegetable oil as the first ingredient. These margarines contain very little trans fat compared to stick margarines or those that list a partially hydrogenated oil as the first ingredient. Trans-fat-free margarines (such as Promise and Smart Beat margarines) are an even better choice, if you can find them.

Recently, two new margarines have arrived on supermarket shelves that may help promote healthy cholesterol levels. Benecol Spread (made by McNeil Consumer Products, a division of Johnson & Johnson) and Take Control Spread (made by Lipton, a division of Unilever) are margarines with unique ingredients that help lower cholesterol levels. Benecol Spread contains a substance derived from pine tree sap that inhibits cholesterol absorption in the gut. Studies show that consuming three servings per day for at least two weeks may help lower LDL cholesterol levels by up to 14 percent. Take Control Spread contains a soybean extract that also inhibits cholesterol absorption. Studies suggest that just two servings per day for at least three weeks may lower LDL levels by up to 10 percent. For more information on these products and the other products made with these beneficial substances, visit the product Web sites at www.benecol.com or www.takecontrol.com .

There are two types of fiber—soluble and insoluble:

• **Soluble fiber** combines with water and fluids in the intestine to form gels that can absorb other substances and trap them. The trapped substances include bile acids that contain a lot of cholesterol. Thus, soluble fiber is particularly good as a way of lowering cholesterol because, as bile acids are excreted from the body, the liver uses up cholesterol to make more bile acids.

Two types of soluble fiber have been proven to have substantial benefits:

• *Whole-grain oat products such as oatmeal, Cheerios cereal (and its clones), and products containing oat bran:* These products are so effective that the Food and Drug Administration (FDA) has allowed certain foods rich in such soluble fiber to make the health claim that, when used in conjunction with a low-fat diet, these foods may further lower your risk of heart disease.

The eggstraordinary news about eggs

Are you wondering why I don't suggest that you eat fewer eggs? A single large egg has 215mg of cholesterol, so health professionals have long advised patients with cardiovascular disease to avoid eggs due to their high cholesterol content. The traditional recommendation for all people, in fact, was to eat no more than 3 or 4 whole eggs a week. (Unlimited cholesterol-free egg whites were okay.) And following this recommendation is still a good idea if you have established coronary artery disease or diabetes.

But a number of well-designed, very large studies have found, overall, that egg consumption is not related to elevated cholesterol levels and cardiovascular disease risk. The bottom line is that consuming up to an egg a day poses no increased risk for cardiovascular disease. (The one exception is for people with diabetes. Research has shown that, for some unknown reason, the cholesterol level of people with diabetes is more affected by dietary cholesterol intake. If you have diabetes, limit yourself to 4 egg yolks per week.)

This may be great news if you're an egg lover who has been feeling deprived lately. But watch what you eat with those eggs. Skip the traditional high-fat accompaniments such as bacon, sausage, buttered toast, and hash browns. Enjoy eggs instead with other healthful foods like whole-grain, unbuttered toast and fresh fruit.

• *Psyllium:* Another natural fiber that helps to lower your cholesterol, psyllium can be found in certain breakfast cereals (such as Kellogg's Bran Buds) and is also available in supplements such as Metamucil. Note that the supplemental forms of psyllium are not for everyone, because they may cause gas and other uncomfortable side effects for some individuals and because they may also interfere with certain heart and blood pressure prescriptions by slowing the absorption of certain drugs. Talk with your doctor before taking a psyllium supplement, and go easy on psyllium cereals.

• **Insoluble fiber,** what many people call "roughage," contains benefits that are not related to heart disease. For example, this type of fiber helps trap water in the stools, providing more bulk and helping food move through the digestive system more quickly. This effect may help lower the risk of colon cancer.

Both soluble and insoluble fiber are found in a wide variety of foods. The most fiber-rich foods include

- Whole grain breads
- Berries
- Black beans and other legumes
- Lentils

- Nuts and seeds

Limiting Your Intake of Sodium

Researchers estimate that about 30 percent of adults in the United States are *salt-sensitive,* which means that their blood pressure is raised when they consume more sodium. The American Heart Association recommends no more than 2,400 milligrams of sodium per day—a little more than the a teaspoon of table salt (2,300 milligrams). The average American consumes 6,000 to 8,000 milligrams of sodium per day.

High blood pressure, or hypertension, is often called the "silent killer" because it does not typically cause any noticeable symptoms. By any name, high blood pressure is a major risk factor for heart disease. Over 25 percent of adult Americans suffer from high blood pressure. And the older you are, the more likely you are to have it. In addition to being a risk factor for heart disease, high blood pressure is a major risk factor for stroke and kidney failure as well. For optimal health, you should strive to keep your blood pressure below 120/80 mm Hg.

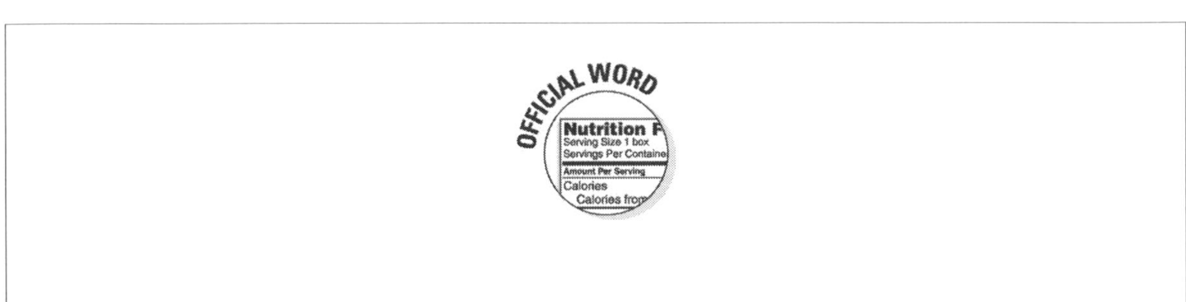

Your eating patterns and food choices can help you prevent high blood pressure or control it if you have it. Cutting back on two nutrients and eating more of many others can help you reduce your blood pressure:

- Cut back on added salt and salty foods.
- Reduce the total amount of fat you eat.
- Eat more fruits and vegetables—a lot more.

You should still watch your sodium intake even if your blood pressure isn't high. Too much salt is not beneficial for anyone, and cutting back may be beneficial for many.

Many of the recipes in this book list salt as an optional ingredient. Keep in mind that the sodium nutrition information provided for recipes where salt is optional is based on *no added salt.* Most chefs argue that adding salt adds a depth of flavor and interest to a recipe that no other ingredient can match. In some cases, I agree. However, in many cases, you can use less salt without negatively affecting the taste of the final dish. Research has shown that people can lose their preference for salt simply by cutting back little by little. If you usually add ten shakes of salt to a pot of homemade soup, try using seven or eight shakes the next time you make it, continuing to reduce the amount of salt you add every time you make it, until you get used to the taste of foods made with less salt.

Protecting Your Arteries with Powerful Antioxidants

Oxygen is essential for life, but, in certain circumstances, it can wreak havoc on our bodies. Many reactions in the body that require oxygen create substances called *free radicals.* Also found in cigarette smoke and polluted air, free radicals can damage artery walls, initiate the growth of precancerous cells, and are believed to be responsible for aging. Wherever an artery wall is damaged by a free radical, LDL-cholesterol will collect. When enough LDL cholesterol collects in an artery, that artery becomes clogged, which can lead to a heart attack or stroke.

Antioxidants are substances that combat the negative effects of free radicals. Research supports the notion that a diet rich in antioxidant nutrients is one of the best defenses against free radical damage in the body. The major antioxidant nutrients include vitamin A (also known as *beta-carotene*), vitamin C, and vitamin E. (See Table 2-2 for a list of foods rich in antioxidants.)

Fruits and vegetables are the best sources of vitamin A (in its beta-carotene form) and vitamin C. Nuts, seeds, and certain oils are the best sources of vitamin E. A diet rich in citrus fruits and bright green, yellow, or orange vegetables provides adequate amounts of vitamin A and vitamin C, but it is difficult to get enough vitamin E in a low-fat diet. Many health professionals strongly recommend that adults over age 50 take a vitamin E supplement that supplies 200 to 400 International Units (IU) every day. Vitamin E is the most powerful antioxidant nutrient, and getting adequate amounts through supplementation has been associated with reduced risk of cardiovascular disease. (Table 2-2)

Table 2-2 Foods Rich in Antioxidants

Foods Richest in Vitamin A and Beta-Carotene	Foods Richest in Vitamin C	Foods Richest in Vitamin E
Apricots	Asparagus	Egg yolks
Broccoli	Broccoli	Sunflower seeds
Cantaloupe	Cantaloupe	Vegetable oils (look for oils with added vitamin E)
Carrots	Enriched fruit juices (look for juices with 100 percent vitamin C)	Wheat germ
Egg yolks	Grapefruit	Whole-grain foods (for example, whole-wheat bread)

Foods Richest in Vitamin A and Beta-Carotene	Foods Richest in Vitamin C	Foods Richest in Vitamin E
Mango	Kiwi fruit	
Milk (vitamin A is added to all milk in the United States)	Oranges, orange juice	
Oranges, orange juice	Potatoes	
Pumpkin	Spinach	
Spinach	Strawberries	
Squash	Sweet potatoes	
Sweet potatoes		
Yams		

Table 2-2

Hooking up with the fighting phytochemicals: Nature's gift to health

Phytochemicals are substances created by plants to protect themselves from bacteria, viruses, fungi, and insects. The thousands of phytochemicals in the plant foods we eat may help protect us from a wide range of diseases, including heart disease. Many phytochemical compounds act as antioxidants. Others act as anticancer agents in a wide variety of ways. And where can you find phytochemcials?

One great source is soybeans and the food products made from soybeans, including tofu and soy milk, which are filled with a variety of phytochemicals that reduce the risk of certain cancers and heart disease. Different forms of soy contain different phytochemical components. Check out Chapter 9 for recipes that use tofu, a versatile protein-rich, cholesterol-free substitute for meat.

Here are some other great sources of phytochemicals:

- Berries, including cranberries and blueberries
- Black or green tea (but not herb tea)
- Citrus fruits
- Vegetables, such as broccoli, cabbage, cauliflower, and onions
- Fresh herbs
- Garlic
- Legumes, such as navy beans, kidney beans, and lentils
- Nuts
- Orange and yellow fruits and vegetables like apricots, mango, carrots, and sweet potatoes
- Red grapes and red wine
- Soy foods, such as tofu, soy milk, and soy protein powder
- Tomatoes

• Whole grains, including whole wheat, oats, and barley

To help you identify recipes in this cookbook that are rich in antioxidant vitamins, we include nutrition information for recipes that contain more than 20 percent of the Daily Value for vitamin A, vitamin C, or vitamin E. A few recipes contain 20 percent or more of all three ingredients and are must-tries because of their nutrient-richness.

Putting Science to Work in Your Daily Food Choices

It's one thing to read the kind of information I provide in this chapter; it's another thing entirely to make it a part of your daily life. Implementing these healthy lifestyle choices can be daunting. But keep in mind that wise old saying that the journey of a thousand miles starts with a single step. To help you begin this journey, in the next few sections, I take you through a few simple steps that get you off and running.

Can I just supplement my way to heart health?

With few exceptions, the best way to eat your way to a healthier heart is by making better food choices. A standard multivitamin/mineral supplement is fine to take if you want a little insurance. But many studies show that greater benefits, such as those I cover in this chapter, come from eating the nutrients in fruits, vegetables, and other foods, *not* from supplements. Also, don't think that a supplement can save you from the negative effects of a bad diet.

You may, however, want to consider taking as a supplement three nutrients: calcium, vitamin E, and folate, for reasons I describe below:

- **Calcium.** If you're a post-menopausal woman not on hormone-replacement therapy, your daily need for calcium is 1,500 milligrams, which is equal to five 8-ounce glasses of skim milk. For most women, that level of calcium intake is difficult without a little help from a supplement. Look for one that also contains vitamin D, which is needed to absorb the calcium.
- **Vitamin E.** If you're over 50 and have a family history of heart disease, taking a vitamin

E supplement is a good idea, because vitamin E has been associated with a reduced risk of heart disease. Look for gel caps that contain 200 to 400 international units (IU).

• **Folate.** Folate, also called folic acid, helps lower the blood levels of *homocysteine,* an amino acid that at high levels has been shown to increase the risks of heart attacks. (Folate is also essential for pregnant women to help prevent certain birth defects.) You can get folate in green leafy vegetables, dried beans, peas, and orange juice, but it's hard to consume enough. You may want to consider eating a fully fortified whole-grain cereal or taking 400 micrograms (mcg) of folate in a supplement.

Evaluating your current eating habits

Your first step should be to do a self-evaluation to see if you're currently eating a balanced diet that includes foods from all the major food groups (grains, vegetables, fruits, dairy products, and protein-rich foods). To help you assess your current eating habits, I provide a checklist for meat-eaters (see Figure 2-2) and another for ovo-lacto vegetarians (see Figure 2-3).

Using the checklist (make several copies before you start), keep a record of everything you eat for at least three days. Then look over the completed checklists to see where your strengths and weaknesses are. Are you eating a balance of foods from all food groups? Or are you falling short in some areas? For example, if most days you don't get any servings of dairy products (and ice cream doesn't count!), but you ate at least the minimum of everything else, that's great. All you need to do is concentrate on getting more dairy products. However, if your diet is bottom heavy, and you're falling short in many of the nutrient-rich food groups at the top of the checklist, you have some work to do. Consider meeting with a registered dietitian who can help you navigate a sea of dietary changes.

Planning to make some changes

What changes will you make? I suggest you take a two-step approach to making your diet more heart-healthy:

1. **Work first on balancing your diet, if you need to.**
2. **Work to consume the most nutrient-rich foods you can within each group.** The checklists indicate characteristics of the most nutrient-rich foods within each group, to get you started.

Enjoying your new lifestyle

While you're planning your goals, use the recipes in this book for inspiration and enjoyment. We provide over 100 recipes that fit into a heart-healthy way of eating. You'll find taste treats that range from simple entrées and side dishes to elaborate party dishes. Each recipe has clear, easy-to-follow instructions and most demonstrate heart-healthy cooking techniques that you can use to modify some of your own favorite recipes. (Figure 2-2 & 2-3)

DAILY DIETARY GOALS CHECKLIST

To use this checklist each day to assess the healthfulness of your diet, simply check off foods as you eat them. Examples of common serving sizes are listed under the daily goal for each group. Chapter 3 contains more serving size guidelines. Your primary goal is to get *at least* the minimum number of servings in each of the first four groups every day. Your secondary goal is to choose the most nutrient-rich foods within each group.

Date of Record:

FOOD GROUP	DAILY GOAL	DAILY CHECKLIST
Bread, cereal, rice, and pasta *Best Choices: whole grain foods*	**6 to 11 servings per day** ■ 1 slice of bread ■ ½ English muffin ■ ½ cup rice, pasta, hot cereal ■ ¾ cup cold cereal	□□□□□□□□ □□□
Vegetables *Best Choices: bright green, yellow, orange, or red vegetables, and legumes*	**3 to 5 servings per day** ■ ½ cup cooked vegetables ■ 1 cup raw vegetables ■ 1 cup vegetable soup ■ ¾ cup vegetable juice	□□□□□
Fruit *Best Choices: citrus fruits, berries and tropical fruits*	**2 to 4 servings per day** ■ 1 small piece of fruit ■ ½ cup fruit cup or sauce ■ ¼ cup dried fruit ■ ¾ cup fruit juice	□□□□
Milk, yogurt, and cheese *Best Choices: low-fat or nonfat products*	**2 to 3 servings per day** ■ 1 cup milk or yogurt ■ 1 ounce cheese ■ ½ cup cottage cheese	□□□
Meat, poultry, fish, and eggs *Best Choices: cold water fish, lean cuts of beef, pork, and poultry*	**Up to 6 cooked ounces per day** ■ 1 egg = 1 ounce	□□□□□□
Fats and oils *Best Choices: olive or canola oil, nuts, and seeds*	**Up to 8 added servings per day** ■ 1 teaspoon margarine or oil ■ 1 tablespoon salad dressing ■ 2 teaspoons peanut butter ■ 1 tablespoon nuts or seeds	□□□□□ □□□
Water	**At least 8 servings per day** ■ 8 fluid ounces	□□□□□ □□□
Foods below this line are not essential for a healthy diet. Enjoy in moderation!		
Sweets	**No more than 200 calories per day**	
Alcohol	**No more than 2 drinks per day**	□□

Figure 2-2: Dietary goals checklist for meat-eaters.

OVO-LACTO DAILY DIETARY GOALS CHECKLIST

To use this checklist each day to assess the healthfulness of your diet, simply check off foods as you eat them. Examples of common serving sizes are listed under the daily goal for each group. Chapter 3 contains more serving size guidelines. Your primary goal is to get *at least* the minimum number of servings in each of the first four groups every day. Your secondary goal is to choose the most nutrient-rich foods within each group.

Date of Record:

FOOD GROUP	DAILY GOAL	DAILY CHECKLIST
Bread, cereal, rice, and pasta *Best Choices: whole grain foods*	**6 to 11 servings per day** ■ 1 slice of bread ■ ½ English muffin ■ ½ cup rice, pasta, hot cereal ■ ¾ cup cold cereal	☐☐☐☐☐☐☐☐ ☐☐☐
Vegetables *Best Choices: bright green, yellow, orange, or red vegetables, and legumes*	**3 to 5 servings per day** ■ ½ cup cooked vegetables ■ 1 cup raw vegetables ■ 1 cup vegetable soup ■ ¾ cup vegetable juice	☐☐☐☐☐
Fruit *Best Choices: citrus fruits, berries, and tropical fruits*	**2 to 4 servings per day** ■ 1 small piece of fruit ■ ½ cup fruit cup or sauce ■ ¼ cup dried fruit ■ ¾ cup fruit juice	☐☐☐☐
Milk, yogurt, and cheese *Best Choices: low-fat or nonfat products*	**2 to 3 servings per day** ■ 1 cup milk or yogurt ■ 1 ounce cheese ■ ½ cup cottage cheese	☐☐☐
Protein-rich alternatives to meat *Best Choices: tofu or tempeh, beans, peas, lentils, egg whites*	**Up to 6 servings per day** ■ ½ cup cooked legumes ■ ½ cup soft tofu ■ ½ cup firm tofu ■ 1 egg or 2 egg whites	☐☐☐☐☐☐
Fats and oils *Best Choices: olive or canola oil, nuts, and seeds*	**Up to 8 added servings per day** ■ 1 teaspoon margarine or oil ■ 1 tablespoon salad dressing ■ 2 teaspoons peanut butter ■ 1 tablespoon nuts or seeds	☐☐☐☐☐ ☐☐☐
Water	**At least 8 servings per day** ■ 8 fluid ounces	☐☐☐☐☐ ☐☐☐
Foods below this line are not essential for a healthy diet. Enjoy in moderation!		
Sweets	**No more than 200 calories per day**	
Alcohol	**No more than 2 drinks per day**	☐☐

Figure 2-3: Dietary goals checklist for ovo-lacto vegetarians.

Chapter 3

Cooking Heart-Healthy Meals

In This Chapter

- Using the power of the pyramid for healthy eating
- Getting a primer on the basic food groups
- Following the Rule of Fourths for easy nutritional balance
- Substituting lower-fat ingredients for the higher-fat ones you're accustomed to
- Trying out five key heart-healthy cooking techniques

When I say "heart-healthy cooking," what images flash into your mind? Some dull, tasteless meal, stripped of all fat, and dry as sawdust? Well, banish that terrible image, because the best heart-healthy cooking and eating need not boycott any food, including fat. The best heart-healthy eating, the kind you can maintain and enjoy for a lifetime, embraces the approach championed by the American Dietetic Association as a recent National Nutrition Month theme: "All Foods Fit." This approach to eating and cooking emphasizes balance and variety and includes all food groups as part of a healthy lifestyle. You'll find the "All Foods Fit" approach represented in the great variety of recipes in this book.

As I discuss in Chapter 2, the catch is that some foods are more fit than others for your heart-healthy plan. This chapter explores how to achieve this balance using a model eating plan—the Food Guide Pyramid—then looks at practical ways to select the most healthful foods and the most heart-healthy techniques for preparing them.

Making Sense of the Food Guide Pyramid

Who said pyramids are only found in Egypt? Based on the evidence of hundreds of scientific studies conducted over many years, the United States Department of Agriculture (USDA) has constructed a modern pyramid: the Food Guide Pyramid, shown in Figure 3-1. The Food Guide Pyramid illustrates the amounts and types of foods our bodies need to achieve optimal health. I think of this pyramid guide as a model eating plan because it shows you the proportion and balance you should achieve in what you eat. Nobody is going to eat exactly the amounts or food types described in the pyramid every single day. But over a week or a month, the pyramid illustrates how you should build your menu—from the ground (or grains) up, so to speak.

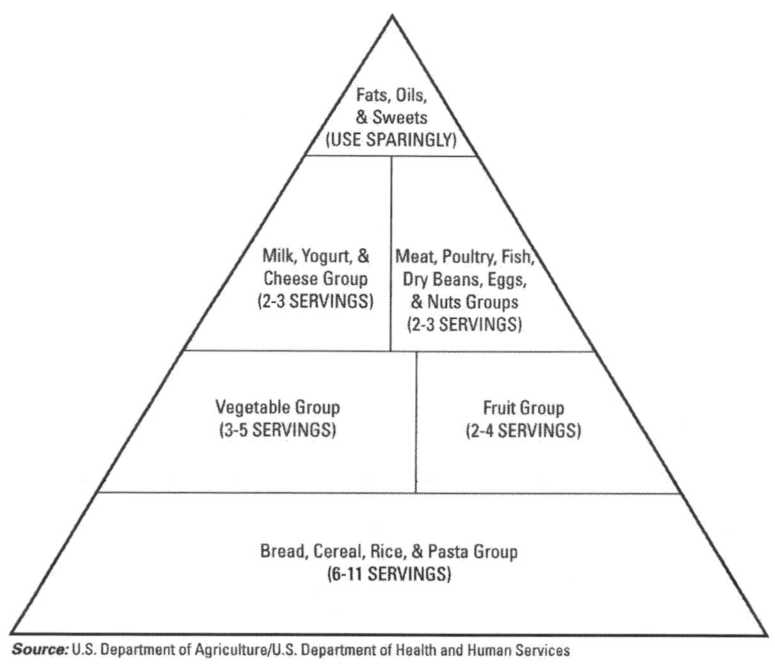

Figure 3-1: The Food Guide Pyramid.

The world over, bread is called the "staff of life," and for good reason. The food group containing bread, grain, cereal, and pasta is the body's first (and best) source of energy. This food group should provide the foundation of a healthy diet and be the source of at least half of your calories. Choose *at least* six servings from the grain food group each day.

Stacked above the grain group are vegetables and fruits. This vitamin-and nutrient-dense level should be your second source of energy. Choose *at least* five servings of fruits and vegetables each day.

Heading to the peak of the pyramid, the next stop is the dairy and meat groups (or, if you are vegetarian, think of it as the protein group). Because these groups exist closer to the top of the pyramid, you need to consume fewer calories from these groups—a little goes a long way. Choose at least two servings from the dairy group and two servings from the meat/protein-rich foods group each day. (Figure 3-1)

At last, you reach the peak. Here you find the fats, oils, and sweets. Choose sparingly from this group. You'll get fats and oils from foods in some of the other groups and don't necessarily need additional fats and oils. Many sweets provide only sugar calories and little else. Sweets are fine once in a while, but don't let them take the place of other nutrient-rich "sweets" like fresh fruits.

If you consume energy-producing foods, starting from the base group and working your way up to the top, your body will be well nourished and quite satisfied by the time you reach the pyramid's peak.

Although building your personal food pyramid may seem complicated at first, this process becomes easier as you discover how to balance your food choices (think of them as your building materials) to construct a solid, nutritious pyramid. For example, building a real pyramid using only mud would be difficult, if not impossible. You need other materials to form the structure and keep it stable. Now, think of the Food Guide Pyramid. Would it be well balanced and strong if you consumed too much of one type of the food and not enough of another? If your body lacks a variety of food sources, it will eventually show signs of deterioration, leaving you at greater risk of exhaustion and serious illness.

You can take advantage of three keys to making the Food Guide Pyramid work for you:

- **Gather your foods from *all* food groups.**
- **Balance your grocery store cart and your plate.** Eat the right amounts from each group, weighting your intake from the base (taking in more of these foods) to the peak (consuming less of these).
- **Consume the appropriate serving or portion sizes and number for your age, sex, height, bone structure, and physical status.** The Food Guide Pyramid (refer to Figure 3-1) shows the servings appropriate for a range of intakes from 1,500 calories (the lower serving number) to 3,500 calories (the higher serving number).

The number of servings indicated by the Food Guide Pyramid can seem large—a sure recipe for weight gain—unless you realize that the technical definition of a serving used by food professionals is much smaller than we citizens in the land of the bigger burger, overstuffed potato, and all-you-can-eat buffet realize. After all, you'd never consider a measly 1/2 cup of spaghetti a serving, would you? But that's the standard that the Food Guide Pyramid uses. That means you usually eat two to three standard servings when you eat a modest spaghetti dinner. For a helpful image adjustment, pay close attention to the serving sizes indicated in the information on each food group provided in the following sections.

Taking a Look at the Basic Food Groups

Food is a media darling. Claim a new discovery about the benefits or dangers of a particular food or type of food and you're assured an instant audience. With all the food buzz about, separating some perennially popular misconceptions and myths from the facts can be difficult. The following sections offer a quick guide to the most important concepts.

The bread and grain group

Daily requirement: 6 to 11 servings

Serving size: 1 slice bread; 1 ounce ready-to-eat cereal; 1/2 cup cooked cereal, rice, or pasta

Myth: Breads, grains, and other starches (the carbohydrates) cause weight gain.

Facts: Carbohydrates have two forms, based upon their chemical structure: simple and complex. When they are digested, both types of carbohydrates turn into *glucose,* a form of sugar. This blood sugar, one of the body's main sources of fuel, is carried into each cell by a hormone called *insulin.*

• **Simple carbohydrates,** which are digested quickly, come in several forms:

• *Fructose,* found in fruit or fruit juice

• *Lactose,* found in dairy products

• *Sucrose,* found in honey, molasses, maple syrup, and granulated sugar

The simple sugars from dairy products or fruits provide a number of beneficial nutrients. But simple sucrose carbohydrates that are found in refined sugar products, such as processed snack foods and drinks, have little nutritional value. The "emptiness" of sucrose calories is one reason that simple carbohydrates from sucrose are known as the "bad" carbohydrates.

• **Complex carbohydrates,** the "good" carbohydrates, are usually packed with more vitamins, minerals, fiber, and other nutrients than simple carbohydrates contain. Plus, complex carbohydrates take longer to digest. Complex carbohydrates include vegetables, breads, cereals, beans and other legumes, and pasta. Most of the complex carbohydrates in these food items come from a substance called *maltose,* and they ultimately break down into *glucose,* that important blood sugar.

Carbohydrates provide most of the energy needed in our daily lives. So getting carbohydrates from foods in the bread and grain group is crucial to sound nutrition. Even if you ban breads, pastas, and other starches from your menu (which I don't recommend), your body will continue to receive carbohydrates from other essential food groups. If you eat only the right quantities and limit the butter, cheese, or cream sauces that often accompany carbohydrates such as breads and pasta, carbohydrates will nourish you, not cause you to gain weight.

The vegetable group

Daily requirement: 3 to 5 servings

Serving size: 1 cup (a fist-size amount) raw vegetables; 1/2 cup cooked vegetables; 6 ounces vegetable juice

Myth: All vegetables provide the same nutrients; they're all the same.

Facts: Not all vegetables, even within the same species, are nutritionally equal. Color clues you in to the best nutritional values. Usually, the more brilliantly colored a vegetable is, the greater its nutritional value. A pale iceberg lettuce, for example, does not have nearly the nutritional kick of a dark green lettuce or spinach. (Plus, brilliantly colored vegetables usually have a bigger taste kick than their paler counterparts.)

Cooking techniques also play an important part in a vegetable's nutritional integrity. The longer you cook a vegetable, the greater the nutrient breakdown. What does that mean for you? The longer you cook a vegetable, the less of its nutrients you receive. Using too much cooking liquid can also drown a significant amount of the vegetable's vitamins and minerals. So, to retain all the nutrients possible, steam, microwave, roast, or sauté your vegetables just until tender.

The fruit group

Daily requirement: 2 to 3 servings

Serving size: 1 piece fresh fruit the size of a tennis ball; 1 small banana; 1/3 cantaloupe or similar melon; 1/2 cup chopped fruit or berries; 6 ounces fruit juice, 1/4 cup dried fruit

Myth: Consuming three servings of fruit a day is impossible.

Facts: One 9-inch banana is the equivalent of two servings of fruit. A medium glass of juice can easily hold 10 to 12 ounces—and that's 2 servings! Upping your fruit intake is easy. Particularly when you consider that fruit makes a great, vitamin-rich snack. For the biggest nutrient benefit, choose fresh fruits over fruit sauces and juices; fresh fruit contains the most fiber.

Select fresh fruits and fruit juices, and frozen, canned, or dried fruits. Dried fruits pack the same number of calories as fresh fruit, but in a smaller volume (because the water, which takes up space, is absent), so use dried fruits sparingly. Try chopping a few dried apple rings into cereals and baked items. Avoid fruits packed or processed with heavy syrups and sugar-sweetened juices (look for a label that says the fruit is packed in "light" syrup or in unsweetened juice).

The protein group

Daily requirement: 2 to 3 servings

Serving size: 2 to 3 ounces cooked lean meat, poultry, or fish (roughly the size of a deck of cards); 1 whole egg, 2 egg whites or 1/4 cup egg substitute; 1/2 cup cooked beans; 2 tablespoons seeds or nuts; 4 ounces tofu

Myth: Nuts and red meats are high-fat sources of protein that you should avoid in order to reduce your risk of heart disease and/or obesity.

Facts: When consumed in moderation, both nuts and red meats can be great for your body. Nuts contain mostly monounsaturated fat, which helps to raise your HDL ("good") cholesterol. One tablespoon of nuts provides 5 grams of fat, mostly monounsaturated.

Red meats, on the other hand, contain variable amounts of saturated fat—the fat that raises the "bad" cholesterol (LDL). But many people overlook the fact that white meats contain saturated fat as well. In fact, the amount of saturated fat in meat—red or white—can vary greatly depending on the cut, which is why knowing the cut of beef, chicken, or pork you're using is important. For example, compare the fat and saturated fat in two different cuts of beef and two different cuts of chicken: (Table 3)

Cut of Meat	Serving Size	Total Fat	Saturated Fat
Skinless, light-meat chicken, broiled	3 1/2 ounces	4.5 grams	1.3 grams

Cut of Meat	Serving Size	Total Fat	Saturated Fat
Dark meat chicken, with skin, broiled	3 1/2 ounces	16 grams	4.4 grams
Top round beef, broiled	3 1/2 ounces	5 grams	1.7 grams
Beef, chuck blade, roast, braised	3 1/2 ounces	13.3 grams	5.2 grams

Table 3

Ounce for ounce, poultry, beef, pork, or other meats may contain different amounts of total fat, saturated fat, and cholesterol, depending on the cut of meat. So, read nutrition labels and familiarize yourself with the leanest cuts of the meats you enjoy.

Animal foods, including beef, are excellent sources of protein, iron, zinc, and B vitamins, as are beans, nuts, and seeds. So if you are vegetarian or are cutting down on meat, be sure to get your protein from other sources, including tofu, tempeh, beans, peas, lentils, eggs, egg whites, soy protein powder, and vegetable burgers.

The dairy group

Daily requirement: 2 to 3 servings

Serving size: 8 ounces low-fat or nonfat milk; 1 cup low-fat or nonfat yogurt; 1/2 cup low-fat or nonfat cottage cheese; 1 1/2 ounces low-fat or nonfat cheese

Myth: There's not much nutritional difference between whole milk and 1 percent milk, so drinking whole milk is okay.

Facts: An 8-ounce cup of whole milk has more than 5 grams of saturated fat, whereas the same amount of skim milk has less than 0.5 gram. Plus, whole milk and skim milk have exactly the same amount of protein for example, but skim milk has more calcium. So choosing low-fat or nonfat dairy products eliminates the unwanted fat (especially saturated fat) and calories without sacrificing great nutritional value. Low-fat and nonfat dairy products taste good, too, especially if you give your palette a chance to adapt.

Cheese is a great source of flavor and nutrients. Try small portions of reduced-fat cheeses.

If you are crazy about the taste of cheese on vegetables, try a little sprinkle of a highly flavored, grated hard cheese (such as Parmesan or Romano) for lots of flavor for only a fraction of the saturated fat and calories of cheddar cheese sauce.

Fats and sweets

Daily requirement: No set daily requirements; use in moderation.

Myth: Eating heart-healthy means giving up sweets and rich treats.

Fact: All foods fit in a healthy diet, so enjoy your favorite desserts—even Double Death by Chocolate—in moderation. As long as you build your daily and weekly menu around the five nourishing food groups, the occasional extra treat fits in well.

Following the Rule of Fourths

As patients sit in the offices of my laboratory's research dietitians, gazing at walls covered with helpful versions of the Food Guide Pyramid, what sound do you suppose I hear most often? A big sigh! The pyramid looks so simple. So why do so many folks have a hard time balancing their food choices? Some say they don't have the time to plan or prepare elaborate meals—or even simple, balanced ones. Trying to keep track of how much you have eaten throughout the day and wondering if it all fits within the Food Guide Pyramid can be extremely challenging. But after you get the hang of it, following the pyramid at each meal is really quite simple. Here's my secret: Use the Rule of Fourths.

Look at your 9-inch dinner plate and visually divide it into quarters. Fill two quarters with vegetables. Go for rich colors—brilliant red and yellow peppers, tomatoes, squash, and dark greens such as broccoli, spinach, and salad greens. Fill a third quarter with a protein source. A typical 3-ounce serving of meat fits nicely; it's about the size of a deck of cards. Finally, fill the fourth quarter of your dinner plate with a source of grains. Because grains are the base of the pyramid, you may need more than one grain serving per meal; two to three is sufficient. One cup of wild rice should work. Or you can have one serving of grain in the form of rice or pasta, and add a whole-grain roll to your meal. For a nutritious dessert, try 1 cup of low-fat yogurt with cut-up fruit.

When you're brown-bagging or grabbing a meal on the go, you can apply the rule of fourths without a plate. Let's say you're planning to eat a sub sandwich and a bag of chips. Take a close look at the color and variety in your meal. A salami sub on white bread with mayonnaise and potato chips obviously lacks color (barbecue flavoring doesn't count) and, therefore, important nutrients. To apply the Rule of Fourths, select a whole-grain roll or bread if possible, then select a lean cut of meat. That's two fourths.

Now add color in the vegetable fixings. Ask for fresh tomatoes, peppers, onions, mushrooms, and dark greens. Hold the sauces unless they are barbecue, salsa, vinegar, mustard, or other non-creamy dressings. If you must have oil, ask for olive oil, and ask for it on the side. Instead of having chips for your daily sandwich accompaniment, try low-fat, baked tortillas or pretzels. Or really go for the extra nutrients and pair your sub with low-fat, calcium-rich chocolate milk.

Making Simple Recipe Substitutions and Modifications

When most people hear the word "substitution," they think, "Substitute? But I want the real thing!" I hear this kind of comment a lot, especially, "Oh, I use *real* milk," when the person really means she uses whole milk instead of one of the reduced-fat versions. Does that mean skim milk doesn't come from cows? What are real burgers, real hollandaise sauce, or real dessert? Actually, modified recipes are just as real as the ones your grandmother used to make.

You can make many modifications that won't change the taste of your favorite comfort foods but *will* make them healthy for your heart. For example, rather than whipping potatoes with whole milk and butter, try using skim milk, chicken broth, nonfat sour cream, or soy milk. You may find a version you like even better.

Also, take a look at the wonderful adaptations the chefs have made in the heart-healthy recipes in this book. Instead of traditional cream sauces and gravies, you'll find lots of tasty salsas, fruit sauces, and spicy marinades. These alternatives offer treats for both your taste buds *and* your arteries.

Table 3-1 contains simple and great-tasting substitutions that enhance your palate as well as your body. Also, check out Chapter 18 for ten simple recipe substitutions that you can put to use every day.

Table 3-1 Heart-Healthy Recipe Substitutions

Instead of...	Use...
Sour cream	Nonfat sour cream
Full-fat hard cheeses	Low-fat cheeses; nonfat ricotta cheese; feta cheese
Whole milk	Fat-free (skim) or reduced-fat milk; low-fat or nonfat soy or rice milk
Copious amounts of oil or butter for sautéing	Cooking spray; broth; wine; small amount of olive oil
Mayonnaise	Nonfat ranch dressing; light sour cream; light mayonnaise
French fries	Baked potato wedges
Snack chips	Baked chips; pretzels; soy nuts
Hamburgers	90 percent lean ground beef or turkey; vegetable burgers
Dips made with sour cream or cheeses	Salsa; low-fat cottage cheese dips; nonfat sour cream dips
Spam, salami, or bologna	Lean baked ham; turkey
Prime rib slices	Lean beef or flank; London broil slices
Oil-packed tuna	Water-packed tuna
White toast with margarine	Whole wheat toast with 1 teaspoon of peanut butter

Instead of...	Use...
Whole milk or cream in coffee	Evaporated skim milk or nonfat flavored liquid creamers
1 whole egg	2 egg whites or 1/4 cup egg substitute
Bacon, 4 slices	Canadian bacon, 2 slices; vegetable protein strips

Table 3-1

In some dishes, changing an ingredient or two may affect the outcome. But change isn't bad if you still achieve great taste. Variety keeps life interesting. Don't be afraid to experiment. But if you can't adapt a favorite comfort food, eat it only occasionally, and look for some new favorites that use more healthful methods of preparation.

Putting Some Heart-Healthy Cooking Techniques to Use

You can use the same techniques employed by the chefs who contributed to this book when you cook at home. Try them out when you prepare some of your family favorites. Traditional gourmet food preparations, like the use of butter, lard, heavy whipping cream, large portions of meat and heavy gravies, can be eliminated without eliminating the great taste. The chefs who have contributed to this book feature lighter methods of preparation. For example, some sauces start with tropical fruit purees (which are easy to make with a blender or food processor). Oils are used modestly. Fried items appear only rarely, and grilling, broiling, steaming, poaching, sautéing, and baking take center stage in preparing dramatic, delicious, and often simple dishes. The following sections provide the information you need to use these techniques in your everyday life.

You really can have your cake and eat it, too!

After you get past the media hype about which foods you can or cannot have and evaluate your current pattern of eating based on the Food Guide Pyramid (using the checklists in Chapter 2), you may find that your current diet is more balanced than you imagined. Or you may need to modify the amounts of a few items or substitute a few things.

But whether you need only a few modifications or a complete menu makeover, you'll have the most success and get the most pleasure (which is very important) if you avoid nutritional claims that discourage important food groups. The fickle finger of popular favorites moves continuously from food to food, first praising one food and condemning another, only to do the exact opposite a few months later.

Take a look at the progression of recent claims that have ridiculed your favorite foods. For years fats were the subject of every dieter's scorn. "Fat-Free Is the Way to Be" read the headlines. Soon, fat-free products fought for space on supermarket shelves. Even products that never had fat to begin with (like hard candy) were labeled "fat-free" in an attempt to capitalize on the craze. If you believed everything you read, you would have thought that fat-free products would reverse the obesity epidemic in America. Unfortunately, people forgot that fat-free isn't calorie-free. They chowed down on the fat-free goodies, consuming more and more calories in ever larger portions. Hey, if it's fat-free why not eat a whole pint of ice cream at one sitting or half a package of cookies?

When people awakened from this madness, they looked for a different villain in the continued rise of obesity and said, "Aha! Continued weight gain must come from sugar and too many starches!" So carbohydrates were banned from the food list of any in-the-know dieter, and the spotlight of favor turned to proteins.

The popularity of high-protein diets surged. Proponents proclaimed beneficial weight loss, increased energy, and greater muscle mass. But the fads overlooked the fact that too much protein can harm your kidneys and cause nitrogen build-up, which can lead to various other complications. The excess nitrogen generated by such diets also requires additional fluid to flush it from the body. As a consequence, much of the weight loss attributed to a high-protein diet may result from water loss.

What all of these fad approaches to controlling and losing weight neglect to mention is that severely restricting *any* food group will lead to temporary weight loss. That's why short-term successes of the high-protein, high-fat, and low-carbohydrate diets are not surprising.

Based on principles proven over and over, the Food Guide Pyramid gleams high above trendy food claims. The advice to eat a variety of foods from the basic food groups in recommended portions sounds too simple, and yet including such a wide variety of foods in your diet provides the necessary vitamins and minerals your body needs each day. Don't forget that the pyramid includes sweets and other treats that can easily fit into a heart-healthy diet. So try to avoid isolating important food groups and focus on which food group items have the greatest nutritional value, practicing portion sizes as you go.

Grilling or broiling

Grilling is a great way to cook meats, fish, poultry, and vegetables. And the best part: Excess fat from the meat or marinade drains off during cooking. If you are grilling outside, the hot coals provide smoky scents. You can also use scented wood chips to create various tastes, such as apple wood and mesquite. Grilling on stovetop grill pans or broiling also produces wonderful results—even when it's cold outside.

Steaming

To steam food, place it 1/2 to 1 inch above the water, stock, or other liquid, to enhance flavors. Add herbs or wine to the liquid and cook on the stovetop or in the oven.

You can also steam in the microwave simply by washing your produce, placing it in a shallow, covered microwave dish, and cooking according to microwave directions. Vegetables and fish are usually ready after 5 minutes on medium to high heat.

Poaching

A great way to cook meats and poultry is to simmer them in stock. Simmer fish in a vegetable stock or wine, and simmer eggs in lightly salted water with vinegar. You may poach in the oven or on the stovetop. Simply submerge the item being poached partway in the liquid and cover if you wish.

Sautéing

Sautéing is a quick way to cook almost anything. Unfortunately, most people use butter or other not-so-healthy fat sources when sautéing. A little olive oil or canola oil is a great way to start. Don't use too much, however. Start sautéing with 1 or 2 teaspoons of oil, and be sure to use a nonstick (or very well-seasoned) pan. I like using an oil spray canister (Misto, for example) to which I add olive oil or, sometimes, herb-or roasted-garlic-infused oils. Because you add oil to the apparatus, the oil is fresher and less expensive than aerosol sprays. (Check out Chapter 21 for more information on these handy canisters.) Sauté on a medium flame for best results. If the food starts to stick, add a little wine, stock, or water.

Using oil to sauté is easy and convenient, yet because it's highly caloric you must be careful to use very small amounts. A great alternative to oil is frozen broth cubes. Simply pour extra stock into an ice-cube tray and cover with plastic wrap. When frozen, transfer to a resealable freezer bag. Pop a frozen cube or two into a heated pan and start cooking.

Baking

Baking offers a good way to achieve food with a fried texture without the extra fat. Start with poultry or fish, baste in egg white, and roll in seasoned cracker crumbs. Place on a nonstick skillet or cookie sheet, and bake according to the recipe.

You can bake in one of several ways, depending on the desired result of your dish. For example, you can leave your dish uncovered and place it in the oven to achieve a crispy surface. You may also wrap your dish so that the steam cooks the food. Try wrapping poultry or seafood in spinach leaves, grape and cabbage leaves, or phyllo dough (just don't moisten with gobs of oil or butter in the traditional method). You can also use aluminum foil or parchment paper to wrap your food for steaming.

Spice up your healthy heart creations

If you want to kick up the flavor of heart-healthy foods, try these fat-free flavorings during preparation or at the table:

- Red pepper flakes

- Herbs (fresh basil, cilantro, thyme, parsley, rosemary, or sage)
- Reduced-sodium soy sauce
- Fresh fruit or vegetable salsas
- Fresh garlic
- Fresh ginger
- Vinegar
- Fruit preserves
- Spices (freshly ground black pepper, cinnamon, cumin, chili pepper, and chilies)

Chapter 4

A Grocery Store Guide to Healthy-Heart Shopping

In This Chapter
- Taking a new look at grocery shopping
- Solving the market maze
- Reading the labels
- Doing some alternative grocery shopping—beyond the supermarket

Although we *all* have to shop for groceries, our individual shopping styles may vary greatly. Take a look at the following descriptions of shopping styles and see where your shopping fits.

- **Born-to-shop excursion:** Shopping is a major event for these folks. Surfing the week's sale flyers and clipping coupons is a part of daily life for those who were born to shop. Their refrigerators sport scrolling grocery lists that detail everything from absolute necessities to those sinful chocolate cookies they think they'll try (after all ... there's a coupon). When they reach the store, they take their time walking the aisles considering each and every option.

- **After-work supermarket blitz:** The after-work blitzers may or may not have a plan or a list, but they tend to swing by the market after work and grab something to make for dinner or just enough food to last a couple of days. Spending a long time searching the aisles and deciphering food labels makes these speed demons scream. They would rather make three quick trips to the store than one longer one.
- **Meal-to-meal pick-up:** People who fall into this category shop, or rather decide what to eat, from meal to meal. Their refrigerators hold only a jar of Dijon mustard, a half loaf of bread, nearly spoiled milk, and two limp carrots. A shopping cart is a foreign object to these non-planners. They usually grab breakfast on their way to work and go out for lunch. For dinner, they shop just for that one meal or settle for that canned soup or pasta mix in the cupboard.

Supermarket traps for the unprepared shopper

Supermarkets are designed to snag you, making you buy things you may not need. Studies have shown over and over that such impulse buying, abetted by the store's savvy marketing ploys, can bust both your budget and your healthy eating plan.

But you can avoid the common supermarket traps by following our simple tips:

• **Trap:** Because you can't find a handy basket, you settle for a large cart. But even if you only need a few items, a large cart invites you to fill it up, causing you to buy things you don't want or need.

Tip: Keep a cotton bag in your car and bring it in to the store when you only need a few small items. Then, even if you can't find a basket, you can fill up your bag and avoid the large carts altogether.

• **Trap:** If your only reason for going to the store is to grab a gallon of milk, you'll have to walk to the farthest corner of the store to get it. Although milk is one of the most common items shoppers need, placing it far away makes you walk through the rest of the store, where you may be tempted to buy other items.

Tip: Look for newer grocery stores that have small cases of milk at the front of the store. Grab what you need when you walk in the door and head straight for the checkout line.

• **Trap:** En route to pick up just a few small items, you pass a sale display reading "two for one." What a deal! More aisles, more flashy "super sale" displays, and suddenly you no longer qualify for the express checkout.

Tip: Jot down a list of the few items you need before you enter the store. Only buy what you have on the list. Make note of the sale items if you wish, and review those notes when you get home. Removing yourself from the store may give you the perspective you need to tell whether those items are really things you need.

Whatever *your* shopping style, you can use the tips in this chapter to your advantage. I don't hit you with things you already know, such as to choose the skinless chicken breasts over the frozen fried chicken dinner. I *do,* however, share lots of tips to help you use the supermarket to benefit your healthy-heart cooking and avoid the traps that lie in wait for the hurried and the hungry. These tips help you purchase the best quality food for your health, at the best price, in the most stress-free manner.

Planning Ahead to End Market Madness

There you go, groaning again. But whatever your shopping style, you can benefit from planning ahead. Keeping a grocery list posted to the refrigerator is actually a great idea. Try the following suggestions before you head to the supermarket the next time:

- **Map out your meals for at least two weeks.** You don't have to eat the meals in the order you list them if you hate regimentation, but this meal plan can give you ideas for making shopping and preparation faster and easier. Plus, it gives you the opportunity to be sure your diet is balanced and healthy. As you plan, use the recipes in this book and others you like as well.
- **Make notes of the ingredients you need.** After you know which meals you'll be preparing in the coming weeks, you can make a list of the ingredients you need. Keep this list posted to your refrigerator. Then, when you run out of certain key ingredients, you can just add them to the list to make your next shopping trip more efficient.
- **Use your list to map out (mentally at least) the most efficient shopping route through your favorite market.** Doing this can help you avoid the supermarket's favorite traps, and it saves time, too. If you want to go the extra mile, put the foods on your list in the order that you'll find them as you walk your supermarket's aisles.

Sticking to the Perimeter

The layout of the typical supermarket can actually make shopping for heart-healthy foods a cinch, whether or not you plan ahead. Visualize the interior of the supermarket you frequent and the types of foods located along its outer walls. In most supermarkets, fruits and vegetables, fresh meats, dairy products, freshly baked items, and deli selections are located around the perimeter. This typical layout means that eating healthy can be as quick and easy as a spin around the *perimeter* of the market.

Did you notice that most of the foods located around the market's perimeter are also whole foods rather than processed items? Most foods in their natural state have little or no added fats, sugar, sodium, or other preservatives. And sticking to such unprocessed food items can help you buy nutrient-dense, high-quality groceries without having to do a lot of label reading. I don't want to downplay the importance of label reading or your knowledge of which cuts of meat, for example, have less saturated fat. I just want to note that if you're running short of time and inspiration, you'll make better choices if you skip the center aisles and stick to the market's perimeter.

The following sections take a look at some tips for making shopping the perimeter work for your heart-healthy cooking goals (and I've broken down these sections into food groups).

Color your basket with produce

Eating more fruits and vegetables is one of the most important things you can do for your heart. But don't think of fruits and vegetables as medicinal; think of them as essential to eating pleasure. If you doubt that fruits and vegetables can taste good, glance through the recipes in this book to see some of the exciting ways the chefs use them.

At first, fresh produce may seem more expensive than other items. After all, a single bunch of carrots or cantaloupe may cost more than three boxes of macaroni and cheese. In actuality though, fruits and vegetables are quite priceless when you consider how packed they are with valuable nutrients without the high fat and sodium found in many convenience foods.

Here are some tips to help you get the most nutrient and money value from your produce purchases:

- **Buy produce in season.** The quality of produce is usually better in season, and its cost is lower. If you want peaches in winter, for instance, or brussels sprouts in July, you'll pay a premium for them.
- **Purchase the sale items.** Markets promote weekly specials on produce. A sale can make winter grapes from South America a great deal.

- **Select brightly colored fruits and vegetables.** Generally, the richer the color of the fruit or vegetable, the richer it is in nutrients. So get the most nutritional bang for your produce buck by choosing ones that are bright in color.
- **Make a menu plan and select only the produce on your list.** This strategy helps ensure that none of your selections goes to waste.

Do the deli right

Did you know that the deli counter can be another great stop for heart-healthy food? When you grab ticket number 40 and they are serving number 29, take the time to explore all the different types of cold cuts and cheeses available. Beyond the bologna and American cheese, you'll find many good selections. And it's convenient, too.

Check out these tips for getting the most from the deli counter:

- **Choose turkey breast, chicken breast, lean roast beef, and lean ham.** These meats are excellent sources of protein and make great sandwich stuffers. Try pastrami-cured turkey for that great pastrami flavor with a fraction of the fat.

- **Ask the deli to slice lean meats in 1-ounce slices.** This tactic helps you keep track of your daily goal of 2 to 3 servings (or 4 to 6 ounces) of meat.
- **Experiment occasionally with some of the reduced-fat cheeses.** Ask the deli to slice the cheese in 1-ounce slices (the size of a prepackaged American cheese slice) so you can keep track of how much you eat.
- **Beware of prepared tuna, chicken, macaroni, egg, and potato salads.** The added salad dressing and mayonnaise in these salads can give them twice the fat per serving of artery-clogging cold cuts such as salami.
- **Try pre-made meals or salads.** These pre-made treats can be excellent side dish choices. Watch out, however, for large portion sizes and extra oil, even when it's heart-healthy canola or olive oil. Choose lightly oiled dishes with a lot of bright vegetable colors, and steer away from the pre-made barbecued wings and fried foods. If, after the first bite, your lips are glistening, keep your side portion around 1/2 cup.

Select heart-healthy cuts of meat

As I discuss in Chapter 3, a variety of meats can have a place in heart-healthy cooking. The goal is to make sure that you choose lean cuts. Table 4-1 compares some top meat choices.

Table 4-1 Fat and Cholesterol Content in Meat and Meat Substitutes

Meat	Cooked Weight	Total Fat (grams)	Saturated Fat (grams)	Cholesterol (milligrams)
Lean beef, sirloin	3 ounces	4.1	1.4	71
Lean beef, top round	3 ounces	4.1	1.5	73
Ground beef, 90 percent lean	3 ounces	8.0	3.0	65
Ground beef, 96 percent lean	3 ounces	3.3	1.1	57
Lean pork, tender-loin	3 ounces	4.1	1.4	67
Lean pork, center-cut loin chop	3 ounces	8.6	3.0	71
Skinless turkey breast	3 ounces	1.0	0.3	73
Ground turkey, 93 percent lean	3 ounces	6.3	1.7	76
Boneless, skinless chicken breast	3 ounces	3.8	1.1	72
Garden Burger Patty	2.5 ounces	3.5	1.6	7
Tofu, extra-firm	3 ounces	8.1	1.2	0

Table 4-1

Check out these tips for making good meat choices:

• **Select whole cuts rather than ground meat.** Ground meat is a good place for the market to hide—and sell—fat. If you select a ground meat, be sure that you get the leanest possible kind. Even then, you may want to be cautious. Although markets are responsible for accurate food labeling, recent news reports have exposed some grocery stores that mix several types of animal tissue and label it as 100 percent beef, lamb, or turkey. If you have a good local butcher, purchase your ground meat there, or buy a lean steak, such as top round, at the supermarket and ask the people at the meat counter to grind it for you.

• **Shop weekly meat sales with caution.** The favorite sales items are usually chicken thighs or wings, 85 percent lean hamburger, sausage, and "value pack" pork chops. Unfortunately, these items are often the highest in fat and saturated fat. Plus, you're often paying for bone, skin, and lots of visible fat. Watch for good sales on skinless, boneless chicken breasts, lean cuts of beef, pork tenderloin, and boneless loin of pork.

• **Buy only modest portions of meat.** Aim for individual servings of about 3 ounces. Most meats shrink by 25 percent after cooking. If you're cooking a meal for four, start with one pound or 16 ounces of raw meat. This will become 12 ounces after cooking, which is equal to 3 ounces per person. If you're buying steaks, consider sharing with someone because that big, juicy steak may be enough for two or three people. Or when you select a boneless pork loin or large beef roast, for instance, plan to use it for a couple of meals and save some in the freezer.

If you don't have a scale, a 3-ounce serving is close to the size of a deck of playing cards or the palm of your hand. What does this translate to? Think of 1/2 skinless chicken breast or 1 chicken leg with thigh; 3/4 cup flaked fish; or 2 thin slices lean roast beef.

Hook your catch of the day at the seafood counter

Although fish and seafood can be expensive, its health benefits make it worth the price. Like produce, the weekly sale selection is usually quite affordable. And because all fresh fish and seafood is wonderful for you, you won't be missing out with the special catch.

Salmon, tuna, and swordfish are particularly good sources of heart-healthy omega-3 fatty acids, which reduce triglycerides and inhibit platelet "stickiness" (both of which contribute to coronary artery disease). These sources are generally higher in fat than white fillets, such as haddock, sole, cod, turbot, and halibut, yet all fish are excellent sources of protein and help reduce the risk of heart disease.

Enjoy shrimp, crawfish, and lobster in moderation. In the past, these delicacies were left out of the school of healthy seafood because they are higher in cholesterol than most other types of seafood. But because they are extremely low in saturated fat, eating them occasionally is fine. Make a note that one serving of shrimp (3 ounces or about 12 large shrimp) contains 130 milligrams of cholesterol; your daily recommendation is 300 milligrams or less.

Cut fat in the dairy aisle

In most supermarkets, you've reached the homestretch when you hit the dairy section, which is loaded with essentials for most market baskets—milk, cheese, eggs, yogurt, cottage cheese, sour cream, and margarine. All you need is a good pair of eyes—for label reading—and you're down the aisle in a flash. Read the labels to select nonfat and low-fat items. Look for the words "fat-free, low-fat, and reduced-fat" on dairy products such as milk, yogurt, and sour cream. Look for "low-fat, reduced-fat, and part-skim" cheeses. If you're a cheese connoisseur and you want full-fat, flavor-rich cheeses like Gruyère, Stilton, or Brie, keep in mind that these cheeses contain 8 grams of total fat and 5 grams of saturated fat *per ounce.* If you go this route, keep moderate portion sizes in mind.

What about fish oil supplements?

No evidence exists to indicate that fish oil supplements have the same heart-healthy benefits as fresh fish. And like any oil, fish oils are loaded with calories. So I recommend that you eat the real thing instead of opting for the supplement. Any of the great seafood recipes in this book are tasty– definitely more rewarding than popping a pill.

Gotcha focaccia

Focaccia bread is rising in popularity at many bakeries. This Italian bread looks very healthy and very tempting with its drizzle of olive oil, rosemary, and, often, tomatoes. And it is. But, depending on the baker, focaccia and other specialty breads may be loaded with fat. (The fat is often healthful olive oil, but just remember that it's not calorie-free.)

Most people find that low-fat or nonfat cottage cheeses, sour creams, and yogurts have great taste and comparable consistency to the full-freight items. And the low-fat dairy foods still contain the other important nutrients, such as calcium, which not only helps build healthy bones but also may help control blood pressure.

Get your grains at the bakery

Ahhh, the bakery. Another one of my favorite sections. Who can resist the smell of fresh-baked breads? And why should you? Breads, bagels, muffins, and more make up the base of the Food

Guide Pyramid and offer great heart-healthy benefits. Just keep in mind the following tips when selecting your grains:

- **Choose freshly made multigrain or whole wheat breads and bagels.** Multigrains and whole grains are good sources of fiber and other nutrients. Low-fat muffins are better choices than regular, high-fat muffins, and bran muffins are better than white.
- **Bypass the brownies, doughnuts, croissants, and other pastries.** Look for lower fat treats such a low-fat muffins, angel food cake, or lower fat cookies such as ginger snaps.

Make your own treats and desserts using the low-fat cooking techniques in Chapter 3 and the recipes we provide in this book. Add the ingredients to your shopping list. If you don't have a family full of teenagers to share the home-baked goodies with, freeze some. Baked goods freeze nicely when wrapped in clear plastic wrap and then aluminum foil.

Paying Attention to the Labels

Planning ahead is especially important when you enter the supermarket's trap zone: the center aisles. Of course, many food staples and otherwise nutritious foods *do* reside in the center aisles, but they are surrounded by brownie boxes and jars of gravy and faux cream sauces.

So how can you make your way through those center aisles, picking up the nutritious foods you want and leaving the rest behind? Master the art of label scanning. Label scanning can help you avoid errors in the aisles. Here are the most important facts you want to scan:

- Serving size
- Total fat
- Saturated fat
- Sugar
- Sodium
- Fiber

These and other nutrients are clearly listed on the sample Nutrition Facts label illustrated in Figure 4-1.

Food label information plays an important role in weight management and disease prevention and treatment. In 1990, the Nutrition Labeling and Education Act, the Food and Drug Administration (FDA), and the U.S. Department of Agriculture (USDA) established extensive food labeling changes. Jointly, these departments required that most foods list their ingredients and nutritional value per serving. The regulations also defined the meaning of certain terms that marketers love to use to entice you to buy their products. Table 4-2 lists the definitions of some common terms or nutritional key words that you may see on product packaging.

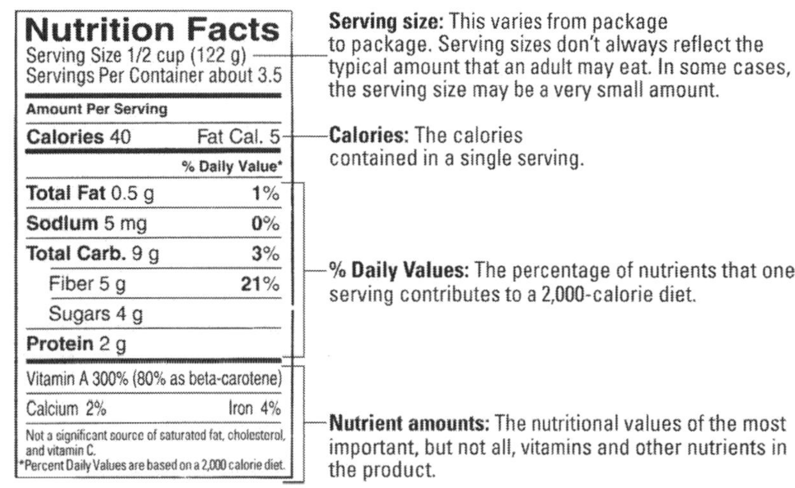

Figure 4-1: A Nutrition Facts food label.

Table 4-2 Definitions of Key Words Used on Food Labels

Key Words	What They Mean
Calorie-free	Less than 5 calories per serving
Light	33 percent fewer calories or 50 percent less sodium or 50 percent less fat (all compared to the regular full-calorie, full-sodium, or full-fat product)
Fat-free	Less than 0.5 gram of fat per serving
Low-fat	3 grams (or less) of fat per serving
Reduced-fat	25 percent less fat per serving than the higher fat product
Lean	Less than 10 grams of fat, 4 grams of saturated fat, and 95 milligrams of cholesterol per serving

Key Words	What They Mean
Extra-lean	Less than 5 grams of fat, 2 grams of saturated fat, and 95mg of cholesterol per serving
Low-sodium	140 milligrams per serving, with no sodium chloride
High-fiber	5 grams (or more) of fiber per serving

Table 4-2

If, after looking over the key words in Table 4-2, you're thinking you'll never memorize all those numbers, don't worry. You don't have to. A little practice in scanning labels, and actually noticing what you're buying, will help you select more heart-healthy foods and avoid ingredients that increase your risk for heart disease.

Label reading can produce a shock when you pick up some of your favorite convenience foods. You don't want to part with your Monday night favorite, the Gargantuan Fried Chicken Dinner even though it packs 900 calories, 55 grams of fat, 14 grams of saturated fat, and 2,600 milligrams of sodium. Relax. Today's freezer section offers healthier versions that taste great and can actually make you feel better than your old standby. Use the labels to check out all your options.

When "light" isn't "lighter"

The term *light* on a label does not always refer to calories, fat, or sodium content and can sometimes refer to taste or color. For example, Extra-Light Virgin Olive Oil has nothing to do with calories, sodium, or fat. The term actually refers to the type of olive or how the oil is refined, giving it a "lighter" flavor.

Fiber fact

Breads, cereals, crackers, rice, bulgur wheat, and other grains or grain products are good fiber sources if they provide 2.5 to 4.9 grams of fiber per serving.

Shopping for Groceries beyond the Supermarket

Grocery shopping doesn't always have to take place in large impersonal supermarkets. I actually prefer wonderful little markets and roadside stands. The closer to the farm you get, the better the taste and nutritional value, generally speaking. Check out the following tips for shopping beyond the supermarket:

- **Check in the Yellow Pages of your local telephone directory or in a community newspaper for gourmet stores that sell local produce and other products.**
- **From spring to autumn, visit farm stands and farmers' markets for the freshest harvest from the earth.** If you have a freezer, buy extra and make batches of soups, sauces, and other great dishes from this book to freeze and enjoy when the growing season has passed.
- **Look for a year-round produce stand or greengrocer in your community.** Even though these merchants may select most of their produce from wholesale markets, many stress quality and variety, as well as a good price.
- **Look for new types of markets that feature organically grown produce and meats.** Wild Oats is one nationwide chain that offers both natural foods and the practical groceries you need every day at an affordable price. Among their expansive selection of organically grown foods, you can find

products free of irradiation, hydrogenated oils, chemical additives, and preservatives. (You can find Wild Oats on the Web at www.wildoats.com.) Other markets with a similar style include Trader Joe's, Nature's Heartland, and Whole Foods Market. Look for comparable markets in your community.

Chapter 5

How to Plan a Heart-Healthy Meal

In This Chapter

- Stimulating all of your senses in the meals you plan
- Taking advantage of foods when they're in season
- Knowing the basics of meal planning
- Planning a menu from beginning to end

Many people associate meal planning with entertaining a crowd, but meal planning can be as simple as deciding what to make for your lunch. Whether you're planning a meal for one or one hundred, the basic principles are the same: you want to present great-tasting food that looks appealing in a comfortable, pleasant environment.

Martha Stewart, the food and style expert, has noted that entertaining, including meal planning, has one goal: to please a person or a group. I believe that reaching that goal is most important for you and your family, because that's whom you feed everyday. Aren't you worth it?

You may be thinking, "But I don't have *time* to plan." Actually taking a few moments to plan ahead, can *save* time and frustration in the long run. If you take a few moments each week to jot down some ideas, not only will you feel creative and in control, but you'll avoid those awful dashes at the end of the day when you stand undecided and hungry in the market before Chef Du Jour's ready-to-nuke entrées and side dishes—and nothing looks good. That's just the beginning of the benefits that meal planning offers.

To help you get started, this chapter reviews the basic precepts for meal planning and then delves into the specifics of planning an individual meal, including choosing a focus or theme, identifying appropriate foods and recipes, shopping, preparing the food, and preparing the setting.

A Good Meal: More Than a Matter of Taste

Planning a meal that successfully pleases yourself and others means coming up with something that satisfies not just the taste buds but all five senses: taste, smell, touch, sight, and hearing. In my estimation, more healthy eating plans are sabotaged by boredom and frustration than by personal busyness or other factors. If you really enjoy something, you'll find time to do it. So the following sections look at how food appeals to the five senses—eliminating boredom along the way.

Taste

Taste or flavor, of course, is the primary reason people choose the foods they do. A number of studies have shown that taste or flavor influences food choices more than cost, convenience, and (much to the frustration of dedicated dietitians) nutritional value.

Whatever foods you like, you can enhance, improve, and ensure better flavor by following some of these great tips:

- **Use the freshest possible fruits, vegetables, meats, fish, and other ingredients.** Anyone with a home garden, for example, can attest to the superior flavor of freshly picked produce compared to supermarket produce that may have been picked two to three weeks earlier. Freshness is also critical to the flavor of fish, which I recommend that you consume two or three times a week. If your fish or shellfish smells sweet, you are in for a treat. If it smells fishy, even the best recipe won't give great results.

- **Use fresh herbs and spices to enhance flavor.** Dried herbs and spices are also fine as long as they have not become stale. If you rub a bit of dried herb between your fingers and don't immediately smell a fragrance, it is probably stale and won't increase the flavor of your food in any meaningful way. Throw it out and get a fresh supply.
- **Use salt in moderation.** Our contributing chefs would say that using salt greatly improves flavor, and I agree. However, if you have high blood pressure and have been advised by your physician or registered dietitian to use less salt, then do so. Using fresh ingredients and fresh herbs and spices does more for flavor than using salt on stale food.

Smell

Contrary to what you may think, your taste buds are not the chief determinant of how food tastes to you. Experts estimate that as much as 80 percent of what people perceive as "taste" is actually determined by smell. You can test this theory yourself by holding your nose and tasting a favorite food. You should notice a marked decrease in what you "taste." You may also notice this loss of taste when you have a cold and a stuffy nose. More than the germ is "bugging" your appetite. You're also not as hungry because food isn't as appealing when you can't smell it.

The aroma of freshly brewed coffee in the morning, the comforting smell of freshly baked bread, the appetizing scent of simmering stew whet the appetite and practically pull folks into the kitchen. Serving a variety of foods that give off appealing and complementary aromas is an important goal to strive for when planning a meal. Although not all foods will give off an aroma, make sure you haven't chosen recipes whose aromas overpower or compete with each other. Some foods (cabbage and parsnips come to mind) even have a negative reputation with some people because they give off such a strong odor when cooking, even though they are much milder when eaten. Choosing the right recipe or having a strong kitchen exhaust fan can counter those problems.

Touch

Touch, texture, or feel refers to how food feels in your hands, in your mouth, and in your throat. Think about a glass of cold lemonade on a hot summer day—the cool wetness of the glass in your hand, the refreshing tartness and sweetness of the lemonade in your mouth, and the soothing coolness as the lemonade passes down your throat. In the dead of winter, however, hot cider or cocoa usually appeals more.

Texture as much as taste can influence our likes or dislikes of certain foods. Many children, for example, reject certain foods not really because of how they taste but because of how they feel in their mouths. Choosing complementary textures within a meal can enhance its appeal.

Sight

In most instances, serving food that looks good is just as important as serving food that tastes good. Attributes of appearance include color, portion size, shape, consistency, and contrast. Imagine a meal in which all the foods served are mashed, white, and presented on white plates. How unappetizing! So think about the appearance of both individual items and the entire meal as you plan. And check out these tips:

- **Use a variety of colorful fruits and vegetables in a meal to give the meal a vibrant, attractive appearance.** You get all those important health-promoting nutrients from fruits and vegetables, too.
- **Use garnishes to zip up the appearance of a meal.** A slice of lemon, a sprig of fresh herbs, a sprinkle of chopped parsley, or a melon wedge can do wonders to a dull plate.
- **If you have more than one set of dishes, select the tableware or accent dishes that make your meal look the most attractive.** Food almost always looks better on a beautiful china plate than it does on a Styrofoam one. So break out the good dishes, if you can. Or choose brightly colored,

inexpensive dishes from a discount store the next time you need to replace the ones you've broken.

Sound

And you thought the sound of food resembled the sound of silence? Well, sound is probably the least important attribute of a dish, but it does exist. Think of those food sounds that delight us: the popping of popcorn, the snappy crunch of breakfast cereal, the sizzle of a steak hitting the grill, or the crisp sound of Champagne as it is poured into a flute.

If you're struggling to find ways to incorporate sound into a meal, however, make it easy on yourself and play some soothing background music to create a relaxing environment as you eat.

Shopping in Season

Seasonal cooking refers to using foods that are in season, and it's a practice most of our contributing chefs strongly support. When you shop for foods in season, you get the best quality and the most flavor for the most reasonable price. The disadvantage of seasonal cooking is that you may have a brief window of opportunity to use a specific food. For example, fresh Copper River King Salmon from Alaska is available for just 3 to 4 weeks each year in late May to early June. Of course, many other types of salmon are available to choose from throughout the year, but if your heart is set on Copper River Kings, you'd better move quickly and hope it's May or June! (Even then, you probably need to know someone special, because most of this superb fish goes to fine restaurants.)

More common vegetables from the supermarket, such as tomatoes, asparagus, and kale are noticeably better in season. Although modern transportation and storage methods have made many fruits and vegetables available year-round, knowing the prime season for an item can guide you in selecting a recipe to use it in. Just choose the recipes that really show off the vegetables or fruits that are in season.

To identify the availability of fresh fruits and vegetables throughout the year, refer to Table 5-1, which was compiled using information from the United States Department of Agriculture. (Table 5-1 a, b & c)

Table 5-1 Availability of Fresh Fruits and Vegetables

Vegetable	*Availability*	*Fruit*	*Availability*
Alfalfa sprouts	Year-round	Apples	Year-round; in season throughout much of the United States in the fall
Artichokes	March–May	Apricots	June–September
Arugula	May–October	Avocados	Year-round
Asparagus	February–July	Bananas	Year-round
Beans	Year-round	Blackberries	July–September
Beets	Year-round	Blueberries	June–August
Belgian endive	Seasonal	Cantaloupe	May–November
Broccoli	Year-round	Cherries	June–August
Brussels sprouts	Year-round; in season throughout much of the United States in the fall and winter	Cranberries	September–December
Cabbage	Year-round; in season throughout much of the United States in the fall and winter	Currants	June–August
Carrots	Year-round	Dates	Year-round
Cauliflower	Year-round	Figs (fresh)	July–October
Celery	Year-round	Gooseberries	May–August

Table 5-1 (a)

Table 5-1 *(continued)*

Vegetable	*Availability*	*Fruit*	*Availability*
Collard greens	Year-round; in season throughout much of the United States in the fall and winter	Grapefruit	Year-round; in season throughout much of the United States in the fall, winter, and spring
Cucumbers	Year-round	Grapes	June–March
Dandelion greens	Year-round; in season throughout much of the United States in the spring	Honeydew melon	June–December
Eggplant	Year-round	Kiwifruit	Year-round
Garlic	Year-round	Kumquats	May–August
Jicama	Year-round	Lemons	Year-round
Kale	Year-round; in season throughout much of the United States in the fall and winter	Limes	Year-round
Kohlrabi	July–November	Mandarin oranges	November–May
Leeks	Year-round	Mangos	January–August
Lettuce	Year-round	Nectarines	May–September
Mushrooms	Year-round	Oranges	Year-round; in season throughout much of the United States in the fall, winter, and spring
Mustard greens	Year-round; in season throughout much of the United States in the fall and winter	Papayas	May–June, October–December
Okra	June–November	Peaches	May–September
Onions	Year-round	Pears	July–March
Parsley	Year-round	Persimmons	April–June

Table 5-1 (b)

Vegetable	*Availability*	*Fruit*	*Availability*
Parsnips	Year-round	Pineapples	Year-round
Peas	March–September	Plums	May–September
Peppers	Year-round	Pomegranates	August–December
Plantain	Year-round	Raspberries	June–September
Potatoes	Year-round	Rhubarb	April–June
Radishes	Year-round	Strawberries	Year-round; in season throughout much of the United States in the spring and early summer
Rutabaga	Year-round	Tangelos	October–April
Scallions (green onions)	Year-round	Tangerines	October–March
Spinach	Year-round; in season throughout much of the United States in the fall and spring	Watermelon	May–October
Summer squash	Year-round		
Sweet corn	Year-round; in season throughout much of the United States in the summer		
Sweet potatoes	Year-round; in season throughout much of the United States in the fall		
Swiss chard	Year-round		
Tomatoes	Year-round; in season throughout much of the United States in the summer		
Turnips	Year-round		
Watercress	Year-round		
Winter squash	August–March		

Table 5-1 (c)

Getting a Meal-Planning Overview

Keep in mind two concepts when planning healthful meals: You want to provide an overall balanced and nutritious meal and meet any particular dietary needs that you, your family, or your guests may have. The following sections guide you through this process.

Providing nutritious and balanced meals

Developing a meal that is nutritious and balanced is very easy if you follow a few simple guidelines:

- **Serve at least four different foods at each meal.**

To ensure you are getting a variety of essential nutrients, serve a variety of foods. For example, if you want to serve pasta with a basic tomato sauce, add some freshly grated Parmesan cheese (for calcium and protein) and a salad or steamed green vegetable (for vitamins, minerals, and fiber). Preparing at least four foods also helps to meet sensory needs for a variety of flavors, appearances, textures, and aromas.

You can also use the Rule of Fourths (see Chapter 3 for more information) to ensure a meal is balanced. Imagine a dinner plate divided into four sections. One section should contain a protein-rich food, one section should contain a starchy food, one section should contain a vegetable, and the fourth section should contain either a fruit or another vegetable.

• **Balance higher fat choices with lower-fat or nonfat choices.**

If you want to serve a rich dessert, make sure the rest of the foods on your menu are lower in fat and calories. For example, if you want to impress your in-laws with your award-winning cheesecake for dessert, serve a mixed green salad with low-fat vinaigrette or balsamic vinegar, poached or grilled fish, steamed vegetables, and whole grain rolls. The low fat content of the salad and main course nicely offsets the high fat content of the cheesecake.

• **Take the long-term view. Follow the macro-plan rather than the micro-plan.**

Sometimes, in their eagerness to follow heart-healthy nutrition guidelines, people slip into behaving like food cops. If a particular food or recipe doesn't have 10 percent or less of its calories from saturated fat and 30 percent or less from any fat, it's banished from the shopping cart or table. Taking such a negative, restrictive view is much too limiting. Your goal is to enjoy healthful food. You can include higher-fat and calorie-dense foods in healthy eating. *It's not the individual food or the individual meal that is most important, but the average pattern of eating that you achieve over each day, each week, and each month.* Being able to include all sorts of recipes in a heart-healthy approach to eating is another reason to engage in some longer-range meal planning, rather than just thinking about each meal as the time to prepare it rolls around.

Meeting special dietary needs

If you or a member of your family has specific medical conditions or allergies, or other special food needs, you must take those into account in meal planning as well. When you entertain, you want to extend that courtesy to your guests. Here are some tips on planning for a few of the most common conditions:

- **Heart disease or high cholesterol:** I've started with the easiest condition to accommodate. Simply choose a variety of low-fat recipes from this cookbook! All of the recipes in this book (with the exception of those in Chapter 10) have 10 percent or less of calories from saturated fat and 30 percent or less of calories from fat. If you want to prepare something special from Chapter 10, you can use any of the other recipes in this book as part of that meal, as long as the entire meal has 30 percent or less of its total calories from fat.
- **High blood pressure:** Those who have high blood pressure usually need to strive for low-sodium meals. This need is also fairly easy to accommodate. Simply avoid using salt while cooking and allow your guests to add their own salt at the table. Many chefs will tell you that adding salt to foods before and during the cooking process improves the flavor more than if you add it at the table. But if you need to limit sodium, avoiding salt while cooking is your best bet. Keep in mind

the high sodium content of certain ingredients like soy sauce, broths, bouillon cubes, and mustard, which you may need to avoid in order to meet a low-sodium request. Furthermore, 40 percent of people with increased blood pressure also have increased cholesterol levels, so watching saturated fat intake is also important.

- **Diabetes:** In general, people with diabetes can eat most healthful foods, but they must watch portion sizes carefully. Simply eliminating any dishes that use sugar is not enough, because the carbohydrate in all foods turns into sugar in the bloodstream. Watching portion sizes is the most important thing to do. If you have diabetes, you should follow carefully the instructions of your physician and dietitian in planning your meals. If you are entertaining guests with diabetes, ask them about their typical meal patterns and types of foods they eat and plan the meal accordingly. Don't single out guests with diabetes by offering them different dishes. Instead, serve everyone a more healthful alternative. For example, you may serve a fresh fruit cup for dessert rather than a fruit pie.
- **Lactose intolerance:** If one of your guests is lactose intolerant, that means he or she has a difficult time digesting the sugar (lactose) in dairy foods. Milk is the most important food to avoid as you plan your menu. Many people with

lactose intolerance can digest the small amounts of lactose found in yogurt and cheese, but check with your guests to see what they tolerate best. If the answer is no lactose, avoid using any dairy products in your meal. Soy milk often provides an excellent alternative in recipes calling for milk.

- **Food allergies:** Food allergies can limit some foods, but they rarely make it impossible to plan menus that are balanced. Depending on the food allergy, you may have to work a little harder to find the right recipes and to vary your meal plans, but you can do it. Asking guests if they have any allergies *before* you plan that special meal can at the very least help you avoid embarrassment. It may even help prevent your guest from becoming ill because of what you've served.
- **Peanut allergy:** I list this allergy separately because it can be very serious—even life threatening. For safety's sake, if you are planning a meal for someone with a peanut allergy, do not serve any peanuts in any form (nuts, peanut butter, peanut oil, and so on) in the meal and don't even have nuts in your home, if possible. For some individuals, a peanut allergy is so severe that even breathing the air in a room where peanuts are stored can bring on symptoms of the allergy, including difficulty breathing.

Planning an Individual Meal

Now that we've discussed the major concepts to keep in mind when planning *any* meal, it's time to think about planning an individual meal. To plan a meal, there are four tasks you need to accomplish before you can sit down to eat, and I cover them in the following sections.

Create a theme or focus for your meal

If you have a theme or focus for a meal, a menu can start to write itself. Now before you get all excited about going to such extremes, let me say that you already choose themes, whether you call it that or not. When you think, "It's hot, so I could make grilled lemon chicken. Now what goes well with that?" you are starting to create a theme or focus. Coming up with an idea around which to center a meal makes the planning process easier.

If you take a moment to look through all those recipes you've clipped and page through cookbooks like this one, you can begin to build some future meal plans around various themes. Thousands of potential themes and variations exist, including the following:

- Harvest Festival
- A Tribute to Spring
- Comfort Foods for Cold Winter Nights
- Beat-the-Heat Summer Foods
- New England Seafood Fest
- A Taste of the Mediterranean

- California Cuisine
- A Tribute to Southwest Cooking
- Soy Foods Feast
- Variations on Vegetarian Favorites
- Antioxidant-Rich Food Fest
- Celebrating Whole-Grain Goodness

Keep in mind that although a theme gives you a basis for planning a meal and writing a menu, not every element needs to fit perfectly. For example, if you're making a French meal but prefer wine from California, serve a California wine. On special occasions (or even everyday ones), you may want to incorporate music and decorations (flowers, table linens, candles, and so on) that work well with the theme. These decorations need not be elaborate, but they can help make mealtimes special and relaxing, almost an oasis in a busy day.

Write your menu

You probably already write down your menu when you're planning a special dinner party, but taking time out as I suggested in the last section to create a number of meals at once can be a real time-saver. You don't have to plan meals for particular days of the week if you don't want to, but just have them ready, like a meal plan savings account ready for withdrawal. To help you keep track, Figure 5-1 provides a handy meal planning sheet you can use to jot down your ideas. Make as many copies as you like.

Acquiring unusual ingredients

You may want to use a recipe that requires unusual, obscure, and hard-to-find ingredients. If you have access to the Internet, you can probably find almost any ingredient known to humankind and a company that will sell it to you

A number of specialty food stores and catalogs are great places to purchase unusual ingredients as well. We list a number of these sources of unique ingredients in the appendix.

Meal Planning Worksheet

Date of Meal:		Time of Meal:
Occasion:		
Theme:		
Guest List:		

Menu	Specific Menu Items	Sources
Appetizer(s)		
Entrée(s)		
Side Dishes		
Dessert(s)		
Beverage(s)		

Decorations :		Sources

Shopping List

Figure 5-1: A meal-planning worksheet.

For ease in planning a single meal, choose an entrée first and then select appetizers, side dishes, soups, salads, desserts, and beverages that go well with the entrée. Of course, every menu does not need multiple courses (most everyday meals probably won't), but for nutritional balance remember to use at least four different foods.

If you're serving a dish with many ingredients, that one dish could be a meal. For example, a vegetable lasagna with reduced-fat cheese or a chicken and vegetable soup with dumplings could be considered a full meal. All you need to add is a beverage.

If you're serving individual whole foods, such as grilled fish, a steamed vegetable, rice, and fresh fruit, be sure to follow the four-item rule (see the "Providing nutritious and balanced meals" section earlier in this chapter).

Many chefs recommend using one element consistently throughout the menu. For example, let's say you're going to serve salmon in a lemongrass broth as an entrée. Perhaps lemon flavor could be your common thread. Use lemon as the acid in the vinaigrette dressing for the salad. And for dessert, how about a store-bought lemon sorbet, dressed up with shaved lemon peel for garnish?

Identify the sources of menu items

Even if you love cooking, unless you have lots of time, you won't make every item in every meal from scratch. So you need to identify which recipes or items you want to make and which items you want to buy. And if you despise cooking but love entertaining, you only need to identify markets, delis, and caterers who can provide the menu items you want.

Here are some ideas on how to put the meal on the table without doing all the work yourself:

- **For a family meal, ask each family member to help with a different task.** Even the youngest child can help set the table.
- **Rotate the preparation of dinner among the members of your family throughout the week.** Children as young as seven or eight can take a turn making dinner (although the menu may always be spaghetti with a salad).

- **For an informal dinner with friends, ask your guests to bring an item or two.**
- **Plan a more formal dinner in partnership with friends.** Each of you can provide part of the meal so no one has to do all the work alone.
- **Pick up some items at the market or have them delivered.** A number of suppliers of very high-quality prepared foods and gourmet ingredients will deliver right to your door. Check to see if your local grocery store will deliver groceries to your house. You may even be able to submit your order via the Internet.

Set the scene

No meal is too insignificant to set the scene. Your goal is to create a comfortable environment in which to enjoy the fabulous menu you've created. Tablecloths or place mats and linen napkins are great for more formal dining, but something as simple as a jar holding fresh flowers when you're serving food on paper plates at a picnic table is perfect for an informal outdoor meal. Or even putting that low-fat lentil soup you heated for a quick lunch into a bowl rather than eating it right out of the pan can give your meal a lift.

Lowering stress, as I mention throughout this book, can promote better health and well-being and may help prevent heart disease. If setting the scene seems like too much bother, don't stress about it. What most people care about is the food. If you put your heart and soul into creating a great tasting, nutritious meal, the food itself can set the scene. But if you'd like to add some memorable finishing touches to the meal, consider taking a few extra moments to make your dining environment more relaxing and inviting. You may find that you feed your spirit as well as your body when you do.

Part II

Laying the Foundation: The Main Course

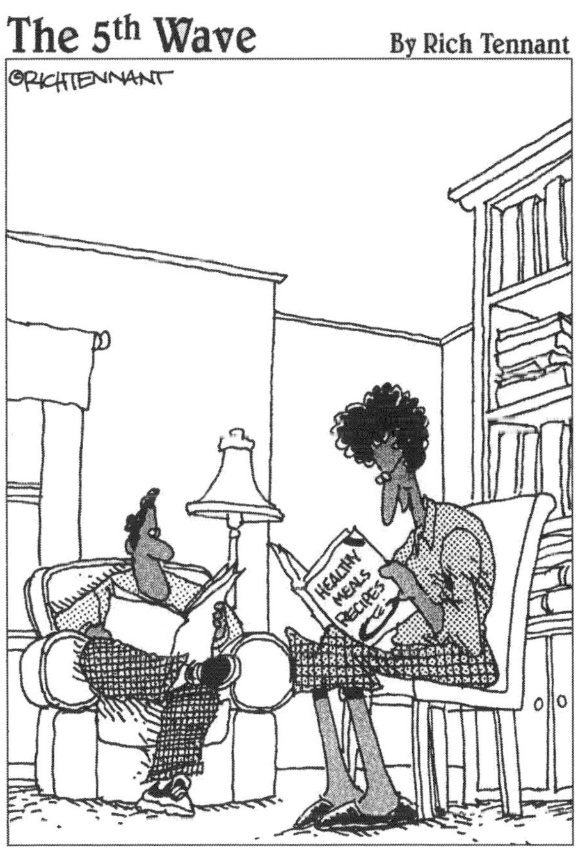

Image 2.1: "Here's one ... 'Poacked Salmon with Kale and Lemon Spiced Rice-Feeds 6 coronary arteries'."

In this part...

The chapters in this part are the real meat of this book (or tofu, for you vegetarians). Here you'll find fantastic recipes for the main course of your meal, with a special chapter of vegetarian entrées (you'll love these recipes whether you're a practicing vegetarian or not). We even provide a chapter of recipes for special occasions—ones that are a little higher in fat than we recommend for every day, but that still make a great meal as a special treat.

Chapter 6

Breakfast and Brunch

In This Chapter
- Breakfasting the heart-smart way
- Enjoying low-fat brunches

Recipes in This Chapter

- Mark's Low-Fat Oat Bran Muffins with Fresh Peaches **(V)**
- Pumpkin Cheesecake Muffins **(V)**
- Peach Scones **(V)**
- Eggs Benedict with Asparagus and Low-Fat Hollandaise Sauce
- Popeye's Favorite Breakfast **(V)**
- Apple Blackberry Soufflé T Sweet Potato Hash Browns **(V)**
- Homemade Granola **(V)**
- Pacific Time's Broiled Pink Florida Grapefruit with Wild Flower Honey **(V)**

***

Eating a healthy low-fat breakfast every day is one of the most important things you can do for your heart and your overall health. Why? People who skip breakfast don't get the calories they need to get the body going early in the morning. As a result, studies show that breakfast-skippers tend to fill up on midmorning snacks that are high in calories and fat, such as doughnuts. Eating breakfast boosts your metabolism early in the day. And boosting your metabolism means you're burning calories at a faster rate, which helps you manage your weight. Plus, breakfast is a good time to consume fiber and fruit, which contribute nutrients for heart health.

This chapter contains some delicious recipes for smart starts for breakfast and brunch. Some of the recipes, such as the muffins, you can make on a more leisurely day and have plenty left over for busy days when you have only minutes for breakfast. Others offer you heart-smart treats for weekends and holidays—or whenever you have a little more time.

Breakfast to Go: Muffins and Scones

Muffins and scones are simple to make and even easier to enjoy. They are the perfect way to start a busy day because you can just grab and go. They also make great snacks. And when fresh fruit is added to the batter, muffins and scones, like the ones in this section, become incredibly nutritious as well as delicious.

Mark's Low-Fat Oat Bran Muffins with Fresh Peaches

Created by Mark Tarbell
Executive Chef/Owner, Tarbell's and Barmouche
Phoenix, Arizona

Oat bran was all the rage in heart health in the late 1980s. But there was a common problem with foods made with a lot of healthful oat bran—few of them tasted very good and people gave up on oat bran in search of the next magic ingredient. These muffins are an exception to that rule. They are possibly the best tasting oat bran muffins ever created! Try them and see for yourself.

Tools: *1 12-cup or 2 6-cup muffin pans, 2 mixing bowls, wooden spoon*

Preparation time: *15 minutes*

Cooking time: *15 minutes*

Yield: *12 muffins*

2 cups oat bran
2 teaspoons baking powder
1 teaspoon cinnamon
1/2 teaspoon kosher salt
1 cup milk
2 egg whites
2 tablespoons canola oil
1/2 cup maple syrup
1 cup diced fresh peaches

1 Preheat oven to 425 degrees.

2 Grease muffin pan(s) with cooking spray.
3 Combine the oat bran, baking powder, cinnamon, and salt in a mixing bowl and stir to blend.
4 In a separate mixing bowl, combine the milk, egg whites, canola oil, maple syrup, and peaches.
5 Pour the peach mixture into the dry ingredients and stir very gently, just to combine. Lumps in the batter are okay.
6 Spoon batter into the muffin pan(s), filling about three-quarters full.
7 Bake 15 minutes or until golden brown on top.

Nutrition at a glance (per serving): *total fat 3g; saturated fat 0 g; protein 4g; dietary fiber 3g; carbohydrate 24g; cholesterol 0mg; sodium 184mg; % of calories from fat 23; % of calories from saturated fat 9; calories 117.*

You can substitute strawberries or blueberries for the peaches in this recipe, in the same amount.

***

Pumpkin Cheesecake Muffins

Created by Angela Kirkpatrick, R.D.
Research Dietitian, Rippe Lifestyle Institute
Shrewsbury, Massachusetts

Cheesecake brings to mind thoughts of decadence and richness, which is exactly what these muffins offer but without all the fat. The use of pumpkin means you're getting a heart-healthy dose of vitamin A. For the best flavor and texture, serve these muffins warm.

Tools: *Medium mixing bowl, 3 6-cup muffin pans, large mixing bowl, cooling rack*

Preparation time: *15 minutes*

Cooking time: *20 minutes*

Yield: *18 servings*

Cream Cheese Filling

1 8-ounce package light cream cheese
1/2 cup sugar
2 tablespoons unbleached flour
2 egg whites
1/4 cup nonfat sour cream
1 teaspoon vanilla

Mix all ingredients in a medium bowl and store in refrigerator while mixing muffin batter.

Muffins

1 cup pumpkin
2/3 cup packed brown sugar

1 1/2 cups milk
1/2 cup applesauce
1 egg
2 egg whites
3 cups flour
1/2 cup sugar
5 teaspoons baking powder
2 teaspoons cinnamon
1 teaspoon salt
1/2 teaspoon cloves
1/2 cup chopped raisins

1 Preheat oven to 400 degrees. Spray the muffin pans, or line with paper cupcake wrappers.
2 In a large bowl, beat the pumpkin, brown sugar, milk, applesauce, egg, and egg whites.
3 Gently stir in the flour, sugar, baking powder, cinnamon, salt, and cloves until just moistened.
4 Add the raisins and stir again.
5 Fill muffin cups 1/3 full.
6 Spoon 1 tablespoon or so of cream cheese filling on top of the batter. Cover the filling with enough batter to fill the muffin cup 2/3 full. Repeat with remaining muffin cups.
7 Bake 20 to 22 minutes or until springy to the touch with a golden brown glow.
8 Remove from muffin pans, place on a cooling rack, and cool slightly before serving.

Nutrition at a glance (per serving): *total fat 3g; saturated fat 1g; protein 6g; dietary fiber 1g; carbohydrate 44g; cholesterol 18mg; sodium 361mg;*

vitamin A (% Daily Value) 65; % of calories from fat 11; % of calories from saturated fat 6; calories 221.

***

Peach Scones

Created by Amy Myrdal, M.S., R.D.
Senior Research Dietitian, Rippe Lifestyle Institute
Shrewsbury, Massachusetts

Scones originated in Scotland and may have been named after the location where Scottish kings were crowned, the *Stone of Destiny* or *Scone.* Scones differ little in ingredients when compared to other quick breads like muffins but tend to be denser and drier. Scones come in many shapes including circles, squares, and classic wedges. Enjoy the following scones with tea. Peach herbal tea is an especially good match.

Tools: *Medium mixing bowl, 2 forks, small mixing bowl, whisk, nonstick baking sheet*

Preparation time: *30 minutes*

Cooking time: *12 minutes*

Yield: *8 scones*

2 cups flour
2 tablespoons sugar
1 tablespoon baking powder
1 teaspoon baking soda
1/2 teaspoon salt

3 tablespoons stick margarine (not reduced-fat margarine), cold, cut into small pieces

1 cup chopped peaches, fresh or canned, well drained

1/2 teaspoon almond extract

2 eggs

1/2 cup fat-free buttermilk (or skim milk)

1 tablespoon decorating or coarse sugar

1 Preheat oven to 425 degrees.

2 In a medium bowl, mix together flour, sugar, baking powder, baking soda, and salt.

3 Add the margarine and cut it into the flour mixture using two forks. Mix until the margarine is well incorporated and the mixture gets crumbly.

4 Add the peaches and almond extract, and stir to combine.

5 In a small bowl, beat the eggs; whisk in the buttermilk. Pour the egg and milk mixture into the dry ingredients. Gently combine until moistened, gathering dough together into a ball.

6 Set mixture aside for about 5 minutes.

7 Divide dough in half. On a floured surface shape each half into a circle, approximately 1-inch thick. Use your hands to gently pat out the dough.

8 Cut each round of dough into four wedges.

9 Place the wedges on a nonstick baking sheet. Sprinkle with decorating sugar. (If you don't have decorating sugar, you can use granulated sugar.)

10 Bake for about 12 minutes, or until lightly golden brown.

11 Serve warm. Scones can be reheated in a toaster oven.

Nutrition at a glance (per serving): *total fat 6g; saturated fat 1g; protein 6g; dietary fiber 1g; carbohydrate 32g; cholesterol 54mg; sodium 557mg; % of calories from fat 26; % of calories from saturated fat 4; calories 206.*

***

Decorating sugar is simply coarse, large grain sugar that, when used on top of a baked item, does not melt onto the surface but instead keeps its shape and adds a "crunch" to the top. Decorating sugar is also called *coarse sugar, sugar crystals,* or *crystal sugar* and can be found in most supermarkets. It also comes in colors (which is especially fun if you have children).

Five-minute breakfast ideas

For days when you have to eat on the run, here are six quick and nutrient-rich breakfast ideas. Notice that each of these breakfasts includes foods from at least three food groups, which helps ensure nutrient richness:

- A fortified cereal topped with fresh fruit, a few chopped nuts, and low-fat milk.

• A toasted whole grain bagel with natural peanut butter, topped with raisins, and a glass of low-fat milk.

• Low-fat or nonfat yogurt topped with low-fat granola and fruit.

• A fruit and low-fat yogurt smoothie with wheat germ.

• A toasted English muffin with a poached egg, a slice of low-fat cheese, and a glass of orange juice.

• A slice or two of cold cheese-and-veggie pizza and a glass of orange juice.

Leisurely Breakfasts and Brunches

When you don't have to dash off to work, everyone enjoys a leisurely breakfast. A special breakfast or brunch can make a special start to a great weekend day for just you and your family or for a gathering of friends. The following recipes will help you provide breakfasts or brunches that are both decadently fun to eat and good for you.

Eggs Benedict with Asparagus and Low-Fat Hollandaise Sauce

Created by Amy Myrdal, M.S., R.D.
Senior Research Dietitian, Rippe Lifestyle Institute
Shrewsbury, Massachusetts

The next time you have friends over for a weekend brunch, serve them this elegant dish with freshly squeezed orange juice for a colorful and healthful meal. The use of asparagus as an accompaniment also provides a serving of vegetables early in the day—helping you reach the healthful goal of at least five vegetables every day.

Tools: *Medium saucepan, electric mixer, medium stainless steel or glass bowl, steamer or steamer basket, large nonstick skillet, medium sauté pan*

Preparation time: *20 minutes*

Cooking time: *15 minutes*

Yield: *4 servings*

Low-Fat Hollandaise Sauce

1/4 cup homemade or canned chicken broth or stock

1/4 cup fresh lemon juice

1/2 cup liquid egg substitute

2 teaspoons canola oil

1/4 teaspoon mustard

Salt and pepper to taste

1 In a medium saucepan, bring the broth and lemon juice to a rolling boil. Allow to boil about 5 to 6 minutes or until liquid volume is reduced by half.

2 While the broth and lemon juice are reducing, whisk the egg substitute in a medium stainless steel or glass bowl until the egg triples in volume. You can use a hand-mixer or a standing mixer to do this.

3 When the broth has reduced, whisk in the oil and the mustard. Then *slowly* add the reduced broth to the egg mixture, whisking the entire time. Season with salt and pepper to taste.
4 The sauce will thicken as it sits and cools; either make it immediately before serving or warm over low heat while whisking to thin the sauce if you make it ahead of time.

Eggs Benedict with Asparagus

4 English muffins
8 large eggs
8 1/2-ounce slices Canadian bacon
1/2 cup Low-Fat Hollandaise Sauce (see recipe above)
16 asparagus spears
Salt and pepper to taste
4 cups freshly squeezed orange juice

1 Split English muffins and toast.
2 Place asparagus spears in a steamer and steam for 3 to 5 minutes, depending on their thickness. They should be tender but firm.
3 While muffins are toasting and asparagus is steaming, place the eggs in a large nonstick skillet filled with 1/2 inch simmering water. Cover and cook for 2 to 3 minutes or until the egg whites are firm and white.
4 Warm the Canadian bacon slices in a medium sauté pan over medium heat, about 1 minute per side. Place 2 English muffin halves on each plate and top each half with a slice of bacon.

5 When the eggs are ready, drain and place over the bacon. Place 4 asparagus spears between the muffins on each plate. Season the top of the eggs and the asparagus with salt and pepper. Top each muffin with 1 tablespoon Low-Fat Hollandaise Sauce. Serve immediately with 1 cup freshly squeezed orange juice per person.

Nutrition at a glance (per serving, includes juice): *total fat 16g; saturated fat 4g; protein 29g; dietary fiber 3g; carbohydrate 55g; cholesterol 436mg; sodium 994mg; vitamin A (% Daily Value) 32; vitamin C (% Daily Value) 161; folic acid (% Daily Value) 48; % of calories from fat 29; % of calories from saturated fat 7; calories 491.*

***

Popeye's Favorite Breakfast

Created by Amy Myrdal, M.S., R.D.
Senior Research Dietitian, Rippe Lifestyle Institute
Shrewsbury, Massachusetts

The cartoon character Popeye is known for his love of spinach, a vegetable that purportedly made and kept him strong. This breakfast combines spinach with other nutrient-rich foods, such as orange juice, to create a breakfast that will keep *you* strong all morning long.

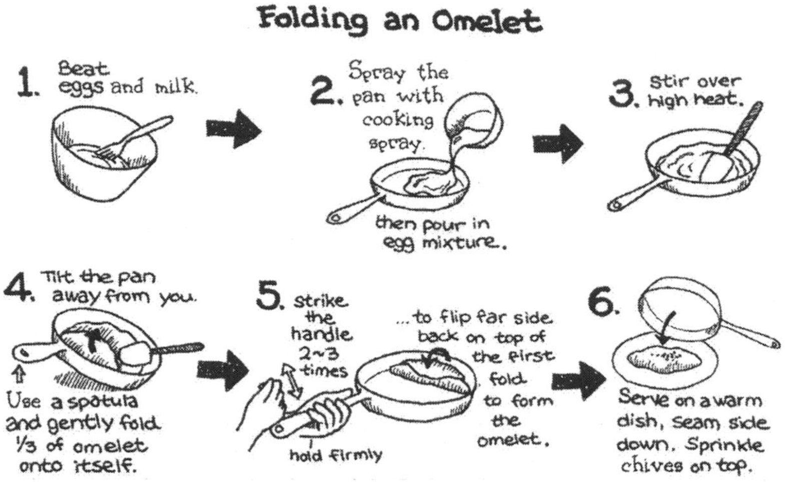

Figure 6-1: Folding an omelet isn't as hard as you may think.

Tools: *Small bowl, whisk, large nonstick skillet, 8-inch nonstick skillet, rubber spatula*

Preparation time: *10 minutes*

Cooking time: *10 minutes*

Yield: *1 serving*

1 egg

2 egg whites

1 tablespoon milk

1/2 cup frozen, chopped spinach, thawed (or 4 cups fresh spinach, coarsely chopped)

2 tablespoons light (reduced-fat) cream cheese

Salt and pepper to taste

Fresh chive sticks for garnish (optional)

2 slices whole wheat bread, toasted

1 tablespoon of your favorite jam

6 fluid ounces (3/4 cup) orange juice (or your favorite fruit juice)

1. Combine egg, egg whites, and milk in a small bowl. Beat well with a fork or wire whisk until well combined. Set aside.
2. If using *fresh* spinach, place spinach in large nonstick skillet, drizzle with a few drops of water, cover, and steam over high heat until wilted. If using *frozen* spinach, heat in microwave or steam, covered, in skillet on stovetop.
3. Drain all excess water from cooked spinach and set aside.
4. Coat an 8-inch nonstick skillet with cooking spray and heat over medium-high heat. When the pan is hot, pour in egg/milk mixture and allow to cook undisturbed for about 30 seconds. Then use a fork or rubber spatula to gently push the sides down toward the center. As you do this, tip the pan on all sides to allow the uncooked egg to reach the sides of the pan. Repeat this until the omelet is set and only moist in the middle, about 2 to 3 minutes. Place the spinach across one side of the omelet and dot with cream cheese. Sprinkle with salt and pepper (optional). Fold the other side over and transfer to a plate (see Figure 6-1 for illustrated instructions for folding an omelet).
5. Garnish the omelet with fresh chives and serve with whole wheat toast with jam and fresh fruit juice.

Nutrition at a glance (per serving, includes toast, jam, and juice): *total fat 13g; saturated* *fat 5g; protein 27g; dietary fiber 8g; carbohydrate 67g; cholesterol 227mg; sodium 865mg; vitamin A (% Daily Value) 180; vitamin C (% Daily Value) 131; folic acid (% Daily Value) 52; % of calories from fat 25; % of calories from saturated fat 10; calories 474.*

***

Check out Figure 6-2 for illustrated instructions for separating an egg.

Figure 6-2: Recipes often call for separated egg yolks or whites. Follow these steps to get only the part you want.

Apple-Blackberry Soufflé

Created by Angela Kirkpatrick, R.D.
Research Dietitian, Rippe Lifestyle Institute

Shrewsbury, Massachusetts

The oats in this soufflé are soaked in milk overnight, so try this delicious dish at a Sunday brunch, when you've had time to start preparing it the night before. It's also a sweet treat you can enjoy guilt-free, because it's so good for you—it's particularly high in heart-healthy soluble fiber.

Tools: *Small mixing bowl, medium saucepan, large mixing bowl, rubber spatula, 2-quart soufflé dish*

Preparation time: *50 minutes*

Cooking time: *45 minutes*

Yield: *4 servings*

3/4 cup quick-cooking oatmeal

1 cup skim milk

1/3 cup light cream cheese

1/4 cup light brown sugar

1/4 cup maple syrup

1/4 teaspoon cinnamon

1/4 teaspoon nutmeg

1/2 teaspoon powdered ginger

1 cup sliced apple wedges

1 cup blackberries (fresh or frozen), thawed and drained

3 egg whites, stiffly beaten

2 teaspoons powdered sugar

1. In a small mixing bowl, combine the oatmeal with the milk. Soak overnight, at least 8 hours, in the refrigerator.
2. Preheat the oven to 325 degrees.

3 Heat the soaked oats in a medium saucepan over low to medium heat. When the oats are heated, add the cream cheese, brown sugar, maple syrup, cinnamon, nutmeg, and ginger to the saucepan, stirring to combine and dissolve the cream cheese.
4 Remove the saucepan from the heat and transfer mixture to a large mixing bowl. Fold in the apple wedges and blackberries. Using a rubber spatula, fold in the whipped egg whites.
5 Spray a 2-quart soufflé dish with cooking spray. Pour the batter into the mold and place the mold in a baking pan. Fill the baking pan with water to come up halfway on the mold. Bake 40 to 45 minutes, until the center springs back when touched.
6 Serve warm with a dusting of powdered sugar.

Nutrition at a glance (per serving): *total fat 4g; saturated fat 2g; protein 9g; dietary fiber 4g; carbohydrate 52g; cholesterol 11mg; sodium 174mg; % of calories from fat 13; % of calories from saturated fat 6; calories 279.*

***

A *soufflé dish* is a round, ovenproof dish with straight sides that allows the soufflé to rise.

Breakfast Sides

If you're planning a large, leisurely breakfast any one of the next three recipes would be a wonderful side dish to serve. Or mix and match them to make a total breakfast when balanced with fruit or juice and milk.

Sweet Potato Hash Browns

Created by Angela Kirkpatrick, R.D.
Research Dietitian, Rippe Lifestyle Institute
Shrewsbury, Massachusetts

In a nation that loves potatoes, hash browns are always a treat for breakfast—diced, scattered, and fried. This recipe gives the old favorite a delicious and nutritious twist by featuring sweet potatoes, which are rich in two important antioxidants, vitamins A and C.

Tools: *Medium saucepan, large nonstick skillet*
Preparation time: *20 minutes*
Cooking time: *15 minutes*
Yield: *8 servings*

1 1/4 pounds sweet potatoes, peeled and halved
1 1/4 pounds white boiling potatoes, peeled and halved
2 tablespoons canola oil or vegetable cooking spray
1 small sweet Vidalia onion, finely chopped
2 tablespoons finely chopped fresh chives
Sea salt and pepper to taste

1 Place peeled, and halved potatoes in a medium saucepan, and cover tops with cold water. Bring to a boil.

2 Once boiling, reduce heat to simmer and continue cooking uncovered for 5 minutes or until parboiled.
3 Drain well and set aside to cool.
4 Cut cooled potatoes into 1/2-inch cubes.
5 Heat the canola oil in a large nonstick skillet. Add the onions and cubed potatoes. Sauté, tossing or stirring often, until onions become translucent and potatoes start to brown and are tender when pierced with a knife, 5 to 7 minutes.
6 Stir in the chives and pepper. Add a sprinkle of sea salt, if desired.

Nutrition at a glance (per serving): *total fat 4g; saturated fat 0g; protein 2g; dietary fiber 2g; carbohydrate 21g; cholesterol 0mg; sodium 7mg; vitamin A (% Daily Value) 188; vitamin C (% Daily Value) 28; % of calories from fat 27; % of calories from saturated fat 0; calories 119.*

***

Homemade Granola

Created by Carrie Nahabedian
Executive Chef, Four Seasons Hotel Los Angeles at Beverly Hills
Los Angeles, California

Try this hearty, healthy version of granola, which, unlike most granolas, is not coated with oil or butter or heavily sweetened with honey or other sweeteners. It makes a wonderful high-energy breakfast. Chef Nahabedian recommends storing the granola in tightly sealed plastic bags or glass jars in a cool place for no longer than ten days.

Tools: *Large mixing bowl, small mixing bowl, shallow baking pan*

Preparation time: *15 minutes*

Cooking time: *45 minutes*

Yield: *8 1/2-cup servings*

6 1/3 cups rolled oats (regular, not instant)
2 tablespoons whole wheat flour
3 tablespoons nonfat dry milk
6 tablespoons sesame seeds
6 tablespoons sunflower seeds
6 tablespoons chopped almonds
1 tablespoon lemon or orange zest, grated
1 tablespoon ground cinnamon
1/2 cup unsweetened apple juice, frozen concentrate, thawed
1/2 cup hot water
8 teaspoons honey
1/2 cup chopped dates or granulated date sugar
3/4 cup currants, dried

1 Preheat oven to 300 degrees.
2 In a large mixing bowl, combine the oats, flour, dry milk, sesame and sunflower seeds, almonds,

lemon or orange zest, and ground cinnamon. Mix well.

3 In a small bowl, stir together the concentrated apple juice, hot water, and honey. Add the granola mixture, stirring to coat evenly.
4 Thinly spread the mixture in a shallow baking pan. Bake until dry and toasted, about 40 to 45 minutes, stirring occasionally.
5 Pour into large mixing bowl and cool slightly before stirring in chopped dates and the currants.
6 Cool completely before storing.

Nutrition at a glance (per serving): *total fat 9g; saturated fat 1g; protein 9g; dietary fiber 7g; carbohydrate 53g; cholesterol 0mg; sodium 20mg; % of calories from fat 26; % of calories from saturated fat 4; calories 311.*

***

Pacific Time's Broiled Pink Florida Grapefruit with Wild Flower Honey

Created by Jonathan Eismann
Chef/Proprietor, Pacific Time
Miami Beach, Florida

Tools: *Paring knife, rectangular ovenproof glass or stainless steel baking dish*

Preparation time: *10 minutes*

Cooking time: *2 minutes*
Yield: *4 servings*
2 large whole pink Florida grapefruit
1 tablespoon sugar
4 tablespoons wild flower honey

1 Preheat broiler.
2 Using a sharp paring knife, remove the peel and inner skin from each grapefruit. Use the same knife (or a fillet knife) to cut each section from its membrane casing.
3 In a rectangular ovenproof dish arrange the grapefruit supremes edge to edge.
4 Sprinkle the sugar and the honey over the grapefruit sections.
5 Place the dish under a broiler for 2 minutes.
6 Remove from the oven, divide evenly among four plates, and serve immediately.

Nutrition at a glance (per serving): *total fat 0g; saturated fat 0g; protein 0g; dietary fiber 1g; carbohydrate 28g; cholesterol 0mg; vitamin C (% Daily Value) 52; % of calories from fat 0; % of calories from saturated fat 0; calories 105.*

***

Supremes of fruit are rindless, skinless sections of the fruit "meat" removed with a paring or fillet knife. Supremes are also known as *fillets.*

Chapter 7

Poultry and Meat

In This Chapter

- Selecting the leanest cuts of poultry and meat
- Storing poultry and meat
- Exploring different ways to cook poultry and meat
- Venturing into specialty meats

Recipes in This Chapter

- Roasted Chicken with Caramelized Garlic and Sage with Lemon Risotto
- Pot-au-Feu of Chicken
- Chili Lime Game Hens with Cranberry Pecan Salsa
- JK's Kicking Jambalaya
- Marinated Grilled Pork Tenderloin with Raspberry Chamborde Sauce
- Chipotle BBQ Pork Tenderloin with Grilled Pineapple Salsa
- Picadillo
- Grilled Flat Iron Steak with Chipotle Glaze Served with Wilted Escarole and Sweet Onion Salad
- Healthy-Heart Beef Stroganoff

• Herb-Crusted Lamb Loin with Braised Fennel and Fresh Mint
• Pan-Roasted Buffalo Steaks
• Zak's Grilled Quail with Mustard and Herb Chutney
***

Long faces show up often in our dietitians' offices at the Rippe Lifestyle Institute. Like many, these men and women are sure that a diagnosis of heart disease means they are sentenced to a lifetime of turkey sandwiches for lunch and plain broiled chicken breasts for dinner. Actually, as I discuss in Chapter 3, all kinds of lean meat—from turkey to beef to specialty meats—have a place in a healthy-heart approach to eating.

This chapter provides a selection of recipes that demonstrate delicious, heart-healthy ways to prepare a variety of meats. The foundation is starting with modest portions of lean cuts. The secret, which our chefs employ masterfully, is to then prepare these cuts with tasty creativity.

Selecting Lean Poultry and Meat

The first step in selecting the best cuts of poultry and meat is to learn which cuts are leanest. The sidebar on the next page provides a handy checklist of lean cuts for both common and specialty meats.

Next, use your eyes and nose. Most people today purchase prepackaged poultry and meat at the supermarket. Even though everything is sealed in plastic, you can use these tips to make good choices.

- **Packages should be clean, well-sealed, and well within the "sell-by" date.** If anything looks or smells bad, leave it in the bin. Reject items sitting in liquid within the package.
- **Select the leanest piece of meat you can see.** If a roast, steak, ham, or chop has large streaks of fat through it, choose another. Fat on the outside, you can trim, but it should be white or creamy not yellow.
- **Select whole chickens and turkeys that have smooth clear skin that is not bruised or discolored.** The color may range from creamy to bright yellow. Skinless chicken pieces should be plump, firm, and not at all slimy.

Which cuts are leanest?

This checklist identifies leaner cuts of poultry and meat. These cuts are not equal to each other but are all on the leaner end of the scale. And we don't need to remind you to trim all visible fat, do we?

Poultry

- Turkey breast, without skin

- Chicken breast, without skin
- Ground turkey, 99 percent or 97 percent lean
- Turkey sausage, 90 percent lean

Beef

- Top round steak or roast
- Eye of Round
- Sirloin
- Flank
- Tenderloin
- 90 percent (or higher) lean ground beef

Pork

- Ham, boneless, precooked, 96 to 97 percent lean
- Canadian bacon
- Pork tenderloin
- Pork boneless loin
- Center-cut loin chops, lean only

Lamb

- Leg roast
- Loin, roast or chop, lean only

Specialty and Game Meats

- Beefalo
- Buffalo
- Wild duck
- Game birds such as quail, dove, pheasant
- Ostrich
- Rabbit
- Venisonm

If you have a specialty butcher, you can ask him or her to help you select with these same criteria in mind.

Storing Poultry and Meat until You're Ready to Cook

For retaining flavor and freshness, plan to cook poultry and meat within a day or two of its purchase. If you don't plan to cook it on the day of purchase, many experts recommend that you remove the poultry or meat from its store packaging, rinse it with water, pat it completely dry, and place it in loose wrapping or a plastic bag. Whether or not you repackage it, poultry and meat should always be stored in the coldest part of the refrigerator, which is generally on the bottom shelf, toward the back.

Freeze the poultry or meat if you will not use it within two days. But don't just toss it in the freezer in the store packaging. Repackage the poultry and meat in appropriate freezer wrapping. For convenience and timesaving when thawing and preparing, freeze in meal-sized or single-serving portions. For example, when you hit a great sale on boneless, skinless chicken breasts, wrap each individually in plastic wrap then place the individual packages within a single resealable plastic freezer bag. Cut a boneless pork loin into a roast and chops and freeze separately. (Or, if you're not an expert meat cutter, ask the person behind the meat counter to cut the meat into the portions you wish.) Such planning ahead makes defrosting just the right amount for any recipe or number of diners quicker and easier. Most cuts of poultry and meat will keep at least two months in the freezer; some will keep a lot longer. For excellent information about freezing and other methods of preserving foods, call your local Cooperative Extension Office, a service of the United States Department of Agriculture and state universities.

For safety, always thaw frozen poultry and meats in the refrigerator, not at room temperature. Also remember to handle raw poultry and meat safely. To avoid the danger of bacterial contamination, don't let knives, utensils, cutting boards, or serving dishes that have been used with raw meat come in contact with cooked meat or other food stuffs. Many health authorities recommend using a separate cutting board for raw meat and poultry. Wash your hands thoroughly with warm water and antibacterial soap after handling raw meat.

Cooking Chicken

If you think chicken has to be dull, any one of the next six recipes will change your mind and show you some of the many excellent ways to cook this versatile bird.

Roasted Chicken with Caramelized Garlic and Sage with Lemon Risotto

Created by Walter Pisano
Executive Chef, Tulio Ristorante
Seattle, Washington

Shocking! A recipe with chicken skin in a heart health book? Don't worry. Although we don't recommend *eating* poultry skin, we certainly don't discourage cooking poultry with the skin on to trap in juices. Doing so does not significantly affect the fat content of the meat but does significantly affect the final flavor. This recipe calls for caramelized garlic and sage tucked under the skin while roasting—talk about flavor!

Tools: *Small heavy saucepan, sauté pan, roasting pan*

Preparation time: *20 minutes*

Cooking time: *45 minutes*

Yield: *8 servings*

4 large whole chicken breasts (bone-in or boneless), with skin, halved

4 cloves garlic, peeled

1/4 cup sugar

2 to 3 fresh sage leaves, chopped

1/2 tablespoon unsalted butter

2 tablespoons olive oil

1 Preheat oven to 375 degrees.

2 Peel and slice the garlic paper thin, then blanch in boiling water for 1 minute. Heat the sugar in a small heavy saucepan until golden brown. Remove from the heat and add the blanched garlic, chopped sage, and butter. Mix well and set aside to cool.

3 Prepare each chicken breast by carefully pulling up the skin in one corner, at the thickest point. Slip approximately 1/2 teaspoon of the caramelized garlic and sage under the skin, being certain to keep the skin attached to the meat as much as possible. You will have extra caramelized garlic and sage, which you can use later or brush on the chicken after searing and before baking.

4 Season chicken with salt (optional) and pepper to taste. Sear each breast, skin side down, in a preheated sauté pan with olive oil.

5 Place seared breast in a roasting pan and roast in a 375-degree oven for 25 to 35 minutes, depending on thickness. When done, allow chicken to rest 4 to 5 minutes before removing the skin, slicing and serving. Serve over Lemon Risotto (see following recipe).

Nutrition at a glance (per serving): *total fat 5g; saturated fat 1g; protein 30g; dietary fiber 0g; carbohydrate 2g; cholesterol 84mg; sodium 76mg; % of calories from fat 25; % of calories from saturated fat 5; calories 181.*

Lemon Risotto

Tools: *Small saucepan, large sauté pan*
Preparation time: *15 minutes*
Cooking time: *30 minutes*
Yield: *8 servings*

6 to 7 cups chicken stock, warmed (homemade or very low-sodium canned broth)
10 ounces (1 3/4 cups) Arborio rice, uncooked
1 bay leaf
1 teaspoon shallot, minced
1/2 teaspoon fresh lemon juice
1 teaspoon preserved lemon (optional)
1 teaspoon lemon zest
2 teaspoons unsalted butter
2 teaspoons fresh Italian parsley, chopped
Salt and pepper to taste

1. In a small saucepan, warm the chicken stock over low heat until ready to use.
2. In a large sauté pan, sauté the minced shallots in butter over medium heat for 2 to 3 minutes.
3. Add the bay leaf and rice and stir until the rice is coated with butter.
4. Slowly add 3 cups of the warmed chicken stock to the sauté pan. Bring to a simmer and cook, stirring often and adding more broth, 1/2 cup at a time as the rice absorbs the liquid. Use only the amount of broth needed to bring the rice to a tender, creamy (but not soupy) texture.
5. Add the remaining ingredients; stir and serve.

Nutrition at a glance (per serving): *total fat 2g; saturated fat 1g; protein 4g; dietary fiber 1g; carbohydrate 31g; cholesterol 3mg; sodium 26mg; % of calories from fat 11; % of calories from saturated fat 6; calories 161.*

***

Arborio rice is *the* rice to use when making risotto. The kernels have a higher starch content than other types of rice; the starch gives risotto its distinctive creamy texture.

Preserved lemons are lemons that have been preserved in a salt and lemon juice brine, possibly with additional spices such as cinnamon, cloves, or coriander. Preserved lemons have a very distinctive flavor and are commonly used in Moroccan cooking. Preserved lemons may be found in specialty food shops or markets that cater to Moroccan clients.

Pot-au-Feu of Chicken

Created by Joe Mannke
Chef/Proprietor, Rotisserie for Beef and Bird
Houston, Texas

This savory combination of fresh vegetables stewed with chicken tastes wonderful on a cool night. *Pot-au-feu* is a French term that simply means dinner in a pot (literally "pot on fire") and typically is made with beef, veal, or chicken. What New Englanders think of as a "boiled dinner" can be considered the American version of pot-au-feu.

Tools: *4-quart stock pot or soup pot*

Preparation time: *2 hours*

Cooking time: *1 hour, 15 minutes*

Yield: *4 servings*

1 small whole chicken (2 1/2 to 3 pounds), trimmed and cleaned with cold water, skin removed

1 teaspoon salt

2 bay leaves

1 teaspoon fresh thyme, or 1/2 teaspoon dried

6 cloves fresh garlic

2 carrots, peeled and cut into 1-inch pieces

6 pearl onions, peeled

2 stalks of celery, cut into 1-inch pieces

2 parsnips, peeled and cut into 1-inch pieces

1 leek, root end trimmed, halved lengthwise, thoroughly washed, white and light green part cut into 1-inch pieces

1/2 head of green cabbage, cut into 4 wedges

1 fennel bulb, quartered

2 medium Be-red (or other red-skinned) potatoes, quartered

1/2 cup fresh or frozen green peas

2 tablespoons chopped fresh parsley, for garnish

1 Place the chicken in a 4-quart stock pot, cover with cold water, and bring to a boil. Reduce heat to simmer.

2 Add the salt, bay leaves, thyme, garlic, carrots, onions, celery, parsnips, leek, cabbage, fennel, and potatoes. Simmer over low heat for 1 hour, skimming the surface as necessary until the chicken is tender and cooked through. Add the peas during the last 3 minutes of cooking.
3 Place four soup plates in a warm oven to preheat for 2 to 3 minutes. Using kitchen tongs or a carving fork, carefully lift the chicken out of the pot, draining any liquid in the cavity back into the soup pot. Transfer the chicken to a large cutting board and carve so that each diner receives half of a breast and half of a leg. Divide the chicken among four preheated soup plates, and ladle broth and vegetables over the chicken.
4 Sprinkle with parsley and serve.

Nutrition at a glance (per serving): *total fat 8g; saturated fat 2g; protein 35g; dietary fiber 11g; carbohydrate 45g; cholesterol 87mg; sodium 782mg; vitamin A (% of Daily Value) 54; vitamin C (% of Daily Value) 117; folic acid (% of Daily Value) 37; % of calories from fat 19; % of calories from saturated fat 5; calories 381.*

***

Fennel is an aromatic plant that has a pale green bulb, celery-like stems, and feathery fronds like dill. It has a sweet flavor that, although like anise, is much more delicate. It's available in the market usually from fall through spring.

Chili Lime Game Hens with Cranberry Pecan Salsa

Created by Kimberly Shaker
Chef, Cowboy Ciao
Scottsdale, Arizona

Prepare the salsa for this dish ahead of time so the flavors can combine, mellow, and marry. Chef Shaker recommends letting the salsa sit at least 1 hour before serving. If you make it first, it will have plenty of time to mellow while the game hens marinate.

Tools: *Medium mixing bowl, blender, sharp knife or kitchen shears, deep bowl, baking sheet*

Preparation time: *1 hour, 25 minutes (including marinating)*

Cooking time: *40 minutes*

Yield: *4 servings*

Cranberry Pecan Salsa

1 cup dried cranberries
1/4 cup orange juice
1/4 cup honey
1 red bell pepper, cored, seeded, and chopped
1/4 cup chopped toasted pecans
1/4 cup chopped cilantro

2 tablespoons lemon zest and the juice from zesting

1 teaspoon salt

Combine all ingredients in a medium mixing bowl, and refrigerate covered for at least 1 hour to allow flavors to combine.

Chili Lime Game Hens

1 cup lime juice

1/2 cup olive oil

3 tablespoons fresh chopped garlic

2 tablespoons ground cumin

1 tablespoon ground cinnamon

2 tablespoons chili powder

2 teaspoons salt

2 teaspoons pepper

4 1-to 1 1/2-pound game hens

1 Combine all ingredients except game hens in a blender. Blenderize and reserve.

2 Clean game hens by removing innards and rinsing under cold running water. Cut out the back bone by placing the hens, breast sides down, on a cutting board. Using a sharp knife or kitchen shears, cut along both sides of the backbone for each hen. Remove the bone. Using your hands, press down, flattening the hens.

3 Place hens in a deep bowl, pour marinade mixture over, and refrigerate for at least 1 hour.

4 Preheat oven to 375 degrees, remove hens from marinade, and place on a baking sheet so they lay flat with skin side up.
5 Cook uncovered for 35 to 40 minutes, until cooked through. (Cooking time varies depending on the size of each bird.)
6 Serve each bird with 1/2 cup Cranberry Pecan Salsa.

Nutrition at a glance (per serving): *total fat 16g (based on removing skin before eating); saturated fat 3g (based on removing skin before eating); protein 46g; dietary fiber 4g; carbohydrate 51g; cholesterol 202mg; sodium 1029mg; vitamin A (% of Daily Value) 37; vitamin C (% of Daily Value) 94; % of calories from fat 27; % of calories from saturated fat 5; calories 527.*

***

JK's Kicking Jambalaya

Created by Jeremy Kirkpatrick
Acton, Massachusetts

This dish can be made a day ahead to allow the flavors to really heat up. Coauthor and registered dietitian, Angela Kirkpatrick testifies that her husband's jambalaya is "kicking" with flavor and creates a perfect meal when paired with salad greens and citrus shallot dressing. The use of fresh, nutrient-rich ingredients and its ease of preparation make this a fast, delicious, and nutritious meal.

Tools: *Medium to large casserole*
Preparation time: *15 minutes*
Cooking time: *30 minutes*
Yield: *6 servings*

1 1/2 tablespoons olive oil
1 large onion, roughly chopped
3 sticks celery, roughly chopped
1 1/2 to 2 medium green bell peppers, seeded and roughly chopped
3 cloves garlic, crushed
1/4 teaspoon white pepper
1/4 teaspoon black pepper
1/8 teaspoon cayenne pepper
1 cup long-grain rice
1 14-ounce can tomatoes
1 large red tomato, diced
6 ounces 90 percent lean, smoked turkey sausage
3 1/4 cups sodium-reduced chicken stock
1 pound chicken breasts cut into 1-inch chunks
1/8 to 1/4 cup fresh chopped parsley

1 In a medium to large casserole, heat the olive oil over medium heat. Add the onions, celery, green pepper, and garlic, and sauté, stirring often, until slightly softened, about 5 minutes.
2 Add the white pepper, black pepper, cayenne pepper, and rice, stirring to mix well.
3 Add the canned tomatoes, diced tomato, sausage, chicken stock, and chicken, and mix well. Bring to

a boil. Reduce the heat to simmering, and cook about 20 to 25 minutes, stirring occasionally until the chicken is done and rice is tender. (The rice should have absorbed most of the liquid by the time it has cooked.) Stir in the parsley and serve.

Nutrition at a glance (per serving): *total fat 10g; saturated fat 2g; protein 28g; dietary fiber 3g; carbohydrate 38g; cholesterol 60mg; sodium 708mg; vitamin A (% Daily Value) 21; vitamin C (% Daily Value) 96; % of calories from fat 25; % of calories from saturated fat 6; calories 353.*

***

Watch out! As the rice cooks you may need to add more water. If you add too much water, uncover the pan just before the rice is done and let it boil rapidly.

Add 1 teaspoon of hot chili peppers if you really like zip!

Cooking Meat

Lean cuts of pork, beef, and lamb can have a place in heart-healthy cooking. Preparing any of the following recipes with these meats will show you how appetizing and satisfying low-fat preparation can be. The chefs' inventiveness will soon have you deserting your old favorites to try some ideas of your own in the kitchen.

Marinated Grilled Pork Tenderloin with Raspberry Chamborde Sauce

Created by Kevin T. Jones
Executive Chef, Aurora Summit
Aurora, Colorado

According to Chef Jones, "This is the perfect recipe for the working man or woman. I suggest preparing the marinade a day in advance, marinating in the morning and grilling it up when you get home. The reason for such a long marinating time (7 to 10 hours) is that the marinade cooks the meat prior to grilling, which results in a very tender product. I usually serve the grilled tenderloin with my Raspberry Chamborde Sauce."

Tools: *Large mixing bowl, gas or charcoal grill or stovetop grill pan*

Preparation time: *10 minutes for preparation, 7 to 10 hours for marinating*

Cooking time: *15 to 20 minutes*

Yield: *6 servings*

Zest and juice of 1 grapefruit

Zest and juice of 3 limes

Zest and juice of 2 oranges

6 fluid ounces raspberry vinegar

1 bunch fresh cilantro, chopped

1 cup honey

3 tablespoons soy or vegetable oil (preferably canola oil)

2 16-ounce pork tenderloins, trimmed of all fat with silver silk skin removed

1 In a large bowl, combine all ingredients except pork and mix with a wire whisk. Set aside.
2 If necessary, remove all fat and the silken skin from the pork tenderloins.
3 Place trimmed tenderloins in a shallow pan and cover with marinade.
4 Refrigerate for 7 to 10 hours.
5 When you're ready to cook the meat, preheat the grill. Place the rack 3 to 4 inches from the heat source. When the grill is hot, grill the tenderloins, turning to brown all sides, for 10 to 12 minutes for medium or 15 to 18 minutes for medium-well

to well-done, depending on your preference. Use a meat thermometer to assure that internal temperature has reached 150 to 160 degrees. Remove from the heat and let rest (cooking will continue) for 5 minutes.

6 Slice into 1 1/2-to 2-inch medallions and serve with Raspberry Chamborde Sauce (see following recipe).

Nutrition at a glance (per serving): *total fat 9g; saturated fat 2.5g; protein 35g; dietary fiber 0g; carbohydrate 20g; cholesterol 96mg; sodium 74mg; vitamin C (% of Daily Value) 26; % of calories from fat 27; % of calories from saturated fat 7; calories 302.*

Raspberry Chamborde Sauce

The sweetness of this sauce complements the subtle spiciness of Chef Kevin Jones's Marinated Grilled Pork Tenderloin. We think this sauce is also wonderful spooned on top of fresh mixed berries and topped off with a small scoop of low-fat frozen yogurt for dessert. Any extra sauce can be kept in the refrigerator for 5 to 7 days.

Tools: *Saucepan, sieve or strainer*
Preparation time: *5 minutes*
Cooking time: *1 hour*
Yield: *6 1/3-cup servings*
1/2 pound (1 3/4 cups) fresh raspberries
2 cups Burgundy wine
6 ounces (1 cup minus 2 tablespoons) sugar

1 Place raspberries, wine, and sugar in medium saucepan.

2 Bring to a boil, reduce to a simmer, and simmer 1 hour. Strain seeds out with a fine sieve or strainer and serve.

Nutrition at a glance (per serving): *total fat 0g; saturated fat 0g; protein 0g; dietary fiber 0g; carbohydrate 34g; cholesterol 0mg; sodium 6mg; % of calories from fat 0; % of calories from saturated fat 0; calories 184.*

***

Chipotle BBQ Pork Tenderloin with Grilled Pineapple Salsa

Created by Paul Agnelli
Executive Chef, Van Gogh's Restaurant & Bar
Roswell, Georgia

The smoky flavor of chipotle pepper (dried jalapeno) and the piquancy of adobo sauce in Chef Agnelli's Chipotle Marinade paired with the unique grilled fresh pineapple salsa give new richness to the meaning of barbecue. Because the marinade will keep for a couple of weeks, you may want to make a little extra so that you can enjoy this barbecue again.

Tools: *Food processor, gas or charcoal grill, shallow baking dish, medium mixing bowl*

Preparation time: *20 minutes plus 1 hour to marinate*

Cooking time: *30 minutes (for the Pork Tenderloin and the Pineapple Salsa)*

Yield: *4 servings*

For the Chipotle Marinade:

*1 6-ounce can chipotle peppers packed in adobo sauce (**Note:** Use only 1 pepper but all of the adobo sauce.)*

2 shallots

2 cloves garlic

1/2 cup apple cider vinegar

1/2 cup tomato paste

1/4 cup brown sugar

1 cup chicken broth

1/4 cup canola oil

1 tablespoon salt

For the Pork Tenderloin:

16 ounces pork tenderloin

For the Grilled Pineapple Salsa:

1 large golden sweet pineapple

2 tablespoons Grand Marnier liqueur

1 small red onion, diced

1 bunch cilantro, roughly chopped

1 medium jalapeno pepper, diced

1 teaspoon salt

1 large lime, juiced

Prepare the Chipotle Marinade:

This marinade can be made up to 2 weeks in advance.

Mix all ingredients in a food processor until smooth. More chipotle peppers can be added for extra spiciness.

Prepare the Pork Tenderloin:

1 Clean the silver skin off the tenderloin.
2 Place the pork in a shallow baking dish.
3 Rub and cover the entire surface with the Chipotle Marinade. Cover with plastic wrap and place in refrigerator for 1 hour to allow the marinade to soak into the pork.
4 Depending on whether you're using a gas or charcoal grill, preheat your grill at the appropriate time. Place the grill rack 3 to 4 inches from the heat source. When your grill is ready, remove the tenderloin from the marinade and place on grill. Grill the tenderloin, turning to evenly brown, to desired doneness, about 12 to 15 minutes for medium.
5 Remove the tenderloin from the grill and allow to rest for 5 to 10 minutes before slicing.
6 When you're ready to serve, slice the tenderloin into medallions.
7 Serve with Chef Agnelli's Grilled Pineapple Salsa.

Prepare the Grilled Pineapple Salsa:

1 Cut top, bottom, and skin off the pineapple.
2 Cut the pineapple into 4 large slices lengthwise, avoiding the core.
3 Place the pineapple in a shallow baking dish and soak or toss with the Grand Marnier.

4 On a hot grill, grill all pieces until tender and evenly brown, about 3 to 4 minutes per side. Remove from the grill and allow to cool.
5 When cool, dice the pineapple and place in a medium mixing bowl.
6 Add the rest of the ingredients and toss well to combine.
7 Store, covered, in the refrigerator until 15 minutes before serving. Warming to room temperature before serving intensifies the flavors of the salsa.

Nutrition at a glance (per serving): *total fat 11g; saturated fat 2g; protein 28g; dietary fiber 3g; carbohydrate 32g; cholesterol 72mg; sodium 1093mg; vitamin A (% of Daily Value) 38; vitamin C (% of Daily Value) 101; % of calories from fat 29; % of calories from saturated fat 5; calories 342.*

***

Reduce the sodium content of this dish by using less salt and low-sodium chicken broth in the marinade.

Picadillo

Created by Amy Myrdal, M.S., R.D.
Senior Research Dietitian, Rippe Lifestyle Institute
Shrewsbury, Massachusetts

Picadillo (pronounced pee-kah-DEE-yoh) is a common dish in many Spanish-speaking countries. This recipe was developed by Amy's mother, who, as a Spanish language instructor for many years, studied not only the language but also the foods of Spanish-speaking countries. The dish makes a great meal-in-a-bowl but also is wonderful as a filling for stuffed green peppers. Extra picadillo freezes and reheats well, so if you make a big batch and can't finish it, just freeze the extra for future healthful "frozen dinners."

Tools: *Sauté pan or skillet, 3-quart saucepan, strainer*

Preparation time: *15 minutes*

Cooking time: *60 minutes*

Yield: *8 servings (1 1/2 cups per serving)*

1 pound ground pork, lamb, or beef (analysis based on using ground pork)

1 yellow or white onion, peeled and finely chopped

3 cloves garlic, peeled and minced

5 carrots, peeled and shredded

1 green pepper, seeded and roughly chopped

1/2 small head of green cabbage, finely chopped

1 teaspoon dried oregano (or 1 tablespoon fresh)
1 teaspoon dried thyme (or 1 tablespoon fresh)
2 bay leaves
2 1/2 cups water
1 28-ounce can tomato puree
1 28-ounce can whole tomatoes
1 tablespoon soy sauce
2 tablespoons red wine or dry sherry
1 cup uncooked rice
Salt and pepper to taste

1 Brown the ground meat in a sauté pan or skillet over medium-high heat. After about 5 minutes, when the meat is fully cooked, transfer to a strainer and rinse under hot running water for 30 seconds to remove excess fat.
2 Place rinsed meat in a 3-quart saucepan over medium heat. Add the chopped onion and garlic and sauté for 5 minutes.
3 Add the remaining ingredients, stir, cover, and bring to a boil. Reduce heat and simmer for 45 minutes. Stir occasionally to prevent sticking or burning on the bottom.
4 Serve with warmed tortillas and your favorite beverage.

Nutrition at a glance (per serving): *total fat 3.5g; saturated fat 1g; protein 18g; dietary fiber 6g; carbohydrate 43g; cholesterol 32mg; sodium 706mg; vitamin A (% of Daily Value) 159; vitamin C (% of Daily Value) 114; % of calories from fat 12; % of calories from saturated fat 3; calories 270.*

***

Grilled Flat Iron Steak with Chipotle Glaze Served with Wilted Escarole and Sweet Onion Salad

Created by Bradley Ogden
Chef/Co-Owner, The Lark Creek Restaurant Group
Larkspur (Marin County), California

The salad in this recipe is a refreshing departure from the typical cold, lettuce-based salad. The Wilted Escarole and Sweet Onion Salad is a warm salad that includes potatoes, which makes this a heartier entrée appropriate for a cool fall or winter evening.

Tools: *Saucepan, baking dish, gas or charcoal grill or stovetop grill pan, large skillet*

Preparation time: *25 minutes*

Cooking time: *20 minutes*

Yield: *4 servings*

For the Salad:

8 small (half-dollar size) red potatoes, rose fir or Yukon gold

1 medium red onion, peeled and cut into 8 wedges

2 tablespoons olive oil

Kosher salt

Pepper

1 head escarole, outside leaves removed, rinsed well and torn into small pieces
2 teaspoons minced garlic
2 tablespoons balsamic vinegar

For the Steak:
24 ounces flat-iron steak, trimmed and cut into 4 steaks (can use flank steak)
Olive oil or olive oil spray (minimal amount)
Kosher salt to taste
Pepper to taste
1/2 cup Chipotle Glaze (see following recipe)

Prepare the Onions and Potatoes for the Salad:

1 Place the potatoes in a saucepan with enough cold salted (optional) water to cover. Bring to a boil, reduce heat, and simmer until just tender (approximately 10 minutes.)
2 Coat the onion wedges with 1 tablespoon of the olive oil. Season to taste with salt (optional) and pepper.
3 Place onions in a baking dish and roast for 10 minutes.
4 Remove onion wedges from the pan, place on a plate, and allow to cool to room temperature.
5 Drain potatoes and allow to cool to room temperature.
6 When potatoes are cool, cut in half. Set aside. Do not refrigerate.

Prepare the Steaks:

1 Arrange grill rack 3 to 4 inches from the heat source. Preheat your grill or stovetop grill pan.
2 Brush steaks with a little olive oil, then season with salt and pepper.
3 When the grill is hot, place steaks on grill. For medium-rare, grill the steaks approximately 4 minutes on each side.
4 Brush the steaks with the Chipotle Glaze just before removing them from the grill.
5 When cooked to desired doneness, remove the steaks from the grill and let steaks rest while you're finishing the vegetables/salad.

Finish Preparing the Salad:

1 Place a large skillet over medium heat, add 1 tablespoon olive oil and heat until hot.
2 Add the potatoes and cook, tossing or gently stirring occasionally, until lightly browned.
3 Transfer the potatoes to a paper-towel-lined plate.
4 Add the escarole and garlic to the skillet and sauté until the escarole just begins to wilt, about 2 minutes. At this point, return the potatoes to the skillet.
5 Add the vinegar to the escarole and lightly mix.
6 Season to taste with salt and pepper.

Plate the Entrée:

1 Set four dinner plates on counter or tabletop.

2 Place equal amounts of wilted escarole, potatoes, and 2 wedges of roasted onion on each serving plate.
3 Cut each portion of steak into 4 slices.
4 Arrange steak slices over the top of the greens, brush with a thin layer of Chipotle Glaze and serve immediately.

Chipotle Glaze

Tools: *2-quart saucepan, strainer, wooden spoon*
Preparation time: *15 minutes*
Cooking time: *20 minutes*
Yield: *2 cups (16 servings, 2 tablespoons per serving)*

1 tablespoon canned chipotle or 1/2 teaspoon minced, dry chipotle
2 tablespoons poblano chili peppers, minced and seeded
2 cloves garlic, peeled and minced
2 tablespoons dark molasses
1 tablespoon soy sauce
1 tablespoon dark brown sugar
1 tablespoon balsamic vinegar
2 teaspoons Dijon mustard
3 tablespoons fresh lemon juice
1 medium ripe tomato, chopped
2 cups water
1/4 teaspoon kosher salt
1/4 teaspoon pepper
1/4 cup chopped cilantro

1 Combine all the ingredients, except the cilantro, in a 2-quart, stainless steel heavy-bottomed saucepan. Place over high heat and bring to a boil.
2 Reduce the heat to low and simmer for 15 to 20 minutes.
3 Remove from the heat and pour the sauce through a fine strainer. Use a wooden spoon to push through as much of the sauce as possible. Discard the solids left in the strainer.
4 Stir the cilantro into the sauce and cool completely before using. The glaze can be stored in the refrigerator for up to 4 days in a tightly covered container or frozen. Reheat over low heat before serving.

Nutrition at a glance (per serving), based on 4 servings of salad with 2 table-spoons glaze per serving: *total fat 18.7g; saturated fat 5.6g; protein 42g; dietary fiber 6g; carbohydrate 52g; cholesterol 97mg; sodium 228mg; vitamin A (% of Daily Value) 25; vitamin C (% of Daily Value) 54; folic acid (% of Daily Value) 27; % of calories from fat 30; % of calories from saturated fat 9; calories 553.*

***

Chipotle chili peppers are dried, smoked jalapeno peppers. They can be purchased dried, pickled, or included in adobo sauce, which is used as a marinade or serving sauce. The dried peppers with their wrinkled, dark brown skin and smoky, sweet flavor add tremendous flavor to stews and sauces. The pickled chipotles make great appetizers. Latin markets, specialty food stores, and some supermarkets carry chipotles in their various forms.

In addition to Chef Ogden's Grilled Flat Iron Steak, try this glaze on grilled beef, pork, or poultry. Brush on the meat just before removing it from the grill. The aroma and flavor of this sauce is incredible! If you haven't met your neighbors yet, you will when they invite themselves over to investigate the amazing scent emanating from your grill when you're using this glaze.

Healthy-Heart Beef Stroganoff

Created by Amy Myrdal, M.S., R.D.
Senior Research Dietitian, Rippe Lifestyle Institute
Shrewsbury, Massachusetts

Low-fat sour cream lightens up this dish, which is traditionally known as high-fat comfort food.

Freshly ground nutmeg adds a gourmet touch and an element of taste surprise.

Tools: *Large pot, large skillet or sauté pan, medium bowl*

Preparation time: *20 minutes*

Cooking time: *25 minutes*

Yield: *6 servings*

1 tablespoon olive oil

3 cloves garlic, minced

1 small onion, chopped

1 pound top round steak, trimmed of all visible fat and cut into 1-x-1/2-x-1/4-inch slices

1 tablespoon all-purpose flour

8 ounces mushrooms, sliced into 1/4-inch slices

1/2 cup red wine (any oak barrel aged red wine such as Merlot or Cabernet Sauvignon)

1/2 cup low-fat sour cream

1/4 teaspoon nutmeg, freshly ground, if possible

1/4 teaspoon thyme

Salt and pepper to taste

3 cups egg noodles

Fresh parsley, for garnish

1 Bring a large pot of water to a boil and season with salt.

2 Heat the olive oil in a large skillet or sauté pan over medium-high heat. When the oil is hot, add the garlic and onion and sauté for 30 to 45 seconds, until aromatic, being careful not to let the garlic burn.

3 In a medium bowl, toss the sliced beef with the flour, salt, and pepper, and then add to the pan, raise heat to high, and cook for 3 to 5 minutes or until the beef is browned.

4 Reduce the heat to medium-high and add the sliced mushrooms. Sauté, stirring often, for 2 to 3 minutes or until the mushrooms soften slightly.

5 Add the wine and cook for 1 minute to allow the alcohol to burn off; then add the sour cream, nutmeg, and thyme.

6 Reduce heat to low and simmer for 10 minutes.

7 While the beef simmers, drop the egg noodles in the boiling water, and cook according to package directions. Drain and portion between 6 serving plates.

8 To serve, spoon the beef mixture over the noodles and garnish with fresh parsley.

Nutrition at a glance (per serving): *total fat 8g; saturated fat 2g; protein 25g; dietary fiber 2.5g; carbohydrate 47g; cholesterol 99mg; sodium 64mg; % of calories from fat 19; % of calories from saturated fat 5; calories 373.*

Whole nutmeg "nuts" (about the size of grapes) can be found in most super-markets in the spice aisle right next to the ground nutmeg. Specially crafted nutmeg graters or small handheld graters can be used to grate the nutmeg and release the fresh, pure aroma of this versatile spice.

Herb-Crusted Lamb Loin with Braised Fennel and Fresh Mint

Created by Todd Gray
Chef/Owner, Equinox Restaurant
Washington, D.C.

Rosemary, thyme, fennel, and mint love lamb and, in this recipe, help create a lamb lover's treat. This recipe combines grilling with oven roasting to produce tender, succulent meat. Because of the typical size of a boneless lamb loin (or rack), you can easily make this recipe for 2, 4, or 6. But any leftover lamb is also delicious when sliced thin for a sandwich.

Tools: *Large baking sheet, gas or charcoal grill, medium nonstick sauté pan, mixing bowl*

Preparation time: *15 minutes*

Cooking time: *45 minutes*

Yield: *6 servings*

18 small red skinned potatoes

24 ounces boneless lean lamb loin, trimmed of all visible fat (equal to about 3 boned racks)

1 teaspoon salt (optional)

1 teaspoon pepper

1 teaspoon olive oil

1 pound fennel bulb, tough outer leaves and core removed, sliced thinly

1 Vidalia onion, peeled and sliced

1/4 teaspoon ground fennel seeds

3/4 cup water

1/4 cup fresh mint leaves, chopped

2 tablespoons Dijon mustard

2 cups dry (unseasoned) bread crumbs

1 tablespoon fresh rosemary, chopped

1 tablespoon fresh thyme, chopped

1 tablespoon Parmesan cheese, grated

1 Preheat oven to 400 degrees. Place potatoes on a large baking sheet and roast for 25 minutes while grilling lamb.

2 Arrange rack 3 to 4 inches from the heat source, and preheat grill to medium.

3 Season lamb loins with salt (optional) and pepper.

4 When grill is hot, grill lamb to medium rare temperature (130 degrees), about 3 to 4 minutes per side.

5 Remove lamb from grill, place on a plate and allow to rest.

6 Meanwhile, heat a medium nonstick sauté pan over medium heat. Add olive oil, fennel, Vidalia onion, fennel seed, and water. Slowly cook fennel

mixture for 20 minutes or until the fennel is tender; add a little more water if necessary to continue cooking.

7 Add mint and cover to keep warm.

8 Brush lamb with Dijon mustard. Mix bread crumbs, rosemary, thyme, and cheese in a bowl and then proceed to roll lamb in the herb crumb mix.

9 Bake the crusted lamb loins until golden brown (approximately 10 minutes) while the potatoes finish roasting.

10 Heat 6 large plates. To serve, spoon a pile of braised fennel in center of each plate.

11 Remove lamb from oven, slice, and place on top of fennel. Serve immediately.

Nutrition at a glance (per serving): *total fat 12g; saturated fat 4g; protein 31g; dietary fiber 3g; carbohydrate 32g; cholesterol 82mg; sodium 939mg (based on no added salt); % of calories from fat 30; % of calories from saturated fat 10; calories 364.*

***

Vidalia onions are grown in a multi-county area surrounding Vidalia, Georgia. The large, yellow onions are valued for their mildness and sweetness, which is said to be the result of low sulfur soils. They are readily available nation-wide from May to June (and beyond with new refrigeration methods) and can be found at most supermarkets and produce markets. Washington State claims the Walla Walla onion rivals the Vidalia in sweetness.

Cooking Specialty Meats

Specialty meats such as buffalo, which is very lean, are beginning to show up on fine restaurant menus across the country. You may wish to give these a try at home. Wild game birds, such as quail, dove, or partridge, even when farm-raised are naturally lean, as is other game such as venison or wild duck. Here are two recipes that give you an opportunity to venture beyond the ordinary. (If you'd rather not, we give you substitutions so you won't miss these great recipes.)

Pan-Roasted Buffalo Steaks

Created by Michael Degenhart
Executive Chef, Restaurant Rue Cler
Denver, Colorado

Buffalo, or American bison, is very lean but tender and tastes much like beef. Chef Degenhart, who created this recipe, says, "My wine suggestions for this dish vary—an older Gigondas (Cotes du Rhone) or, moving into America, one of our versions of the Rhone. Altus Peak makes some interesting wines along this path. Or try a nice, not too oaky Zinfandel." Chef Degenhart suggests serving roasted new potatoes or a green salad with the buffalo steaks.

Tools: *Large nonstick sauté pan, medium nonstick sauté pan*

Preparation time: *20 minutes*

Cooking time: *10 minutes*

Yield: *4 servings*

For the Buffalo Steaks:

4 4-ounce buffalo steaks, tenderloin or sirloin, trimmed of all visible fat

Salt and pepper, to season

1/2 tablespoon olive oil

For the Salsa:

1 tablespoon olive oil

2 portobello mushrooms, stems and gills removed and cut into 3/4-inch dice

2 red onions, peeled and cut into 1/2-inch dice

2 cloves garlic, sliced

1 red or yellow bell pepper, cut into 1/2-inch dice

1 tablespoon balsamic vinegar

2 Roma tomatoes, washed and cut into 1/2-inch dice

1 tablespoon fresh thyme leaves

Salt and pepper, to taste

1. Season buffalo steaks with salt (optional) and pepper and set aside.
2. In a large sauté pan over medium-high heat, add 1/2 tablespoon olive oil and heat until smoking.

3 Carefully add buffalo steaks and sear for 3 minutes on each side for medium rare. Remove from pan and place on a warm plate.
4 In a medium nonstick sauté pan, heat 1 tablespoon olive oil over medium-high heat. Add portobello mushrooms, onion, garlic, and red or yellow pepper, and sauté, tossing or stirring occasionally, for 3 to 4 minutes.
5 Add balsamic vinegar, tomatoes, and fresh thyme and cook for another minute. Season to taste.
6 To serve, place steak in the center of a plate and spoon warm salsa over and around. Serve with new potatoes or a green salad.

Nutrition at a glance (per serving): *total fat 6g; saturated fat 2g; protein 28g; dietary fiber 2g; carbohydrate 10g; cholesterol 95mg; sodium 52mg; vitamin A (% of Daily Value) 38; vitamin C (% of Daily Value) 112; % of calories from fat 26; % of calories from saturated fat 9; calories 209.*

***

A growing number of producers are now raising buffalo for market. A cross between cattle and buffalo, the *beefalo,* is also available. Buffalo is available from specialty meat markets and from mail order sources such as Mount Royal USA "The Venison and Game Meat Connection," 800-730-3337 or online at mountroyal.com.

If you can't wait for buffalo, try this recipe with your favorite lean beef steak—sirloin or filet mignon would be good.

Zak's Grilled Quail with Mustard and Herb Chutney

Created by Michael Degenhart
Executive Chef, Restaurant Rue Cler
Denver, Colorado

Game birds such as quail have long been prized for flavor. They are also naturally lean. Chef Degenhart suggests serving this next dish with his Cinnamon Roasted New Potatoes (see Chapter 14), which like this recipe incorporates the rich spiciness of the Moroccan spice blend, *ras el hanout.* If you would like to pair this entrée with wine, Chef Degenhart recommends a dry, yet spicy Alsatian Riesling, in particular, Hubert Trimbach Riesling. Extra chutney makes a wonderful spread for sandwiches and can be brushed on chicken or lean beef prior to grilling. For perfect timing, prepare the chutney before the quail.

Tools: *Broiler pan, small mixing bowl*

Preparation time: *20 minutes to marinate, 35 minutes overall preparation time*

Cooking time: *10 minutes*

Yield: *4 servings*

For the Quail:

8 semi-boneless or boneless quail

3 teaspoons ras el hanout (or Madras curry powder)

1 teaspoon pepper

2 cloves garlic, chopped

2 teaspoons olive oil

1 teaspoon salt

1 tablespoon lemon juice

For the Mustard and Herb Chutney

Yield: *10 servings (2 tablespoons per serving)*

1 cup whole-grain mustard

1 tablespoon honey

1 tablespoon fresh basil, chopped

1 tablespoon fresh parsley, chopped

2 teaspoons picked fresh thyme leaves

2 teaspoons fresh rosemary, chopped

Pepper to taste

Prepare the Quail:

1. In a plastic bag, combine all ingredients and marinate in the refrigerator for 20 minutes.
2. Preheat broiler.

3 Place quail on broiling pan and cook for 5 minutes on each side until quail are light pink inside. Serve immediately with the chutney.

Prepare the Chutney:

1 Combine the mustard, honey, and herbs in a small mixing bowl and mix well.
2 Season with pepper to taste.
3 Store extra chutney in a covered container in the refrigerator for up to a week.

Nutrition at a glance (per serving): *total fat 10g; saturated fat 2g; protein 46g; dietary fiber 1g; carbohydrate 5g; cholesterol 122mg; sodium 1,016mg; % of calories from fat 30; % of calories from saturated fat 6; calories 304.*

***

Quail are a small game bird with delicate white flesh, although most are farm raised. Quail are available at many specialty meat stores and frozen in super-markets in some regions of the country. You may order quail from Game Sales International at 800-729-2090.

Ras el hanout is a Middle Eastern spice blend. If you can't find it at a Middle Eastern market, Chef Degenhart recommends using madras curry powder instead. Try this recipe with broiled or grilled chicken instead of quail, too.

Chapter 8

Seafood

In This Chapter

- Identifying heart-healthy fish and shellfish
- Purchasing fish the right way
- Marinating seafood to add flavor
- Grilling, roasting, and braising for great taste and variety

Recipes in This Chapter

- Lime-Marinated Shrimp
- Fire-Roasted Ahi Tuna Tenderloin with Ginger Glaze
- Grilled Copper River Salmon with Rhubarb and Ginger Chutney
- Husk-Wrapped Salmon with Toasted Israeli Couscous and Grilled Corn Relish
- Red Snapper with Braised Fennel and Spinach
- Fillet of Red Snapper en Papillote
- Spinach-Wrapped Halibut with Yellow Tomato Sauce and Creamy Asparagus Polenta
- Baked Halibut with Three Colored Peppers and Fingerling and Red Potatoes
- Herb-Encrusted Halibut with Raspberry Sauce

- Pan-Roasted Alaskan Halibut with Red and Yellow Pepper Coulis
- Maine Halibut with Basil Mustard Crust Served with Sherry Onions and Portobello Mushrooms with Baby Spinach
- Lavender-Grappa Glazed Tuna
- Jicama Salsa
- Seared Scallops in Grilled Eggplant (Lasagna-Style) with Mango Salsa
- San Francisco Crab and Wild Fennel Cioppino
- Baked Fillet of Turbot with Gratin of Yukon Potato, Tomato, Lemon, Onion, and Basil

***

Fish and shellfish, when prepared in low-fat ways, are not only delicious but also good for your heart—and your waistline. All seafood is naturally lean. Plus, the little fat that there is in fish contains omega-3 fatty acids, which actually promote heart health. So I am delighted with the recipes contributed by the chefs for this book. They provide a number of varied recipes featuring seafood, and you can find all of them in this chapter.

My family and I enjoy eating fish two or three times a week. Based on the scientific evidence that supports seafood's health-promoting benefits, I recommend that you do the same. Many people order fish or shellfish when they eat out but never, or rarely, eat seafood at home because they think preparing fish is difficult. But with the right techniques, preparing seafood is actually simple. So don't be intimidated. The tips and recipes in this chapter can soon have you cooking fish and other seafood like a pro. When you enjoy a delicious seafood dinner prepared by your own hands, your warm glow of satisfaction will be enhanced by the knowledge that a great seafood dinner is also great for your health.

Understanding the Heart-Healthy Benefits of Fish

Because most fish and shellfish are naturally low in total fat, and particularly low in saturated fat, they have fewer calories and less fat than burgers, steak, pork chops, or even chicken. So eating seafood meals prepared using low-fat methods can be a great way to lower your fat and calorie intake.

But, as I note in Chapters 2 and 4, the real "fishy" secret lies in omega-3 fatty acids, a type of polyunsaturated fat. A steadily growing body of research suggests that eating fish (not fish oil supplements) just a couple of times a week can reduce your risk of heart disease or, if you already have heart disease, can help you control it. Omega-3s may also be helpful in controlling some other conditions, such as arthritis and kidney disease.

Although all saltwater and freshwater fish and shellfish contain *some* omega-3 fatty acids, some species of cold-water fish are particularly rich sources. These rich sources tend to be the fish that we think of as oilier or having darker flesh, such as salmon, mackerel, herring, anchovies, and sardines. But because you only need a small amount of omega-3s to reap the rewards, consuming fish and shellfish with lower levels of omega-3s soon adds up to benefit your heart.

Basically, the fattier the fish, the more health-promoting omega-3 fatty acids it contains. The following list can help you identify fish and shellfish with the most omega-3s. Those fish that are used in at least one recipe in this book are listed in bold. (Table 8)

Highest Levels of Omega-3s	Moderate Levels of Omega-3s	Lower Levels of Omega-3s
Albacore tuna	Alaska king crab	Atlantic cod
Atlantic herring	Blue crab	Brook trout
Atlantic mackerel	Blue mussels	Carp
Atlantic salmon	Bluefish	Channel catfish
Bluefin tuna	Channel catfish	Clams
Lake trout	Flounder	Flounder
Pacific herring	Halibut	Grouper
Pacific mackerel	Oysters	Haddock
Pink salmon	Pollock (often used in surimi, imitation crab)	Mahi mahi
Rainbow trout	Red snapper	Pacific cod
Sablefish	Striped bass	Rockfish
	Swordfish	Scallops

Highest Levels of Omega-3s	Moderate Levels of Omega-3s	Lower Levels of Omega-3s
	Turbot	Shrimp
	Yellowfin tuna	Sole
		Sturgeon

Table 8

Very high temperatures, such as those required for deep-fat frying, can destroy some omega-3s, not to mention adding extra fat to the final dish. The power of omega-3s also gives you one more reason to grill, bake, steam, or braise that fish just till it's done instead of deep frying it.

Purchasing Seafood

To be a good seafood cook, you must first be an even *better* seafood shopper. When fish, shrimp, scallops, or other shellfish you prepare don't taste good, the trouble can usually be traced back to the market. The fish you bought was probably not fresh enough or had not been handled properly. You can't make a great-tasting dish without a fresh-tasting fish. So here are four tips to help you bring home the freshest fish and shellfish.

Use your eyes

Most markets won't let you handle the fish, but you can watch the fish merchant handle the fish and even ask for a few tests. Whole fish should look full, firm, moist, and, well, fresh. The flesh should spring back when touched; the gills should look red to dark red, not gray or brown. The eyes should generally look clear, not milky. Fillets should look plump, firm, and moist, not tired and dry. Don't buy anything sitting in a puddle of water. Avoid frozen products with frozen liquid in the package, indicating the product has thawed and been refrozen.

Ask questions

To check freshness ask the fish merchant or attendant at the seafood counter two important questions: When did the fish come in? Don't buy anything more than a couple of days old. Was it frozen or fresh? Both frozen and fresh fish can be very good. But if the market's "fresh" fish is actually frozen fish that the market has thawed before display, you may want to buy it frozen (particularly fillets or shrimp) and thaw it yourself at home just before you plan to prepare it so that you get the freshest quality.

Consult your nose

The nose knows. Smell provides the truest test of freshness. Fresh fish and shellfish always smell clean and sweet, never "fishy." Avoid anything with a chemical or bleach-like smell, too. Of course, most markets won't let you smell the fish before you buy (but it never hurts to ask). If you can't smell the fish before you buy, I recommend following Julia Child's advice. In *The Way to Cook,* Ms. Child suggests that you unwrap your fish right in the market and give it a sniff. If the fish doesn't smell fresh, take it right to the manager, make a polite complaint, and get your money back.

Make sure live shellfish and mollusks are moving

Crabs and lobsters purchased live should be moving. The shells of oysters, clams, and mussels should be tightly shut, or, if they're open, they should shut when you handle them, indicating they are still alive. Discard any open ones to avoid the danger of consuming any spoiled shellfish.

Storing Fish until You're Ready to Cook

If you've bought fresh fish, you should plan to prepare it the day you purchase it, or within two or three days. Most experts recommend that you store fresh whole fish in the refrigerator in a bed of crushed ice (see Figure 8-1). Use a perforated container and a drip pan so that the fish doesn't get water-logged and your fridge doesn't get flooded. Fillets are best stored on ice, too, but leave the fillets in a watertight plastic bag or container, because contact with the ice damages their taste and texture. If you can't ice the fish, store it in the coldest part of the refrigerator.

If you've purchased frozen fish or shellfish, thaw it out slowly on a bed of ice in the refrigerator, following the same rules as for fresh whole fish or fillets.

Never thaw fish or shellfish at room temperature.

Figure 8-1: Icing fish keeps it fresh.

Gone fishing!

Those who enjoy the art of angling may benefit their hearts three times over:

- Fishing for dinner (or clamming, crabbing, or seining) guarantees the freshest catch of all.
- Fishing provides a bit of moderate physical activity, which promotes a healthy heart.
- Fishing is a relaxing pursuit that takes place in nature, thus reducing stress, one of the risk factors for heart disease.

Just make sure you fish safely and handle your catch safely.

To ensure that your catch comes from safe waters, check state and local government advisories about safe and unsafe areas or types of fish or shellfish.

Treat your catch gently. Don't let it flop about in the boat, bruising itself. Keep it in a live well, if possible, or on ice. Clean the fish promptly. Place fillets in a plastic bag and store on ice. (Figure 8-1)

If you bring home oysters, clams, lobsters, or mussels, be kind to them. They need a cool environment, such as the back of the bottom shelf of your refrigerator. They also need air, so be sure the plastic bag or container in which they've traveled is opened a bit or has air holes punched in it. These critters don't keep long, so plan to buy them the day you'll use them.

If a recipe calls for marinating fish or shellfish, do the marinating in the refrigerator.

Grilling Shrimp and Tuna

Now it's time to get down to business—cooking that delicious, fresh seafood in mouth-watering heart-healthy ways. I start with two simple recipes for shrimp and tuna that feature grilling, my favorite way to prepare seafood. Grilling is also quick and easy.

Shrimp

Hundreds of species of shrimp are found all over the world, so they come in many sizes and colors, ranging from dark green to white. But all shrimp turn pink and tasty when cooked. Shrimp are usually sold by size, determined by number per pound, not by variety. For grilling, select larger shrimp (about 31 to 35 per pound or fewer) rather than smaller ones. Many shrimp today arrive at the market frozen and are then thawed for sale. If that's the case at your market, we recommend buying frozen shrimp and thawing them in the refrigerator or cold water just before cooking. Because shrimp usually come individually frozen, you may enjoy keeping several pounds in the freezer, ready to remove just the number you need for a meal. Use the frozen shrimp within two or three months.

Lime-Marinated Shrimp
Created by Mark Tarbell
Executive Chef-Owner, Tarbell's
Phoenix, Arizona

In this easy recipe, Chef Tarbell combines the simplicity of marinating to add flavor and grilling. The amount of olive oil in this recipe may shock you. But keep in mind that the olive oil is only used in the marinade; the shrimp doesn't absorb much of the oil, but it does absorb a lot of flavor from the other ingredients in the marinade.

Tools: *2 medium mixing bowls, whisk, indoor or outdoor grill or stovetop grill pan*

Preparation time: *15 minutes (plus 1 hour for marinating)*

Cooking time: *5 minutes*

Yield: *4 servings*

1 pound large to extra-large shrimp, peeled and deveined (see Figure 8-2 for illustrated instructions)

1 cup fresh lime juice

1 shallot, minced

2 cloves garlic, minced

2 serrano chilies, stemmed, seeded, and finely chopped

4 scallions, thinly sliced

1/2 cup cilantro, rinsed, destemmed, and finely chopped

1/2 cup parsley, rinsed, destemmed, and finely chopped

2 tablespoons honey

1/2 cup water

1 cup olive oil

Salt and pepper to taste

1 Place the shrimp in a medium mixing bowl and refrigerate.
2 To another medium mixing bowl, add lime juice, shallot, garlic, chilies, scallions, cilantro, parsley, honey, and water.
3 Slowly add the olive oil to above ingredients, whisking continuously. Salt to taste.

4 Pour marinade over shrimp 1 hour before grilling. Remove the shrimp from the marinade and drain 5 minutes before grilling.
5 Place shrimp on a clean, hot grill and cook approximately 2 minutes on each side.
6 Season with salt and pepper to taste. Serve immediately.

Nutrition at a glance (per serving): *total fat 4g; saturated fat 1g; protein 18g; dietary fiber 0g; carbohydrate 10g; cholesterol 161mg; sodium 191mg; vitamin C (% of Daily Value) 23; % of calories from fat 26; % of calories from saturated fat 4; calories 151.*

***

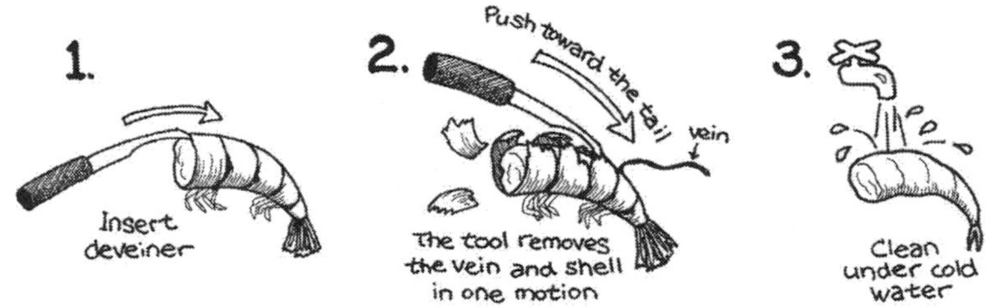

Figure 8-2: How to clean and devein shrimp.

The seeds of serrano and other hot peppers (habanero, chili, and so on) contain oils that can burn the skin and eyes. Wash your hands frequently when working with these peppers to avoid irritating your skin and eyes.

If you don't have an outdoor grill, try this recipe using a stovetop grill pan. It may not have all the smoky taste of a charcoal fire, but it will be delicious.

Tuna

Tuna is a very healthful fish, rich in beneficial omega-3 fatty acids. The broad term *tuna* includes albacore, bluefin, blackfin, bonito, skipjack (also known in Hawaii as *aku*), and yellowfin (sometimes called big eye or ahi). The best sushi-grade tuna comes from the belly (which the Japanese call the *toro*) of yellowfin or bluefin tuna. The belly meat has the most fat and, therefore, the most flavor. Lesser quality sushi-grade tuna comes from any part of a yellowfin or bluefin. The best tuna steaks come from the loin of yellowfin tuna. Dark spots on any piece of tuna indicate a bruise to the flesh in that area, and bruised tuna is considered inferior.

Fire-Roasted Ahi Tuna Tenderloin with Ginger Glaze
Created by Bradley Ogden
Chef/Co-Owner, The Lark Creek Restaurant Group
Larkspur (Marin County), California

Tools: *Small mixing bowl, tongs, gas or charcoal grill, saucepan, strainer*

Preparation time: *10 minutes*

Cooking time: *20 minutes*

Yield: *4 servings*

2 teaspoons olive oil

1 tablespoon soy sauce

1 teaspoon kosher salt

1 teaspoon pepper

1 pound center-cut tuna loin, halved (first-grade sushi-style tuna)

1/2 cup Ginger Glaze (see following recipe)

1 Preheat grill.
2 Combine the olive oil, soy sauce, salt, and pepper in a small bowl. Pour the mixture onto the tuna and then gently rub into the tuna.
3 Using tongs, wipe the grill with an oiled cloth to prevent the tuna from sticking to the grill. If you're using a stovetop grill pan, mist the pan with olive oil.
4 Set the tuna on a hot grill, 3 to 4 inches from the heat.

5 Sear on all sides, keeping the tuna rare, about five minutes. Remove from the grill and place on a platter. If you want the tuna cooked beyond rare, cook on a cooler spot on the grill for 5 minutes longer or until desired doneness is reached.
6 Brush with the Ginger Glaze.

Ginger Glaze

Yield: *1 1/4 cups*

1 teaspoon mustard seeds
1/2 ancho chili, seeds removed
2 tablespoons molasses
1 teaspoon soy sauce
1 tablespoon minced lemongrass (use the tender tip, not the coarse stalk)
1 teaspoon minced garlic
3 tablespoons grated white ginger
1 cup sweet rice wine vinegar
4 tablespoons lemon juice
4 tablespoons chopped cilantro
1/2 teaspoon red pepper flakes
1 cup water

1 Combine all ingredients in a saucepan over medium heat and reduce to 1/2 cup of glaze.
2 Strain and cool.

Nutrition at a glance (per serving): *total fat 8g; saturated fat 2g; protein 28g; dietary fiber 0g; carbohydrate 16g; cholesterol 43mg; sodium 949mg; vitamin A (% of Daily Value) 64; vitamin C (% of Daily Value) 28; % of calories from fat 29; % of calories from saturated fat 7; calories 245.*

***

To reduce the sodium content of this dish, you can omit the salt or decrease the amount of salt. You can also use low-sodium soy sauce in the glaze and the tuna marinade.

America's Favorite Fresh Fish: Salmon

Salmon goes great on the grill, as the following recipes demonstrate. Salmon is also one of the fish richest in heart-healthy omega-3 fatty acids.

Grilled Copper River Salmon with Rhubarb and Ginger Chutney

Created by Greg Atkinson
Executive Chef, Canlis
Seattle, Washington

According to Chef Atkinson, "In Seattle, the arrival of the first Copper River king salmon from Alaska is heralded with more fanfare than a visit from any head of state. The salmon is available at better groceries nationwide from the second week of May until the second week of June. During other times of year, any wild Alaskan king salmon could be prepared in the same way. Copper River salmon is preferred because of its relatively high content of heart-healthy omega-3 fatty acids, which give the fish a rich flavor and a velvety texture. Rhubarb, which is in season at the same time as the elusive Copper River kings, has a refreshing astringent quality that compliments this rich seafood beautifully."

Tools: *Charcoal grill, long spatula, thin-bladed knife, paring knife, medium saucepan*

Preparation time: *15 minutes*

Cooking time: *25 minutes*

Yield: *4 servings*

4 8-ounce fillets of Copper River salmon, or other available fresh salmon fillets

1 teaspoon kosher salt

1 teaspoon pepper

2 teaspoons olive oil (or olive oil in a spray canister)

Rhubarb and Ginger Chutney (see following recipe)

1 Wipe the grill with a cloth dipped in olive oil or spray it with an oil sprayer.
2 Position the grill 4 inches above a bed of glowing coals.
3 Sprinkle the fillets with salt and pepper and rub or spray with olive oil.
4 Place the fillets, skinned-side up, on the grill and allow them to cook for 5 minutes. If the oil ignites,

cool the flames with a little water splashed from a cup or streamed from a squirt gun.

5 With a long spatula, turn the fillets once and allow them to cook for 3 to 5 minutes longer. To check doneness, use a thin-bladed knife to look between the flakes; the center should be moist and still *slightly* translucent (see Figure 8-3).

6 Transfer to a warm platter of serving plates.

7 Top each fillet with 1/4 cup Rhubarb and Ginger Chutney (see following recipe).

Rhubarb and Ginger Chutney

The chutney may be served at once or kept covered in the refrigerator for several days.

Yield: *1 1/2 cups*

2 stalks rhubarb, chopped (about 2 cups)

1/2 cup crystallized ginger, chopped

1/4 cup raspberry vinegar

1/2 teaspoon salt

1 Prepare the rhubarb. Using a paring knife, grasp the end of the rhubarb and pull the strings up the length of the stalk. Chop into 1/2-inch pieces.

2 In a medium saucepan over medium-high heat, stir together rhubarb, ginger, raspberry vinegar, and salt. Cook until rhubarb is very tender and beginning to disintegrate, about 15 minutes.

Nutrition at a glance (per serving): *total fat 15g; saturated fat 2g; protein 39g; dietary fiber 1g; carbohydrate 36g; cholesterol 107mg; sodium 984mg; % of calories from fat 30; % of calories from saturated fat 4; calories 445.*

Figure 8-3: Testing fish for doneness.

Husk-Wrapped Salmon with Toasted Israeli Couscous and Grilled Corn Relish

Created by Brian Houlihan
Executive Chef, The Regal Bostonian Hotel
Boston, Massachusetts

Much to our delight, Chef Houlihan created this simple but scrumptious recipe especially for this cookbook. Chef Houlihan writes, "Cooking the salmon wrapped in the cornhusks enables one to encapsulate the flavor of the fish, enhancing the flavor with the cornhusk. Perhaps the best part of this cooking style is that the salmon will cook perfectly without the addition of any fats or oils." Chef Houlihan encourages home chefs to "make the relish your first project as it picks up more flavor the longer it sits. Making the relish a day before is a good idea."

Tools: *Gas or charcoal grill, medium saucepan, knife, mixing bowl*

Preparation time: *25 minutes*

Cooking time: *35 minutes*
Yield: *4 servings*

4 6-ounce boneless, skinless salmon fillets
Salt and pepper to taste
4 fresh fennel sprigs
Inner husks from 3 corn ears to create an enclosed package for the salmon fillets (see Grilled Corn Relish recipe)

1 Preheat the grill.
2 Season the salmon with salt and pepper to taste.
3 Place one fresh fennel sprig on each portion of salmon, and wrap each portion in a cornhusk. You can use a toothpick soaked in water to fasten the cornhusk around the salmon.
4 Place the husk-wrapped salmon on the grill and cook 6 minutes on each side over medium heat. If you're using a charcoal grill, wait until the coals start to lose some heat before grilling the salmon (you don't want the salmon to overcook).
5 Place the relish on the husk wrapped salmon and accompany with the couscous on the plate. Chef Houlihan writes, "Arrange in any decorative fashion you wish. Remember: You're the artist today. Let the plate be your canvas."

Toasted Israeli Couscous

Couscous is coarsely ground semolina wheat. Israeli Couscous is a large pearl couscous that can be found in specialty stores.

1 tablespoon olive oil
1 cup Israeli couscous

1/4 cup minced onion
1 pinch (1/4 teaspoon) chopped garlic
1 cup water

1 In a medium saucepan over medium heat, heat the olive oil. Add the couscous and toast, stirring, until golden brown, about 3 to 4 minutes.
2 Add the minced onion and a pinch of garlic. Stir to combine.
3 Lower heat to medium-low, add water, and simmer, uncovered, until the couscous is tender. If you start the couscous before you start the salmon, the couscous can cook while the salmon is grilling.

Grilled Corn Relish

Yield: *2 1/2 cups*
3 ears of corn with husks on
1 red bell pepper, diced
1 red onion, diced
1 bunch cilantro
2 tablespoons honey
Juice from 2 limes

1 Preheat the grill.
2 When the grill is ready, place the ears of corn (in their husks) on the grill. Grill the corn, turning occasionally, until the outside leaves are charred, about 15 minutes. Remove the corn from the grill; remove the charred outer leaves and discard them. Be sure to keep the inner leaves to wrap the salmon. Discard the silk.
3 Using a very sharp knife, cut the corn from the cob.

4 In a mixing bowl, mix the corn with the diced red pepper, red onion, cilantro, honey, and lime juice. Cover the bowl and place in the refrigerator until ready to serve.

Nutrition at a glance (per serving): *total fat 10g; saturated fat 2g; protein 44g; dietary fiber 7g; carbohydrate 83g; cholesterol 88mg; sodium 365mg; vitamin A (% of Daily Value) 28; vitamin C (% of Daily Value) 129; folic acid (% of Daily Value) 20; % of calories from fat 15; % of calories from saturated fat 3; calories 587.*

***

Red Snapper in a Snap

I have a pop quiz for you: Which of the following two recipes sounds more complex? "Red Snapper with Braised Fennel and Spinach" or "Fillet of Red Snapper en Papillote"? If you side with the majority in my small informal survey, you probably said, "The Fillet of Snapper en ... whatever." Actually, both recipes use simple techniques that anyone can do. Both use moist heat to cook the snapper to ensure that it stays moist and tender. And both take about the same amount of time—30 minutes. So what's the point of my quiz? To encourage you to explore the techniques that the chefs are sharing. An exotic title may lead you to a recipe or cooking technique you find tasty and easy to use on a regular basis.

Red Snapper with Braised Fennel and Spinach

Created by Carrie Nahabedian
Executive Chef, Four Seasons Hotel, Los Angeles at Beverly Hills
Los Angeles, California

The techniques used to prepare the ingredients for this multi-layered recipe are quite simple, but timing the steps to come out together can be a little tricky. So read the recipe carefully to plan your approach, get all your equipment ready, and prepare all your ingredients before you start cooking. Then enjoy your triumph.

Tools: *Large saucepan, paring knife, large nonstick sauté pan, medium sauté pan, shallow bowl*

Preparation time: *20 minutes*

Cooking time: *30 minutes*

Yield: *6 servings*

9 young fennel bulbs, trimmed and halved lengthwise

Chicken stock (not canned broth), as needed

6 6-ounce red snapper fillets

Juice of one lemon

3 tablespoons olive oil

1 bunch young spinach (at least 1 pound)

1 tablespoon olive oil

3 large tomatoes, peeled, seeded, and diced

1/4 cup reserved fennel cooking liquid

3 tablespoons lemon peel, candied and sliced (see Toque Tip icon following this recipe for instructions)

4 sprigs chervil, stemmed and chopped

Salt and pepper to taste

6 yellow beets, stems trimmed, halved lengthwise, and boiled, for garnish (optional)

Chervil sprigs, for garnish (optional)

1 Place the fennel in a large saucepan, cover with chicken stock (about 1 quart), and bring to boil.
2 Reduce the heat and simmer until tender, 15 to 20 minutes. (Pierce the fennel at their tough core with a sharp paring knife to determine if they are tender.) Remove from heat and set aside to cool in the cooking liquid.
3 Brush the snapper fillets with lemon juice, olive oil, and season with salt and pepper. Heat a large, nonstick sauté pan over medium-high heat, add fillets flesh side down, and sear until browned, about 3 minutes. Then turn the fish over and cook another 3 to 4 minutes, to desired doneness. Do in two batches if the pan is crowded.
4 Remove the fish from the pan, reserving the pan, and set aside on a warmed plate, loosely covered to keep warm.
5 In the sauté pan used to sear the snapper, add the spinach and 1 tablespoon olive oil and sauté over medium-high heat until wilted. Remove from heat, season, and set aside to keep warm.
6 Drain the fennel halves from their cooking liquid, reserving 2 cups of the liquid. In a medium sauté

pan, heat the olive oil over medium-high heat. Add the tomatoes and reserved fennel and sauté for 2 minutes.

7 Add the fennel cooking liquid and the candied lemon peel and bring to a boil.

8 Remove from the heat and add the chervil. Season, set aside, and keep warm.

9 Arrange some spinach in the center of a shallow bowl and place a snapper filet on top.

10 Set 3 fennel halves beside the fillet and spoon the tomatoes and juice on top and around the snapper.

11 Place 2 beet halves beside the fillet and garnish with chervil.

12 Serve immediately.

Nutrition at a glance (per serving): *total fat 10g; saturated fat 1g; protein 34g; dietary fiber 10g; carbohydrate 36g; cholesterol 75mg; sodium 409mg; vitamin A (% of Daily Value) 115; vitamin C (% of Daily Value) 105; vitamin E (% of Daily Value) 23; folic acid (% of Daily Value) 63; % of calories from fat 25; % of calories from saturated fat 3; calories 352.*

Make your own *candied lemon peel* by shaving off only the yellow portion of the rind (the zest) of one lemon with a sharp vegetable peeler or a zester. Avoid the white part of the peel because of its bitterness. If you do peel off some white with the peeler, use a small sharp paring knife to scrape off the white. Roughly chop or slice the shaved lemon peel, then place in warm sugar syrup (equal parts water and granulated sugar—1/2 cup each will work fine for 1 lemon) in a small saucepan. Bring to a rolling boil, then remove from the heat source and let sit for 10 minutes. Drain off the sugar syrup and sprinkle the lemon peel with granulated sugar. Once cooled, you have can-died lemon peel! You can do exactly the same with orange peel.

What if your supermarket has only red beets, but not yellow ones? Reading the preceding recipe, you may decide that red beets wouldn't have quite the right taste or color. What are your options? You could omit the beets. Or you could try something a little different but similar, perhaps some diagonal slices of a fat carrot, steamed.

Ditto with the chervil. If there's no chervil, try parsley.

Fillet of Red Snapper en Papillote

Created by Joe Mannke
Chef/Proprietor, Rotisserie for Beef and Bird
Houston, Texas

Although the name of this recipe makes it sounds exotic and difficult to make, it's quite easy to prepare. *En papillote* is a French term for food baked inside parchment paper. When the parchment paper is tightly sealed, steam is trapped, which quickly cooks the food inside. If you're fresh out of parchment paper, don't use that as an excuse to skip this great recipe—substitute aluminum foil. It's not quite the same, but you'll still have a tasty dish—and we won't tell Chef Mannke.

Tools: *Baking pan, parchment paper, large sauté pan, saucepan, pastry brush, spatula, shallow soup bowl*

Preparation time: *25 minutes*

Cooking time: *15 minutes*

Yield: *4 servings*

4 6-ounce red snapper fillets, skinless
4 sheets parchment paper
2 tablespoons olive oil
1/2 cup flour (for dusting fish fillets)

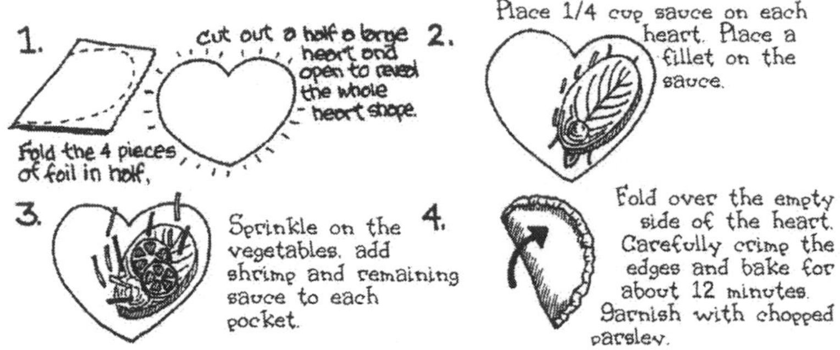

Figure 8-4: Elegant-looking fish in a packet isn't difficult to put together.

1/3 teaspoon white pepper

1 cup fish velouté or canned cream of mushroom soup

1 cup dry white wine

1/2 cup minced shallots

1/2 cup sliced scallions

1/2 cup diced bell pepper

1 cup sliced mushrooms

1 cup parboiled baby shrimp

1 egg white, lightly beaten

1 Preheat the oven to 375 degrees. Place a baking pan in the oven to heat.
2 Wash the fillets under running cold water and pat dry.
3 Cut the parchment paper sheets into heart shapes (see Figure 8-4).
4 Heat the olive oil in a large sauté pan over medium-high heat.
5 Spread the flour in an even layer on a plate. Season the fish fillets with pepper, then lightly dust

them with flour, shaking off any excess. Place them in the sauté pan and quickly sear until lightly browned on one side. Remove the pan from the heat and set aside.

6 In a saucepan, bring the fish velouté (or mushroom soup) and white wine to a boil. Remove from heat.

7 Place a large spoonful (about 1/4 cup) of the fish and wine sauce in the center of one side of the heart-shaped paper.

8 Remove fish fillets from the sauté pan and place on the sauce. Divide the shallots, scallions, bell peppers, mushrooms, and baby shrimp evenly and place on top of the fish.

9 Ladle the rest of the sauce over each of the fish and vegetables.

10 Using a pastry brush, coat the edges of the parchment paper with egg white. Fold the empty side of the heart-shaped paper over to cover the fish, and press the edges together to seal. Make a series of straight folds, one over the other, until you have a tight heart-shaped package.

11 Place the packages on the preheated baking pan and place in the oven for about 12 minutes.

12 With a spatula, transfer to a shallow soup bowl. Use scissors to cut open and serve steaming hot at once.

Nutrition at a glance (per serving): *total fat 11g; saturated fat 2g; protein 43g; dietary fiber 2g; carbohydrate 19g; cholesterol 162mg; sodium 431mg; vitamin C (% of Daily Value) 40; vitamin E (% of*

Daily Value) 20; % of calories from fat 26; % of calories from saturated fat 5; calories 394.

Chef Mannke recommends serving this dish with steamed fresh green beans and new potatoes.

Velouté sauce is one of the five "mother sauces." It is a stock-based white sauce made with either chicken, veal, or fish stock thickened with a flour and oil roux. If you want to give it a try, consult a good standard cookbook. A *roux* is a cooked mixture of equals part fat (often butter or oil) and flour used to thicken a sauce.

***

Halibut: One Fish Five Ways

Halibut was a favorite of our contributing chefs. The distinctive recipes in this section demonstrate the versatility of halibut. Halibut is one of the largest fish we eat. They can grow to up to 1,000 pounds in weight but *chicken halibuts,* which weigh between 2 and 10 pounds are considered the best for eating. Because halibut is also one of the leanest fish we eat, it needs special care during preparation. The low fat content of the flesh gives it a tendency to dry out, but using a moist cooking method, such as wrapping the fish in spinach to steam it or accompanying the halibut with a vegetable-based sauce, remedies this problem easily. The next five recipes demonstrate how varied and versatile a fish can be. What's true for halibut is true for other types of seafood, too.

Spinach-Wrapped Halibut with Yellow Tomato Sauce and Creamy Asparagus Polenta

Created by Jeffrey J. Russell
Ventana Room Chef, Loews Ventana Canyon Resort
Tucson, Arizona

The spinach wrapping not only keeps the halibut moist but, with the contrast of yellow polenta and tomato sauce and asparagus garnish, also makes a very attractive and appealing dish.

Tools: *Medium saucepan, skimmer or slotted spoon, bowl of ice water, tongs, strainer, shallow roasting pan, saucepot, blender, small saucepan, whisk*

Preparation time: *25 minutes*
Cooking time: *40 minutes*
Yield: *4 servings*

4 6-ounce halibut fillets
Salt and pepper to taste
1/2 pound fresh spinach (large leaves)

1 tablespoon shallots, chopped
2 cups white wine, preferably Chardonnay
large yellow tomatoes
6 fresh basil leaves
1 tablespoon garlic, chopped
Salt and pepper to taste
1 bunch asparagus (about 20 spears)
2 cups skim milk
2 tablespoons garlic, chopped
1/2 cup polenta (ground cornmeal)

1 Preheat oven to 400 degrees.
2 Fill a medium saucepan two-thirds full of water and bring water to a boil. Place spinach in boiling water for 5 seconds, using a skimmer or slotted spoon, quickly remove and place in a bowl of ice water to stop cooking process. After 10 seconds, using tongs or a slotted spoon, carefully transfer the spinach leaves from the ice water to a strainer to drain. Try to keep the spinach leaves intact. Set aside.
3 Place asparagus in the boiling water and cook for 2 minutes or until tender but firm (cooking time will depend on the thickness of the asparagus). Drain and transfer to the ice water bath. Drain again and set aside.
4 Season halibut with salt (optional) and pepper.
5 Open the spinach leaves and lay them flat on a counter to make four big squares. (If necessary, you can patch together two or more pieces to form the square.) Place one piece of halibut on

each spinach square. Cover the top and wrap in the sides on each piece of fish.

6 Place the pieces of wrapped fish, seam side down, in a shallow roasting pan just large enough to hold the fish in one layer. Cover with chopped shallots and white wine. Cover top of pan with aluminum foil and set aside.

7 Remove stems and roughly chop the tomatoes. Place in a saucepot with garlic and basil and allow to simmer, stirring often, until slightly thickened and aromatic, about 20 minutes. If your tomatoes are not particularly juicy, add a tablespoon here and there to keep moist and continue cooking.

8 Place tomato sauce in a blender for 10 quick pulses. Add salt (optional) and pepper to taste. Cover and set aside.

9 Place halibut in the preheated oven and roast for 15 minutes while preparing the polenta.

10 Take the cooked asparagus and discard the bottom quarter. Reserve the tips for garnish and puree the remaining stems in a blender with the skim milk.

11 Add garlic to a small saucepan coated with nonstick cooking spray and place on medium heat. When garlic starts to brown, add the milk and asparagus combination and bring to a simmer.

12 Whisk in the polenta and allow to cook over medium heat for 5 minutes. Add asparagus tips, salt (optional), and pepper to taste.

13 On four separate serving plates place equal amounts of polenta in the center of each plate.
14 Place a spinach-wrapped piece of halibut on top of the polenta.
15 Finish with a drizzle of tomato sauce all around the dish.
16 Serve immediately.

Nutrition at a glance (per serving): *total fat 5g; saturated fat 1g; protein 46g; dietary fiber 9g; carbohydrate 29g; cholesterol 57mg; sodium 254mg (based on no added salt); vitamin A (% of Daily Value) 58; vitamin C (% of Daily Value) 79; folic acid (% of Daily Value) 40; % of calories from fat 11; % of calories from saturated fat 2; calories 422.*

Polenta is an Italian dish made from cornmeal. Unflavored, polenta is rather bland and, therefore, is wonderfully suited for mixing with garlic and herbs or an intensely flavored cheese such as Parmesan or Gorgonzola.

Baked Halibut with Three Colored Peppers and Fingerling and Red Potatoes

Created by Nora Pouillon
Chef and Owner, Nora, the only certified organic restaurant in the United States
Washington, D.C.

Baking the halibut in the colorful three pepper sauce imparts a delicious flavor and keeps the fish beautifully moist. Completed with the steamed fingerling and red potatoes, this recipe is low in fat and very rich in vitamins A and C.

Tools: *Medium sauté pan, baking dish, medium saucepan, steamer insert, spatula*

Preparation time: *20 minutes*

Cooking time: *15 minutes*

Yield: *4 servings*

1 medium onion, thinly sliced

2 teaspoons minced garlic

2 green peppers, seeded and cut in julienne

1 red pepper, seeded and cut in julienne

1 yellow pepper, seeded and cut in julienne

1 cup white wine (Chardonnay, Pinot Grigio, Sauvignon Blanc, for example)

2 to 3 tablespoons assorted fresh herbs such as thyme, oregano, and rosemary

Sea salt and black pepper to taste

1 1/2 pounds halibut fillets, cut into 4 portions

16 to 20 small fingerling and red potatoes, unpeeled (about 1 pound)

Small bouquet of assorted fresh herbs such as thyme, oregano, and rosemary, for garnish

1 Preheat oven to 450 degrees.
2 Heat 2 teaspoons of the olive oil in a medium sauté pan over medium heat, add the onion, garlic, and peppers and sauté for about 5 minutes, stirring frequently.
3 Add the wine and herbs, and season to taste with salt and pepper. Bring the mixture to a boil, and cook for about 1 minute, stirring to combine.
4 Remove the pan from the heat.
5 Spoon the pepper mixture and juices into a baking dish large enough to accommodate the fillets in one layer. Arrange the halibut fillets on top. Drizzle with the remaining olive oil and season to taste with salt and pepper. Bake for 8 to 10 minutes or until the fish fillets are cooked through.
6 While the fish is cooking, steam the potatoes in a medium saucepan using a collapsible insert, or boil them for 10 to 15 minutes or until a fork can be inserted easily.
7 Assemble the plates by using a spatula to transfer each halibut fillet with the pepper mixture and juices under it to the center of a large warm dinner plate. Surround the fish with the potatoes and garnish with a small bouquet of fresh herbs.

Nutrition at a glance (per serving): *total fat 9g; saturated fat 1g; protein 40g; dietary fiber 3g; carbohydrate 41g; cholesterol 54mg; sodium 108mg (based on no added salt); vitamin A (% of Daily Value) 49; vitamin C (% of Daily Value) 353; % of calories from fat 18; % of calories from saturated fat 2; calories 440.*

***

A recipe like the next one, which calls for an abundance of fresh herbs, is perfect for a home chef with a thriving herb garden. If you don't have your own herb garden, either befriend a green-thumbed neighbor or start your own. Herb gardening is a very relaxing, stress-reducing activity that can be done in a window box, a small backyard strip, or on a large community plot. I've attempted starting an herb garden with seeds but have found that buying starter plants is the quickest, easiest way to start a flourishing garden. Of course, if your herb garden is nonexistent, most supermarkets carry the three familiar fresh herbs Chef Shaker features.

Herb-Encrusted Halibut with Raspberry Sauce

Created by Kimberly Shaker
Chef, Cowboy Ciao

Scottsdale, Arizona

The fragrant herb crust and a quick searing before baking impart flavor and seal the moisture into the halibut fillets. The fresh raspberry sauce gives this recipe the perfect lightness for spring and early summer—when, of course, raspberries are in season.

Tools: *Medium saucepan, blender, sieve, large sauté pan, baking dish*

Preparation time: *10 minutes*

Cooking time: *25 minutes*

Yield: *4 servings*

4 6-ounce fresh boneless, skinless halibut (or salmon) fillets

4 tablespoons chopped fresh thyme

4 tablespoons chopped fresh oregano

2 tablespoons chopped fresh Italian parsley

1 pint (2 cups) fresh raspberries, rinsed and drained

1/4 cup sugar

1/2 cup homemade chicken stock or canned broth

3 tablespoons chopped shallots

2 tablespoons olive oil

Salt and pepper to taste

1. Preheat oven to 350 degrees.
2. Place thyme, oregano, and parsley on a large plate and mix together.
3. Rinse the fish with cold water and season with salt (optional) and pepper.

4 Place fish fillets on the herb mixture and press lightly. You only need to cover the top of the fish with herbs. Place the fish in the refrigerator while you make the sauce.
5 Place 1 tablespoon of the olive oil in a medium saucepan; add the chopped shallots and sauté over medium heat for about 2 minutes. Add the chicken stock, the sugar, and 1 1/2 pints of the raspberries. Cook slowly over low heat, stirring often, for about 10 minutes or until the sauce starts to thicken and the sugar is dissolved.
6 Place the raspberry sauce in a blender and puree until smooth. Pass the sauce through a sieve to remove seeds. Taste for desired sweetness and add salt and pepper to taste. Set aside.
7 Place a large sauté pan over medium-high heat and add 1 tablespoon of olive oil. When the pan is hot, place the fish in the pan, herb side down. Cook for 1 minute, being very careful to not burn the herbs. Turn the fillets over and cook for another 1 to 2 minutes, until lightly brown.
8 Transfer fillets to a baking dish (unless your sauté pan is ovenproof) and bake at 350 degrees for 5 to 6 minutes or until fish is done.
9 To serve, place remaining raspberries in warm sauce and spoon onto the bottom of dinner plates. Place the fish on top.

Nutrition at a glance (per serving): *total fat 9g; saturated fat 1.5g; protein 33g; dietary fiber 5g; carbohydrate 21g; cholesterol 90mg; sodium*

149mg; vitamin C (% of Daily Value) 39; vitamin E (% of Daily Value) 20; % of calories from fat 28; % of calories from saturated fat 4; calories 303.

Chef Kimberly Shaker recommends serving the fish with a mixed green salad or fresh steamed vegetables and potatoes.

***

Anything but halibut?

What's good for the halibut is good for the turbot. And probably other lean, light, and fine-textured fish such as sea bass, tile fish, cod, scrod, and even shark. Recipes for fish tend to be as versatile as the fish themselves. When choosing an alternate fish for a recipe that looks good, try to match the fish in texture, leanness, and quality of its flesh. In other words, you could substitute turbot for halibut because turbot is light and lean like halibut, but oily mackerel would be a mistake.

Pan-Roasted Alaskan Halibut with Red and Yellow Pepper Coulis

Created by David Gross
Executive Chef, City Grill

Atlanta, Georgia

The even heat provided by a heavy cast-iron skillet can help you pan roast the delicate halibut to perfection. But if all you have is a heavy, non-stick skillet or sauté pan, go ahead—your results will still be tasty and elegant.

Tools: *Large cast-iron skillet, roasting pan (if needed), medium saucepan, blender*

Preparation time: *20 minutes*

Cooking time: *35 minutes*

Yield: *8 servings*

8 6-ounce portions Alaskan halibut
Salt and pepper to taste
2 tablespoons pure canola oil (to pan roast)
Parsley and thyme sprigs, for garnish (optional)

1 Preheat oven to 375 degrees. Season the fish with salt and pepper. Heat the canola oil in a large cast-iron skillet over medium-high heat. Add the halibut and pan roast it over medium heat until golden brown on one side. Use two pans or do fish in two batches if all the fillets do not fit easily in your skillet.

2 Turn the halibut fillets over and transfer pan to the oven. (Transfer fish to roasting pan if your skillet is not ovenproof.) Cook for 4 minutes, or until fish easily flakes. Then lower heat to 200 degrees and keep warm until ready to serve.

3 On 8 large serving plates arrange the 2 coulis in desired pattern. Use 1/2 cup of each coulis

for each serving. Less coulis may be needed to cover the bottom of each plate depending on the size of your dinner plates.

Red Pepper Coulis

Yield: *4 cups*

1 teaspoon canola oil

4 cups red bell peppers, diced small (approximately 5 peppers)

2 cups yellow onions, diced small

1 tablespoon garlic, minced

2 1/4 cups homemade chicken stock or canned broth

1/4 cup white wine

Salt and white pepper to taste

1 Place medium saucepan on medium heat. When the pan is hot, add canola oil, red peppers, onion, and garlic.
2 Sauté, stirring and adding a little of the chicken stock if necessary to prevent sticking or burning, until vegetables soften, approximately 10 minutes.
3 Add the white wine to the pan and stir to loosen any ingredients or flavorful juices stuck to pan. Add the chicken stock and reduce down in quantity by half.
4 Remove from heat and blend smooth in blender.
5 Season to taste with salt and pepper.
6 Cool rapidly and hold off to side until ready to serve.

Yellow Pepper Coulis

Yield: *4 cups*

1 teaspoon canola oil

4 cups yellow bell peppers, diced small (approximately 5 peppers)

2 cups yellow onions, diced small

1 tablespoon garlic, minced

2 1/4 cups homemade chicken stock or canned broth

1/4 cup white wine

Salt and white pepper to taste

Follow instructions as listed for the red pepper coulis. To save time, make both coulis at the same time but in separate saucepans.

Nutrition at a glance (per serving): *total fat 8g; saturated fat 1g; protein 36g; dietary fiber 4g; carbohydrate 18g; cholesterol 90mg; sodium 177mg; vitamin A (% of Daily Value) 89; vitamin C (% of Daily Value) 474; vitamin E (% of Daily Value) 23; % of calories from fat 25; % of calories from saturated fat 3; calories 293.*

***

Maine Halibut with Basil Mustard Crust Served with Sherry Onions and

Portobello Mushrooms with Baby Spinach

Created by Gary Donlick
Executive Chef, 103 West Restaurant
Atlanta, Georgia

The use of mustard and fresh basil to create a crust on the halibut is a simple technique that can be used with chicken and other types of fish. Experiment with different types of mustard and different herbs to create your own "crust" recipe.

Tools: *Baking pan, large sauté pan, tongs*

Preparation time: *15 minutes*

Cooking time: *10 minutes*

Yield: *4 servings*

4 7-ounce halibut fillets

Kosher salt and black pepper to taste

1 teaspoon fresh basil, cut into thin chiffonade strips (see Figure 8-5 for illustrated instructions)

2 tablespoons of coarse grain mustard, preferably Pommery

1 cup dry white wine

1. Preheat oven to 450 degrees.
2. Season each fillet with kosher salt and black pepper.
3. Mix basil and mustard together and then spread thin even layers on the halibut fillets.
4. Place on baking pan and add 1 cup white wine.

5 Cook fish 10 minutes for each 1 inch of thickness, until fish just flakes and is no longer translucent. *Do not overcook.*
6 When fish is cooked, serve immediately, with side of Sherry Onions and Portobello Mushrooms with Baby Spinach.

Sherry Onions and Portobello Mushrooms with Baby Spinach

Preparation time: *5 minutes*

Cooking time: *10 minutes*

1 tablespoon extra virgin olive oil

2 medium onions, sliced

2 large portobello mushrooms (with stems removed), sliced

1 pound baby spinach (with stems removed)

Sherry vinegar, to taste

1 Place a large sauté pan over medium heat. Add olive oil and sliced onions. Stir and cook for 2 to 3 minutes.
2 Add portobello mushrooms. Cook, stirring often, for 5 to 6 minutes, then add spinach, tossing with kitchen tongs or two forks to evenly wilt.
3 Stir in the sherry vinegar.
4 Divide evenly among 4 plates to top the halibut.

Nutrition at a glance (per serving): *total fat 7g; saturated fat 1g; protein 44g; dietary fiber 13g; carbohydrate 9g; cholesterol 105mg; sodium 384mg; vitamin A (% of Daily Value) 60; vitamin C (% of Daily Value) 50; % of calories from fat*

16; % of calories from saturated fat 2; calories 316.

Serving suggestion: *Although Chef Donlick uses this combination of onions, mushrooms, and spinach to top his "Maine Halibut with Mustard Crust," you may also like to serve it as a side dish to accompany a number of entrées, such as fish or chicken.*

Figure 8-5: Chiffonade is a fancy term for a simple procedure.

Pommery mustapd is also known as *Moutarde de Meaux.* It is a grainy French mustard found in some supermarkets and specialty shops. Pommery mustard is considered the most superior of the coarse-grained mustards, with a unique taste all its own. The eighteenth-century French "foodie" Brillat-Savarin called this mustard "the gourmet's mustard." Using a different type of mustard in this recipe is *not* advised by the chef.

Sea Salsa

Creating and using salsa and sauces with fish and shellfish is a great low-fat way to vary the flavor and flair of a dish. On evening when you just feel like quickly broiling a fillet, for instance, salsas are a quick and flavorful way to dress up such a simple preparation technique. But saucing and salsas also enhance more creative and inventive recipes, as the next two recipes show.

Lavender-Grappa Glazed Tuna

Created by Bernard Kantak
Executive Chef, Cowboy Ciao
Scottsdale, Arizona

This recipe has several wonderful components that you combine to prepare the final dish. Read the recipe through carefully and prepare your lavender-grappa glaze and salsa before you start grilling and everything will come off to perfection.

Tools: *2 small saucepans, strainer, small stainless steel or ceramic bowl, outdoor grill or stovetop grill pan, tongs*

Preparation time: *15 minutes*
Cooking time: *25 minutes*
Yield: *4 servings*

1 cup white wine
1 cup grappa
1/2 cup honey

1/4 cup dried lavender flower
1/3 cup reduced-sodium soy sauce
1/8 cup lime juice
1/8 cup orange juice
1/8 cup Bonny Doon framboise (or a similar raspberry liqueur)
1/2 cup sugar
1/2 teaspoon arrowroot
4 6-ounce tuna steaks (preferably Ahi tuna)
1 teaspoon olive oil
Kosher salt to taste (optional)
Pepper to taste

1 Combine wine, grappa, honey, and lavender in a small saucepan.
2 Bring to a boil and reduce by a half (about 1 1/4 cup).
3 Strain into a small stainless steel or ceramic bowl. Set aside.
4 Combine soy sauce, lime juice, orange juice, framboise, sugar, and arrowroot in a small saucepan and bring to a boil. Lower heat to a simmer and cook, stirring frequently, until slightly thickened, 2 to 3 minutes. Transfer to a small bowl.
5 Chill in refrigerator until ready to use.
6 Preheat grill. When grill begins to warm up, oil the grates by rubbing them with a clean vegetable-oiled cloth. For safety's sake, use tongs to rub the cloth over the grates. For best results, be sure your grill grates are clean before oiling them.

7 Rub each tuna steak with a touch of olive oil and season with salt (optional) and pepper. Place steaks on the grill rack and mark each side by cooking for about 1 minute.

8 Brush each side of the tuna with glaze, turning the tuna on the grill, repeating 2 times. For medium rare, total cooking time should be about 1 1/2 minutes per side; for medium, about 2 minutes per side.

9 When ready to serve, drizzle with sweet soy sauce.

Nutrition at a glance (per serving): *total fat 2g; saturated fat 0g; protein 41g; dietary fiber 0g; carbohydrate 65g; cholesterol 77mg; sodium 860mg; % of calories from fat 3; % of calories from saturated fat 0; calories 652.*

Serve with Chef Kantak's Jicama Salsa (see following recipe). In addition to the Jicama Salsa, Chef Kantak serves this dish with fresh sautéed vegetables.

***

Be very cautious when boiling the liqueur, grappa, honey, and lavender. The liquid may ignite! If this happens, remove the pan from the burner and cover with a lid.

Dried lavender flower can be ordered online at Dean and Deluca's Web site (www.deandeluca.com) or by calling 800-221-7714.

Arrowroot is a starchy product, usually in flour form, that is used as a thickening agent in sauces and puddings. A good substitute for cornstarch because it is colorless and tasteless, arrowroot can be found in most large supermarkets and Asian markets.

Grappa is colorless, high-alcohol Italian liqueur that is distilled from the residue that is left in the winepress after juice has been removed for the wine. Grappa can be found at most fine liquor stores.

Jicama (pronounced *HICK-a-ma*), often referred to as the Mexican potato, is a large vegetable with thin brown skin and white crunchy flesh. Many chefs use jicama (shown in Figure 8-6) to add a sweet and nutty flavor to a dish. Jicama is a great source of vitamin C and potassium. It can be found in most large supermarkets and in Mexican markets from November through May.

Figure 8-6: Jicamas look like potatoes, but unlike potatoes, jicamas can be eaten raw.

Jicama Salsa

Tools: *Medium mixing bowl*
Preparation time: *15 minutes*
Cooking time: *None*
Yield: *4 servings*
1 medium jicama, diced small
1/2 medium red onion, diced small
1 jalapeno, stemmed, seeded, and minced
1 garlic clove, minced
1 small red bell pepper, stemmed and seeded, diced small
1/4 bunch cilantro, stems removed
Juice of 1 lime
1/2 cup orange juice
1 teaspoon olive oil
1 cup cantaloupe, diced small
Salt and pepper to taste

Combine all ingredients in a medium mixing bowl and season to taste.

Nutrition at a glance (per serving): *total fat 2g; saturated fat 0g; protein 2g; dietary fiber*

9g; carbohydrate 25g; cholesterol 0mg; sodium 74mg; vitamin A (% of Daily Value) 29; vitamin C (% of Daily Value) 188; % of calories from fat 15; % of calories from saturated fat 0; calories 117.

***

Seared Scallops in Grilled Eggplant (Lasagna-Style) with Mango Salsa

Created by Thierry Bregeon
Executive Chef, Bistro 45
Pasadena, California

If you have time, prepare the mango salsa a day ahead of time to allow the flavors to marry.

Tools: *Blender, 2 small mixing bowls, outdoor grill or stovetop grill pan, baking dish, medium nonstick skillet*

Preparation time: *30 minutes plus 30 minutes for marinating*

Cooking time: *15 minutes*

Yield: *2 servings*

Mango Salsa

Yield: *2 cups (about 1/2 cup per serving)*

1 mango

1/2 cup orange juice

1/2 cup fresh lemon juice

1 red onion, peeled

1 fresh tomato, cored
1 red bell pepper, seeded and cored
1 green bell pepper, seeded and cored
1 teaspoon fresh cilantro
1 teaspoon chopped fresh garlic
Salt and pepper to taste

1 Wash, peel, and slice the mango (see Figure 8-7 for illustrated instructions).
2 In a blender, combine the sliced mango with the orange juice and lemon juice and mix thoroughly.
3 Finely dice the red onion, tomato, and bell peppers, and place in a small bowl. Add the blended mango and juice mixture. Toss to combine.
4 Add the fresh cilantro and chopped garlic and toss again.
5 If possible, allow the salsa to sit covered in the refrigerator for 24 hours before serving.

Scallops and Eggplant

4 teaspoons olive oil
2 cloves garlic, chopped
2 teaspoons fresh thyme, chopped
2 teaspoons fresh basil
Salt and pepper to taste
2 small eggplants
10 ounces fresh scallops, rinsed, drained, and patted dry
2 sprigs fresh basil for garnish

1 Preheat the grill. Preheat the oven to 350 degrees.
2 In a small bowl, combine the olive oil, garlic, fresh thyme, fresh basil, salt, and pepper.

3 Peel the eggplants. Cut each eggplant into 2 long, lengthwise slices. Each slice should be a uniform thickness, about 1 to 1 1/2 inches thick. (You may have to cut off excess egg-plant to achieve uniform thickness.)
4 Brush the eggplant lightly on each side with the herb and oil mixture, reserving remaining marinade for the scallops.
5 Sear the eggplant directly on the grill, 1 minute on each side. Set aside, covered.
6 Transfer the eggplant to a baking dish, cover with foil wrap, and place in the oven approximately 8 minutes.
7 While the eggplant roasts, marinate the scallops. Place the scallops in a small container with the extra herb and oil mixture and refrigerate for 30 minutes.
8 Place a medium nonstick skillet over medium-high heat. When hot, add the scallops, searing them for 1 1/2 to 2 minutes, until the outer rim turns a golden brown, then turn them over and cook another 1 1/2 minutes or until it just springs back when lightly touched. In a skillet over medium heat, lightly sear the scallops on both sides. Note: Be careful not to overcook the scallops; they are chewy when overcooked.
9 To present and serve, place one slice of eggplant on a warm plate and spoon half of the scallops onto the eggplant. Top the scallops with another slice of eggplant and a scoop of the Mango Sal-

sa. Do the same for the second plate. Garnish each plate with a sprig of fresh basil. Serve and enjoy or, as Chef Bregeon would say, "Et voila, bon appetit!"

Nutrition at a glance (per serving): *total fat 12g; saturated fat 2g; protein 22g; dietary fiber 15g; carbohydrate 67g; cholesterol 23mg; sodium 225mg; vitamin A (% of Daily Value) 138; vitamin C (% of Daily Value) 283; vitamin E (% of Daily Value) 21; folic acid (% of Daily Value) 33; % of calories from fat 25; % of calories from saturated fat 4; calories 427.*

***

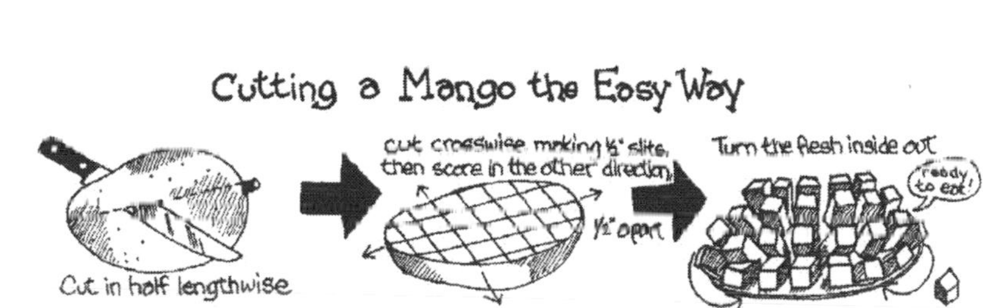

Figure 8-7: Avoid a lot of hassle by using this mango-cutting method.

Flavorful Combos

Some of most delicious seafood dishes combine several types of fish and shellfish in delicious stews. Others combine a single fish with a variety of vegetables. Here are two American classics that reflect our heritage as a nation of immigrants; first a cioppino, then a gratin.

San Francisco Crab and Wild Fennel Cioppino

Created by Jody Denton
Executive Chef/CEO, Restaurant LuLu
San Francisco, California

According to Sharon Tyler Herbst, author of The New Food Lover's Companion, Italian immigrants in San Francisco were the first to create cioppino, a stew classically made with fresh tomatoes and variety of fish and shellfish. Chef Denton's version incorporates French and Tunisian flavorings to give the stew an intense aroma and intriguing blend of flavors.

Tools: *Large heavy-bottom saucepan, food mill*

Preparation time: *45 minutes*

Cooking time: *45 minutes*

Yield: *6 servings*

3 tablespoons extra-virgin olive oil

1 white onion, thinly sliced

1 leek, well rinsed, white and light green portion only, thinly sliced

1 fennel bulb, thinly sliced

10 cloves garlic

Pinch of saffron

1 tablespoon ground fennel seeds

1 teaspoon pepper

2 tablespoons harissa

1 bunch fresh thyme

1 bunch Italian parsley, chopped

1 tablespoon orange zest

6 salt anchovy fillets, not rinsed

1 pound boneless fish fillet such as rockfish, mullet, snapper, or halibut, cut into 2-inch chunks

2 whole cooked Dungeness crabs (about 1 pound each) or 10 ounces crab meat (If using whole crab, purchase and have the seafood market steam them for you the day you will use them.)

1 1/2 quarts fresh, ripe tomato puree

1/2 pound clams

1/2 pound mussels

1/4 cup Pernod liqueur

1/4 cup chopped wild fennel tops (or cultivated fennel tops)

4 cups fresh sourdough bread croutons (about 6 to 8 slices of bread)

1/2 teaspoon chopped garlic

1 teaspoon fresh chopped thyme

1 Preheat oven to 350 degrees.

2 In a large heavy-bottom saucepan, heat 2 tablespoons of the olive oil over medium heat. Add the onion, leeks, sliced fennel bulb, and garlic and cook, stirring often, until translucent, about 5 minutes. Add the saffron, fennel seed, and pepper and cook for another 2 to 3 minutes.

3 Add the harissa, the bunch of thyme, parsley, orange zest, anchovies, and fish. Cover with water and bring to a boil. Once boiling, reduce the heat and simmer for about 15 minutes.

4 While this cooks, "crack" the precooked crab by removing the claws and dividing the legs at the joints, and cracking all with a mallet; remove the back from the body, discard all soft matter, and divide body in half and reserve.
5 Pass the entire contents of the saucepan through a food mill to puree. The food mill will remove seed coverings, stems of herbs, and so on; discard these.
6 Return the puree to the pot, add the tomato puree, and bring to a boil. To the boiling puree, add the cracked crab or crabmeat, clams, mussels, and Pernod, reduce to a simmer, and cook for 10 minutes (or until the clams and mussels open).
7 Adjust the seasoning.
8 While cioppino is simmering, toss the croutons in a bowl with the remaining olive oil, chopped thyme, garlic, and pepper. Toast in a 400 degree oven on a baking sheet until golden brown, about 8 minutes.
9 Ladle the soup into large shallow soup bowls, distributing the crab, clams and mussels evenly. To finish, scatter the croutons on top of the soup.

Nutrition at a glance (per serving): *total fat 13g; saturated fat 2g; protein 30g; dietary fiber 6g; carbohydrate 36g; cholesterol 87mg; sodium 420mg; vitamin A (% of Daily Value) 32; vitamin C (% of Daily Value) 96; vitamin E (% of Daily Value) 20; folic acid (% of Daily Value) 23; % of calories from fat 30; % of calories from saturated fat 5; calories 391.*

Note: *Nutritional analysis based on use of halibut. Fat content may be higher if another type of fish is used.*

***

A *food mill* (sometimes called a *mechanical sieve*) is a manually operated kitchen tool used to remove skin, seeds, and fiber from foods. It has a hand-turned paddle that forces food through a strainer. A food mill can be found in specialty kitchen shops.

Harissa is an intensely spicy hot sauce made from olive oil, hot chilies, garlic, cumin, coriander, and caraway. The sauce, with origins in Tunisian cooking, can be found in canned or jarred form in Middle Eastern markets and specialty cooking shops.

Pernod is a licorice-flavored liqueur that can be found in fine liquor and wine stores.

Baked Fillet of Turbot with Gratin of Yukon Potato, Tomato, Lemon, Onion, and Basil

Created by Sylvain Portay
Chef of The Dining Room, The Ritz-Carlton, San Francisco
San Francisco, California

With its accompanying vegetable gratin, this recipe looks and tastes wonderful, and it's not difficult to prepare. Turbot is a highly prized flatfish with firm, lean white flesh and a delicate flavor. Turbot is caught in the waters of the Atlantic Ocean off the coast of Europe and is often sold frozen in United States markets. Some fish markets may call flounder caught in the Pacific "turbot," but this is not the same as the Atlantic-caught fish. If turbot is not in your market, go ahead and try the recipe with flounder or halibut.

Tools: *Medium saucepan, 1 1/2-inch diameter cookie cutter, chef's knife, ovenproof 6-x-6-x1 1/2-inch casserole dish*

Preparation time: *20 minutes*

Cooking time: *20 minutes*

Yield: *4 servings*

3 medium Yukon gold potatoes, peeled
Salt and pepper to taste
3 small white onions, peeled and thinly sliced
2 medium ripe red tomatoes, thinly sliced
4 basil leaves
1/2 lemon, peeled and thinly sliced
1 fennel stick
1 8-ounce turbot fillet
Olive oil in an oil sprayer
2 tablespoons chicken stock or water

1 Preheat oven to 350 degrees.
2 In a medium saucepan, bring 1 quart of water to a boil. Season with salt (optional). Trim both ends of the potatoes and place upright on a cutting board. With a 1 1/2-inch diameter cookie cutter, cut the potatoes to form a complete cylinder. Using

a knife, slice the potatoes to 1/4-inch thickness. Transfer to the boiling water. Drain and set aside.

3 Using an ovenproof 6-x-6-x-1 1/2-inch casserole dish, oil the bottom and side of the dish with a small amount of olive oil. Season with salt (optional) and pepper, to taste.

4 Line the casserole dish with sliced ingredients beginning with the potatoes, lining them up and overlapping them left to right. Start a second row using the tomatoes, overlapping them from left to right. Start a third row using the onions overlapping them from left to right. Repeat layering starting with the potatoes and ending with the onions.

5 Place one piece of basil leaf in each corner of the casserole dish behind the tomatoes.

6 Place one piece of sliced lemon and one piece of fennel stick in the center of the casserole dish.

7 Season the turbot fillet with salt (optional) and pepper, and mist or brush with olive oil. Lay fillet on top of the ingredients and drizzle with chicken stock or water.

8 Cover the casserole dish with aluminum foil and bake in a 350-degree oven for 15 to 20 minutes or until the fish is cooked through.

9 Serve this dish family-style by placing the baking dish on the table and allowing diners to serve themselves.

Nutrition at a glance (per serving): *total fat 2g; saturated fat 0g; protein 14g; dietary fiber 6g;*

carbohydrate 49g; cholesterol 27mg; sodium 111mg; vitamin C (% of Daily Value) 70; % of calories from fat 7; % of calories from saturated fat 0; calories 267.

***

A fennel stick is simply the green stem of a stalk of fresh fennel. Pale green fresh fennel stalks with their darker feathery leaves on top look like celery. Fresh fennel gives a lighter, more delicate flavor than dried fennel or fennel seeds. If you don't like the anise/licorice flavor of dried fennel, you may appreciate the subtler flavor of fresh fennel.

Using the cookie cutter to give all the vegetables a similar shape and size makes an elegant dish, but if you don't have a cookie cutter, you can achieve a similar but rougher effect by shaping the potatoes with a knife to match the diameter of the onion and tomato. Also use a 8-x-8-x-2-inch baking pan if you don't have the smaller casserole dish specified.

Chapter 9

Vegetarian Entrées

In This Chapter

- Enjoying the nutritional benefits of vegetarian eating
- Cooking creatively without meat

Recipes in This Chapter

- Vegetable Burger with Lentils and Portobello Mushrooms **(V)**
- Spicy Vegetarian Pinto Bean Chili Por **(V)**
- Farfalle Ai Pisellini **(V)**
- Cannellini Spinach Penne **(V)**
- Angel Hair Pasta with Fresh Tomatoes, Basil, and Garlic **(V)**
- Roasted Vegetable Calzones **(V)**
- Moo Shu Vegetables with Chinese Pancakes **(V)**
- Curried Tofu and Vegetable-Stuffed Pitas with Cashews and Raisins **(V)**

***

Whether you choose to eat meat-free as a way of life or for just a few meals each week, going vegetarian can be a heart-healthy way to eat. One big plus of vegetarian cooking is the abundant use of a variety of vegetables and whole grains that are rich in vitamins, minerals, antioxidants, and other heart-healthy phytochemicals, and often fiber. Vegetarian cooking is also usually lower in saturated fat and cholesterol than the typical Western diet that contains meat.

Today, because of the availability of a rich variety of foods in most markets, cooking creatively and eating well while cooking vegetarian is easier than ever before. Consider how your local supermarket has probably expanded the variety of foods it offers in just the past ten years. Today, items such as elephant garlic, fresh basil, mint, and other herbs, several varieties of rice and other whole grains, and exotic fresh fruits and vegetables from around the world are easy to find and relatively inexpensive to buy. Good vegetable sources of protein such as tofu, tempeh, and soy milk have taken their place on the shelves beside or near the dairy products. Taking advantage of this rich variety, the vegetarian entrées in this chapter demonstrate that vegetarian cooking can be a culinary adventure and taste treat for anyone who wants to eat well—and heart healthy.

Including Vegetarian Meals in Heart-Healthy Eating

Inserting two or three vegetarian meals or entrées into your weekly menu is a smart practice for the healthy-heart cook. Using meat substitutes in place of meat offers two big nutrition benefits: less saturated fat and less cholesterol, two dietary components that are closely linked with heart disease. Although saturated fat is found in some plant foods (coconut milk or palm oil, for example), animal products account for the majority of saturated fat in the typical American diet. Cholesterol, you remember, comes only from animal products. Therefore, cooking and eating a vegetarian meal or entrée a couple of times a week can help you meet your goals of limiting your saturated fat and cholesterol intake.

Whether you are a lacto-ovo vegetarian (which means you eat dairy products and eggs) or a vegan (which means you eat no animal products whatsoever), you can follow a balanced, nutritious eating plan than supports your heart health and your overall health. The key for such an eating plan, as for all healthy eating plans, is to consume a variety of foods that provide a balance of nutrients. Doing so helps ensure you get all the protein you need as well as most other nutrients. Depending on your age and the type of vegetarian diet you eat, you need to be careful to get enough iron, vitamin B-12 (which is necessary for healthy blood cells and mental function), and vitamin D (which you need for calcium absorption).

You can also adapt the Food Guide Pyramid for vegetarian use. Several government agencies and private health promotion groups have produced variations on the Food Guide Pyramid (see Chapter 3 for more discussion of the pyramid itself) that adapt this guide to the requirements of a healthy vegetarian eating plan. You can find the useful vegetarian food guide pyramid developed by the Oldways Preservation & Exchange Trust in cooperation with the Harvard School of Public Health together with other resources on their Web site at www.oldwayspt.org.

For anyone thinking about adopting a vegetarian eating plan, I recommend that you consult some good resources on vegetarian nutrition and meal planning. Two good resources are *Being Vegetarian* written for the American Dietetic Association by Suzanne Havala and *Almost Vegetarian: A Primer for Cooks Who Are Eating Vegetarian Most of the Time, Chicken & Fish Some of the Time & Altogether Well All of the Time* by Diana Shaw (for full details see the appendix). You can also find many useful resources on the Web site of the Vegetarian Resource Group at www.vrg.org.

Cooking Vegetarian Entrées

The recipes in this chapter will warm your heart and do it some good, too. They start with two great American comfort foods featuring legumes, then offer several very different pasta dishes with a Mediterranean flavor, and finish with two recipes that draw on Chinese and Middle Eastern cuisines. Try them all and treat your palate to a mini world tour.

Vegetable Burger with Lentils and Portobello Mushrooms

Created by Hans Spirig
Executive Chef, Maison & Jardin Restaurant
Altamonte Springs, Florida

These hearty meatless burgers go great in a bun with all the fixings. For a complete meal serve them with a broth-based vegetable soup or a salad. These burgers could also make great appetizers if you make smaller patties.

Tools: *Small baking pan, medium sauté pan, large mixing bowl, large nonstick sauté pan*

Preparation time: *30 minutes*

Cooking time: *1 hour*

Yield: *6 burgers*

1/2 pound dry lentils, cleaned (1 1/3 cup raw or 3 1/4 cups cooked)

1 portobello mushroom cap, brushed clean, bottom gills shaved off

2 tablespoons olive oil

1 small Vidalia onion, chopped

1 small red pepper, diced

3 cloves garlic, chopped

1 small celery root, peeled and diced
1 carrot, peeled and diced
1/4 cup balsamic vinegar
3/4 cup unseasoned bread crumbs
1 egg
1 egg white
1/3 cup chopped cilantro
1 teaspoon ground cumin
Salt and pepper to taste
1 red onion, peeled and thinly sliced
1 tablespoon clarified unsalted butter
1 tablespoon brown sugar

1 Preheat oven to 425 degrees.
2 Simmer lentils in 4 cups salted (optional) water over medium-high heat for about 50 minutes. The lentils should be very tender, almost mushy. Drain off any remaining liquid.
3 Lightly spray the portobello or brush with olive oil and place on a small baking pan. Roast in the oven until tender, about 20 minutes. Remove, allow to cool slightly, and then cut into cubes.
4 When the lentils are cooking and the portobellos are roasting, heat 1 tablespoon olive oil in a medium sauté pan over medium-high heat.
5 Add the Vidalia onion, red pepper, garlic, celery root, and carrots and sauté, tossing or stirring often, until tender, about 8 minutes.
6 When the vegetables are tender, place them in a large mixing bowl, and deglaze the pan with

the balsamic vinegar. Reduce the vinegar by half, then add it to the vegetables.

7 When the lentils are tender, strain any excess liquid (if there is any) and place the lentils in the mixing bowl with the sautéed vegetables. Add the cubed portobello mushrooms, 1/2 cup bread crumbs, the egg and egg white, cilantro, cumin, and salt and pepper to season. Mix well.

8 Place a large nonstick sauté pan with 1 tablespoon of olive oil over medium-high heat. Form 6 patties, dip each patty in the remaining bread crumbs, coating each on both sides. Place the patties into the pan and sauté until well browned on the bottom, about 3 minutes. Turn, lower heat slightly, and cook until heated through and browned on the other side, about 4 minutes.

9 When all the patties have cooked, sauté the red onions in the clarified butter with the brown sugar. Cook until the onions become light brown.

10 To serve, spoon some of the caramelized onion mixture on top of each patty.

Nutrition at a glance (per serving): *total fat 6g; saturated fat 2g; protein 14g; dietary fiber 10g; carbohydrate 40g; cholesterol 41g; sodium 151mg; vitamin A (% of Daily Value) 51; vitamin C (% of Daily Value) 50; folic acid (% of Daily Value) 52; % of calories from fat 22; % of calories from saturated fat 7; calories 263.*

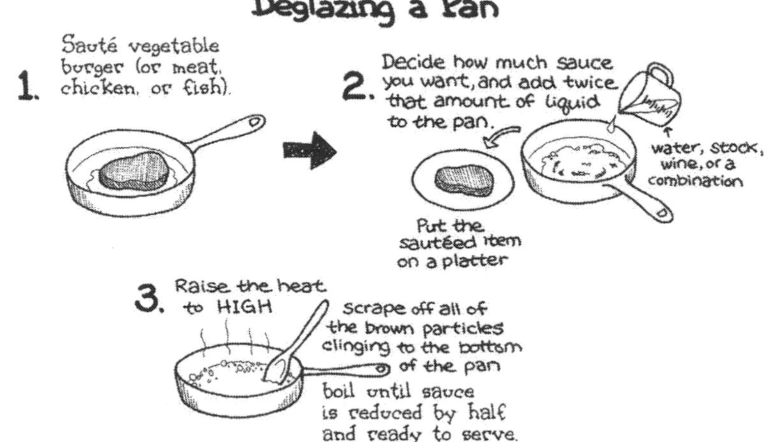

Figure 9-1: Deglazing a pan enables you to add the flavorful brown bits to your sauce.

Figure 9-2: Using a hand blender, making your own bread crumbs is easy.

Deglazing is done by heating a small amount of liquid (the balsamic vinegar) in the pan and stirring to loosen browned bits of food on the bottom (see Figure 9-1). The resulting mixture is often used as a base for a sauce to accompany the food cooked in the pan.

How to make fresh bread crumbs: Put fresh white, French, or Italian bread in your food processor and process until crumbs form. The resulting crumbs will be much fresher than store-bought bread crumbs, which tend to go stale very quickly. One average slice of white bread will yield 1/2 cup of bread crumbs. You can store extra fresh bread crumbs in an air-tight container in your refrigerator for 2 to 3 days or in your freezer for 2 to 3 months. (See Figure 9-2 for illustrated instructions for making bread crumbs with a hand blender.)

***

Clarified butter is unsalted butter, slowly melted to evaporate the water and separate the milk solids, which settle on the bottom of the pan. A golden liquid will form on top of the milk solid and is poured off and used for frying. The taste is less buttery, but the removal of the milk solid prevents the butter from burning.

Spicy Vegetarian Pinto Bean Chili

Created by Amy Myrdal, M.S., R.D.
Senior Research Dietitian, Rippe Lifestyle Institute
Shrewsbury, Massachusetts

This hearty, heart-healthy chili is packed with antioxidants, folic acid, and fiber. This recipe makes a large batch of chili, but it can be stored in the refrigerator for up to four days or frozen and reheated at a later time. If you're not a spicy-food lover, simply leave out the jalapeno peppers and red pepper flakes. To add richness to the chili, top with a small amount (a couple tablespoons) of grated, reduced-fat cheddar cheese

Tools: *Large stockpot, soup pot, or Dutch oven*
Preparation time: *20 minutes*
Cooking time: *1 hour, 10 minutes*
Yield: *8 servings*

2 tablespoons canola oil

1 medium onion, finely chopped

4 cloves garlic, finely chopped

1 tablespoon red pepper flakes

2 jalapeno peppers, seeded, cored, and diced (see Figure 9-3 for illustrated instructions on seeding jalapeno peppers)

1 large green bell pepper, seeded, cored, and chopped

1 large red bell pepper, seeded, cored, and chopped

4 stalks celery, trimmed and sliced
4 carrots, peeled and grated
1 28-ounce can crushed tomatoes
1 12-ounce can tomato paste
3 1/2 cups water
6 cups cooked pinto beans (or canned, drained beans)
1 15 1/2-ounce can whole kernel corn, drained
1 teaspoon pepper
1/2 teaspoon salt
1 1/2 teaspoons oregano
2 teaspoons sugar
1 bay leaf

1 Heat the canola oil over medium-high heat in a large stockpot, soup pot, or Dutch oven. Add the chopped onions and garlic and sauté for 2 to 3 minutes.
2 Add the red pepper flakes, jalapeno, green and red peppers, celery, and carrots, and continue cooking, stirring often, for another 1 to 2 minutes.
3 Add the crushed tomatoes and stir well.
4 Add the remaining ingredients.
5 Stir again, cover, reduce heat to low, and allow to simmer for at least 1 hour. Stir occasionally to prevent sticking or burning.
6 Serve warm. Be sure to remove the bay leaf before serving.
7 Refrigerate or freeze extra chili.

Nutrition at a glance (per serving): *total fat 5g; saturated fat less than 1g; protein 16g; dietary* *fiber 18g; carbohydrate 67g; cholesterol 0mg; sodium 987mg; vitamin A (% of Daily Value) 179; vitamin C (% of Daily Value) 207; vitamin E (% of Daily Value) 24; folic acid (% of Daily Value) 73; % of calories from fat 12; % of calories from saturated fat 2; calories 351.*

Figure 9-3: How to seed a jalapeno pepper without getting burned.

Pasta

Pasta, in all its seemingly infinite shapes and types, provides a wonderful resource for healthful vegetarian entrées. The following recipes give you just a sampling of the possibilities.

Farfalle Ai Pisellini

Created by Marius Pavlak, Executive Chef, and Laura Maioglio, Owner
Barbetta Restaurant
New York, New York

By combining wheat-based pasta with green peas, a legume, this Italian recipe gives you a tasty, nutritionally balanced main dish. *Farfalle* are bowtie-shaped pasta noodles. *Pisellini* are tiny green peas (The suffix "ini" in Italian indicates that the object is small. You've probably noticed it in the names of various types of pasta such as farfallini or spaghettini). Be sure to read the recipe through and plan your timing of the steps, so that all the components finish more or less together.

Tools: *Large skillet, large mixing bowl, blender, straining basket, large sauté pan or medium saucepan*

Preparation time: *20 minutes*

Cooking time: *30 minutes*

Yield: *4 servings*

8 ounces farfalle, also known as bow-ties (The chefs recommend Barilla farfalle #65. See Figure 9-4 for an illustration of farfalle.)

10 ounces fresh shelled peas (or 1 10-ounce box of frozen tiny baby peas)

2 shallots, chopped

1 small Spanish onion, chopped

1 cup unsalted chicken broth

1/2 bunch Italian (flat-leaf) parsley, chopped

2 stems basil, chopped

3 ounces whole sugar snap peas, for garnish

2 tablespoons extra-virgin olive oil

Salt and pepper to taste

1 Bring 4 quarts of salted water to a boil.

2 Heat the olive oil in a large skillet over medium heat. Sauté shallots and onion until they are soft, about 5 minutes, adding a little water as needed to prevent browning.

3 Pour chicken broth into skillet and boil for 5 minutes.
4 Prepare a large bowl of ice water. Add 3/4 of the peas and boil for 5 minutes, simmering. Transfer to a container and place in the ice bath to preserve green color. Do not throw away the ice bath.
5 Transfer cooled mixture to a blender, add chopped parsley and basil, and blend well. Set this puree aside.
6 Place the remaining peas in a straining basket and place in the boiling water for 5 minutes; remove the basket, drain, and set aside.
7 Blanch sugar snap peas in the same manner for 2 minutes. Transfer to a small container and place it in the ice water bath for 30 seconds to stop cooking process. Remove from water, drain, and set aside. (See Figure 9-5 for illustrated instructions of blanching and shocking.)
8 While preparing the pea sauce, cook farfalle in lightly salted (optional) boiling water until al dente, 10 to 13 minutes depending on the brand. Drain well when done cooking.
9 In a large sauté pan or medium saucepan, stir together the cooked farfalle, whole peas, and puree, stirring lightly to coat. Bring to a simmer, then quickly remove from the heat.
10 Divide evenly among 4 dinner plates and add blanched sugar snap peas for a garnish.

Nutrition at a glance (per serving): *total fat 8g; saturated fat 1g; protein 13g; dietary fiber 7g;*

carbohydrate 58g; cholesterol 0mg; sodium 77mg; vitamin A (% of Daily Value) 20; vitamin C (% of Daily Value) 49; folic acid (% of Daily Value) 20; % of calories from fat 21; % of calories from saturated fat 3; calories 355.

***

Figure 9-4: The bow-tie pasta, also known as farfalle.

Figure 9-5: Blanching and shocking can heighten the color of vegetables to stop the cooking process.

Cannellini Spinach Penne

Created by Melanie Mulcahy
Nutrition Intern, Rippe and Lifestyle Institute
Shrewsbury, Massachusetts

Penne are large macaroni tubes that are cut on the diagonal. Combining the wheat-based pasta with the beans, a legume, provides a complete protein. Adding colorful spinach and the other ingredients makes this recipe a nutritional powerhouse, rich in vitamins C and A and folic acid.

Tools: *Small nonstick skillet, large stockpot or soup pot, large nonstick skillet*

Preparation time: *5 minutes*

Cooking time: *20 minutes*

Yield: *4 servings*

1 14 1/2-ounce can diced tomatoes

1/2 19-ounce can cannellini (white kidney) beans, drained and rinsed

1/2 10-ounce bag fresh spinach, rinsed and chopped

1/2 pound penne pasta

1/2 cup crumbled feta or goat cheese

4 tablespoons toasted pine nuts

1. Toast pine nuts in a small skillet over medium heat until fragrant, about 3 to 4 minutes. Set aside.
2. Bring a large pot of water to a boil. Season with salt and add the pasta, cooking until al dente, tender but firm.

3 In a large skillet, combine tomatoes and beans; bring to boil. Reduce heat and allow to simmer for 10 minutes.
4 Add spinach to the sauce, cooking for about 2 minutes or until slightly wilted. Make sure to constantly stir the mixture.
5 Serve on 4 separate plates. Place penne on plate and top with sauce, feta, and toasted pine nuts.

Nutrition at a glance (per serving): *total fat 11g; saturated fat 4g; protein 20g; dietary fiber 9g; carbohydrate 69g; cholesterol 17mg; sodium 400mg; vitamin A (% of Daily Value) 74; vitamin C (% of Daily Value) 41; folic acid (% of Daily Value) 38; % of calories from fat 22; % of calories from saturated fat 8; calories 444.*

***

Angel Hair Pasta with Fresh Tomatoes, Basil, and Garlic

Created by Amy Myrdal, M.S., R.D.
Senior Research Dietitian, Rippe Lifestyle Institute
Shrewsbury, Massachusetts

This is a very light entrée that can be paired with a soft breadstick, fresh fruit, and a glass of chilled white wine, like a Pinot Grigio, for a simple yet elegant meal on a hot summer evening, when light fare is most appealing. Using just-picked vine-ripened tomatoes is the key to making this simple entrée. Fresh basil and good quality extra-virgin olive oil are also important. But fresh, sweet ripe tomatoes are essential for the best flavor.

Tools: *Large bowl, medium saucepan, slotted spoon*

Preparation time: *10 minutes*

Cooking time: *15 minutes*

Yield: *4 servings*

4 ripe red tomatoes, blanched, peeled, seeded, and chopped

8 ounces angel hair pasta

4 teaspoons extra-virgin olive oil

2 tablespoons fresh basil, de-stemmed and chopped

2 cloves fresh garlic, minced

Pepper to taste

2 sprigs fresh basil, for garnish

Freshly grated parmesan cheese (optional)

1 Fill a large bowl with cold water and ice cubes. Set aside.

2 Fill a medium saucepan 3/4 full with water and place on stove over high heat. Bring water to a boil. When boiling, drop tomatoes in water. Blanch for 30 seconds or until skins start to crack. Using a slotted spoon, remove from boiling water and place in ice water bath to stop the cooking process.

3 When you remove the tomatoes from the water, add the pasta. Cook until al dente, about 4 to 5 minutes or according to package instructions.
4 Remove tomatoes from ice water after 1 minute and peel. Cut tomatoes in half and squeeze out seeds; chop and set aside.
5 When pasta is cooked, drain and combine with tomatoes, olive oil, basil, and garlic in a large serving bowl. Toss together. Top with black pepper and garnish with basil. Serve immediately.
6 Top with freshly grated Parmesan cheese, if desired.

Nutrition at a glance (per serving): *total fat 6g; saturated fat 2g; protein 9g; dietary fiber 4g; carbohydrate 52g; cholesterol 0mg; sodium 13mg; vitamin C (% of Daily Value) 40; folic acid (% of Daily Value) 20; % of calories from fat 18; % of calories from saturated fat 6; calories 294.*

***

Roasted Vegetable Calzones

Created by Amy Myrdal, M.S., R.D.
Senior Research Dietitian, Rippe Lifestyle Institute
Shrewsbury, Massachusetts

These calzones take some time to make but are well worth the effort. They're great warm or cold and can easily be reheated in a toaster oven or conventional oven. The smoked mozzarella cheese complements the rich flavor of the roasted vegetables nicely, but you can use whatever cheese you like. Unlike traditional calzones, these don't use any pizza sauce inside. As the vegetables roast, they release their juices to form a rich, flavorful sauce.

Tools: *Medium mixing bowl, whisk, oiled bowl, 2 large mixing bowls, large baking sheet, small saucepan, baking sheet or pizza stone*

Preparation time: *1 hour 45 minutes*

Cooking time: *about 50 minutes*

Yield: *4 servings*

For the Dough:

1 cup warm (125 to 130 degrees) water

1 teaspoon sugar

1 teaspoon salt

1 package (1 tablespoon) yeast

2 3/4 cups all-purpose flour

2 tablespoons olive oil

For the Filling:

1 large green bell pepper, cored, seeded, and cubed

1 large red bell pepper, cored, seeded, and cubed

1/2 medium red onion, cubed

1 large portobello mushroom cap, brushed clean and cubed

2 ripe red tomatoes, cored and cubed
4 to 6 cloves of garlic, peeled and quartered
1 tablespoon olive oil
2 teaspoons dried basil
1 teaspoon dried oregano
Freshly ground black pepper to taste
6 ounces smoked mozzarella cheese, grated

For the Dipping Sauce:

1 teaspoon olive oil
1 clove garlic, peeled and minced
1/4 cup red onion, peeled and finely chopped
1 1/2 cups tomato puree
2 teaspoons sugar
1 teaspoon dried basil
1/2 teaspoon dried oregano
1 bay leaf

Prepare the Dough:

1 In a medium mixing bowl, combine the warm water, sugar, and salt. Stir to dissolve the sugar and salt. Sprinkle in the yeast, stir gently, and allow to sit for 1 minute.
2 Add 1 cup of the flour and whisk to combine.
3 Add the olive oil and whisk again.
4 Add another 1 cup of the flour and stir well.
5 Add the final 3/4 cup of flour and stir until a dough ball begins to form. Then transfer the dough to a clean, flour-dusted surface and knead to combine all the flour. Knead the dough by pushing into the dough ball with one fist and then pulling the dough

on top of itself. Use your other hand to turn the dough one-quarter turn. Continue kneading the dough for at least 8 minutes. The dough will become somewhat glossy and will resist being pulled and pushed. (See Figure 9-6 for illustrated instructions of kneading.)

6 Transfer the dough ball to an oiled bowl, cover with plastic wrap and a clean kitchen towel. To expedite the rising process, fill a larger bowl halfway with hot tap water, and place the bowl holding the dough into the larger bowl. Set aside and allow the dough to rise for 50 to 60 minutes or until doubled in size.

Prepare the Filling:

1 Preheat the oven to 450 degrees with one oven rack at the highest level.

2 Prepare all vegetables as described in the ingredient list. (You don't need to chop the vegetables finely. One-inch cubes are a good size to strive for.)

3 Place chopped vegetables in a large mixing bowl. Drizzle with olive oil and add dried herbs and pepper. Toss well to coat all vegetables with herbs and oil.

4 Transfer the vegetables to a large baking sheet, place in oven, and roast for 15 minutes.

5 Remove from oven and allow roasted vegetables to cool on baking sheet. Reduce oven temperature to 375 degrees.

Prepare the Dipping Sauce:

1 In a small saucepan, combine the oil, garlic, and onion and sauté over medium heat until the onions become translucent.
2 Add remaining ingredients. Reduce the heat to low and simmer for 20 minutes.

Prepare and Serve the Calzones:

1 Divide the dough into four pieces. Using your hands, form each piece of dough into a 6-inch circle.
2 Place the circle on a baking sheet or pizza stone. Spoon 1/4 of the filling onto one side of the circle. Top with 1 1/2 ounces of grated mozzarella cheese. Fold dough in half over filling. Use a fork to press the edges together. Repeat until all 4 calzones have been formed.
3 Spray or brush the tops of the calzones with olive oil. Use the tip of a sharp knife to poke three holes in the top of each calzone.
4 Bake calzones in the oven for 25 to 30 minutes or until golden brown on top.
5 Serve warm with 1/4 cup dipping sauce per calzone.

Nutrition at a glance (per serving): *total fat 20g; saturated fat 6g; protein 26g; dietary fiber 8g; carbohydrate 93g; cholesterol 23mg; sodium 1,202mg; vitamin A (% of Daily Value) 92; vitamin C (% of Daily Value) 245; folic acid (% of Daily Value) 36; % of calories from fat 28; % of calories from saturated fat 9; calories 648.*

***

Figure 9-6: Knead dough by pushing down, folding, and rotating 1/4 turn.

Pacific Rim Treats

The many cultures of the Pacific Rim have long featured vegetarian dishes as part of their traditional cuisines. We have drawn on traditional approaches and ingredients, such a soy-based tofu, to give you two very different entrées to sample with the hope that you will seek out more on your own.

Moo Shu Vegetables with Chinese Pancakes

Created by Amy Myrdal, M.S., R.D.
Senior Research Dietitian, Rippe Lifestyle Institute
Shrewsbury, Massachusetts

Many cultures have a version of the pancake. Americans make *flapjacks* and *griddle-cakes;* Hispanics make *tortillas;* Norwegians make *lefse;* Russians make *blini;* Icelanders make *ponnukokur;* French make *crepes;* and Chinese make *moo shu pancakes,* which are also known as *Peking doilies.*

If you're in a hurry, this recipe can be simplified by using flour tortillas in place of the pancakes. But when you have time, try making the pancakes from scratch. They taste great warm and freshly made. The trick to great *moo shu* pancakes is rolling them as thin as possible.

Tools: *Medium mixing bowl, wooden spoon, small mixing bowl, chef's knife, rolling pin, nonstick skillet, large mixing bowl, large skillet or wok*

Preparation time: *1 hour 15 minutes*

Cooking time: *20 minutes*

Yield: *4 servings*

For the pancakes:

2 cups all-purpose flour (for the dough)

1 cup plus 1 tablespoon boiling water

1/2 cup all-purpose flour (for rolling)

For the vegetables:

1/2 ounce dried wood ear mushrooms, rehydrated in hot water (or use 4 ounces fresh crimini or portobello mushrooms instead)

4 cups shredded Chinese cabbage (see Figure 9-7)

1 tablespoon rice wine vinegar

1 tablespoon peanut or canola oil

3 cloves garlic, minced

1 tablespoon minced ginger

4 scallions (green onions), trimmed and sliced
3 carrots, peeled and shredded
4 eggs, lightly beaten
1 cup bean sprouts
1 tablespoon soy sauce
1 tablespoon hoisin sauce

For spreading on pancakes:

4 tablespoons hoisin sauce

Prepare the pancakes:

1 Place 2 cups flour in a mixing bowl. Add 1 cup boiling water and stir with a wooden spoon until a dough ball forms. Add another 1 tablespoon of boiling water if the dough seems too dry. Allow dough to sit a few moments to cool.
2 Transfer the dough ball to a clean counter and knead until soft, but don't work it too much (2 minutes should be long enough).
3 Place the dough in a clean bowl, cover with a clean, damp kitchen towel, and let rest for 20 minutes.
4 Remove the rested dough from the bowl and form the dough into a long cylinder about 2 inches in diameter. Using a sharp knife, cut the dough into 12 disks.
5 Place a little flour on the counter and, using your hands, pat a dough ball into a flat disk about 1/4 inch thick. Use your rolling pin to roll out the dough as thinly as possible. Roll from the center and add more flour as you roll to keep the dough

from sticking. You should end up with a very thin pancake about 8 inches in diameter.

6 Cook the pancake in a dry nonstick skillet over medium heat. Cook for 1 minute per side. Stack cooked pancakes on a plate.

7 If you have leftover pancakes, wrap them in plastic wrap and refrigerate them. To reheat, steam about 10 minutes in a bamboo or other steamer to soften before using. The pancakes can also be prepared, frozen, and steamed without thawing.

Prepare the vegetables:

1 While the dough is resting, soak the mushrooms in hot water to rehydrate them and pre pare all the vegetables. When soft, drain the mushrooms and set aside.

2 Place the shredded Chinese cabbage in a bowl and add 1 tablespoon rice wine vinegar. Set aside.

3 In a large skillet or wok, heat 1 tablespoon peanut or canola oil over high heat. Add the garlic, ginger, and scallions and stir fry for 10 seconds. Add the carrots and mushrooms next and stir fry another 10 seconds.

4 Add the eggs and stir fry for 1 minute, until just set.

5 Add the cabbage, bean sprouts, soy sauce, and hoisin sauce. Stir fry another 30 seconds or so.

Plate and serve:

1 Spread 1 teaspoon hoisin sauce on each pancake. Add a generous scoop of *moo shu* vegetables to

each pancake. Fold over one third of the pancake to form the end, then fold up each side and place on the plate, seam side down.

2 Repeat with remaining 11 pancakes, or let your guests roll their own pancakes.

Nutrition at a glance (per serving): *total fat 12g; saturated fat 3g; protein 21g; dietary fiber 6g; carbohydrate 80g; cholesterol 212mg; sodium 683mg; vitamin A (% of Daily Value) 196; vitamin C (% of Daily Value) 74; folic acid (% of Daily Value) 36; % of calories from fat 21; % of calories from saturated fat 5; calories 505.*

***

Figure 9-7: Chinese cabbage is great for wrapping packages (not the kind that you mail—the food kind).

Curried Tofu and Vegetable-Stuffed Pitas with Cashews and Raisins

Created by Melanie Mulcahy
Nutrition Intern, Rippe Lifestyle Institute
Shrewsbury, Massachusetts

This recipe features a technique—freezing—that extends the range of recipes in which tofu can be used. Freezing tofu alters the protein structures, which gives the tofu a more meaty texture. The tofu becomes more porous and will soak up more marinade than when it hasn't been frozen. One normal change in the tofu is that it turns a slight brown, so don't get concerned if it looks just like steak!

Tools: *Cheesecloth, shallow baking pan, large nonstick skillet or wok*

Preparation time: 12 *hours to prepare the tofu, 20 minutes to prepare the dish*

Cooking time: *10 minutes*

Yield: *6 servings*

16 ounces firm or extra-firm tofu
2 teaspoons olive oil
1 cup broccoli, chopped
1/4 cup red onion, finely diced
1 carrot, peeled and sliced
1 red bell pepper, sliced
1 cup bok choy (see Figure 9-8), chopped
1 cup pea pods
1 tablespoon whole wheat flour

2 teaspoons curry powder
1/2 cup water
1/4 cup cashews, chopped
1/2 cup seedless golden raisins
6 7-inch whole wheat pita pockets

To freeze tofu:

1 Remove tofu block from package and drain.

2 Wrap tofu in cheesecloth and place between 2 cutting boards (or other flat, heavy objects). Place a shallow baking pan under the boards to create a place for the excess water to collect. Allow the tofu to drain for 30 minutes on each side.

3 Remove tofu from cheesecloth and wrap in plastic wrap, then aluminum foil. Set tofu in freezer, for at least 8 hours or until ready to use. (Tofu can remain in the freezer for up to 6 months.)

4 When ready to prepare, remove the tofu from the freezer and take off the foil. Thaw in the microwave (on defrost setting) approximately 2 minutes on each side.

To prepare stuffed pitas:

1 Heat a large skillet or wok over medium-high heat. When hot, coat the pan with 1/2 tablespoon of olive oil.

2 Add the broccoli, onions, and carrots and sauté, stirring, for 2 minutes.

3 Add the remaining vegetables and sauté, stirring often, until desired tenderness. Remove sautéed vegetables from the skillet or wok and set aside.
4 Cut the thawed block of tofu into equal size cubes. Set aside.
5 Reduce heat to medium and add the remaining 1/2 tablespoon of olive oil. Sprinkle in the flour and cook, stirring constantly, until lightly browned, 3 to 4 minutes.
6 Mix in curry powder. Then, while stirring continuously, slowly add the water.
7 Add the chopped tofu and cook until warm and well coated with curry sauce.
8 Add the cashews, raisins, and vegetable mixture and coat evenly.
9 Cut approximately 1 inch off the top of each pita and stuff it with the tofu and vegetable mixture. If desired, warm the pitas in the oven for a few minutes before stuffing them.
10 Serve immediately.

Nutrition at a glance (per serving): *total fat 13g; saturated fat 2g; protein 21g; dietary fiber 9g; carbohydrate 56g; cholesterol 0mg; sodium 405mg; vitamin A (% of Daily Value) 68; vitamin C (% of Daily Value) 106; folic acid (% of Daily Value) 20; % of calories from fat 29; % of calories from saturated fat 5; calories 399.*

***

Figure 9-8: Bok choy is great in stir-fries and soups.

Chapter 10

Special Occasion Dishes

In This Chapter

- Celebrating special occasions with special recipes
- Including higher-fat dishes in a healthy-heart diet
- Balancing higher-fat and low-fat dishes for celebratory meals

Recipes in This Chapter

- Yellow Tomato and Fennel Gazpachos**(V)**
- Baby Spinach and Citrus Salad with Wheatberries and Red Onion Confit**(V)**
- Arugula Salad with Melons and Lime Dressing **(V)**
- Rice Vermicelli and Salad Rolls with Peanut Sauce
- Smoked Salmon Tartare
- Diver-Caught Maine Sea Scallops with Grapefruit
- Taylor Bay Scallops with Uni and Mustard Oil
- Lemon-Grilled Cornish Hens

- Spinach Salad with Pears and Walnuts and Yellow Raisin Vinaigrette**(V)**
- Tangerine Chicken Escabéche
- Grilled Beef Tenderloin with Arugula, Marinated Red Onions, and Balsamic Vinaigrette
- Caramelized Onion, Ham, and Portobello Mushroom Tart
- Sautéed Halibut with Roasted Fennel and Swiss Chard
- Steamed Trout Stuffed with Root Vegetables and Truffle Vinaigrette
- Seared Ahi Tuna with Tomatoes, Lime, and Basil
- Yellowfin Tuna with Green Gazpacho Sauce
- Spinaci Alla Perugina**(V)**
- Orzo Salad with Lemon Tarragon Vinaigrette**(V)**
- Portobello Mushroom Carpaccio with Shallot Relish, Sun-Dried Tomatoes, and Aged Balsamic**(V)**

Special occasions—from the end of the work week (TGIF) to birthdays and anniversaries—demand great food. But great food is not always low-fat food. And in a healthy-heart approach to eating, it doesn't have to be. Instead, you want to make sure that your overall diet over the course of a day, a week, or a month stays within the guidelines of less than 30 percent of total calories from fat and less than 10 percent of total calories from saturated fat as recommended by the American Heart Association, the

American Dietetic Association, and other nutrition groups. In other words, you can balance low-fat and higher-fat food choices to achieve a heart-healthy diet.

In this chapter, I show you how to incorporate into a heart-healthy lifestyle dishes that have more than 30 percent of total calories from fat. The fat in these recipes is mostly of the type that promotes heart health—monounsaturated fat from such sources as olive oil or canola oil or fat from fish that are rich in omega-3 fatty acids. In most cases, you can plan a meal that, as a whole, contains less than 30 percent of calories from fat by including one of these recipes and choosing from other recipes in the book for your menu. And you can certainly fit one or more of the recipes into a day's meals and stay within the guidelines. At the end of each recipe, I give a suggested menu to show you how.

Some of these recipes also seem appropriate for celebrations because they call for more time in preparation or more special ingredients than you might select for everyday meals. I look at these recipes as good opportunities to enjoy creative time in the kitchen (or to put family and friends to work in helping out). I also suggest that, as usual, you read each recipe through and plan before you begin cooking—that's the surest route to an enjoyable time in the kitchen and a successful dish. Now, go celebrate!

Starters

Most of the salads, soups, and appetizers in this section demonstrate one of the paradoxes of labeling dishes "high fat": A dish can have relatively few grams of fat and yet still have a high percentage of calories from fat. That happens because these recipes feature foods such as salad greens, tomatoes, vegetables, and scallops that are very low in calories. So, adding even a little olive oil, for example, in preparing the salad or appetizer can provide a sizable portion of the recipe's calories. When you have a dish that is low in total fat, even though that fat may provide a higher percentage of the calories, it's easy to incorporate the dish into a menu that meets healthy-heart guidelines.

Yellow Tomato and Fennel Gazpacho

Created by Peter Zampaglione
Chef, Atlanta Grill at The Ritz-Carlton, Atlanta (Downtown)
Atlanta, Georgia

Gazpacho, as it originated in Spain, is a cold, uncooked soup that traditionally features a basic mixture of fresh tomatoes, cucumbers, and green peppers, plus seasonings. Chef Zampaglione has taken this traditional dish in a creative new direction that features yellow tomatoes (rather than red), yellow peppers, fennel, and creamy goat cheese to make a cold starter perfect for a summer celebration.

Tools: *Blender, plastic or glass container*

Preparation time: *2 hours chilling time, 15 minutes preparation time*

Cooking time: *None*

Yield: *8 servings*

3 medium yellow tomatoes, cored and roughly diced

1 large cucumber, peeled, seeded, and roughly diced

1/2 fennel bulb, cored and roughly diced

1/2 medium white onion, roughly diced

1 yellow bell pepper, seeded and diced

2 cups fresh or store-bought carrot juice

1/3 cup white wine vinegar

2 cloves garlic, peeled

1/4 cup olive oil

1 jalepeno, seeded

1 1/2 teaspoons salt

1/2 teaspoon white pepper

2 ounces hard goat cheese, crumbled

1 Two hours prior to serving, place one half of all ingredients, except the goat cheese, into a blender.

Slowly increase the speed until the mixture is pureed. Transfer mixture to a plastic or glass container. Repeat the process with the remaining half of the ingredients. If the mixture appears too thick or lumpy, slowly add water and continue blending until smooth.

2 Transfer the rest of the mixture to the plastic or glass container, cover and refrigerate until ready to serve.

3 To serve, ladle the chilled mixture into small serving bowls. Top each serving with 1 ounce of crumbled goat cheese.

Nutrition at a glance (per serving): *total fat 10g; saturated fat 3g; protein 4g; dietary fiber 2g; carbohydrate 13g; cholesterol 8mg; sodium 448mg; vitamin A (% of Daily Value) 150; vitamin C (% of Daily Value) 94; % of calories from fat 62; % of calories from saturated fat 19; calories 145.*

Suggested Celebration Menu: *Serve this gazpacho with French bread (in the form of a baguette) or hard rolls. Add an entrée of Red Snapper with Braised Fennel and Spinach (see Chapter 8) or Baked Filet of Turbot with Gratin of Yukon Potatoes (see Chapter 8). For dessert, try Chilled Melon Soup with Anise Hyssop (see Chapter 15), which carries out the anise/fennel theme.*

***

Baby Spinach and Citrus Salad with Wheatberries and Red Onion Confit

Created by Alfonso Constriciani
Executive Chef-Proprietor, Opus 251 at the Philadelphia Art Alliance and Circa
Philadelphia, Pennsylvania

This recipe requires making four separate items and combining them. Although it does take some time to make, the end result is definitely worth the effort! Prepare this salad on a lazy Sunday afternoon while listening to some relaxing instrumental jazz.

Tools: *Large nonstick skillet, shallow dish, small mixing bowl, medium saucepan, plastic or glass container, cookie sheet or small sauté pan, small bowl*

Preparation time: *30 minutes*
Cooking time: *2 hours*
Yield: *4 servings*

Red Onion Confit

2 tablespoons canola oil

2 1/2 red onions, cut into thin strips

3/4 teaspoon fresh thyme leaf, leaves removed from sprigs

1 tablespoon brandy

1/4 cup Burgundy wine

2 tablespoons raspberry vinegar

1 tablespoon red wine vinegar
2 tablespoons honey

1 In a large skillet, heat the oil over medium-high heat until almost smoking. Add the onions and sauté with the thyme leaf until the onions turn translucent, about 5 minutes.
2 Carefully flambé by adding brandy, igniting the ingredients, and quickly extinguishing by covering the skillet with a lid. (To do this safely, remove the pan from the burner, add the brandy, return the skillet to the burner, ignite with a match held with tongs to keep the flames at arm's length away, and then cover with a lid to extinguish the flames.) Add the remaining ingredients and simmer, uncovered, stirring occasionally, over low heat for 15 minutes or until onions are very soft.
3 Transfer to a shallow dish and place in the refrigerator to cool while preparing the dressing and salad.

Citrus Dressing

Yield: *About 1/2 cup*
Zest of 1 orange
1/2 orange, minced
Zest of 1 lemon
1/2 lemon, minced
2 tablespoons fresh lemon juice
1 tablespoon fresh garlic, minced
2 tablespoons citrus oil or canola oil
2 tablespoons olive oil
1 tablespoon rice wine vinegar

2 tablespoons parsley, finely chopped
Salt and pepper to taste

Combine all ingredients in small bowl and mix well. Set aside while preparing rest of salad.

Marinated Wheatberries

3 cups water
2/3 cup uncooked wheatberries
1/2 cup Citrus Dressing (see preceding recipe)

1 Place the water and wheatberries in a medium saucepan over medium heat. Simmer until the wheatberries are tender and have tripled in size, about 1 hour and 15 to 30 minutes.

2 After the wheatberries are fully cooked, place them in a plastic or glass container with 1/2 cup of the Citrus Dressing. Marinate in the refrigerator for 20 to 30 minutes.

Salad

1 tablespoon pine nuts
1 grapefruit, peeled and filleted
2 oranges, peeled and filleted
1 pound baby spinach, washed and dried
Remaining Citrus Dressing (see previous recipe)
Red Onion Confit (see previous recipe)
Marinated Wheatberries (see preceding recipe)
Pepper to taste

1 Place the pine nuts on a cookie sheet in a 400 degree oven for 2 to 3 minutes until lightly toasted. Remove from the oven and cool. (You may also

toast the pine nuts in a small, dry sauté pan over medium heat until fragrant, about 3 to 4 minutes.)

2 Prepare the grapefruit and orange fillets by cutting away, with a sharp knife, both the outer skin and the white pith of the fruits. Then gently cut around each section to separate the flesh from the membrane that encloses it. Reserve in a small bowl.
3 Toss the spinach in a large bowl with the remaining Citrus Dressing, and then divide the salad equally among 6 chilled salad plates.
4 Arrange the citrus fillets around the spinach. Top with Marinated Wheatberries and Red Onion Confit.
5 Garnish each salad with toasted pine nuts and finish with pepper. Serve immediately.

Nutrition at a glance (per serving): *total fat 16g; saturated fat 2g; protein 5g; dietary fiber 7g; carbohydrate 34g; cholesterol 0mg; sodium 53mg; vitamin A (% of Daily Value) 96; vitamin C (% of Daily Value) 114; vitamin E (% of Daily Value) 21; folic acid (% of Daily Value) 36; % of calories from fat 48; % of calories from saturated fat 6; calories 300.*

Suggested Celebration Menu: *Because this salad is complex, why not pair it with a simple grilled salmon fillet or breast of chicken and steamed vegetables, such as green beans or summer squash? For celebratory elegance, use baby vegetables.*

***

Wheatberries are whole, unprocessed kernels of wheat. Wheatberries can be purchased at natural food stores. Be sure to clean the berries before cooking, if necessary.

Arugula Salad with Melons and Lime Dressing

Created by Nora Pouillon
Chef and Owner, Nora—the only certified organic restaurant in the United States
Washington, D.C.

This beautiful salad is simple and quick to make—and it looks and tastes wonderful. It's also very rich in heart-healthy vitamins A and C, folic acid, and soluble fiber.

Tools: *Small mixing bowl, melon baller*
Preparation time: *10 minutes*
Cooking time: *None*
Yield: *4 servings*

For the Lime Dressing:

2 tablespoons of lime juice
1 tablespoon water
1/4 teaspoon sea salt
1/4 teaspoon pepper
3 tablespoon canola oil
1 tablespoon minced fresh mint leaves

For the Salad:

1/2 medium cantaloupe, seeds removed
1/2 medium honeydew, seeds removed
1 medium wedge watermelon
3/4 pound arugula or mesclun mix, washed and spun dry

1 Mix the lime juice, water, salt (optional), pepper, canola oil, and mint in a small bowl. Taste for seasoning.
2 Use a melon baller to make balls from each kind of melon.
3 To assemble, toss the arugula with the lime dressing. Divide the salad among four large salad plates. Garnish each plate with an assortment of melon balls.

Nutrition at a glance (per serving): *total fat 11g; saturated fat 1g; protein 4g; dietary fiber 3g; carbohydrate 27g; cholesterol 0mg; sodium 190mg; vitamin A (% of Daily Value) 46; vitamin C (% of Daily Value) 140; folic acid (% of Daily Value) 28; % of calories from fat 48; % of calories from saturated fat 4.*

Suggested Celebration Menu: *The fat in this salad comes entirely from the dressing so serve it with a lower fat entrée from the poultry and meat, seafood, or vegetarian entrée chapters of this book. Add whole grain rolls and any dessert for a complete banquet.*

***

Changing the ratio of oil to acid in a dressing recipe will reduce the fat content. Try a three-to-one ratio of oil to lime juice in this recipe.

"That which we call a rose, [b]y any other name would smell as sweet," wrote Shakespeare. The same is true of fresh *coriander,* which is called for in this recipe. In the United States, coriander is more commonly called *cilantro.* (*Chinese parsley* is another name for the same fresh herb.) It is readily available in most supermarkets.

Rice Vermicelli and Salad Rolls with Peanut Sauce

Created by Ignatius Chang

Chef-Owner, Nancy Chang's
Worcester, Massachusetts

This recipe offers you a refreshing new way to serve a salad—Chef Chang's interpretation of fresh Asian summer rolls. Due to the delicate nature of the rice sheets used to wrap the rolls in this recipe, these rolls should be made right before serving. Keep in mind that they can dry out easily and tear. The creamy Peanut Sauce is rich in taste as well as heart-healthy monounsaturated fats.

Tools: *Large mixing bowl, large saucepan, medium mixing bowl, colander or strainer*

Preparation time: *20 minutes, depending on how fast you can assemble the rolls*

Cooking time: *3 minutes*

Yield: *8 servings*

2 ounces uncooked rice vermicelli noodles

1 large carrot, peeled and shredded

1 tablespoon sugar

1 tablespoon fish sauce

8 8-inch round rice paper sheets

8 large romaine or iceberg lettuce leaves, washed, thick stalks removed

12 ounces roast pork, thinly sliced

4 ounces (approximately 12.3 cups) bean sprouts

Handful (16 or so) of mint leaves

8 cooked king prawns, peeled, deveined, and halved (or 8 jumbo shrimp)

1/2 cucumber, cut into fine strips

Coriander leaves, for garnish
Peanut Sauce (see following recipe)

1 Soak rice vermicelli in a large bowl filled with warm water until the noodles soften.
2 While the vermicelli noodles are soaking, fill a large saucepan with water and bring to a boil. When the water is boiling and the noodles have softened, drop the noodles into the boiling water and cook for 1 to 2 minutes or just until they are tender and lose their raw taste.
3 Drain the noodles, rinse under cold running water and drain again.
4 In a medium bowl, combine the vermicelli, carrots, sugar, and fish sauce. Toss well.
5 Dip one of the rice sheets in a bowl of warm water, then lay it flat on the table or countertop. Place on the rice sheet 1 lettuce leaf, 1 to 2 scoops of the noodle mixture, a few slices roast pork, some of the bean sprouts, and several mint leaves. Keep in mind that all filling ingredients need to be divided into 8 servings—try not to shortchange the person who will get the eighth roll!
6 Start rolling up the rice sheet into a cylinder. When half the sheet has been rolled up, fold both sides of the sheet toward the center and lay two prawn halves along the crease.
7 Add a few strips of cucumber and some coriander. Continue to roll up the sheet to make a tight packet. Place the roll on a large serving plate and

cover with a damp dishtowel to keep the roll moist while you assemble the rest of the rolls.

8 Repeat Steps 5 through 7 until all the rolls have been assembled.

9 To serve, cut each roll in half. Serve with Chef Chang's Peanut Sauce (see the following recipe).

Nutrition at a glance (per serving): *total fat 6g; saturated fat 2g; protein 17g; dietary fiber 1g; carbohydrate 16g; cholesterol 47mg; sodium 108mg; vitamin A (% of Daily Value) 36; % of calories from fat 30; % of calories from saturated fat 10; calories 183.*

Peanut Sauce

Tools: *Small saucepan*

Preparation time: *10 minutes*

Cooking time: *5 minutes*

Yield: *8 servings (approximately 2 tablespoons per serving)*

1 tablespoon vegetable oil (preferably canola oil)

3 cloves garlic, peeled and finely chopped

1 to 2 red chili peppers, seeded and finely chopped

1 teaspoon tomato puree

1/2 cup water

1 tablespoon creamy peanut butter (preferably freshly ground peanut butter)

2 tablespoons hoisin sauce

1/2 teaspoon sugar

Juice of 1 lime

2 ounces (approximately 6 tablespoons) roasted, unsalted peanuts, finely chopped or ground

1 In a small saucepan over high heat, heat the oil. Add the garlic, chili peppers, and tomato puree and cook for 1 minute, stirring continuously.
2 Add the water and bring to a boil.
3 Stir in peanut butter, hoisin sauce, sugar, and fresh lime juice. Mix well.
4 Reduce heat and simmer for 3 to 4 minutes.
5 Transfer the sauce into a small serving bowl, top with the ground peanuts, and allow to cool to room temperature before serving.

Nutrition at a glance (per serving), based on 8 servings, approximately 2 table-spoons per serving: *total fat 7g; saturated fat 1g; protein 3g; dietary fiber 1g; carbohydrate 5g; cholesterol 0mg; sodium 111mg; vitamin A (% of Daily Value) 23; vitamin C (% of Daily Value) 40; % of calories from fat 73; % of calories from saturated fat 10; calories 86.*

Suggested Celebration Menu: *The delicious Peanut Sauce is what gives this recipe more than 30 percent of calories from fat. You might begin by planning to use less than 2 table-spoons per serving of sauce. Then serve for an entrée Lime Marinated Shrimp (see Chapter 8) with rice and steamed vegetables.*

***

You may want to make these rolls when you have roast pork leftovers, if you don't have a market where you can purchase roast pork; or, you can make the rolls with just the shrimp. If you make them with just shrimp, only 12 percent of the calories will come from fat.

Hoisin sauce, also known as Peking sauce, is a sweet and spicy mixture of soy-beans, garlic, chili peppers, and spices commonly used in Chinese cooking. Hoisin sauce can be used as a condiment or as a flavoring ingredient for meat, poultry, or seafood dishes. Most large supermarkets and all Asian markets carry this popular sauce.

Special Seafood Starters

In recent years, many Westerners have discovered the elegance and fresh taste of the traditional starters for a Japanese meal—sashimi and sushi. Both dishes feature the very freshest and highest quality fish served raw. Other cuisines such as those of Scandinavia also feature fresh fish such as salmon or herring cured, not by cooking, but by smoking and pickling. For healthy adults, who have no immune system problems, dishes featuring raw seafood, which is naturally lean and often rich in omega-3 fatty acids, can be a wonderful part of heart-healthy eating and gourmet dining.

The following three recipes give you an opportunity to sample this style. Most everyone will enjoy the first recipe, which sounds adventurous but features a familiar favorite, smoked salmon, presented in the style of a tartare. The next two recipes, however, are for the adventurous, because the seafood in these recipes is served uncooked. For that reason, you must be sure that you have the very freshest seafood from a reputable source if you plan to prepare them.

Smoked Salmon Tartare

Created by Joe Mannke
Chef/Proprietor, Rotisserie for Beef and Bird
Houston, Texas

Nothing says *celebration* like this delicious appetizer that combines velvety smoked salmon with a traditional symbol of rich reward—caviar. The dish is very simple to prepare, but the presentation couldn't look more sophisticated.

Tools: *Food processor*
Preparation time: *15 minutes*
Cooking time: *None*
Yield: *6 servings*

10 ounces smoked salmon, such as lox or Nova Scotia

3 tablespoons chopped chives

3 tablespoons drained horseradish (fresh or bottled)

3 tablespoons sour cream

1 tablespoon fresh lemon juice

2 ounces caviar of your choice

6 slices whole grain toast, cut into quarters

6 crisp leaves Boston lettuce

6 black olives, pitted

2 boiled eggs, cut into wedges

1 vine ripe tomato, cut into 6 wedges

6 sprigs fresh dill

1 Place the lettuce leaves on 6 chilled plates.
2 Prepare the salmon tartare by placing smoked salmon in the bowl of a food processor and chop by pulsing briefly 2 or 3 times for 2 seconds each, or dice finely with a chef's knife. Don't overprocess or chop so that salmon is mangled or mealy.
3 Place equal amounts of smoked salmon tartare on the lettuce.
4 In a small bowl, combine the sour cream, lemon juice, chives, and horseradish. Drizzle over the salmon tartare.
5 Garnish with boiled egg, olives, tomato, and fresh dill.
6 Place a spoon of caviar on top of the tartare and serve with the toast wedges.

Nutrition at a glance (per serving): *total fat 8g; saturated fat 2g; protein 18g; dietary fiber 6g; carbohydrate 16g; cholesterol 140mg; sodium 654mg;*

% of calories from fat 36; % of calories from saturated fat 9; calories 202.

Suggested Celebration Menu: *For an entrée serve Marinated Grilled Pork Tenderloin (see Chapter 7) and steamed vegetables. Select a healthy-heart dessert of your choice from this book.*

***

Diver-Caught Maine Sea Scallops with Grapefruit

Created by David Waltuck
Chef/Co-Owner, Chanterelle
New York, New York

If you enjoy Japanese sashimi (raw fish), you may enjoy trying this recipe. Chef Waltuck comments on the critical importance of using diver-caught, not commercially caught, scallops, which are served sashimi style (uncooked). He writes, "Use very large, very fresh scallops that have not had water or bleach added, as often found in commercially available scallops." The fishmonger or seafood specialist in your local supermarket can help you find diver-caught scallops in your local area.

Tools: *Zester or grater, small mixing bowl, clean scallop shells for serving plates (optional)*

Preparation time: *10 minutes*

Cooking time: *None*
Yield: *8 servings*
1 pound very large, very fresh sea scallops
1 large pink grapefruit
1 teaspoon finely grated ginger
1/2 cup extra virgin olive oil
Salt to season
1 small bunch chives, chopped
1/2 ounce red tobiko, for garnish (optional)

1 Using a zester or a grater, remove the zest from the grapefruit and set aside.
2 Using a sharp knife, remove the white pith from the grapefruit, then cut between the membranes to remove the citrus sections. Cut each section into 1/8-inch bits and set aside.
3 Squeeze the juice from what remains of the grapefruit and set aside.
4 In a small mixing bowl, combine the grapefruit zest, grapefruit sections, grapefruit juice, fresh ginger, and olive oil. Season to taste with salt.
5 Slice the scallops thinly (about 1/8-inch thick) against the grain into round slices.
6 Arrange the scallop slices on clean scallop shells or small salad plates.
7 To serve, mix the dressing again and spoon over the scallops.
8 Garnish with chopped chives and red tobiko.

Nutrition at a glance (per serving): *total fat 7g; saturated fat 1g; protein 7g; dietary fiber 0g; carbohydrate 4g; cholesterol 9mg; sodium 75mg* *(based on no added salt); vitamin C (% of Daily Value) 25; % of calories from fat 59; % of calories from saturated fat 8; calories 107.*

Suggested Celebratory Menu: *Serve an entrée of Husk-Wrapped Salmon with Toasted Israeli Couscous (see Chapter 8) and a side salad of Mesclun with No Oil Lemongrass Dressing (see Chapter 13).*

***

Red tobiko is the Japanese name for the eggs or roe from flying fish, a type of tropical fish that is very popular in the Caribbean and the Philippines. Red tobiko can be found at most Japanese markets. If you can't find this ingredient, don't despair; it's optional.

Taylor Bay Scallops with Uni and Mustard Oil

Created by Rocco DiSpirito
Executive Chef, Union Pacific
New York, New York

For this special dish, which is one of Chef DiSpirito's signature recipes, very fresh scallops (see Figure 10-1 for tips on identifying scallops) and uni (sea urchins) are essential because the scallops and uni are served sashimi style (uncooked).

Tools: *Cheesecloth, strainer, coffee filter*

***Preparation time:** 12 hours to make tomato water, 10 minutes to prepare*

***Cooking time:** None*

***Yield:** 4 servings*

2 tomatoes, overripe

1 teaspoon mirin, at room temperature

Cayenne pepper, to taste

Coarse sea salt, to taste

Black pepper, to taste

20 small scallops, cleaned by fishmonger (retain the shells for serving)

4 sea urchins, cleaned by fishmonger

2 ounces seaweed, ogonori, rinsed free of salt

4 teaspoons mustard oil, at room temperature

1/2 teaspoon black mustard seed, freshly ground

Crushed ice, for presentation

1. Pulse overripe tomatoes with coarse sea salt in a food processor.
2. Suspend tomato mixture in cheesecloth and set in strainer overnight allowing liquid to drop into a large bowl (see Figure 10-2).
3. Pass liquid through a coffee filter to remove all solids.
4. Season with mirin, cayenne pepper, sea salt, and freshly ground black pepper. Set aside.
5. Rinse all scallop shells well. Set aside.
6. Arrange 1 scallop and 1 piece of uni (sea urchin) in each well-rinsed scallop shell.

7 Pour tomato mixture over the scallop and sea urchin and drizzle several droplets of mustard oil over the top.
8 Garnish with crusted black mustard seed.
9 Repeat with remaining 19 scallops.
10 On 4 small servings plates place a bed a crushed ice. Top with seaweed. Arrange 5 scallop shells in a circle on seaweed bed and serve immediately.

Nutrition at a glance (per serving): *total fat 6g; saturated fat 0g; protein 11g; dietary fiber 1g; carbohydrate 6g; cholesterol 14mg; sodium 158mg; vitamin C (% of Daily Value) 20; % of calories from fat 48; % of calories from saturated fat 0; calories 113.*

Suggested Celebration Menu: *Serve the appetizer with fresh baguettes or hard rolls, which will balance the fat, and then choose any entrée and side you like from the rest of the cookbook.*

***

Uni (sea urchins) can be purchased from Browne Trading. Call 207-766-2402 or visit their Web site at www.brownetrading.com. Mustard oil can be purchased from Kundan Foods. Call 310-609-3900.

Be sure that any mustard oil you purchase from any source is intended for food consumption and contains no or very little erucic acid; if a brand is marked for massage or has an FDA warning, don't use it.

Mirin and fresh seaweed can be found at Japanese and Asian markets or in the Asian section of some supermarkets. Black mustard seeds may be found in Asian markets (use brown mustard seeds if you can't find black ones).

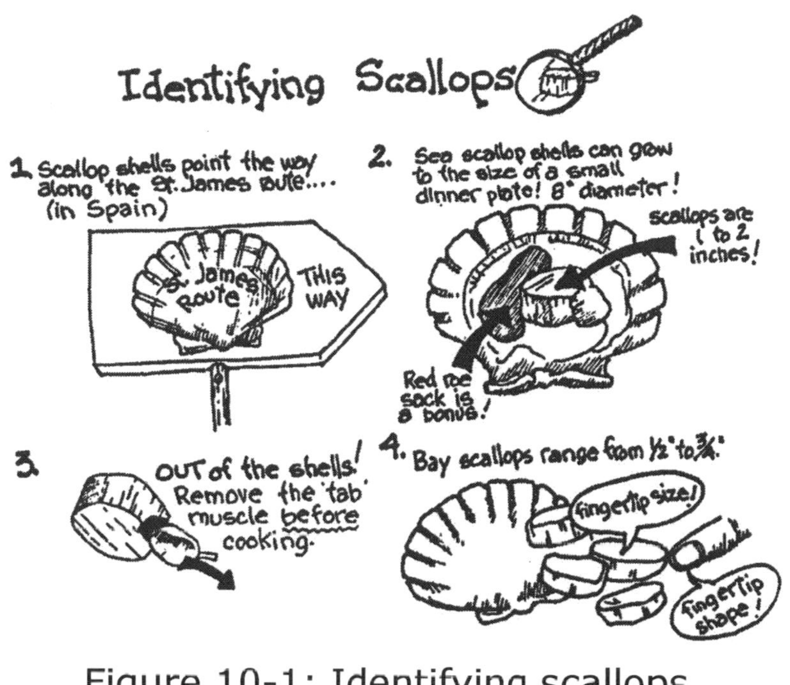

Figure 10-1: Identifying scallops.

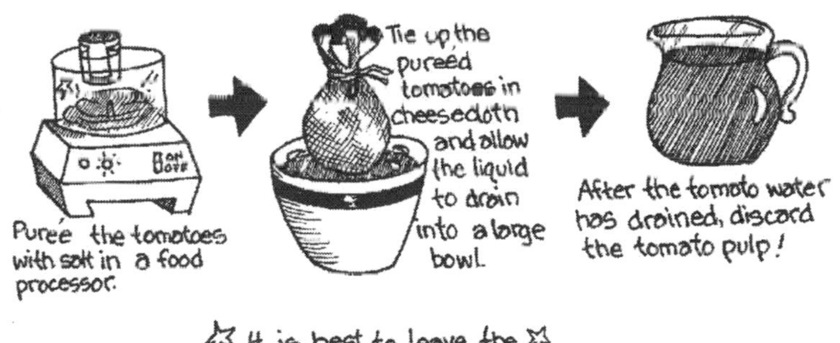

Figure 10-2: Tying and draining tomatoes.

Entrées

Because the entrée is usually the focus of a special meal, when you select a rich dish for dinner, it's wise to watch what you eat during the rest of the day to leave "room" for the special treat. Besides, isn't anticipation a happy part of celebration?

Lemon-Grilled Cornish Hens

Created by Peter Zampaglione
Chef, Atlanta Grill at The Ritz-Carlton, Atlanta (Downtown)
Atlanta, Georgia

This recipe is perfect as the centerpiece in an alfresco celebration. Even if you don't wish to dine outside, the Cornish hens and salad that Chef Zampaglione created and recommends as an accompaniment (Spinach Salad with Pears and Walnuts and Yellow Raisin Vinaigrette, following) are easily prepared and will free you up from the kitchen to enjoy your guests.

Tools: *Gas or charcoal grill*

Preparation time: *3 hours to marinate, 20 minutes to prepare*

Cooking time: *20 minutes*

Yield: *4 servings*

2 Rock Cornish game hens (approximately 12 ounces each), halved

Zest from 3 lemons

3/4 cup olive oil

1/2 cup parsley, chopped

1 tablespoon garlic, chopped

1/4 cup onion, chopped
1/2 teaspoon salt
1/2 teaspoon pepper

1 Mix the lemon zest, olive oil, parsley, garlic, onions, salt, and pepper into a paste.
2 Place halved hens on a flat dish and spoon lemon mixture over the hens. Allow the hens to marinate in the refrigerator for 3 hours prior to grilling.
3 When you're ready to grill the hens, remove them from the refrigerator and wipe or brush off excess marinade.
4 Place hens skin-side down on grill and cook for 18 to 20 minutes, turning them every 2 minutes.
5 After 20 minutes, if hens are not completely cooked, continue grilling and turning until finished.
6 Place half a hen onto each dinner plate. If serving with Chef Zampaglione's Spinach Salad, place warm hens next to the cold salad on each plate.
7 Serve immediately.

Nutrition at a glance (per serving): *total fat 14g (not including the skin); saturated fat 2g (not including the skin); protein 22g; dietary fiber 0g; carbohydrate 1g; cholesterol 101mg; sodium 209mg; % of calories from fat 57; % of calories from saturated fat 8; calories 220.*

***

Spinach Salad with Pears and Walnuts and Yellow Raisin Vinaigrette

Tools: *Salad bowl, whisk*
Preparation time: *1 hour marinating time, 30 minutes preparation time*
Cooking time: *None*
Yield: *4 servings*

Yellow Raisin Vinaigrette

1/2 cup yellow raisins
1/2 cup sherry vinegar
1/4 cup vegetable oil (preferably canola oil)
1 tablespoon walnut oil (optional)
1/4 tablespoon cinnamon
3 1/2 tablespoons honey
Salt and pepper to taste

1 In a medium bowl, whisk together all ingredients.
2 Allow vinaigrette to sit for 1 hour before preparing salad.

Spinach Salad

1 1/2 cups pears, diced
1 teaspoon fresh lemon juice
1/2 cup unsalted walnuts, roasted and chopped
1 pound baby leaf spinach, fresh and washed
Yellow Raisin Vinaigrette (see preceding recipe)

1 Toss pears with lemon juice to prevent pears from browning.
2 In a large bowl, toss pears, walnuts, and spinach together. Set aside until ready to serve.

3 When you're ready to serve the salad, add the Yellow Raisin Vinaigrette to the salad and toss well.
4 Plate equal portions on 4 salad plates. Serve immediately after plating.

Nutrition at a glance (per serving): *total fat 27g; saturated fat 2g; protein 5g; dietary fiber 5g; carbohydrate 48; cholesterol 0mg; sodium 69mg; vitamin A (% of Daily Value) 138; vitamin C (% of Daily Value) 45; vitamin E (% of Daily Value) 27; folic acid (% of Daily Value) 44; % of calories from fat 58; % of calories from saturated fat 4; calories 421.*

Suggested Celebration Menu: *Chef Zampaglione has created a meal rich in flavor and eye appeal. It's also rich in healthy monounsaturated and polyunsaturated fats, antioxidant nutrients, and folic acid. Even with a low-fat side dish, such as steamed quinoa, or some warm whole grain bread or rolls, this meal will have more than 30 percent calories from fat. So plan the rest of your day to allow for it. Eat a healthy breakfast of fruit, juice, and whole grain cereal with skim milk. Then enjoy a light lunch of a low-fat soup, such as vegetable or lentil, and a salad or nonfat yogurt and fruit.*

***

Tangerine Chicken Escabéche

Created by Allen Susser
Executive Chef/Owner, Chef Allen's Restaurant

Aventura, Florida

About this recipe, Chef Susser writes, "The romancing of citrus dates back many centuries. The Chinese were the first to write poetically of their love for these golden fruits. The tangerines from which this inspiration originated came from the Mediterranean. The cooking method of escabéche, like the fruit tangerine, came to the New World from that region. The technique of escabéche was used to preserve foods. The word *escabéche* comes from the medieval Arabic *sikbay,* which was derived from the Persian meaning *sour.* (Now *there's* a word with a long history.) This dish is an excellent one to serve chilled the next day."

Tools: *Large nonstick skillet*

Preparation time: *20 minutes*

Cooking time: *40 minutes*

Yield: *4 servings*

2 medium tangerines

1 whole chicken cut in 1/8ths (2 legs, 2 thighs, 2 wings, 2 breast halves)

1 tablespoon kosher salt

1/2 tablespoon pepper

1 teaspoon ground cumin

1/4 cup olive oil

2 medium sweet onions, thinly sliced

1 medium carrot, julienned

2 cloves garlic, minced

1 small Scotch bonnet, seeded and minced

1/3 cup white wine vinegar

2 tablespoons extra-virgin olive oil (optional; Note: nutrition analysis based on not adding the oil)

1/4 bunch fresh cilantro leaves

1 Finely dice enough of the tangerine peel for 2 tablespoons.
2 Squeeze the juice from the tangerines and reserve.
3 Season the chicken with salt, pepper, and cumin.
4 In a skillet over medium heat, heat the olive oil. Place the chicken in the pan and brown each side.
5 Remove the chicken from the skillet and transfer to a large plate. Pour the reserved tangerine juice over the pieces. Return the skillet to medium heat.
6 Add the onions, carrots, and garlic, and cook, stirring often, until very soft, about
5 minutes.
7 Add the Scotch bonnet, the tangerine zest, and white wine vinegar.
8 Bring to a simmer and cook for 2 to 3 minutes.
9 Add the chicken back into the pan with the tangerine juice.
10 Cover and cook over medium-low heat, simmering until chicken is cooked through, about 15 to 20 minutes.
11 Place the chicken on a large serving platter.
12 Arrange the vegetables around the chicken.
13 Drizzle with extra-virgin olive oil (optional) and garnish with fresh cilantro leaves.

Nutrition at a glance (per serving): *total fat 23g (not including the skin); saturated fat 4g (not including the skin); protein 37g; dietary fiber 3g;*

carbohydrate 15g; cholesterol 108mg; sodium 1184mg; vitamin A (% of Daily Value) 82; vitamin C (% of Daily Value) 69; % of calories from fat 50; % of calories from saturated fat 9; calories 410.

Suggested Celebration Menu: *Begin with Mixed Spring Greens with Lime-Cilantro-Yogurt Dressing (see Chapter 13) and add a side of steamed couscous or brown and wild rice to the entrée. For dessert, try Poached Pears with Orange Yogurt Sauce (see Chapter 15).*

***

Grilled Beef Tenderloin with Arugula, Marinated Red Onions, and Balsamic Vinaigrette

Created by J.P. Samuelson
Chef de Cuisine, D'Amico Cucina
Minneapolis, Minnesota

Many people think *steak* when they plan a special meal. This recipe will have you grilling with distinction. To save time on the day of your dinner, you may want to make the vinaigrette a day ahead and refrigerate. Because you want the onions and tenderloin to be ready to eat at the same time, be sure to read the recipe through and plan your steps as instructed to achieve that happy result.

Tools: *Gas or charcoal grill or stovetop grill pan*
Preparation time: *1 hour, 15 minutes (includes marinating time)*
Cooking time: *30 minutes*
Yield: *2 servings*

Marinated Red Onions

2 red onions, peeled and cored
1 teaspoon sugar
1 teaspoon freshly ground sea salt (optional)
1 tablespoon extra-virgin olive oil
1 tablespoon sherry vinegar

1 Preheat oven to 350 degrees. Slice onions 1/2-inch thick and place in a nonreactive dish.
2 Season with the sea salt and sugar.
3 Let stand for 5 minutes and then drizzle with olive oil and sherry vinegar.
4 After the onions have marinated for 1 hour, grill them on both sides or sear them in a very hot cast-iron pan.
5 Transfer the onions to a small baking dish and roast for 15 to 20 minutes.
6 Remove from the oven, set aside, and hold at room temperature until you're ready to serve.

Balsamic Vinaigrette

Yield: *1 cup*
1/2 cup balsamic vinegar
1/2 cup grapeseed oil
2 teaspoons extra-virgin olive oil
1 shallot, diced

1 tablespoon fines herbes, freshly diced (see note at the end of recipe for more information)
1/2 teaspoon freshly ground sea salt (optional)
1/2 teaspoon fine sugar

1 Place chopped shallots in a mixing bowl and add the sea salt (optional) and sugar.
2 Let stand for 5 minutes, then add the balsamic vinegar and *fines herbes.*
3 Slowly whisk in the olive oil and grapeseed oil.
4 Place in a sealed container in refrigerator. Extra dressing can be safely refrigerated for 2 days with herbs or up to 1 week without herbs.

Beef Tenderloin

2 6-ounce beef tenderloin fillets, trimmed of all visible fat
Freshly ground sea salt and white pepper to taste
1/4 pound mixed salad greens including arugula
1/4 cup Balsamic Vinaigrette (see preceding recipe)
Marinated Red Onions (see previous recipe)

1 Begin by either placing a cast-iron pan or stovetop grill pan over medium heat or by preheating the grill.
2 Season beef with sea salt and white pepper.
3 Place beef on the hottest part of the pan or grill. ***Note:*** The grill or pan needs to be very hot so that the beef doesn't stick. You can prevent sticking by lightly oiling the grill or pan when hot. To safely oil a hot grill, add a small amount of vegetable oil to a clean cloth and use tongs to rub the oiled cloth across the grill grates.

4 Cook beef for approximately 4 to 5 minutes or to medium-rare.
5 When finished cooking, let the beef rest on a clean plate for 2 to 3 minutes.
6 Brush the beef lightly with two tablespoons of Balsamic Vinaigrette.
7 To serve, place the onions in the middle of two plates. Dress the greens and arugula with up to 2 tablespoons Balsamic Vinaigrette or less. Season to taste with sea salt and white pepper. Arrange the mixed greens around the onions. Place the beef on top of the onions and pour the liquid on the plate over the beef. Serve immediately.

Nutrition at a glance (per serving), based on 2 entrée servings: *total fat 34g; saturated fat 7g; protein 39g; dietary fiber 3g; carbohydrate 15g; cholesterol 97mg; sodium 252mg; vitamin A (% of Daily Value) 37; vitamin C (% of Daily Value) 30; vitamin E (% of Daily Value) 36; folic acid (% of Daily Value) 27; % of calories from fat 59; % of calories from saturated fat 12; calories 518.*

Suggested Celebration Menu: *With a side of fresh bread, this recipe is a complete meal. So plan the meals for the rest of your day to allow for this delicious dinner. Start with a breakfast of juice, whole grain cereal with skim milk, toast, and coffee. For lunch, try a turkey sub sandwich with lettuce and tomato dressed with mustard and balsamic vinegar.*

***

Fines herbes is a mixture of finely chopped fresh herbs typically added to a dish right before serving to preserve the delicate flavor of the herbs. Chef Samuelson recommends using the "classic quartet," a mixture of chives, chervil, tarragon, and parsley

As the name suggests, *grapeseed oil* is extracted from grape seeds. Most grapeseed oil is imported from Italy, France, and Switzerland. Although some oils may have a slight taste of the grape, most are rather bland. You can substitute canola oil for grapeseed oil if you want.

Caramelized Onion, Ham, and Portobello Mushroom Tart

Created by Angela Kirkpatrick, R.D.
Research Dietitian, Rippe Lifestyle Institute

Shrewsbury, Massachusetts

Tarts are perfect for any meal, but are great for brunch, especially when balanced with nutritious side dishes. This recipe also demonstrates a way to use phyllo pastry with-out slathering it in fat-laden butter. Although this recipe gets more than 30 percent of its calories from fat because it is so low in calories, it is actually low in total fat. It's easy to pair it with low-fat sides to make a delicious menu that meets your heart-healthy goals.

Tools: *Large nonstick skillet, tart pan/pie pan with removable bottom*

Preparation time: *45 minutes*

Cooking time: *10 minutes*

Yield: *8 servings*

1 large Spanish onion, peeled, halved, and thinly sliced

2 teaspoons olive oil

12 ounces of extra-lean deli-cut ham

2 cloves of roasted garlic

4 tablespoons wine (red or white) or vegetable stock

1 tablespoon of fresh rosemary or 1 teaspoon dried

3 tablespoons bread crumbs

1 teaspoon sugar

6 ounces portobello mushrooms, sliced

1 portobello mushroom cap, sliced

2 sheets of phyllo dough, thawed

1 tablespoon minced fresh basil

3 ounces of reduced-fat Jarlsberg cheese, shredded
1 bay leaf
Pepper to taste
1 teaspoon kosher salt

1 Preheat oven to 450 degrees. Spray large nonstick skillet with cooking spray and place over high heat. Add onion, oil, wine, bay leaf, and rosemary and sauté, keeping pan covered and stirring occasionally, for 10 minutes.
2 Uncover and cook over medium heat, stirring frequently, until onions caramelize and are light brown, about 20 minutes.
3 Once caramelized, add sugar to the onions followed by the garlic, and cook 3 to 5 minutes, stirring often, over medium-high heat until onions are golden brown. Scrape into bowl and set aside.
4 Using the same skillet (unwashed), spray with nonstick spray and sauté mushrooms until brown (3 to 4 minutes). Set aside.
5 Spray a removable-bottom pan with nonstick spray. Lay the first sheet of phyllo so that it covers only half the pan, draping over the pan's edge about an inch. Sprinkle the phyllo with 1 tablespoon of bread crumbs and spray with nonstick spray. Fold the draping part back into the pan and sprinkle another tablespoon of breadcrumbs. Shape edges inside pan and spray.
6 Repeat with second sheet of dough, on the opposite side of the pan.

7 Reduce heat to 375 degrees and let dough bake until golden brown, about 5 minutes. Remove from oven.

8 Spread onions over surface of dough, followed by mushrooms. Place 1-inch slices of ham and cheese over mushrooms and sprinkle with basil.

9 Return tart to oven for 5 more minutes or until cheese melts. Cool before slicing.

Nutrition at a glance (per serving): *total fat 6g; saturated fat 2g; protein 11g; dietary fiber 2g; carbohydrate 8g; cholesterol 25mg; sodium 693mg; % of calories from fat 40; % of calories from saturated fat 13; calories 136*

Suggested Celebration Menu: *For a great brunch, the savory flavor of the ham, basil, onion, and melted Jarlsberg goes deliciously with a side of fresh berries, nonfat yogurt, and whole grain toast. Give your guests a choice of several 100 percent fruit juices, too, such as orange, grapefruit, apple, and pineapple-orange.*

> If you don't wish to use portobello mushrooms, try any other combination of mushrooms. The tart will still be delicious.

Sautéed Halibut with Roasted Fennel and Swiss Chard

Created by Michael Foley
Executive Chef, Printer's Row
Chicago, Illinois

Halibut, as we noted in Chapter 8, is one of the very leanest and tastiest fish. One aspect that elevates this dish to a celebratory meal is the many small details in preparation and presentation. Although the instructions for the following recipe are presented in a step-by-step fashion, you'll save time by completing many of the steps simultaneously. Before you start cooking, study the instructions to get a feel for what you need to do and when. Then put on your toque and cook like a pro.

Tools: *Nonstick skillet or sauté pan, strainer*
Preparation time: *30 minutes*
Cooking time: *15 minutes*
Yield: *4 servings*

Fennel Curls

Make these first, as soon as you've prepared the fennel for the Fennel Broth and Roasted Fennel, because they need to chill in ice water for about an hour.

Ice water
Reserved fennel stem (from following recipe)

1 Run a *very* sharp knife down the sides of the fennel stalks, forming curls.
2 Soak shaved fennel in ice water for 1 hour (no more), then drain and set aside.

Fennel Broth and Roasted Fennel

1 large fennel bulb, with stalks
2 tablespoons extra-virgin olive oil
2 cloves garlic
1 medium onion, chopped
2 ripe tomatoes, chopped
1/3 cup white wine
Herb sachet with 1 tablespoon crushed coriander seeds, 2 sprigs thyme, and 1 dried bay leaf all tied in cheesecloth
2 1/2 cups chicken stock or canned chicken broth

1 Trim the fennel stalks from the bulb and reserve. ***Note:*** Trim the tough outer layer of the bulb and cut into 4 wedges.
2 Heat a nonstick pan. Add 1 tablespoon olive oil, garlic, and onions and sauté over medium heat until garlic and onions are soft, about 5 minutes.
3 Add tomatoes, wine, and sachet. Bring to a boil, lower heat to simmer, and cook 2 to 3 minutes.
4 Add the fennel quarters and just enough of the chicken stock to cover. Bring to a boil.

5 Reduce the heat to low and cook, turning fennel pieces over once, until they can easily be pierced with a thin-bladed knife, 7 to 10 minutes.
6 Transfer the fennel to a bowl and cover.
7 Strain the liquid, reserving 2/3 cup for the vinaigrette.
8 Caramelize the fennel. Heat the remaining 1 tablespoon olive oil in a small sauté pan over high heat. Add the fennel and brown on all sides. Loosely cover and keep warm until ready to plate the entrée. Don't let the fennel get overdone, though. Reheating the fennel before plating it is preferable to letting it sit over the heat for too long.

Halibut

1 tablespoon olive oil
4 6-ounce fillets of halibut
Sea salt and fresh pepper to taste
Several whole green or purple basil leaves and several flat leaf (Italian) parsley sprigs with stems for garnish

1 Season halibut fillets with salt and pepper and allow fillets to come to room temperature before cooking, to help the fish cook thoroughly without overcooking.
2 Heat the olive oil in a large, nonstick sauté pan over medium-high heat. When almost smoking, add the halibut fillets and cook 4 to 5 minutes per side, until lightly browned, firm, and juicy.

For the Swiss Chard:

2 cups water

1 tablespoon butter

1 1/2 pounds Swiss chard, washed and stems removed

Sea salt and fresh pepper to taste

1 Combine the water and the butter in a medium saucepan. Bring to a boil, add the Swiss chard and cook until tender, about 2 to 3 minutes.
2 Remove from heat, drain, and chop into bite-size pieces. Transfer to a bowl and season with salt and pepper.

Coriander Vinaigrette

***Yield:** 1 cup*

2/3 cup reserved fennel stock

4 tablespoons olive oil

2 tablespoons lemon juice

1 1/2 teaspoons coarsely crushed coriander seed

2 tablespoons minced shallot

1 small garlic clove

Sea salt and fresh pepper to taste

1 Combine all ingredients in a small mixing bowl and whisk until well combined.
2 Store extra vinaigrette in a covered container in the refrigerator. Use within 3 to 4 days.

Plate the Entrée:

1 Place equal amounts of chopped Swiss chard, rim deep, in large soup bowls.
2 Add 1 piece of caramelized fennel.

3 Top with a halibut fillet and drizzle fillets with 2 tablespoons of the Coriander Vinaigrette.
4 In a small bowl, toss the shaved fennel with the basil and parsley.
5 Top the halibut with the fennel-herb mixture and serve immediately.

Nutrition at a glance (per serving), based on 4 servings with 2 tablespoons Coriander Vinaigrette per serving: *total fat 25g; saturated fat 5g; protein 40g; dietary fiber 6g; carbohydrate 19g; cholesterol 98mg; sodium 807mg; vitamin A (% of Daily Value) 98; vitamin C (% of Daily Value) 78; vitamin E (% of Daily Value) 38; % of calories from fat 48; % of calories from saturated fat 10; calories 462.*

Suggested Celebration Menu: *Let this elegant dish star. Select a simple starter such as Homemade Dill and Celery Seed Hummus (see Chapter 12), then serve the entrée with French bread or hard rolls. Eat a low-fat breakfast and lunch.*

***

Steamed Trout Stuffed with Root Vegetables and Truffle Vinaigrette

Created by Marcel-Henri Cochet
Chef de Cuisine, Rigsby's
Columbus, Ohio

Truffles, rare delicacies long prized by gourmets, add an indescribable richness to recipes. When you deserve a reward, treat yourself to this special steamed trout recipe. This dish says, "I am worth it." Because the steamed fingerling potatoes that Chef Cochet recommends serving with this dish take about 20 to 25 minutes to steam, you will want to start them about 15 minutes before starting to steam the trout. If you have a bamboo steamer with two racks (sections), you can do potatoes and trout in the same steamer.

Tools: *Bamboo steamer, large sauté pan or skillet*

Preparation time: *25 minutes*

Cooking time: *15 minutes*

Yield: *1 serving*

2 teaspoons butter

1 small whole trout (approximately 8 ounces), gutted and cleaned

1 leek, white part only, julienned

1 strip leek green, blanched in boiling water until soft, about 2 minutes

4 mushrooms, brushed clean, stems removed, caps cut into julienne minutes

1 medium carrot, peeled and cut into julienne

1 small celeriac, peeled and cut into julienne

Salt and pepper to taste

Seaweed (optional)

2 tablespoons Truffle Vinaigrette (see following recipe)

1 In a large sauté pan, melt the butter over medium heat. Add the leeks, mushrooms, carrots, and celeriac, and cook until transparent and softened, 5 to 7 minutes. Season to taste with salt and pepper and set aside.
2 Lay the trout on a flat surface, open the fillet, sprinkle with salt and pepper, and then fill the trout with the sautéed vegetables. Cover the fillet with the other side of the trout, secure the trout with a ribbon made of a blanched leek stem, and set aside.
3 Fill the bamboo steamer with water and a handful of seaweed. Bring the water to a gentle simmer, lay the trout in the basket and steam covered for 7 to 8 minutes.
4 Place the trout on a plate with cooked fingerling potatoes, if desired, off to the side. Drizzle 2 tablespoons of the Truffle Vinaigrette over the trout and potatoes. Serve immediately.

Truffle Vinaigrette

Extra vinaigrette can be stored in the refrigerator for a week but we recommend adding the truffle right before serving.

Yield: *1 1/3 cups*
1/3 cup apple vinegar
1 cup olive oil
2 teaspoons shallot, minced
1 teaspoon Dijon mustard
1 teaspoon black truffle, chopped
Salt and pepper to taste

Combine all ingredients in a small mixing bowl or food processor and whisk or process until smooth.

Nutrition at a glance (per serving): *total fat 42g; saturated fat 10g; protein 44g; dietary fiber 4g; carbohydrate 14g; cholesterol 134mg; sodium 223mg (based on no added salt); vitamin A (% of Daily Value) 201; vitamin C (% of Daily Value) 33; vitamin E (% of Daily Value) 27; folic acid (% of Daily Value) 21; % of calories from fat 63; % of calories from saturated fat 10; calories 604.*

Suggested Celebration Menu: *With a fat content of 42 grams per serving, this unique entree is a once-a-year indulgent treat, particularly when the cost of the truffles is considered. So let the entrée star. Start with a simple green salad such as Mesclun Salad with No-Oil Lemongrass Dressing (see Chapter 13). Include the fingerling potatoes recommended. Enjoy Chocolate Meringue Mousse (see Chapter 15) for dessert. And keep the rest of the day low fat.*

***

Truffles are *very* expensive fungi that grow near the roots of oak, chestnut, beech, and hazel trees in certain parts of Italy and France. Both dogs and pigs are used to "root" for the irregularly shaped truffles whose pungent scents attract the rooters. Pigs are better at locating truffles than dogs but are more likely to eat the truffles! Dean and Deluca (800-221-7714) carries both black and white truffles at competitive prices. (From any vendor, be prepared to pay up to about a hundred dollars for an ounce or less of black truffle, about half that for white truffles.) Dean and Deluca also sells white and black truffle oils, which cost considerably less and which could be used in place of the olive oil and truffles in the vinaigrette. You also may be able to locate imported fresh truffles at specialty markets from late fall to mid-winter.

Celeriac is the ugly, brown knobby root of a special celery cultivated only for its root. Celeriac is available September through May and can be found in many large supermarkets and specialty produce markets.

Seared Ahi Tuna with Tomatoes, Lime, and Basil

Created by Frédéric Lange
Executive Chef, The Hay-Adams Hotel
Washington, D.C.

If you enjoy your beefsteak rare but have never tried tuna prepared rare or medium rare, we encourage you to try this recipe. We think you will enjoy it. For the best flavor in this recipe where the tuna is the star, the chef specifies the finest, freshest shashimi grade tuna. The expense for top grade, very fresh tuna is worth it. Besides, you don't celebrate every day.

Tools: *Large nonstick skillet or sauté pan, broiler pan*

Preparation time: *15 minutes*

Cooking time: *5 minutes*

Yield: *4 servings*

4 4-ounce 1/3 inch thick, center-cut pieces Ahi tuna

6 cups diced red tomato (6 to 8 tomatoes)

Juice of 2 limes

4 tablespoons olive oil

10 fresh basil leaves, chopped

Sea salt and black pepper to taste

1 In a small bowl combine 1 tablespoon olive oil, the lime juice, salt, and pepper. Brush the marinade onto the slices of tuna about 5 minutes before cooking.

2 Fill a large pot with water and bring to a boil. Fill a large bowl with water and ice and set aside.

3 Peel and seed the tomatoes by removing the dark core at the top of the tomatoes with a small paring knife. Make an "X" on the bottom. Drop them into rapidly boiling water for about 30 seconds or so depending on the ripeness until the skin comes off easily. Re move the tomatoes from the boiling water and plunge into the ice bath.

4 After 10 seconds remove the tomatoes from the ice bath, remove the skin, and then slice the outer flesh from the core to avoiding getting any seeds (see Figure 10-3 for illustrated instructions). Dice the tomato flesh into medium-sized cubes. Preheat the broiler.
5 Add 2 tablespoons olive oil to a large sauté pan over high heat. Add the diced tomatoes and cook, tossing or gently stirring for about 30 seconds. Season with salt and pepper. Add the basil. Remove the pan from the heat and set aside while searing the tuna.
6 Place the tuna in a flat pan and place under a hot broiler until hot, 15 seconds or so. Turn the tuna over and cook for another 10 to 15 seconds. ***Note:*** The center of the tuna should remain red (medium rare to rare).
7 To plate the tuna, place a large spoonful of tomatoes on each serving plate and place a piece of tuna on top. Add 1 tablespoon olive oil to the sauté pan with the tomato juices and warm slightly. Dab the warmed juice over the tuna. Finish with a sprinkle of fresh basil and serve immediately.

Nutrition at a glance (per serving): *total fat 20g; saturated fat 3g; protein 29g; dietary fiber 3g; carbohydrate 13g; cholesterol 43mg; sodium 72mg; vitamin A (% of Daily Value) 84; vitamin C (% of Daily Value) 93; vitamin E (% of Daily Value) 20; % of calories from fat 52; % of calories from saturated fat 8; calories 343.*

Suggested Celebration Menu: *Serve this entrée with a green salad and a starchy side such as Organic Root Vegetable Risotto (see Chapter 14) or Stuffed Cylinder Potatoes with Duxelle Mushrooms and Vegetable Jus (see Chapter 14). Select a dessert from Chapter 15.*

***

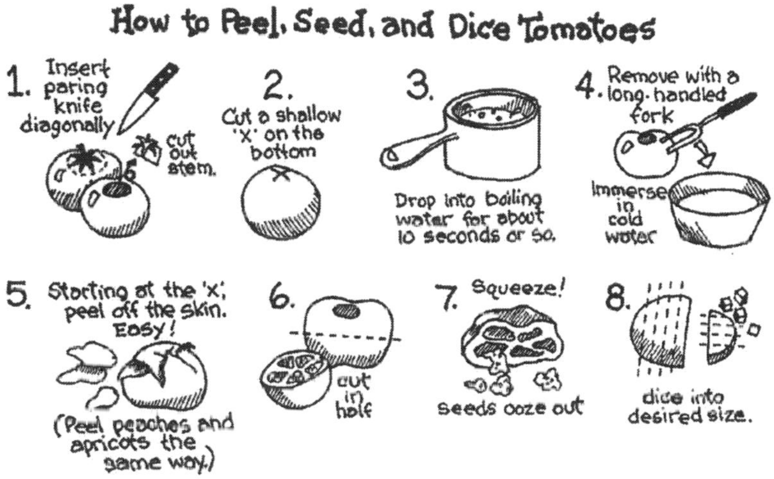

Figure 10-3: How to peel, seed, and dice tomatoes.

Yellowfin Tuna with Green Gazpacho Sauce

Created by Douglas Organ
Executive Chef, Laurel Restaurant & Bar
San Diego, California

A unique spicy green gazpacho sauce and a tomato relish distinguish this recipe for yellowfin tuna.

Though sophisticated, both sauce and relish are very easy and quick to make. As Chef Organ directs, be sure to get very fresh, sashimi-grade tuna for the best flavor. If yellowfin tuna is not available, you may try another variety where you can get fresh, sashimi-grade loin. (For more about varieties of tuna, see the discussion in Chapter 8.)

Tools: Blender, sieve, ovenproof sauté pan
Preparation time: *25 minutes*
Cooking time: *10 minutes*
Yield: *8 servings*

Gazpacho Sauce

1/2 English cucumber, seeded and chopped
1/2 pound tomatillos, cored and quartered
1 ripe avocado, peeled, pitted, and chopped
1/2 small Spanish onion, chopped (use other half in Tomato Relish)
3 scallions, chopped
1/2 serrano chili, seeds removed (use other half in Tomato Relish)
1/4 bunch cilantro
1/4 bunch Italian parsley
1 small garlic clove, peeled
1/2 cup olive oil
1 teaspoon sherry vinegar
Pinch cayenne and white peppers to taste
1 teaspoon kosher salt

1 Combine all ingredients in the bowl of a blender and puree until very smooth.

2 Push through a fine sieve and adjust the seasonings. Set aside until ready to serve.

For the Tomato Relish:

2 medium ripe tomatoes, peeled, seeded, and cut into julienne (refer to Figure 10-3 for instructions for peeling and seeding)

1/2 Spanish onion, thinly sliced

1/2 serrano chili, minced

1 clove garlic, thinly sliced

1 tablespoon fresh parsley, finely minced

1 tablespoon fresh cilantro, finely minced

2 tablespoons olive oil

1/2 teaspoon kosher salt

In a mixing bowl, combine all ingredients and mix well. Set aside until ready to serve.

Tuna

3 pounds fresh sashimi-grade yellowfin tuna loin, well trimmed

Coarsely ground black pepper

Kosher salt to taste

2 tablespoons olive oil

6 sprigs of fresh cilantro for garnish

1 Preheat the oven to 450 degrees.
2 Heat the olive oil in a large ovenproof sauté pan over medium-high heat until almost smoking.
3 Season the tuna loin with salt and pepper and sear on all sides.
4 Transfer the pan into the oven and roast to the desired doneness; for medium-rare, 5 to 7 min-

utes depending on the thickness of the center loin cut.

5 When the tuna has reached desired doneness, remove from the oven and place on a cutting board.
6 Divide the gazpacho sauce in the center of 8 dinner plates, and then divide the tomato relish into the middle of the sauce.
7 Slice the tuna into 8 equal pieces and set on top of the tomato relish.
8 Drizzle with a bit of extra-virgin olive oil and garnish each with a sprig of cilantro.

Nutrition at a glance (per serving): *total fat 29g; saturated fat 5g; protein 41g; dietary fiber 2g; carbohydrate 7g; cholesterol 65mg; sodium 373mg; vitamin A (% of Daily Value) 102; vitamin C (% Daily Value) 50; vitamin E (% of Daily Value) 22; % of calories from fat 58; % of calories from saturated fat 10; calories 453.*

Suggested Celebration Menu: *Start with Dana's Sangria (see Chapter 11) and Spicy White Bean Dip (see Chapter 12) served with baked corn tortilla chips. Then serve bread with the entrée. Finish this celebratory meal with Red Fruits Soup (see Chapter 15).*

***

Tomatillos, also known as Mexican tomatoes, look like green tomatoes. They have a thin, parchment-like covering. Tomatillos have a subtle lemon, apple, and herb flavor and are used in many southwestern dishes. When raw, tomatillos add a desirable acidic flavor to salads and sauces. Canned tomatillos are available in ethnic markets, and are sporadically available year-round in specialty stores and some supermarkets. Tomatillos are a rich source of vitamin A and vitamin C.

Side Dishes

When you have a side dish that wants to star, pair it with a simple entrée to balance the meal both in taste appeal and to meet healthy-heart nutritional guidelines. We give you suggestions with each recipe.

Spinaci Alla Perugina

Created by Saleh Joudeh
Chef/Owner, Saleh al Lago
Seattle, Washington

Fresh spinach enjoys a happy marriage with the rich Italian air-dried ham, prosciutto, in this stylish side dish. Close your eyes, take a bite, and you might be in Tuscany or Umbria. The dish is also rich in such healthful nutrients as Vitamins A and C and folic acid.

Tools: *Large sauté pan*

Preparation time: *15 minutes*

Cooking time: *7 minutes*

Yield: *4 servings*

4 bunches spinach (about 1 pound), cut in half and washed (approximately 8 cups)

6 ounces sliced prosciutto, diced
1 tablespoon garlic, minced
2 tablespoons olive oil
2 teaspoons pine nuts
Pinch crushed red pepper
Lemon juice to taste
Salt and pepper to taste

1 Trim any visible fat from prosciutto and then dice it.
2 In a very large sauté pan, heat olive oil over medium-high heat. Add the garlic, pine nuts, prosciutto, and red pepper, and cook, stirring, until garlic is lightly browned, about 4 minutes.
3 Add spinach and quickly toss.
4 Sprinkle with salt, pepper, and lemon while tossing. Immediately remove from heat and serve.

Nutrition at a glance (per serving): *total fat 12g; saturated fat 2g; protein 12g; dietary fiber 2g; carbohydrate 3g; cholesterol 25mg; sodium 687mg; vitamin A (% of Daily Value) 101; vitamin C (% of Daily Value) 29; folic acid (% of Daily Value) 30; % of calories from fat 67; % of calories from saturated fat 11; calories 161.*

Suggested Celebration Menu: *Serve with a entrée such as Lime Marinated Shrimp (see Chapter 8) or Lavender Grappa Glazed Tuna with Jicama Salsa (see Chapter 8) and Italian bread.*

***

To wash spinach, fill a large bowl or sink with cold water and let the spinach rest on top of the water. Gently move the spinach around without touching the bottom of the bowl or sink. This technique will allow the dirt to fall off of the spinach and stay at the bottom of the bowl.

Prosciutto (shown in Figure 10-4) is an Italian ham that has been salt-cured and air-dried. Because prosciutto becomes tough when overcooked, it should be added into a dish during the last cooking stage. Prosciutto can be found in most supermarkets and also in Italian markets. Prosciutto contributes most of the sodium in this dish.

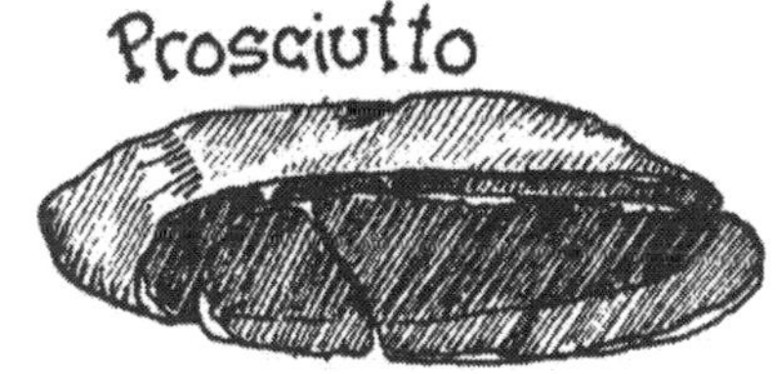

Figure 10-4: Prosciutto.

Orzo Salad with Lemon Tarragon Vinaigrette

Created by David Gross

Executive Chef, City Grill
Atlanta, Georgia

This colorful pasta salad also stars fresh crisp green beans and asparagus. Select the freshest, most tender green beans and asparagus you can find for great results. Chef Gross recommends serving this side dish with his Pan-Roasted Alaskan Halibut with Red and Yellow Pepper Coulis (see Chapter 8).

Tools: *Saucepan, food processor*

Preparation time: *20 minutes*

Cooking time: *15 minutes*

Yield: *4 servings*

1 1/2 cups uncooked tri-colored orzo

1/2 cup haricot verts (green beans), diced small

1/2 cup asparagus, stems sliced, tips halved lengthwise and reserved separately

Salt and pepper to taste

1/2 cup Lemon Tarragon Dressing (see following recipe)

1 Cook orzo in boiling salted water according to package instructions. When the orzo has finished cooking, drain and rinse under cold running water to shock the orzo and stop the cooking process.

2 While the orzo is cooking, blanch the *haricot verts* and asparagus. Bring about 1 quart of water to a boil, season with salt, and add the *haricot verts* and asparagus stems. Cook for 2 minutes, add the tips, and cook another 2 minutes. Drain and

transfer to an ice water bath. Drain, transfer to a large bowl.

3 Add the orzo to the bowl with the vegetables and mix well.

4 Hold at room temperature to allow mixture to cool until ready to serve.

5 When ready to serve, add the dressing to the orzo salad and mix well to incorporate the dressing. Serve and enjoy!

Lemon Tarragon Dressing

Yield: *1 1/2 cups dressing*

1 1/4 cup canola oil

1 tablespoon lemon zest

1 teaspoon garlic, minced

1 tablespoon shallots, minced

1/2 cup Champagne vinegar

1 tablespoon tarragon, finely chopped

Salt and pepper to taste

1 Combine all ingredients except canola oil in a food processor or bowl. Mix to combine.

2 With the food processor running or while continuously whisking, very slowly add the canola oil to make an emulsion.

3 Set aside until ready to serve.

Nutrition at a glance (per serving): *total fat 18g; saturated fat 1g; protein 6g; dietary fiber 2g; carbohydrate 32g; cholesterol 0mg; sodium 4mg; vitamin E (% of Daily Value) 20; % of calories from fat 52; % of calories from saturated fat 3; calories 311.*

Suggested Celebration Menu: *Because the Orzo Salad and Pan-Roasted Alaskan Halibut create a meal rich in monounsaturated fat, plan to eat a low-fat breakfast and lunch, such as fruit, toast, and whole grain cereal with skim milk for breakfast and yogurt, fruit, and bagel crisps for lunch.*

***

Orzo is the Italian word for barley, but the orzo in this recipe refers to the pine-nut-shaped pasta. Orzo also resembles rice and can be used in place of rice in many recipes. To cook orzo, follow directions on package. Like other pastas, orzo doubles in size after cooking.

Portobello Mushroom Carpaccio with Shallot Relish, Sun-Dried Tomatoes, and Aged Balsamic

Created by Edward Gannon
Executive Chef, Four Seasons Hotel
Boston, Massachusetts

Doesn't a carpaccio sound like a recipe appropriate for a celebration? A traditional Italian carpaccio features very thinly sliced beef. Chef Gannon has taken this technique and adapted it to beefy portobello mushrooms creating a marvelous vegetable side that looks as beautiful as it tastes. It's also beautifully rich in heart-healthy vitamins A, C, and E and folic acid.

Tools: *Gas or charcoal grill or stove top grill pan*

Preparation time: *30 minutes to marinate mushrooms*

Cooking time: *35 minutes*

Yield: *4 servings*

4 whole portobello mushrooms, stemmed, caps trimmed of gills, then thinly sliced

4 tablespoons (1/4 cup) balsamic vinegar

4 tablespoons (1/4 cup) olive oil

1/2 cup fresh basil

Salt to season

1 cup shallots, julienned

1/2 cup balsamic vinegar

2 tablespoons sugar

1 tablespoon pepper

1 cup sun-dried tomatoes, julienned

4 cups mixed greens

4 small slices of Tuscan bread, toasted or grilled

1/2 cup chives, minced

1/4 cup balsamic vinaigrette

Salt and pepper to taste

Prepare the Portobello Mushrooms:

1 In a small bowl, whisk together the balsamic vinegar, olive oil, basil, and salt and pepper. Transfer to a small shallow baking dish and add the thin slices of portobello mushrooms. Allow the mushrooms to marinate for 30 minutes.

2 Preheat grill or stovetop grill pan. Place mushrooms on grill rack and cook until tender, about 1 to 2 minutes per side.

Prepare the Shallot Relish:

1 While mushrooms are marinating, combine shallot, vinegar, sugar, and pepper in a small saucepot.
2 Bring to a boil, lower heat to maintain a low boil, and reduce down until a thick relish-like consistency is achieved. This process should take approximately 20 to 30 minutes

Prepare the Croutons:

Grill or toast Tuscan bread croutons until golden brown.

Put the dish together for presentation:

1 Arrange portobello slices around center of chilled dinner plates.
2 Dollop the shallot relish over the portobellos.
3 Sprinkle sun-dried tomatoes on top of the mixture.
4 Toss greens with vinaigrette. Arrange in center of the plates.
5 Place a grilled crouton against the greens.
6 Sprinkle chives around the plate and serve.

Nutrition at a glance (per serving): *total fat 22g; saturated fat 3g; protein 9g; dietary fiber 7g; carbohydrate 43g; cholesterol 2mg; sodium 573mg (based on no added salt); vitamin A (% of Daily Value) 52; vitamin C (% of Daily Value) 53; vitamin E (% of Daily Value) 20; folic acid (% of Daily Value)*

38; % of calories from fat 53; % of calories from saturated fat 7; calories 374.

Suggested Celebration Menu: *Because the grill is already hot to prepare this dish, serve it with a simple grilled fish such as swordfish or salmon.*

***

Tuscan bread is a round loaf of Italian bread with a very crusty crust and airy interior. Any type of Italian bread would be an acceptable substitute.

Part III

Adding the Extras: Recipes for Before and After the Main Course

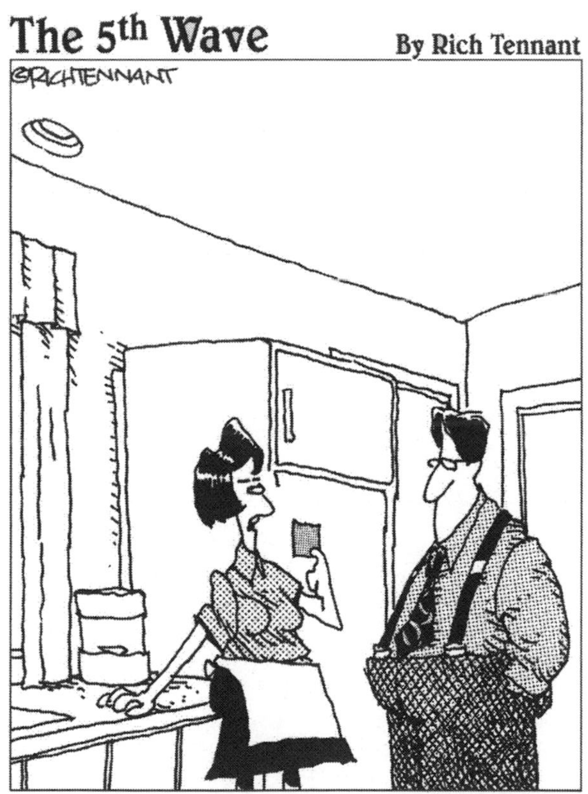

Image 3.1: "I don't care if it does contain greens and, fruit I just don't trust a recipe that comes on the back of a pack of cigarettes."

In this part...

In this part, you gather all the recipes you need to make an ordinary meal special. Here you'll find heart-healthy recipes for everything from drinks to side dishes to desserts. Head into the kitchen with this book at your side and you're sure to come out admired by your family and friends.

Chapter 11

Beverages

In This Chapter
- Drinking to your health
- Making nutritious, low-fat drinks.

Recipes in This Chapter

- Fruit and Yogurt Smoothie **(V)**
- Chocolate Banana Soy Shake **(V)**
- Citrus Tea **(V)**
- Blackberry Lemonade **(V)**
- Dana's Sangria **(V)**

***

Beverages can be nutritional or refreshing—or both! This chapter gives you a sampler of healthy-heart beverages—from smoothies and shakes, which can be a big part of a nutritious meal, to refreshing thirst quenchers for hot days. Drinking plenty of fluids, including lots of pure water, is essential to keeping your body properly hydrated, which is important to good health.

Delicious, Nutritious Smoothies and Shakes

Rich and delicious, a fruit-filled smoothie or shake made the low-fat way can power-pack a meal or snack with nutrients such as calcium, protein, vitamins, and phytochemicals. Familiar comfort food has never been so good for you.

Calcium is often lacking in the typical American diet. If you've shied away from milk as an adult, turn to yogurt for the calcium you need. Calcium not only keeps bones strong and healthy but also helps control blood pressure.

Fruit and Yogurt Smoothie

Created by Amy Myrdal, M.S., R.D.
Senior Research Dietitian, Rippe Lifestyle Institute
Shrewsbury, Massachusetts

We guarantee no recipe in this book is easier to prepare than this one.

Tools: *Blender*
Preparation time: *5 minutes*
Cooking time: *None*
Yield: *2 servings*
1 banana
1/2 cup frozen strawberries or peaches
1 cup plain, nonfat yogurt
1/4 cup orange juice

Combine all ingredients in a blender and blend until smooth and frothy.

Nutrition at a glance (per serving): *total fat 1g; saturated fat 0g; protein 8g; dietary fiber 3g; carbohydrate 30g; cholesterol 2mg; sodium 95mg; vitamin C (% of Daily Value) 81; folic acid (% of Daily Value) 23; % of calories from fat 6; % of calories from saturated fat 0; calories 152.*

***

The benefits of soy have been shown for many years to help fight certain cancers, soothe the symptoms of menopause, boost the immune system, and lower cholesterol. Experts recommend having at least one serving of soy a day (8 ounces soy milk or 4 ounces tofu, for example), but if this is your first experience with soy, try for 2 to 3 servings of soy each week. Getting 2 to 3 servings of soy per week should be easy; choices range from soy milk and tofu to the newest soy-based products located throughout the frozen foods section of most supermarkets. Soy milk is sold primarily in shelf-stable containers, but it recently has made a few appearances in the milk cooler as well.

Chocolate Banana Soy Shake

Created by Melanie Mulcahy
Nutrition Intern, Rippe Lifestyle Institute
Shrewsbury, Massachusetts

This tasty shake is great for breakfast or a snack and is a good way to incorporate heart-healthy soy into your diet. After you have made this shake two or three times by the recipe, try experimenting with your own combinations of fruit and soy milk.

Tools: *Blender*
Preparation time: *5 minutes*
Cooking time: *None*
Yield: *1 serving*

1 large banana, cut into chunks
1 cup vanilla soy milk
1 tablespoon chocolate syrup
1 teaspoon smooth peanut butter

1 Place banana chunks in freezer overnight or until completely frozen.
2 Combine all ingredients in a blender and blend until a smooth consistency is reached.
3 Pour into a large glass and enjoy.

Nutrition at a glance (per serving): *total fat 8g; saturated fat 1g; protein 10g; dietary fiber 7g; carbohydrate 48g; cholesterol 0mg; sodium 74mg; vitamin C (% of Daily Value) 21; % of calories from fat 27; % of calories from saturated fat 5; calories 279.*

***

Refreshing Beverages

The human body is essentially water—60 percent by weight for men, 55 percent by weight for women. So we need to consume a huge amount of water each day from a variety of sources. In addition to drinking the recommended eight 8-ounce glasses of water each day, we recommend that you enjoy other refreshing and healthful beverages such as those included in this section. The first two can make a pleasant change from the usual coffee, tea, or soda. The final recipe for a red-wine-based party drink that adds the nutritional punch of fruit makes a delightful light libation for a celebratory occasion.

Citrus Tea

Created by Marcus Samuelsson
Executive Chef, Aquavit
New York, New York

This recipe for tea uses fresh lemon and lime juice, adding a splash of healthful vitamin C, an important antioxidant nutrient. On hot summer days, you may enjoy making a pitcher early in the morning and keeping it in the refrigerator for refreshment throughout the day.

Tools: *Medium saucepan, strainer, large pitcher*

Preparation time: *10 minutes to prepare, 50 minutes to chill*

Cooking time: *5 minutes (to boil water)*

Yield: *4 servings*

Juice from 2 limes

Juice from 1 orange

4 cups water

1 stalk chopped lemon grass

4 bags orange-flavored herb tea

2 tablespoons sugar

Lemon, lime, or orange slices, for garnish (optional)

1 Combine lime juice, orange juice, water, lemon grass, herb tea, and sugar in a medium saucepan and bring to a boil over high heat.
2 Once boiling, turn off the heat and let it sit on the burner for 5 minutes.
3 Pour the tea mixture through a strainer, place in a large pitcher, and chill in refrigerator for about an hour.
4 When chilled, pour over ice and serve.
5 Garnish glasses with lemon, lime, or orange slices on the rim, if you like.

Nutrition at a glance (per serving): *total fat 0g; saturated fat 0g; protein 0g; dietary fiber 0g; carbohydrate 9g; cholesterol 0mg; sodium 6mg; % of calories from fat 0; % of calories from saturated fat 0; calories 36.*

***

Blackberry Lemonade

Created by David Gross
Executive Chef, City Grill
Atlanta, Georgia

Lemonade and summer fun go hand in hand. The addition of blackberry puree gives this old favorite a new twist. Enjoy this beverage, which is rich in vitamin C, after a leisurely walk on a warm summer evening with family or friends.

Tools: *Medium saucepan or pot, blender or food processor, strainer, large pitcher*

Preparation time: *30 minutes*
Cooking time: *10 minutes*
Yield: *10 servings*

1-pound package of frozen blackberries
8 teaspoons plus 1 1/2 cups granulated sugar
1/3 cup plus 3 quarts water
2 cups freshly squeezed lemon juice

1 Place blackberries, 8 teaspoons of the granulated sugar, and 1/3 cup of the water in a medium saucepan or pot, place over medium heat, and let come to a boil. Immediately reduce heat to low and simmer, stirring often, for about 10 minutes.
2 Remove from heat and let cool for about 20 minutes.
3 When cooled to room temperature pour mixture into a blender or food processor and puree for about 1 minute.

4 Pour through a strainer to remove seeds and pulp. Pour into large pitcher.
5 Add to the pitcher the remaining 1 1/2 cups of granulated sugar, the lemon juice, and the remaining 3 cups of water. Mix. Pour over ice and enjoy!

Nutrition at a glance (per serving): *total fat 0g; saturated fat 0g; protein 0g; dietary fiber 1g; carbohydrate 42g; cholesterol 0mg; sodium 12mg; vitamin C (% of Daily Value) 36; % of calories from fat 0; % of calories from saturated fat 0; calories 163.*

***

Chef Gross writes, "Depending on how you like your lemonade to taste, you might want to add more lemon juice for a more tart flavor or more sugar for a sweeter flavor."

Dana's Sangria

Created by Amy Myrdal, M.S., R.D.
Senior Research Dietitian, Rippe Lifestyle institute
Shrewsbury, Massachusetts

The inspiration for this recipe came from coauthor Amy Myrdal's friend, Dana Zartner. According to Amy, "Among friends my age, Dana is absolutely the best hostess and party planner I know. Enjoying a meal with Dana is one of my favorite events in life, especially if she is doing the cooking!" And this is a party beverage with a purpose—it is rich in vitamin C.

Tools: *Small saucepan, wooden spoon, large pitcher*

Preparation time: *5 minutes*

Cooking time: *2 minutes (if preparing the syrup)*

Yield: *8 servings*

1/2 cup water
1/2 cup sugar
1 medium orange
1 medium lime
1 medium lemon
1 cup fresh cherries with stems
4 to 6 cups of ice cubes
1 750-mL bottle red wine (preferably a Rioja)
1/4 cup brandy (optional)
3/4 cup sparkling mineral water
Sprigs of fresh mint, for garnish

1 In a small saucepan over medium-high heat, combine the 1/2 cup water and the sugar. Bring to a boil and stir with a wooden spoon to completely dissolve the sugar. Remove from heat and set aside, allowing to cool before using.

2 Wash the orange, lime, lemon, and cherries. Slice the orange, lemon, and lime into 1-inch thick slices. Set aside.
3 Fill a large clear glass pitcher half full with the ice cubes. Add the orange, lemon, and lime slices.
4 Stir in the wine and brandy, then add the sparkling water.
5 Taste for sweetness and stir in the sugar-water mixture, if desired. Then add the whole cherries.
6 Pour into 12-ounce glasses and serve. Add a sprig of mint to each glass for garnish.

Nutrition at a glance (per serving): *total fat 0g; saturated fat 0g; protein 1g; dietary fiber 1g; carbohydrate 11g; cholesterol 0mg; sodium 8mg; vitamin C (% of Daily Value) 30; % of calories from fat 0; % of calories from saturated fat 0; calories 119.*

***

Rioja is the major red-wine-producing region of Spain, located in north central Spain. Any red wine from Rioja is acceptable for this recipe, but younger wines from coastal vineyards are better because they tend to be fruitier. They also tend to be less expensive than their oak-barrel-aged counterparts. Traditionally, sangria, which means "blood red," is made with red wine, but you can make *blanco* or white sangria with white Rioja wines for a refreshing change.

What is the best alcohol for your heart? Alcohol from *any* type of alcoholic beverage—whether it's wine, beer, or hard liquor—helps thin the blood and, therefore, helps protect the heart from blood clots and clogged arteries. Red wine is particularly beneficial because it contains phytochemical compounds from grapes. The antioxidant properties of these compounds may help protect arteries from the damaging effects of LDL cholesterol. Dark beers are also a good source of these phytochemicals. Just remember to drink in moderation in order to protect your liver from the damaging effects of alcohol.

Chapter 12

Appetizers and Snacks

In This Chapter

- Making heart-healthy dips
- Preparing elegant, low-fat appetizers

Recipes in This Chapter

- Spicy White Bean Dip **(V)**
- Homemade Dill and Celery Seed Hummus **(V)**
- Garlic, Sun-Dried Tomato, and Herb Cheese Spread **(V)**
- JIcama Chips with Fresh Salsa **(V)**
- Warm Oysters in Kumquat and Verjus Sauce
- Lafayette's Chesapeake Oysters with Asian Scallion Sauce
- Chilled Hapa Shrimp Rolls with Thai Citrus Dipping Sauce

***

When it's time to party—or just put your feet up with a treat while you watch a movie or the big game on TV—this chapter has a healthy-heart light bite that's perfect for the occasion. Some are very simple and quick to prepare and others take more time, but each tempts the palate and is good for your heart and waistline.

Appetizers, hors d'oeuvres, antipastos, meze—by any name—give you more opportunities to enjoy treats that seem sinfully rich but are really good for you. When you've tried each of these recipes, you may even be inspired to create your own heart-healthy appetizers and snacks.

Dips, Salsas, and Spreads

Chips, dips, salsas, and spreads don't have to be the same old thing—as the following recipes demonstrate. With a few minutes in the kitchen and some simple ingredients, you can create snacks or party treats that have more flavor and zip than the typical fat-filled sour cream dip or ordinary store-bought salsa.

Spicy White Bean Dip

Created by Amy Myrdal, M.S., R.D.
Senior Research Dietitian, Rippe Lifestyle Institute
Shrewsbury, Massachusetts

This recipe couldn't be easier to prepare. If you want to make a quick appetizer for a party, this is the recipe for you. Paired with crackers, breadsticks, or fresh vegetable sticks, it makes a healthful, satisfying appetizer or snack.

Tools: *Food processor*

Preparation time: *10 minutes*

Cooking time: *None*

Yield: *8 servings (1/4 cup each)*

1 19-ounce can canellini (white kidney) beans, rinsed and drained

2 cloves garlic

1 teaspoon fresh lemon juice

2 to 3 drops Tabasco sauce (optional)

1/4 teaspoon paprika

1/4 cup water (optional)

Sprig of parsley, for garnish

Whole grain crackers or garlic breadsticks

1 In the bowl of a food processor, combine beans, garlic, lemon juice, Tabasco sauce, and paprika; puree. Add water to thin the dip to desired consistency.

2 Transfer dip to a serving dish, garnish with parsley, and serve with whole grain crackers or garlic breadsticks.

Nutrition at a glance (per serving): *total fat 0g; saturated fat 0g; protein 5g; dietary fiber 4g; carbohydrate 13g; cholesterol 0mg; sodium 137mg; folic acid (% of Daily Value) 41; % of calories from fat 0; % of calories from saturated fat 0; calories 74.*

***

Look in the ethnic foods section of the market if you don't find canellinis with the other beans. You may also substitute great northern beans (white) or try this dip with pintos or red beans if you're in the market for a different flavor and look.

Homemade Dill and Celery Seed Hummus

Created by Melanie Mulcahy
Nutrition Intern, Rippe Lifestyle Institute
Shrewsbury, Massachusetts

The flavor of hummus in this recipe is a new twist on an old favorite. (And if hummus isn't one of your familiar favorites, give it a try. We can almost guarantee it *will* be.) Smeared on crackers or pita bread or used as a vegetable dip, hummus is a great way to increase your intake of fiber-rich legumes. Hummus also makes a flavorful substitute for mayonnaise in sandwiches or wraps.

Tools: *Strainer, food processor or mixing bowl*
Preparation time: *15 minutes*
Cooking time: *None*

Yield: *12 servings (2 tablespoons each)*
1 15-ounce can chick peas
2 tablespoons fresh minced garlic
2 tablespoons sesame tahini paste
1/2 lemon, juiced
1 teaspoon dried dill
2 teaspoons dried celery seeds
2 tablespoons minced fresh parsley
Pepper to taste

1 Drain and rinse chickpeas under tap water in a strainer.
2 Combine all ingredients in a food processor or mixing bowl. Puree or manually mash until the mixture becomes smooth and creamy.
3 Serve immediately or refrigerate in an airtight container until ready to serve. The hummus can safely be stored for up to seven days in the refrigerator.

Nutrition at a glance (per serving): *total fat 1.3g; saturated fat 0g; protein 2.7g; dietary fiber 3g; carbohydrate 9g; cholesterol 0mg; sodium 116mg; % of calories from fat 20; % of calories from saturated fat 0; calories 61.*

***

Sesame tahini paste or tahini is simply ground sesame seeds. Tahini is used to add flavoring to Mediterranean foods like hummus and baba ghanoush. Its consistency is similar to peanut butter. You can purchase tahini in most supermarkets, or you can make your own by pureeing hulled sesame seeds.

Garlic, Sun-Dried Tomato, and Herb Cheese Spread

Created by Angela Kirkpatrick, R.D.
Research Dietitian, Rippe Lifestyle Institute
Shrewsbury, Massachusetts

This delicious spread features yogurt "cheese," which is versatile and surprisingly easy to prepare in the home kitchen. We enjoy this recipe served with crackers and as a dip for fresh vegetables.

Tools: *Strainer, coffee filter, kitchen shears or knife, aluminum foil, baking sheet, food processor*

Preparation time: *10 to 15 minutes (plus 1 hour to strain yogurt)*

Cooking time: *60 minutes*

Yield: *12 servings (2 tablespoons each)*

3/4 cup nonfat plain yogurt

6 cloves garlic

3/4 cup nonfat cottage cheese

2 tablespoons fresh chopped herbs, such as basil or cilantro

1/2 teaspoon salt, or to taste

1/2 teaspoon pepper, or to taste

2 tablespoons chopped, sun-dried tomatoes

2 tablespoons chopped canned roasted red peppers

1 Preheat oven to 350 degrees.
2 Place yogurt in a strainer lined with a coffee filter. Set aside to drain for 1 hour.
3 While yogurt is draining, roast the garlic by removing the loose, outer skin of the whole bulb, leaving the bulb whole. With kitchen shears or a knife, carefully cut off the top 1-inch of each attached clove. Place the entire bulb on a piece of aluminum foil, and drizzle 1 tablespoon water over the top. Bring up the sides of the foil to seal the bulb in the foil. Place on a baking sheet and bake at 350 degrees for 60 minutes. Allow to cool, then squeeze the paste from each clove.
4 Combine the drained yogurt, roasted garlic, cottage cheese, and herbs in a food processor and blend until smooth. Add salt and pepper to taste.
5 Stir in the sun-dried tomatoes and red peppers. Cover and refrigerate until ready to serve.

Nutrition at a glance (per serving): *total fat 0g; saturated fat 0g; protein 2g; dietary fiber 1g; carbohydrate 3g; cholesterol 1mg; sodium 112mg; % of calories from fat 0; % of calories from saturated fat 0; calories 23.*

***

Try the preceding recipe as the basis for your favorite dips, substituting the yogurt cheese for full-freight sour cream or cream cheese in your recipe.

Jicama Chips with Fresh Salsa

Created by Amy Myrdal, M.S., R.D.
Senior Research Dietitian, Rippe Lifestyle Institute
Shrewsbury, Massachusetts

This salsa tastes better if made a day ahead of time and tastes best if made with vine-ripened tomatoes. After the jicama is peeled, try to eat it within a day or two.

Tools: *Medium glass mixing bowl, small glass mixing bowl*

Preparation time: *15 minutes*
Cooking time: *None*
Yield: *6 servings*
2 jicama
4 ripe red tomatoes, chopped

1 small orange (or yellow) bell pepper, seeded and chopped

1 jalapeno pepper, seeded and chopped

1 shallot, finely chopped

1 tablespoon fresh lime juice

1 teaspoon olive oil

2 tablespoons fresh cilantro, chopped

Salt and pepper to taste

1 Peel jicama and slice into 1/4-inch-thick "chips." Set aside.

2 In a medium glass mixing bowl, combine the chopped tomato, bell pepper, jalapeno pepper, and shallot.

3 In a small glass mixing bowl, whisk together the lime juice and olive oil. Stir in the cilantro, and add to the vegetable mixture. Season with salt and pepper, and toss well to combine.

4 Place salsa in a covered container in the refrigerator until ready to serve.

5 To serve, place the jicama chips on a serving platter with a bowl of salsa nearby for easy dipping.

Nutrition at a glance (per serving): *total fat 1g; saturated fat 0g; protein 3g; dietary fiber 12g; carbohydrate 25g; cholesterol 0mg; sodium 19mg; vitamin A (% of Daily Value) 28; vitamin C (% of Daily Value) 165; % of calories from fat 8; % of calories from saturated fat 0; calories 115.*

***

Elegant Party Appetizers

When your dinner party calls for something a little more special, consider one of the three following recipes. Though very different, each looks terrific when plated for presentation and, more importantly, tastes great and is heart-healthy. These recipes aren't hard to prepare, but they may require a little more time than preparing dips or spreads. That's time so well spent, however, that you'll want to throw yourself a party just to try them.

Warm Oysters in Kumquat and Verjus Sauce

Created by Jacky Robert
Executive Chef, Maison Robert
Boston, Massachusetts

Tools: *Oyster shucker, medium saucepan, small bowl*

Preparation time: *30 minutes*

Cooking time: *20 minutes*

Yield: *8 servings*

24 Wellfleet oysters (about 3 ounces each, in the shell)

5 to 6 fresh kumquats

1/4 cup water

1/2 cup plus 1 tablespoon sugar.

3 tablespoons finely chopped shallots

1 tablespoon pepper
1/4 cup Verjus wine or apple cider vinegar
Kosher salt, for plating

1 Preheat oven to 400 degrees.
2 Shuck the oysters. (See Figure 12-1 for illustrated instructions.) Keep the oysters in the bottom shell. Reserve oysters in the refrigerator until ready to use.
3 Wash kumquats under cold running water. Cut in half and remove the pits.
4 In a medium saucepan, prepare the syrup by boiling the sugar with the water. When the sugar has dissolved, add the halved kumquats and boil for another 15 minutes.
5 Drain the kumquats and discard the syrup. In a small bowl, combine the shallots, pepper, Verjus, and kumquats. Mix well.
6 Cover each oyster with 1 teaspoon of the kumquat sauce.
7 Place the oysters on a roasting pan. Bake for 5 minutes.
8 Serve on individual serving plates on a bed of kosher salt to insure stability.

Nutrition at a glance (per serving): *total fat 2g; saturated fat 0.7g; protein 6g; dietary fiber 1g; carbohydrate 14g; cholesterol 45mg; sodium 181mg; % of calories from fat 20; % of calories from saturated fat 6; calories 98.*

***

Considered a delicacy for thousands of years, oysters are typically named for their place of origin. *Wellfleet oysters* are Atlantic oysters that come from Cape Cod, near Chef Robert's Boston location. Oysters of all types are both farmed and gathered from the wild. Although modern refrigeration has made oysters available year-round, they are at their most succulent and flavorful in the famous "months containing an R" (September through April) because they spawn in the summer.

Kumquats belong to the citrus family of fruit. They have a bright orange sweet rind and a tart (even bitter) flesh. For this reason, they are usually served cooked in dishes rather than raw. They are in season from November through March.

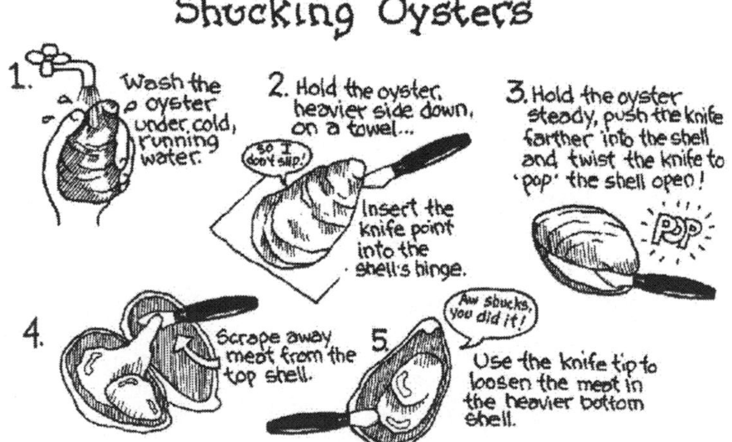

Shucking Oysters
1. Wash the oyster under cold, running water.
2. Hold the oyster, heavier side down, on a towel...
So I don't slip!
Insert the knife point into the shell's hinge.
3. Hold the oyster steady, push the knife farther into the shell and twist the knife to 'pop' the shell open!
POP
4. Scrape away meat from the top shell.
5. Aw shucks, you did it!
Use the knife tip to loosen the meat in the heavier bottom shell.

Figure 12-1: Shucking oysters is a cinch with the help of an oyster shucker.

Lafayette's Chesapeake Oysters with Asian Scallion Sauce

Created by Frédéric Lange
Executive Chef, The Hay-Adams Hotel
Washington, D.C.

We enjoy the Asian flavor of this recipe. The fresh oysters with their taste of the sea are set off by the tangy scallion and black bean sauce.

Tools: *Food processor, steamer basket or bamboo steamer*

Preparation time: *15 minutes (plus 2 to 3 hours to soak the black beans)*

Cooking time: *3 minutes*

Yield: *6 servings*

30 teaspoons Asian Scallion Sauce (see the following recipe)

30 large Chesapeake oysters (shucked on the half shell)

1 red pepper, julienned

1 small bunch of fresh scallions (green onions), julienned

1 Place 1 teaspoon Asian Scallion Sauce on each oyster with red pepper and scallions for garnish.
2 Steam oysters in steamer basket or bamboo steamer for 3 minutes.
3 Serve immediately.

Asian Scallion Sauce

6 ounces (about 2 1/3 cups) salted Chinese black beans (also called fermented black beans)

1 clove fresh garlic

4 tablespoons dry sherry wine

2 tablespoons sesame oil

6 tablespoons soy sauce

6 ounces (about 1 2/3 cups) fresh ginger, peeled and julienned

1 Soak the black beans in water for 2 to 3 hours.
2 Place the soaked black beans, garlic, wine, sesame oil, and soy sauce in a food processor. Puree.
3 Add the fresh ginger to the sauce; mix.

Nutrition at a glance (per serving): *total fat 3g; saturated fat 1g; protein 9g; dietary fiber 1g; carbohydrate 10g; cholesterol 55mg; sodium 365mg; vitamin A (% of Daily Value) 26; vitamin C (% of Daily Value) 74; % of calories from fat 26; % of calories from saturated fat 9; calories 104.*

***

Chinese black beans, also called fermented black beans, are dried, salted beans that can be purchased at any Asian market or in the specialty/ethnic food section of your local supermarket.

You'll have quite a bit of extra sauce left over from the preceding recipe. Brush it on salmon or tuna steaks, grill or pan-fry, and enjoy! You can also add the sauce to stir-fry dishes—it's especially good with stir-fried pork tenderloin and green beans.

James and Stacey McDevitt, the creators of the following recipe, recently lost a very dear member of their family to a massive heart attack. Timothy Alan Hawkins died at the age of 39, leaving behind a wife and two children. James and Stacey contributed recipes to this book with the hope that it will help readers realize that leading a healthful lifestyle, which includes eating a healthful diet, can help prevent such a tragedy.

Chilled Hapa Shrimp Rolls with Thai Citrus Dipping Sauce

Created by James and Stacey McDevitt
Chef/Owners, Restaurant Hapa
Scottsdale, Arizona

Certainly, these Hapa Shrimp Rolls are a delightful addition to heart-healthy cuisine. They are so good, that we occasionally like to serve two rolls per person as a main course for a family dinner, in addition to serving them as party appetizers.

Tools: *Steamer basket, medium mixing bowl, whisk*

Preparation time: *30 minutes to chill shrimp, 15 minutes to prepare rolls, 5 minutes to prepare dipping sauce*

Cooking time: *5 minutes*

Yield: *8 servings*

8 extra-large shrimp, poached and chilled
8 12-inch rice paper rounds
2 cups green papaya, julienned
1 cup daikon radish sprouts
1 1/3 cup carrot, julienned
1 1/3 cup bean sprouts
1/2 cup packed fresh mint leaves
1/2 cup packed fresh basil leaves
1/2 cup packed fresh cilantro leaves

1 Poach shrimp by steaming in a small amount of water until they turn whitish pink, about 3 to 5 minutes. Chill for 30 minutes before using.
2 Soak rice paper in cold water for 10 to 15 seconds, until flexible. Remove from water, place on a clean towel, and let rest about 30 seconds.
3 Place 1 shrimp in the middle of each rice paper; cover with 1/4 cup of the green papaya, 2 tablespoons of the radish sprouts, 1 1/2 tablespoons of

the carrot, 1 1/2 tablespoons of the bean sprouts, 1 tablespoon of the fresh mint, 1 tablespoon of the fresh basil, and 1 tablespoon of the fresh cilantro.

4 To form a roll, roll the rice paper up halfway to cover the filling, fold in the ends, and finish rolling. Repeat Steps 3 and 4 with the remaining rolls.

5 Place the rolls, seam side down, on a serving plate.

Thai Citrus Dipping Sauce

Yield: *2 cups*

4 limes, juiced

1 cup fresh squeezed orange juice

1/4 cup sugar

2 teaspoons chili paste

3 ounces fish sauce

1/3 cup rice wine vinegar

2 tablespoons fresh mint leaves, chopped

2 tablespoons olive oil

Place all ingredients in a medium mixing bowl and whisk until combined.

Nutrition at a glance (per serving): *total fat 5g; saturated fat 0g; protein 8g; dietary fiber 2g; carbohydrate 31g; cholesterol 37mg; sodium 530mg; vitamin A (% of Daily Value) 65; vitamin C (% of Daily Value) 74; % of calories from fat 24; % of calories from saturated fat 0; calories 191.*

***

Chapter 13

Soups and Salads

In This Chapter

- Creating heart-healthy soups
- Making salads rich in health-promoting nutrients
- Designing low-fat and nonfat salad dressings

Recipes in This Chapter

- Curried Squash Soup with Cilantro
- Pumpkin Soup **(V)**
- Butternut Squash Soup with Black Currants and Pine Nuts
- Mushroom Soup with Herb Croutons
- Sweet Corn and Chanterelle Soup with Red Pepper Flan **(V)**
- Mesclun Salad with No-Oil Lemongrass Dressing
- Mixed Spring Greens with Lime-Cilantro-Yogurt Dressing **(V)**
- Arugula Salad with Purple Figs and Red Onions **(V)**

• 1789 Restaurant Asparagus and Gingered Grapefruit Salad with Miso Vinaigrette and Ginger Lime Glaze

• Curried Israeli Couscous Salad **(V)**

• Grilled Chicken Salad with Eggplant, Cucumber, and Mint Yogurt Served in a Whole-Wheat Pita

• Crab Salad with Mango, Avocado, and Tropical Fruit Puree

• Crabmeat Salad with Green Mango Souscaille

***

As great meal starters or as meals in themselves, soups and salads play a versatile role in our daily diets. They can also play an important role in heart-healthy eating, because they offer a variety of ways to help you reach the goal of consuming five or more servings of vegetables and fruits each day.

Soups and salads can help make meals a time apart from the day's hustle and bustle, too. Serving a delicious low-fat soup or attractive salad as a starter, for instance, may elevate an everyday dinner to a more special time for you and your family. When you're trying to lose weight or maintain a healthy weight, soups and salads can add substance and interest to meals so that you feel you're giving yourself a treat rather than depriving yourself.

Soups and salads also offer a good opportunity to turn your creativity loose. Every cook—from beginner to accomplished gourmet—can make a good soup or tasty, eye-appealing salad. With a little courage, you can follow your imagination and create new recipes, using the wonderful array of vegetables and fruits that modern transportation makes available in today's markets. The recipes in this chapter can be your guide and inspiration.

Soups

When our prehistoric ancestors discovered that the combination of a pot and fire (or hot rocks) made possible culinary delights far surpassing charring some meat or roots on the coals, they may have discovered the world's first great comfort food—soup. Each of the world's cultures has wonderful traditional soups. You can approach soup in so many great ways that we can't possibly cover them all in a short chapter. But the soup recipes we do include in this chapter illustrate several different aspects of soup's possibilities.

Have you had your soup today? No. Well, read on and pick one of these to start.

Getting your beta-carotene: The winter squash family

The recipes in this section are very different from each other. Yet each of the recipes features vegetables from the family of winter squash, which are rich in beta-carotene and other nutrients (see Figure 13-1 for an illustration of various winter squash varieties). These recipes illustrate how varied you can make soups, even when working with similar ingredients.

Figure 13-1: Varieties of winter squash.

Curried Squash Soup with Cilantro
Created by Amy Myrdal, M.S., R.D.
Senior Research Dietitian, Rippe Lifestyle Institute
Shrewsbury, Massachusetts

The first recipe in the winter squash family provides an abundance of vitamin A, vitamin C, and fiber—three nutrients essential for a healthy heart. The soup freezes well and makes a great fall meal. You can freeze this soup in plastic containers for up to three months. To reheat, transfer to a covered stockpot and cook over low heat until completely thawed and thoroughly warmed.

Tools: *4-quart saucepan, blender or food processor*

Preparation time: *15 minutes*
Cooking time: *40 minutes*
Yield: *8 servings*
1 tablespoon olive oil
1 medium onion, finely chopped
3 cloves fresh garlic, minced
1 teaspoon curry powder
1 teaspoon ground cumin
2 medium carrots, peeled and chopped
4 cups acorn squash, peeled, seeded, and chopped
4 to 5 cups water plus 4 cubes chicken bouillon (or 4 cups canned chicken broth)
3 tablespoons fresh cilantro, chopped
1/4 teaspoon hot sauce (such as Tabasco sauce) (optional)
Sprigs of cilantro for garnish

1 Pour the olive oil in a large, heavy 4-quart saucepan. Add the onion, garlic, curry, and cumin, and sauté 2 minutes over medium heat. Add the carrots and squash, and sauté an additional 3 minutes.
2 Add the water and bouillon (or chicken broth) and bring to a boil. Reduce the heat and simmer until tender, about 25 to 30 minutes.
3 Transfer the mixture to a blender and puree until smooth, adding a little more water or broth if necessary to thin to desired consistency. Return to the saucepan and add the cilantro and hot sauce.

4 Spoon into large, flat soup bowls, and garnish with sprigs of cilantro.

Nutrition at a glance (per serving): *total fat 2.5g; saturated fat less than 0.5g; protein 4g; dietary fiber 4g; carbohydrate 14g; cholesterol 0mg; sodium 525mg; vitamin A (% of Daily Value) 55; vitamin C (% Daily Value) 23; % of calories from fat 27; % of calories from saturated fat 5; calories 89.*

***

You can substitute other varieties of squash such as butternut or buttercup, or you can use canned pumpkin or squash as well. You may also substitute low-sodium bouillon cubes or low-sodium chicken broth.

Pumpkin Soup

Created by RoxSand Suarez
Chef/Owner, RoxSand
Phoenix, Arizona

Many people think "Fall" when they think of pumpkins, but this savory soup can be made any time of year using frozen or canned pumpkin if fresh pumpkins aren't readily available

Tools: *Large roasting pan, soup pot, food processor or blender*

Preparation time: *25 minutes*

Cooking time: *1 hour, 15 minutes*

Yield: *8 servings*

1 small (2 1/2 to 3 pound) pumpkin, peeled, seeded, and cut into 2-inch chunks

2 large onions, coarsely chopped

6 cloves fresh garlic

2 large potatoes, peeled and cut into 1-inch cubes

4 large sprigs rosemary

2 tablespoons olive oil

8 cups vegetable stock

1 bunch thyme

Salt and pepper, to taste

1 Preheat oven to 400 degrees.
2 Combine pumpkin, onions, garlic, potatoes, rosemary, and olive oil in a large bowl and toss evenly to coat.
3 Roast for 50 minutes or until vegetables are lightly brown and somewhat tender.
4 Transfer roasted vegetables to a soup pot
5 Cover with vegetable stock, stir, and bring to a boil. Lower temperature and simmer and cook until flavors blend, about 20 to 30 minutes.
6 Puree in batches (enough to half-fill your blender or processor bowl) in blender or food processor.

Return mixture to soup pot to keep warm and season with salt and pepper to taste. Serve warm.

Nutrition at a glance (per serving): *total fat 4g; saturated fat 1g; protein 3g; dietary fiber 5g; carbohydrate 25g; cholesterol 0mg; sodium 997mg; vitamin A (% of Daily Value) 490; vitamin C (% of Daily Value) 22; % of calories from fat 26; % of calories from saturated fat 7; calories 136.*

***

Butternut Squash Soup with Black Currants and Pine Nuts

Created by Kimberly Shaker
Chef, Cowboy Ciao
Scottsdale, Arizona

This recipe calls for *black currants,* which are a type of European bush fruit that is very popular in the British Isles. Cassis, a French liqueur, is made from black currants. Though one species of black currant is native to North America, they have never been cultivated and are not very popular as wild fruit.

Tools: *Baking sheet, food processor or blender, 4-quart saucepan*

Preparation time: *25 minutes*
Cooking time: *55 minutes*
Yield: *6 servings*

2 butternut squash
2 sweet potatoes
1 yellow onion
2 quarts unsalted fresh chicken stock or canned chicken broth
1/4 cup brown sugar or honey
Fresh sage (optional)
Salt and white pepper, to taste
3 cups 1 percent milk
1/4 cup toasted pine nuts, for garnish
1/2 cup black currants or golden raisins, for garnish

1 Preheat oven to 375 degrees.
2 Cover a baking sheet with parchment paper.
3 Cut squash in half lengthwise. Remove the seeds and place the cut side down on the parchment-covered baking sheet.
4 Place baking sheet in oven and roast 45 minutes or until squash are tender. Test for tenderness by inserting a fork into the thickest part; if you can insert the fork easily, the squash is the right tenderness.
5 While the squash is baking, peel the potatoes and onion. Cut the potatoes and onion into 2-to 3-inch pieces and place in a 4-quart stock pot with the chicken stock or broth, brown sugar or honey, sage (optional), salt, and pepper. Cook until tender and soft enough to puree, about 25 minutes. If the potatoes and onion are tender before the squash is ready, simple turn the heat off under the pot

and let it remain on the burner until ready to add the squash.

6 When the squash is cool enough to handle, scoop out the flesh and add it to the pot of potatoes and onion. Mix together well and cook for another 5 minutes.

7 Remove potato-onion-squash mixture from the stove and puree in food processor in small batches until smooth. Place pureed mixture in a saucepan over low heat. Add milk to thin soup out, a little at a time. Taste for seasoning and add salt or pepper, if desired.

8 Place pine nuts in a medium sauté pan over medium heat until the pine nuts are lightly browned, gently and continuously shaking the pan while the pine nuts are toasting, about 3 to 4 minutes. When the pine nuts are toasted, they begin to emit a nutty scent.

9 Serve in warmed soup bowls. Garnish with black currants or golden raisins and toasted pine nuts.

Nutrition at a glance (per serving): *total fat 5g; saturated fat 1g; protein 7g; dietary fiber 4g; carbohydrate 47g; cholesterol 5mg; sodium 81mg (based on no added salt); vitamin A (% of Daily Value) 314; vitamin C (% of Daily Value) 46; % of calories from fat 18; % of calories from saturated fat 4; calories 244.*

***

You can save time the day of serving by baking the butternut squash ahead of time. If the squash is already baked and cooled, making the soup only takes 30 minutes.

Black currants are available in some supermarkets and specialty food stores. If you can't find black currants, the chef recommends substituting golden raisins.

Creating soups rich in variety and nutrients

The only limit to the variety of soups you may create in your kitchen is your imagination. The following two soups, which include such favorite fresh produce as mushrooms and sweet corn, only hint at the variety of styles and flavors possible. Each, too, is rich in nutrients, low in fat, and heart healthy.

Mushroom Soup with Herb Croutons
Created by Amy Myrdal, M.S., R.D.
Senior Research Dietitian, Rippe Lifestyle Institute
Shrewsbury, Massachusetts

This recipe tastes best when created using a variety of fresh mushrooms (see Figure 13-2 for an illustration of mushroom varieties). Many people mistakenly think of mushrooms as vegetables but they are really fungi that, unlike vegetables, can grow in the absence of light. When buying mushrooms look for firm mushrooms with closed caps whose gills aren't visibly separated. Many supermarkets feature a wide variety of mushrooms these days from white button mushrooms to exotic chanterelles. Be adventurous and try some you've never tried before in this wonderful soup.

Tools: *Medium (3-to 4-quart) saucepan, baking sheet*

Preparation time: *20 minutes*
Cooking time: *50 minutes*
Yield: *6 servings*
1 1/2 pounds domestic and exotic mushrooms
1 tablespoon olive oil
1 clove garlic, finely chopped
1 shallot, chopped
1 teaspoon butter
1/2 teaspoon dried thyme

4 cups reduced-sodium beef broth
Salt and freshly ground pepper, to taste

1 Clean the mushrooms by brushing them off with a brush or paper towel. Do not wash the mushrooms under water.
2 Trim off the tips of the mushroom stems, and then cut the mushrooms into 1/4-inch slices.
3 Add olive oil and butter to a medium stockpot over medium heat. Add the garlic and shallots, and sauté, stirring, until they begin to turn brown, about 3 minutes.
4 Add the mushrooms and dried thyme to the stockpot, stirring well. Reduce the heat to low, cover, and cook for 15 to 20 minutes, stirring occasionally. The mushrooms will begin to release their water. Cook until the mushrooms are soft. The cooking time varies depending on the type of mushrooms you buy. Domestic mushrooms tend to soften quicker than exotic mushrooms. If you need to extend the cooking time and the liquid has evaporated, add a few tablespoons of liquid (broth, water, or wine) to continue cooking.
5 When the mushrooms have softened considerably, add the beef broth. Season with salt and freshly ground pepper to taste. Simmer, uncovered, for an additional 10 to 15 minutes. While the soup is simmering, prepare the croutons.

Herb Croutons

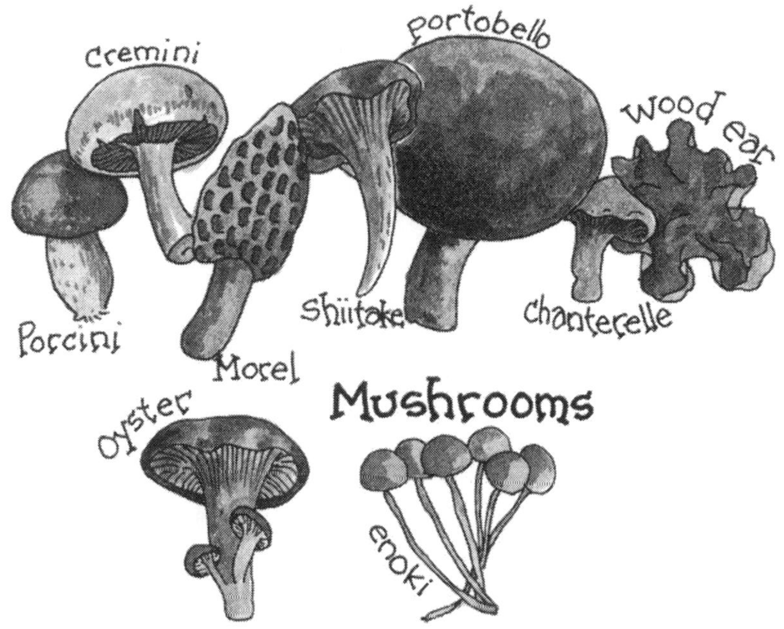

Figure 13-2: Mushrooms are available in many sizes, shapes, colors, and flavors.

6 slices Italian bread
Olive oil in a spray canister
1/2 teaspoon dried thyme
1/2 teaspoon dried parsley

1 Preheat the oven to 400 degrees.
2 Slice the bread into 1/2-inch slices. Then cut the bread into 1-inch-x-1-inch squares. Place the bread on a baking sheet, mist with the olive oil, and sprinkle with thyme and parsley.
3 Bake the croutons for 10 minutes, or until they are dry and lightly browned.
4 When the croutons are ready, ladle the soup into soup bowls, top with croutons, and serve.

Nutrition at a glance (per serving): *total fat 5g; saturated fat 1g; protein 7g; dietary fiber 3g; carbohydrate 22g; cholesterol 2mg; sodium 292mg; % of calories from fat 29; % of calories from saturated fat 6; calories 153.*

***

Finding a low-sodium broth: At least two brands offer very good low-sodium broth and bouillon. Health Valley makes a lower-sodium broth (about 380mg per cup) packaged in a convenient resealable box. Herb Ox makes a very-low-sodium powdered bouillon (about 5mg per packet). Both work well in this soup.

Sweet Corn and Chanterelle Soup with Red Pepper Flan
Created by Frank McClelland
Executive Chef/Owner, L'Espalier
Boston, Massachusetts

The Red Pepper Flan in this recipe calls for a *bain marie,* which is a French term meaning a water bath.

To create a bain marie, simply fill a shallow pan with warm water and set the dish holding the food inside the pan. This delicate method of cooking is perfect for egg-based dishes such as flan that have the tendency to curdle or break.

Tools: *Bain marie (water bath), 2-ounce ramekins, parchment paper*

Preparation time: *25 minutes*

Cooking time: *1 hour, 30 minutes*

Yield: *6 servings*

1 quart vegetable stock

10 ears of corn

2 leeks, halved lengthwise, washed and sliced into 1-inch lengths (white and light green parts only)

1 cup dry sherry

1 1/2 cups dry white wine

1 1/2 pounds Chanterelle mushrooms, trimmed and brushed clean

4 shallots, thinly sliced

3 cloves garlic, chopped

1/2 cup light cream

Pinch nutmeg, lemon juice, salt, and pepper to taste

2 tablespoons olive oil

1 cup roasted red bell peppers

1 egg yolk

1 whole egg

1 teaspoon arrowroot or cornstarch

Lemon juice, to taste

6 sprigs of basil, for garnish

1. Preheat oven to 450 degrees.
2. Place corn, with the husks on, on a roasting pan and roast for 20 minutes. Remove roasting pan from oven, let the corn cool, remove the husk, and cut away the kernels. Reserve the kernels and corn cobs separately.
3. Heat the olive oil over medium-low heat in a 6-quart saucepan. Add the shallots, garlic, leeks, mushrooms, and corn cobs. Sauté, stirring, for 15 minutes.
4. Add dry sherry to the pot, turn up the heat to medium, and simmer for three minutes.
5. Add dry white wine, and continue cooking to reduce the amount of liquid by a third.
6. Add vegetable stock and let simmer for 20 minutes or until reduced by one third.
7. Remove corn cobs and add corn kernels. Bring back to a simmer and remove from the heat.
8. Puree in a blender till smooth.
9. Place back into pot. Add cream, nutmeg, lemon juice, and salt, and pepper to taste.

Red Pepper Flan

The flan can be made 24 hours in advance and reheated before serving.

1. Place a medium roasting pan filled with 1 inch of water into the oven and then preheat oven to 400 degrees.
2. Add roasted red bell peppers, egg yolks, egg white, arrowroot, and lemon juice to a blender and puree until smooth.

3 Butter the insides of six 2-ounce ramekins (4-inch miniature soufflé dishes), place parchment rounds in the bottom of each ramekin, and lightly coat the insides with flour. Tap out all excess flour.
4 Pour red pepper mixture into ramekins. Place ramekins in water bath in the oven.
5 Turn oven down to 350 degrees and bake for 25 to 30 minutes or until firm.
6 Turn out pepper flans into center of soup bowl. Remove parchment paper. Ladle soup around flan. Top each bowl with a sprig of basil.

Nutrition at a glance (per serving): *total fat 13g; saturated fat 4g; protein 11g; dietary fiber 7g; carbohydrate 59g; cholesterol 84mg; sodium 67mg (based on no added salt); vitamin A (% of Daily Value) 38; vitamin C (% of Daily Value) 123; folic acid (% of Daily Value) 35; % of calories from fat 27; % of calories from saturated fat 8; calories 435.*

***

Chanterelle mushrooms are trumpet-shaped wild mushrooms, bright yellow to orange in color, with a delicate, nutty flavor. The texture is semi-chewy and will toughen if overcooked. Although most Chanterelles are imported from France, they can be found canned or dried in most large supermarkets and fresh in some.

You may order them from Dean & Deluca either online (www.deandeluca.com) or over the telephone (877-826-9246).

The basic rule of cooking with wine is to only use a wine you would drink. Don't be tempted to use an inferior quality wine in cooking. The off-flavor of a wine of inferior quality will come through in the finished product.

Salads

Salads provide daily opportunities to consume raw fruits and vegetables of all kinds. Cooked vegetables can play a role, too, in more than potato salad. But the biggest stumbling block to creating heart-healthy salads is usually the salad dressing. (The problem with potato salad, for instance, is that it is commonly prepared with the large quantities of mayonnaise, which gets 99 percent of its calories from fat.)You can build a mixed green salad loaded with vegetables that are rich in health-promoting antioxidants and phytochemicals, only to drown these benefits in fat-filled creamy blue cheese dressing.

Create your own heart-healthy salad dressing

To create your own healthy-heart salad dressing, first select a fat or a fat substitute. Then combine it in creative ways with one or more of the acids and accents. If using a fat, try 1 part fat to 3 parts acid. If using a fat substitute, combine proportions any way you like. You can also try using less fat and a fat substitute together to give the flavor and texture you like without as much fat. Use as many of the accents as you like whatever your fat/acid combination—be creative.

Fat: Canola oil, extra-virgin olive oil, peanut oil, low-fat mayonnaise, sesame oil (in small amounts for flavor), walnut oil (in small amounts for flavor).

Fat substitute: Nonfat plain yogurt, low-fat buttermilk, nonfat sour cream, miso, silken tofu, nonfat cottage cheese.

Acid: Lemon juice, lime juice, orange juice, wine vinegar, balsamic vinegar, cider vinegar, rice wine vinegar, tarragon vinegar, raspberry vinegar, other flavored vinegar, fish sauce, pineapple juice, wine, fresh salsa, apple juice, fresh tomato juice.

Accent: Basil, dill, oregano, fennel, cilantro, mint, curry powder, minced garlic, green onions, chives, shallots, grated fresh ginger, lemon zest, low-sodium soy sauce, capers, honey, mustard, mustard powder, cumin, roasted garlic, poppy seeds, chili paste, finely chopped fresh fruit, dried fruit.

Accents that add a little fat: Anchovy paste, olives, sesame seeds, tahini (sesame seed butter).

Avoiding these stumbling blocks is easy, however, with the recipes in this chapter. We provide recipes for mixed vegetable salads with creative dressings that use no fat. Where fat is used, the chefs turn to monounsaturated oils, such as olive oil, which promote heart health. Make these salads, enjoy them, and use them as inspiration to create your own healthful salads and dressings.

Two salads with fat-free dressings

If you're looking for a way to reduce the fat in your salads, turning to fat-free dressings is a great place to start. Try the following two recipes for flavorful fat-free options.

Mesclun Salad with No-Oil Lemongrass Dressing
Created by Nora Pouillon
Chef and Owner, Nora—the only certified organic restaurant in the United States
Washington, D.C.

The following recipe calls for fish sauce (also known as nuoc mam), which is a popular ingredient in Thai and Vietnamese cuisine. Fish sauce is available in Asian markets and the Asian foods section of most supermarkets.

Tools: *Blender*

Preparation time: *10 minutes*

Cooking time: *None*

Yield: *8 servings*

1/2 cup water

1/2 cup lemon juice

1/4 cup low-sodium soy sauce or tamari

2 to 5 tablespoons fish sauce, or to taste

1/4 cup rice vinegar

1 to 2 jalapeno peppers, chopped

1/4 cup fresh ginger, peeled and thinly sliced

1 1/2 stalks lemongrass, stiff outer leaves removed, sliced

1 bunch fresh cilantro, stems removed, chopped

1/2 teaspoon garlic, chopped

16 ounces mesclun salad greens, washed and spun dry

1 Combine water, lemon juice, soy sauce or tamari, fish sauce, vinegar, jalapeño peppers, ginger, lemongrass, cilantro, and garlic in a blender; blend well. Reserve in the refrigerator until ready to serve.

2 When ready to serve, toss dressing with mesclun greens.

Nutrition at a glance (per serving): *total fat 0g; saturated fat 0g; protein 2g; dietary fiber 2g; carbohydrate 7g; cholesterol 0mg; sodium 514mg; vitamin A (% of Daily Value) 62; vitamin C (% of*

Daily Value) 61; folic acid (% of Daily Value) 21; % of calories from fat 0; % of calories from saturated fat 0; calories 34.

***

For a milder vinaigrette, Chef Nora recommends removing the seeds from the jalapeño peppers before chopping.

Be careful when handling jalapeño peppers and their seeds. The oils from the seeds can irritate your eyes and skin. Always wash your hands after touching the seeds.

Fish oil and tamari or soy sauce contribute a lot of flavor to this recipe, but they also contribute a lot of sodium. Using 2 tablespoons fish sauce versus 5 makes a big difference in the amount of sodium. Keep in mind that including a high-sodium dish like this in your diet once in a while is fine. People with high blood pressure may want to avoid high-sodium dishes like this, but most people are not adversely affected by high sodium intake.

Mixed Spring Greens with Lime-Cilantro-Yogurt Dressing

Created by Kevin T. Jones
Executive Chef, Aurora Summit
Aurora, Colorado

Here's a creamy, zestful dressing that you can heap on your mixed green salad to your heart's content—literally. Where ordinary "creamy" dressing turn a green salad into a high-fat indulgence, this creamy dressing is low-fat and rich in calcium, not fat.

Tools: *Blender*
Preparation time: *5 minutes*
Cooking time: *None*
Yield: *16 servings*
Zest and juice of 2 limes
2 tablespoons cilantro, chopped
1/2 cup honey
1/4 cup white wine vinegar

Figure 13-3: You use a zester to remove the outer skin of citrus fruit.

1 quart nonfat, plain yogurt

Water (optional)

Assorted mixed greens or your favorite type of lettuce, about 2 cups per salad

1 Zest the limes by gently grating the green outer skin only—not the white inner flesh—from the limes with a zester (see Figure 13-3). Then cut the limes in half; over a small bowl, squeeze the halves with your fist to extract the juice. Remove any seeds from the juice with a fork.

2 Place lime zest and juice, cilantro, honey, white wine vinegar, and yogurt in a blender and blend until well combined. Add a little water to the mixture, if a thinner consistency is desired.

3 Serve with mixed spring greens, romaine lettuce, or bibb lettuce, or use as a dipping sauce for fresh vegetables. Leftover dressing will keep in a tightly closed jar in the refrigerator for 2 or 3 days.

Nutrition at a glance (per serving): *total fat 0g; saturated fat 0g; protein 4g; dietary fiber 0g; carbohydrate 14g; cholesterol 1mg; sodium 48mg; % of calories from fat 0; % of calories from saturated fat 0; calories 68.*

***

Salads that go beyond mixed greens

Beyond lettuce and other leafy greens, salads intended to accompany an entree can feature a wide variety of vegetables, fruits and grains. Although very different from each other, the next four salads all demonstrate how to combine different colors and contrasting textures and flavors into beautiful and delicious salads.

Arugula Salad with Purple Figs and Red Onions
Created by Gordon Hamersley
Executive Chef/Owner, Hamersley's Bistro
Boston, Massachusetts

Figs and onions? You might not immediately think of putting them together but this salad of peppery arugula, sweet figs and savory red onions dressed with a balsamic vinaigrette explodes with flavor. It's so delicious you'd never guess it's rich in fiber.

Tools: *Large, ovenproof sauté pan*
Preparation time: *20 minutes*
Cooking time: *55 minutes*
Yield: *6 servings*
3 red onions
1 tablespoon canola oil
Salt and black pepper, to taste
2 teaspoons fresh thyme

1 tablespoon chopped garlic
2 cups red wine
2 cups water
1 teaspoon Dijon mustard
3 tablespoons balsamic vinegar
1 shallot, peeled and minced
2 tablespoons olive oil
2 cups loosely packed arugula lettuce, washed and dried
12 fresh purple figs

1 Preheat oven to 350 degrees.
2 Cut the onions in half, cutting across the diameter of the onion as if you were going to make onion rings. Heat the cooking oil in a large, ovenproof sauté pan over medium-high heat. Add the onions to the pan cut side down. Brown for 3 to 5 minutes.
3 Turn the onions over; add salt and pepper. Add the thyme, garlic, red wine, and water; bring to a boil, then transfer to the oven and cook for 45 minutes or until the onions are tender and fully cooked.
4 While the onions are cooking, make the dressing. Whisking the mustard and vinegar in a small bowl; add the olive oil in a slow, steady stream. Set aside the dressing.
5 When the onions are done, transfer them from the pan to a plate and allow to cool.

6 Cook the juices over moderate heat until 1/2 cup remains. Allow the liquid to cool, and then whisk it into the dressing.
7 To serve, place the arugula and figs in a mixing bowl. Add enough dressing to coat, about 1/2 cup. Place 1/2 an onion on each plate and arrange the arugula and figs around. Drizzle more dressing around if desired.

Nutrition at a glance (per serving): *total fat 7g; saturated fat <1g; protein 2g; dietary fiber 5g; carbohydrate 27g; cholesterol 0mg; sodium 33mg; % of calories from fat 29; % of calories from saturated fat 4; calories 217.*

***

1789 Restaurant Asparagus and Gingered Grapefruit Salad with Miso Vinaigrette and Ginger Lime Glaze

Created by Ris Lacoste
Executive Chef, 1789 Restaurant
Washington, D.C.

West meets East in this recipe as a favorite western vegetable, asparagus, joins a favorite fruit, grapefruit, in a salad that draws delightfully from Asian cuisine in its use of ingredients such as ginger, lime, and miso. Miso is a Japanese bean paste usually made of soybeans and having the texture of peanut butter.

To save some time the day of serving, prepare the Miso Vinaigrette and Ginger Lime Glaze ahead of time and store in the refrigerator until you're ready to make the salad. Chef Lacoste notes that the Ginger Lime Glaze can also be used as a base for hot or iced tea. Extra Miso Vinaigrette can be used as a salad dressing on simple green salads as well.

Tools: *Saucepan, strainer*
Preparation time: *30 minutes*
Cooking time: *10 minutes*
Yield: *8 servings*
48 spears large asparagus
48 sections pink grapefruit
2 cups Ginger Lime Glaze (See following recipe)
1 cup Miso Vinaigrette (See following recipe)
2 scallions, cut thinly at an angle
1/4 cup mixed white and black sesame seeds

1 Very carefully peel away the tough outer stem of each asparagus just up to the tip. Snap off the bottom of each stem—it will naturally break where the tender part begins.
2 Blanch (briefly cook) asparagus in a large pot of boiling water until the stems just bend, 3 to 4 minutes. Remove and place in an ice bath to stop cooking and preserve green color.
3 Remove asparagus from the ice bath as soon as it is chilled and place in a colander to drain. Keep at room temperature until serving the meal, if just about to serve. Otherwise, refrigerate until 10 to 15 minutes before you're ready to use.

4 Section grapefruit into a strainer over a bowl. Squeeze out as much juice as you can from the fruit pulp into a separate bowl. Make sure the grapefruit sections are whole and cleaned of all pith.
5 Place the sections in a separate bowl and toss with Ginger Glaze (see following recipe).
6 Gently toss the asparagus with 1/2 cup of the Miso Vinaigrette (see following recipe).
7 To plate the salad, dress the bottom of 8 plates with equal amounts of the remaining Miso Vinaigrette. Then arrange a log pile of 6 asparagus spears in the center of each plate on top of the vinaigrette. Remove the grapefruit sections from the ginger glaze, and arrange 6 sections fanned out around the edge of the asparagus on each plate, 3 sections per side.
8 Finish the salad with a sprinkle of scallions and sesame seeds.

Ginger Lime Glaze

This glaze will last up to a year when stored in the refrigerator.

Yield: *2 cups*

8-inch long piece of ginger, peeled and cut into very fine threads

Zest of 4 limes

1 1/2 cups tarragon vinegar

3/4 cup sugar

1 Combine all ingredients in a nonreactive, stainless steel pot. Bring to boil.

2 Remove from heat and let sit for 5 minutes to infuse flavors.
3 Bring back to a boil, remove from heat again, and let sit another 5 minutes.
4 Bring back to a boil for a third time, and then set aside for 30 minutes or until cool enough to cover and refrigerate.

Miso Vinaigrette

When covered, this dressing will last up to 5 days in the refrigerator.

Yield: *2 1/2 cups*

3 inches fresh ginger, peeled and finely diced
1 tablespoon garlic, minced
1 tablespoon miso
1 1/2 tablespoons chili paste with garlic
1/2 bunch cilantro, chopped
6 tablespoons sherry wine
1/2 cup rice vinegar
1/2 cup plus 2 tablespoons fish sauce (nuac nam)
1/4 cup lime juice
1 tablespoon honey
2 tablespoons sesame oil
1/2 cup peanut oil

1 Combine all ingredients in a bowl except for the sesame and peanut oils. Whisk to combine.
2 While whisking continuously, slowly pour in the oils, one at a time, to emulsify.
3 Set aside until ready to use.

Nutrition at a glance (per serving): *total fat 9g; saturated fat 1.5g; protein 6g; dietary fiber 4g;*

carbohydrate 45g; cholesterol 0mg; sodium 561mg (based on no added salt); vitamin A (% of Daily Value) 20; vitamin C (% of Daily Value) 133; folic acid (% of Daily Value) 37; % of calories from fat 30; % of calories from saturated fat 5; calories 269.

***

The miso paste, fish sauce, and chili paste with garlic all can be found in Asian markets or the Asian foods section of many supermarkets. They all add a lot of sodium *and* a lot of flavor to the salad.

Curried Israeli Couscous Salad
Created by Chris Toole and Sandra Holland
Chef/Owners, The Humble Gourmet
Brunswick, Maine

Orange carrots, purple raisins, and green cilantro combine with couscous, a mainstay of Middle Eastern cuisine, to provide a filling salad rich in Vitamin A and fiber. *Couscous* is coarsely ground semolina wheat. Israeli Couscous is a large pearl couscous that can be found in specialty stores.

Tools: *Medium saucepan*
Preparation time: *10 minutes*
Cooking time: *13 minutes*
Yield: *12 servings*

2 cups Israeli couscous (or Middle Eastern couscous)
5 cups water
2 teaspoons curry powder
1/3 cup olive oil
3/4 cup grated carrots
3/4 cup raisins
1/3 cup chopped cilantro, loosely packed
Salt to taste

1 In a medium saucepan, bring water to a boil.
2 Add couscous and let water come to a boil again. Simmer uncovered for 2 to 3 minutes.
3 Remove from heat, cover, and let stand 8 to 10 minutes.
4 Transfer the couscous into a strainer and rinse under running water. Drain thoroughly, then transfer to a medium mixing bowl.
5 In a small bowl, mix curry powder and olive oil.
6 Stir curry-oil mixture into the couscous.
7 Add remaining ingredients, toss well, and season to taste with salt.

Nutrition at a glance (per serving): *total fat 6g; saturated fat 1g; protein 4g; dietary fiber 2g; carbohydrate 31g; cholesterol 0mg; sodium 8mg; vitamin A (% of Daily Value) 23; % of calories from fat 28; % of calories from saturated fat 5; calories 195.*

***

Chicken and seafood salads

Grilled chicken salad and crab salad—two lunch mainstays—rise to heights you didn't think possible in the next three recipes as the chefs create wonderful variations that combine the chicken and crab in exciting new ways with fruits and vegetables.

Grilled Chicken Salad with Eggplant, Cucumber, and Mint Yogurt Served in a Whole-Wheat Pita
Created by Rene Bajeux
Executive Chef, Windsor Court Hotel
New Orleans, Louisiana

On the hot, humid days of summer chicken salad always "hits the spot." This chicken salad incorporates ingredients that are always appealing in the summer—including crisp, crunchy, cool cucumber, peppers, and mint.

Tools: *Grill or grill pan, large sauté pan*

Preparation time: *20 minutes plus 4 hours to marinate the chicken*

Cooking time: *20 minutes*

Yield: *8 servings*

2 pounds boneless, skinless chicken breasts (about 6 5-ounce breasts)

1/4 cup olive oil (for the marinade)

2 tablespoons plus 2 teaspoons yellow curry powder
1 tablespoon olive oil (for sautéing)
2 3/4 cups eggplant, diced (see Figure 13-4 for instructions)
2 1/2 teaspoons fresh garlic, finely minced
1 cup cucumber, peeled, seeded, and diced
1/2 cup fresh mint, minced
1/2 cup fresh basil, cut into julienne strips
1/4 cup green onion, sliced 1/4-inch thick
1/4 cup carrot, peeled and finely diced
1/4 cup red bell pepper, finely diced
1/4 cup yellow bell pepper, finely diced
1/4 cup nonfat, plain yogurt
2 tablespoons freshly squeezed lemon juice
Salt and pepper to taste
8 medium (5 1/4-inch diameter) whole wheat pitas, halved
16 leaves of red leaf lettuce, for garnish (optional)

1 Wash chicken breasts under cold running water, pat dry, and trim away any visible fat.
2 Combine olive oil and curry powder in a large bowl or shallow container and whisk to combine. Place the chicken breasts in the marinade, turning them several times to evenly coat. Cover and transfer to the refrigerator. Marinate for 4 hours.
3 About 15 minutes before the marinade time is almost up, start your grill or preheat a stovetop grill pan.

4 Remove the chicken from the marinade, season with salt and pepper, and place on the grill. Cook the chicken, turning two or three times, until it is cooked through, about 15 minutes. Set aside to cool slightly. When cool enough to handle, cut into 1/2-inch cubes. Place in a large mixing bowl and refrigerate.
5 Add 1 tablespoon olive oil to a large sauté pan over medium-high heat. Add the diced eggplant and cook, stirring until lightly brown and soft to the touch, about 5 minutes.
6 Add the browned eggplant and the garlic to the mixing bowl with the chicken. Add the diced cucumber, chopped mint, chopped basil, green onion, carrots, and bell peppers. Stir to combine.
7 Fold in the yogurt and lemon juice, and stir to combine.
8 Place salad in refrigerator until ready to serve.
9 To serve, spoon the salad into pita halves.

Nutrition at a glance (per serving): *total fat 10g; saturated fat 2g; protein 31g; dietary fiber 5g; carbohydrate 30g; cholesterol 69mg; sodium 312mg (based on no added salt); vitamin A (% of Daily Value) 20; vitamin C (% of Daily Value) 29; % of calories from fat 27; % of calories from saturated fat 5; calories 330.*

***

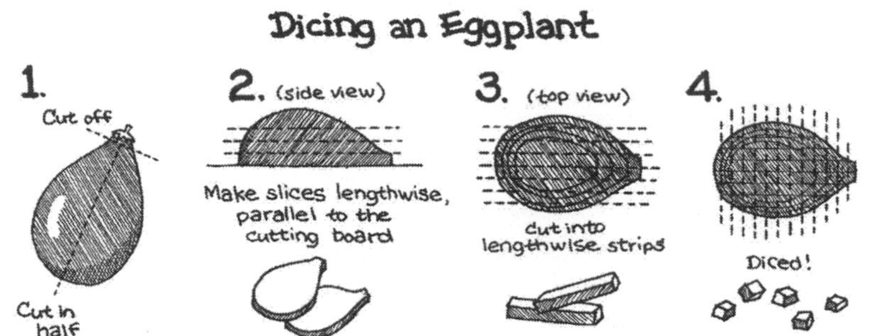
Dicing an Eggplant
1.
Cut off
Cut in half
2. (side view)
Make slices lengthwise, parallel to the cutting board
3. (top view)
cut into lengthwise strips
4.
Diced!

Figure 13-4: Cutting an eggplant into cubes.

Crab Salad with Mango, Avocado, and Tropical Fruit Puree

Created by Patrick O'Connell
Chef Proprietor, The Inn at Little
Washington Washington, Virginia

This is an elegant, tasty salad that makes an eye-appealing lunch—no matter how you serve it. The plating and presentation of the dish we've given you is written for restaurant preparation. If you don't have ring molds and don't want to be so fussy, simply layer the ingredients, as directed, on plates without the molds. You'll get the same layered effect with a more casual approach. If you're interested in buying ring molds, you can find them in kitchen supply stores.

Tools: *2 1/2-inch diameter ring mold, food processor fitted with a metal blade*

Preparation time: *20 minutes*

Cooking time: *None*

Yield: *4 servings*

2 cups jumbo lump crabmeat, carefully picked through, any shell fragments discarded

1 1/2 tablespoons minced jalapeno pepper

2 tablespoons lemon juice

1 1/2 tablespoons fish sauce

2 tablespoons cilantro, roughly chopped

1/4 cup fresh mango, diced

1/2 cup fresh avocado, diced

1 Combine crabmeat, jalapeno pepper, lemon juice, fish sauce, and cilantro in a medium size-mixing bowl. Fold together carefully with a rubber spatula to prevent breaking up the lumps of crabmeat.

2 Place a ring mold (or a round cookie cutter that is about 2 inches tall and 2 1/2 inches wide) on each of 4 chilled plates. With a teaspoon, place 2 tablespoons of avocado at the bottom of the mold. Pack it down lightly with the back of the spoon.

3 Place 1 tablespoon of mango on top of the avocado and press it gently.

4 Place the final layer of the crabmeat mixture and smooth off the top with the flat side of a knife. Lift the ring mold off carefully.

5 Repeat this process on the remaining three plates.

6 Spoon the Mango, Avocado, and Tropical Fruit Puree around the edges of the crab mold and serve chilled.

Tropical Fruit Puree

1 small cantaloupe, halved, seeded, outside skin removed and discarded, flesh cut into large chunks

1/2 small fresh pineapple

Sugar, to taste
2 tablespoons lemon juice
2 tablespoons orange juice
2 tablespoons cilantro, roughly chopped

1 Puree the melon in a food processor fitted with a metal blade. Transfer mixture to a medium size-mixing bowl.

2 Prepare the pineapple by cutting off the top of the pineapple 1 to 2 inches below the flower. Cut off the bottom of the pineapple as well. Cut the pineapple in half lengthwise, then cut in half lengthwise again to make quarters. Use a small knife to cut off the woody core portion from each quarter, and then separate the flesh from the skin by cutting between the two. Cut the quarters into chunks. (See Figure 13-5 for illustrated instructions.)

3 Puree the pineapple, lemon juice, and orange juice together and add it to the melon puree.

4 Add the cilantro, and a pinch of sugar to taste and mix the puree thoroughly.

5 Cover and refrigerate until ready to serve.

Nutrition at a glance (per serving): *total fat 5g; saturated fat 1g; protein 16g; carbohydrate 23g; cholesterol 68mg; sodium 547mg; vitamin A (% of Daily Value) 82; vitamin C (% of Daily Value) 123; folic acid (% of Daily Value) 20; % of calories from fat 24; % of calories from saturated fat 5; calories 186.*

Figure 13-5: How to peel a pineapple.

You can reduce the amount of sodium in this dish by reducing the amount of fish sauce.

Similar to the previous recipe, the plating and presentation of the following dish is written for restaurant preparation. Feel free to take a more casual approach; instead of using ring molds, toss the crab salad together and spoon into the Lime Nage. Or you can use a small ramekin or custard dish as a mold for the crab salad.

Crabmeat Salad with Green Mango Souscaille
Created by Allen Susser
Executive Chef/Owner, Chef Allen's Restaurant
Aventura, Florida

If you are longing to get away to a tropical island, give yourself and some friends a mini-vacation by serving this unusual crab salad.

Tools: *4 3-inch ring molds*
Preparation time: *20 minutes*
Cooking time: 20 minutes
Yield: *4 servings*

2 large unripe mangoes, peeled and diced
2 cloves garlic, minced
1/4 piece Scotch bonnet pepper, minced
3 tablespoons fresh lime juice
1 teaspoon sea salt
1/2 cup water
16 ounces jumbo crabmeat, picked clean
2 tablespoons mayonnaise
1 small red bell pepper, diced
1/2 bunch chives, diced
1/4 teaspoon cayenne pepper
2 cups Lime Nage (see following recipe)

1 In a medium stainless steel bowl, combine the mango, garlic, Scotch bonnet pepper, 2 of the tablespoons lime juice, sea salt, and the water.
2 Cover, place in refrigerator, and allow the mango to marinate for at least 2 hours.
3 In a medium stainless steel bowl, combine the crabmeat, mayonnaise, red peppers, chives, the remaining 1 tablespoon of lime juice, and the cayenne pepper.
4 Mix carefully so as not to break up the crabmeat.
5 Set aside until ready to serve.

6 Drain liquid from mango.
7 Place 4 3-inch ring molds in 4 small low bowls.
8 Using a slotted spoon, divide the mango evenly among 4 ring molds filling about one-third full.
9 Continue to fill the mold with the crabmeat salad.
10 To serve, spoon 1/2 cup of Lime Nage around the mold in each bowl, then remove the mold.
11 Serve immediately.

Lime Nage

Yield: *3 cups*
1 medium Spanish onion, diced
1 large yellow bell pepper, diced
3 tablespoons flat leaf parsley, chopped
1 teaspoon garlic, chopped
3 tablespoons cilantro, chopped
1/4 cup lime juice
2 tablespoons sugar
1/3 cup white wine vinegar
1/4 teaspoon Scotch bonnet pepper, diced
1/4 cup fresh ginger, cut into thin julienne strips
1 tablespoon Kosher salt
3 cups cold water

1 In a large saucepan over high heat combine the onion, pepper, parsley, garlic, cilantro, lime juice, sugar, vinegar, Scotch bonnet, 2 tablespoons ginger, salt, and cold water.
2 Bring to boil, reduce heat to medium, and simmer 20 minutes.
3 Strain and place in refrigerator to cool.

Nutrition at a glance (per serving): *total fat 8g; saturated fat 1g; protein 25g; dietary fiber 3g; carbohydrate 31g; cholesterol 117mg; sodium 1,546mg; vitamin A (% of Daily Value) 111; vitamin C (% of Daily Value) 228; vitamin E (% of Daily Value) 21; folic acid (% of Daily Value) 24; % of calories from fat 25; % of calories from saturated fat 3; calories 283.*

***

Scotch bonnets, called for in this recipe, are small chili peppers 1 to 1 1/2 inches in diameter. They range in color from shades of yellow to red. Scotch bonnets are one of the hottest of the chilies, so wear gloves when cutting and cleaning them, because even the tiniest drop of pepper juice can result in incredible pain if you rub your eye or face after handling them.

Sea salt is exactly what its name suggests; it's the salt left after sea water evaporates. Many chefs prefer the taste of sea salt to iodized table salt. Some say sea salt imparts the taste of the sea, which makes it perfect for use in dishes that include sea food. Sea salt can be purchased at specialty foods stores, some supermarkets and can be ordered from Dean & Deluca either on-line (www.deandeluca.com) or over the telephone (1-877-826-9246).

Reduce the sodium content by using less salt in the Lime Nage.

To julienne is to cut into thin match-stick size strips. To julienne ginger, slice it cross-wise in 1/8-inch thick or smaller slices then cut the slices length-wise into match-stick strips.

Chapter 14

Side Dishes

In This Chapter

- Braising and roasting tasty vegetables
- Exploring new approaches to side dishes

Recipes in This Chapter

- Spaghetti Vegetables **(V)**
- Braise of Spring Vegetables
- Maple Syrup Roasted Acorn Squash **(V)**
- Organic Root Vegetable Risottosh **(V)**
- Stuffed Cylinder Potatoes with Duxelle Mushrooms and Vegetable Jus**(V)**
- Cinnamon-Roasted New Potatoes **(V)**

***

Although it's customary to call accompaniments to an entrée side dishes, they are just as important to the meal's appeal and dietary balance as the main course. Side dishes offer great opportunities for getting fruits, vegetables, and grains and for building your nutritional base of complex carbohydrates. The recipes in this chapter present side dishes that deserve co-star billing in any meal.

Savory Vegetables

Because vegetables are naturally low in fat, featuring them in side dishes also gives you limitless ways to balance the higher fat content of some poultry and meat entrées. Vegetables also provide a rich treasure of necessary vitamins, minerals, antioxidants, and phytochemicals. The following four recipes feature different approaches to preparing savory combinations of fresh vegetables.

Spaghetti Vegetables

Created by MaryAnn Saporito Boothroyd
Chef/Owner Saporito's Florence Club Café
Hull, Massachusetts

Spaghetti vegetables can be served hot or cold as a side dish or tossed with pasta or rice, for a simple low-fat, vegetarian meal. The recipe is presented here tossed with orzo to create a low-fat, energy-rich side dish. Larger servings could definitely be considered a vegetarian entrée. For this recipe, cut the longest, thinnest slices of the vegetables possible (either by hand or with a mandoline) and cut into thin julienne strips. (For an illustration of how to julienne vegetables by hand, see Figure 14-1, and for an illustration of how to use a mandoline, see Figure 14-2.)

Tools: *Mandoline (optional), large mixing bowl, small mixing bowl, whisk, large sauté pan (optional)*

Preparation time: *15 to 25 minutes, depending on whether the dish is served hot or cold*

Cooking time: *15 minutes*

Yield: *6 servings*

1 cup orzo (or 2/3 cup rice)

1 cup leeks, julienne

1/2 cup red onion, julienne

1 cup zucchini, julienne

1 cup carrot, julienne

1 cup red bell pepper, julienne

1/2 cup rice wine vinegar (not required if you serve the dish hot)

1/4 teaspoon minced garlic (optional)

1/4 teaspoon salt

Pepper to taste

2 tablespoons olive oil

1 Cook orzo according to manufacturer's directions. When the orzo is cooked, set aside until ready to toss with the vegetables. If you're making a cold side dish, chill the orzo before tossing it with the vegetables.

2 Julienne the leeks, onion, zucchini, carrot, and red bell pepper, either by hand or with a mandoline.

3 For a cold dish, in a large bowl toss together all of the vegetables and the chilled orzo. In a small bowl, combine the vinegar, garlic, salt, and pepper.

Whisk in the oil. Pour the dressing over the vegetables, toss to combine, and serve.

4 For a hot dish, heat the olive oil in a large sauté pan over medium-high heat. Add the vegetables and cook, tossing or stirring, just until wilted, 2 to 3 minutes. Add a pinch (1/4 teaspoon or so) of fresh minced garlic and season with pepper to taste.

Nutrition at a glance (per serving): *total fat 5g; saturated fat 0.7g; protein 4g; dietary fiber 3g; carbohydrate 25g; cholesterol 0mg; sodium 110mg; vitamin A (% of Daily Value) 97; vitamin C (% of Daily Value) 91; % of calories from fat 29; % of calories from saturated fat 4; calories 155.*

***

A *mandoline* is a compact handheld machine with adjustable blades for cutting or slicing firm fruits and vegetables. Although a mandoline produces very uniform, precise pieces of food, the same can be done with a good knife and a little patience. A mandoline blade is very sharp, so keep your fingers away from the blade when slicing.

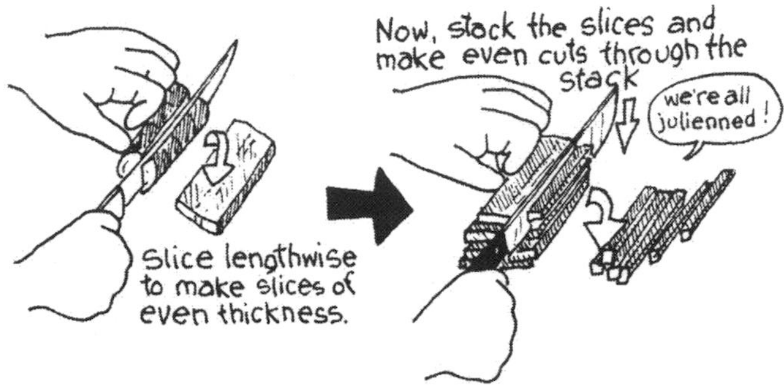

Figure 14-1: Julienne vegetables by stacking slices and cutting into matchstick-sized pieces.

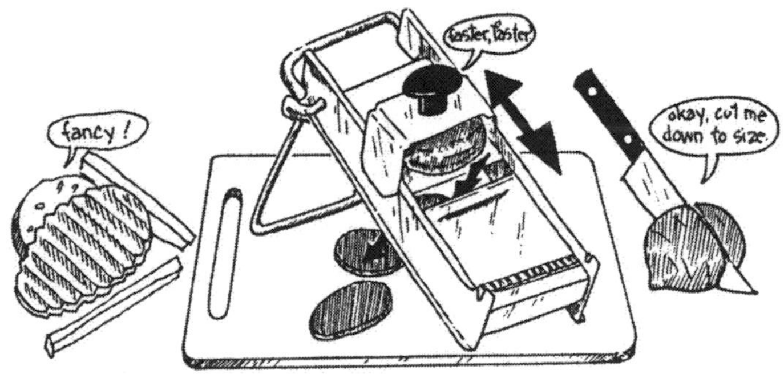

Figure 14-2: How to use a mandoline.

Braise of Spring Vegetables

Created by Sylvain Portay
Chef of The Dining Room, The Ritz-Carlton, San Francisco
San Francisco, California

This recipe requires many baby vegetables and, therefore, can only be made in the spring and early summer when there is an abundance of tender, young vegetables. Some supermarkets and specialty produce markets may carry many of these vegetables, but you may have better luck getting your hands on the freshest, most tender, young vegetables at a gardener's or farmer's market. Regardless of where you live, the point is to use the youngest vegetables available. You don't have to use all the vegetables listed below; be creative and use whatever you can find in season.

Tools: *Ovenproof sauté pan*
Preparation time: *30 minutes*
Cooking time: *10 minutes*
Yield: *4 servings*

4 teaspoons olive oil

4 baby carrots, peeled

4 green onions, root trimmed and cut to 4-inch segments

2 baby gold beets, halved

2 baby Chioggia beets, halved

2 baby turnips

1 baby artichoke, halved

2 small fennel bulbs (see Figure 14-3), sliced to 1-x-1-x-1/2-inch cubes

Salt and pepper to taste

8 green beans, ends trimmed

1 baby green zucchini, halved lengthwise

2 tablespoons green shelling peas

1/4 cup chicken stock or broth

1 tablespoon black truffle shavings (optional)

1 tablespoon sherry vinegar

1 Preheat oven to 450 degrees.

2 In an ovenproof sauté pan, heat 2 teaspoons of the olive oil over high heat. Add carrots and cook for 1 minute; then add the green onions, beets, and turnips and cook for 1 minute. Add the artichokes, fennel, and a pinch of salt (optional). Toss in the green beans, zucchini, and peas. ***Note:*** This cooking order will ensure the vegetables are perfect in color.

3 Sauté vegetables, tossing or gently stirring, for 1 minute; then add the chicken stock and the remaining 2 teaspoons of olive oil. Bring to a simmer and place the pan in the oven for 3 to 5 minutes or until the vegetables are tender.

4 Remove the sauté pan from the oven and place back over high heat. Reduce the liquids until thick. Arrange on a salad plate. To finish, sprinkle truffle shavings, sherry vinegar, a pinch of salt (optional), and black pepper over the dish.

Nutrition at a glance (per serving): *total fat 4.7g; saturated fat 0.7g; protein 4g; dietary fiber 8g;*

carbohydrate 23g; cholesterol 0mg; sodium 220mg; vitamin A (% of Daily Value) 163; vitamin C (% of Daily Value) 51; folic acid (% of Daily Value) 24; % of calories from fat 30; % of calories from saturated fat 4; calories 142.

***

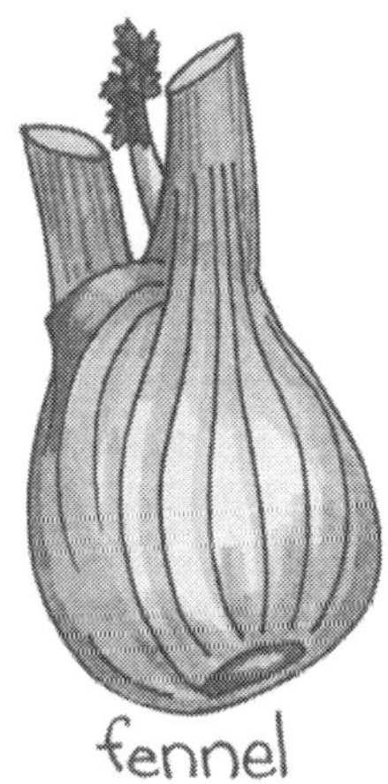

Figure 14-3: Fennel is terrific prepared a variety of ways, and it goes great in salads.

The Chioggia beet is also called the *candy cane beet* because of the concentric rings of red and white that run through the beet. If you can't locate baby Chioggia beets, feel free to use baby red beets.

Maple-Syrup-Roasted Acorn Squash with Fresh Herbs

Created by Amy Myrdal, M.S., R.D.
Senior Research Dietitian, Rippe Lifestyle Institute
Shrewsbury, Massachusetts

This recipe is incredibly easy to make. Using real maple syrup is absolutely a must—maple-flavored pancake syrup just won't do.

Tools: *Baking pan, parchment paper (optional) or aluminum foil*

Preparation time: *10 minutes*

Cooking time: *50 minutes*

Yield: *4 servings*

2 medium acorn squash
4 teaspoons unsalted butter
4 tablespoons pure maple syrup
2 teaspoons coarsely chopped fresh thyme
2 teaspoons fresh oregano leaves
Salt and pepper to taste

1 Preheat oven to 425 degrees.
2 Cover a baking pan with aluminum foil or parchment paper. If using aluminum foil, place the shiny side down.
3 Cut the acorn squash in half and remove seeds and strings.
4 Set squash, cut side up, on baking sheet. Place 1 teaspoon butter and 1 tablespoon maple syrup in each half squash.

5 Sprinkle each squash with 1/2 teaspoon fresh thyme and 1/2 teaspoon fresh oregano.
6 Season with salt and pepper to taste.
7 Place in oven and roast for 50 minutes, or until tender when pierced with a knife. Serve warm as a side dish with roasted chicken, pork, or wild game.

Nutrition at a glance (per serving): *total fat 4g; saturated fat 2g; protein 2g; dietary fiber 10g; carbohydrate 45g; cholesterol 10mg; sodium 36mg; vitamin A (% of Daily Value) 22; vitamin C (% of Daily Value) 40; % of calories from fat 17; % of calories from saturated fat 9; calories 207.*

***

You can use other types of winter squash, but depending on size you may want to quarter instead of halving. A great variation to try is to sprinkle with cinnamon instead of fresh herbs.

Ratatouille

Created by Constantin "Chris" Kerageorgiou

Executive Chef, La Provence Restaurant
New Orleans, Louisiana

Tools: *Medium heavy-bottom saucepan, oven-proof earthenware dish*

Preparation time: *30 minutes*

Cooking time: *1 hour, 30 minutes*

Yield: *6 servings*

2 tablespoons olive oil

2 pounds (3 to 4 small) eggplant, ends trimmed, cut into 1-inch cubes

2 large onions, sliced

6 large cloves garlic (4 cloves sliced or minced and 2 cloves put through a press or pureed)

1 large red bell pepper, cut into slices about 1 inch thick by 2 inches long

1 large green bell pepper, cut into slices about 1 inch thick by 2 inches long

1 1/2 pounds (3 medium-size) zucchini, cut in half lengthwise and sliced 1/2-inch thick

Coarse sea salt to taste

4 large (or 6 medium) tomatoes, peeled, seeded, and coarsely chopped

1 tablespoon tomato paste

1 bay leaf

2 teaspoons fresh thyme leaves, or 1 teaspoon crushed dried thyme

1 teaspoon crushed dried oregano, or 2 teaspoons chopped fresh oregano

1/2 teaspoon crushed coriander seeds

1 Preheat oven to 300 degrees.
2 Heat the oil in a medium heavy-bottom saucepan over medium-high heat. Add the eggplant, onions, garlic, peppers, and zucchini, and sauté, stirring often, for 5 minutes. Season with salt and add the tomatoes, tomato paste, and bay leaf. Bring to a simmer.
3 In a large earthenware dish, combine the sautéed vegetables and the thyme, oregano, and coriander, and bake for about 1 hour, 20 minutes, until they are completely tender.

Nutrition at a glance (per serving): *total fat 5.6g; saturated fat 0.8g; protein 5g; dietary fiber 8g; carbohydrate 28g; cholesterol 0mg; sodium 43mg (based on no added salt); vitamin A (% of Daily Value) 61; vitamin C (% of Daily Value) 196; folic acid (% of Daily Value) 29; % of calories from fat 30; % of calories from saturated fat 4; calories 168.*

***

Coriander seeds come from the coriander plant, a member of the parsley family, which includes cilantro and Chinese parsley. The mildly aromatic tiny yellow seeds release a flavor that resembles a combination of lemon, sage, and caraway. The seeds are available in most supermarkets. Crush them by using a small mortar and pestle.

Rice and Potatoes

Rice and potatoes are among the oldest and most popular starchy staples in the world. Rice has been cultivated since before 5000 B.C. in Asia. And in the Americas, the ancient Incas grew potatoes thousands of years ago. The following three recipes give you some new ways to prepare these old favorites.

Organic Root Vegetable Risotto

Created by Toni Robertson
Executive Chef, Sonoma Mission Inn & Spa
Sonoma, California

Featuring vegetables that grow underground, this risotto can be made year-round but seems particularly appropriate for fall, when many of these vegetables are harvested. Risotto is traditionally made with Arborio rice, a high-starch rice that gives the dish its creamy texture.

Tools: *Large mixing bowl, nonstick baking sheet, medium heavy-bottom saucepan*

Preparation time: *15 minutes*

Cooking time: *60 minutes*

Yield: *4 servings*

4 cups assorted root vegetables (celery root, parsnips, sweet potato, carrots, rutabaga, Jerusalem artichokes, and so on)

1 cup Arborio rice

3 cups vegetable stock, hot

2 tablespoons chopped shallots
1 tablespoon chopped herbs
1 tablespoon olive oil
1/4 cup grated Monterey Jack cheese
Pepper to taste

1 Preheat oven to 450 degrees.

2 Wash, peel, and cut the root vegetables into 2-inch cubes. Place them in a large bowl, spray them with cooking spray (or use 1 tablespoon of olive oil), and toss to evenly coat. Spread in one even layer on a large nonstick baking pan and place in the oven. Roast for 15 minutes, or until they start to brown, then turn them. Lower the heat to 375 degrees and continue roasting until the vegetables are tender when pierced with a knife, about 15 to 20 minutes. Season with pepper to taste.

3 Heat the olive oil in a medium, heavy-bottomed saucepan over medium heat. Add the shallots and cook, stirring, until limp, about 3 minutes. Add the rice and toast it, stirring gently, for approximately 2 minutes.

4 Add 1/2 cup of the vegetable stock and boil until most of the liquid has been absorbed by the rice. Continue adding simmering stock, 1/2 cup at a time, until the rice is tender but firm; the total cooking time of the rice should not exceed 18 minutes. The rice should have movement, but no excess liquid. If the rice requires more cooking, add a touch more liquid and cook for another 1 to 2 minutes. You may not need to use all of the

stock. During the last minute of cooking, stir in the root vegetables and chopped herbs. Remove from the heat and stir in the grated cheese. Season with salt and pepper to taste.

Nutrition at a glance (per serving): *total fat 7g; saturated fat 2g; protein 9g; dietary fiber 7g; carbohydrate 61g; cholesterol 7mg; sodium 130mg (based on no added salt); vitamin A (% of Daily Value) 199; vitamin C (% of Daily Value) 41; folic acid (% of Daily Value) 21; % of calories from fat 19; % of calories from saturated fat 5; calories 339.*

***

Stuffed Cylinder Potatoes with Duxelle Mushrooms and Vegetable Jus

Created by Felicien Cueff
Chef de Cuisine, CITRONELLE
Santa Barbara, California

This recipe raises ordinary potatoes to star attraction by imaginatively shaping them and stuffing them with a classic mushroom *duxelle* and serving them in a fragrant vegetable broth or *jus.* This recipe goes well with an entrée of roasted pork, beef, or lamb and a colorful vegetable salad.

Tools: *Melon baller, cookie cutter, cheese cloth, cotton string*

Preparation time: *30 minutes*

Cooking time: *40 minutes*

Yield: *6 servings*

For the Duxelle:

1 pound mushrooms

3 shallots, diced small

1 teaspoon olive oil

Salt and pepper to taste

For the Jus:

2 whole peppercorns

2 carrots, peeled and sliced

1/4 fennel bulb, cleaned and diced small

1 celery stick, diced small

3 to 4 cloves garlic, peeled and lightly crushed

2 large leeks, cleaned and diced small

4 shallots, peeled and sliced

5 basil leaves

10 tarragon leaves

1 branch thyme

2 teaspoons olive oil

1 cup Chardonnay wine

4 cups water

12 potatoes (approximately 5 inches long), peeled and washed

12 large leeks, cleaned and steamed for garnish (optional)

Prepare the Duxelle:

1 Cut the stems off the mushrooms. Reserve the stems. Peel and cut out the gills inside the mushrooms. Discard the gills.

2 Put the mushrooms in a food processor. Pulse the machine on and off until the mushrooms are coarsely chopped.

3 Heat the olive oil in a large sauté pan. Add the chopped mushrooms and diced shallots and cook over medium heat, stirring occasionally, until dry, about 10 minutes. Add salt and pepper to taste. Set aside.

Prepare the Jus:

1 Wrap the basil, tarragon, and thyme in a piece of cheesecloth and tie closed with cotton string.

2 Pour 2 teaspoons olive oil into a large sauté pan. Add the peppercorns, carrots, fennel, celery, garlic, shallots, and leeks to the olive oil. Cook over medium heat for 2 to 3 minutes, or until the vegetables soften slightly.

3 Add the Chardonnay wine and simmer until it has almost completely reduced. Add the water and cheesecloth-wrapped herbs and simmer for about 10 minutes.

4 Strain the jus through cheesecloth, reserving only the liquid. Place the liquid in a saucepan. Bring to a low boil and reduce for about 5 minutes to intensify the flavor. Add salt and pepper to taste. Set aside.

Prepare the Potatoes:

1 Fill a large pot two-thirds full of tap water, add salt (optional), and place over high heat to bring to a boil.
2 Cut each potato in half crosswise to form two approximately 2-inch long pieces. Then, using a 2-inch diameter cookie cutter, press down evenly to cut each segment into a cylinder that is 2 inches high and 2 inches across. Use a melon baller (see Figure 14-4) to scoop out a crater on one end of each cylinder.
3 Cook the potato cylinders in boiling water for 10 minutes or until tender when pierced with a thin-bladed knife. Drain and set aside.
4 Stuff each cylinder with the duxelle mixture.

Plate the Potatoes:

In warmed individual serving bowls, place 4 potato cylinders. If desired, add 2 leeks to each bowl for garnish and pour a little jus over the potatoes.

Nutrition at a glance (per serving): *total fat 3g; saturated fat 0.5g; protein 9g; dietary fiber 11g; carbohydrate 57g; cholesterol 0mg; sodium 70mg; vitamin A (% of Daily Value) 81; vitamin C (% of Daily Value) 102; folic acid (% of Daily Value) 46; % of calories from fat 9; % of calories from saturated fat 1; calories 294.*

***

Figure 14-4: A melon baller can scrape like a knife, but without the super-sharp edge.

Duxelle is a French term for a mixture of mushrooms, shallots, herbs, and butter (the preceding recipe uses the more healthful olive oil instead of butter) slowly cooked over low heat to form a paste. Chef Cueff removes the gills from the mushroom to eliminate their dark brown color, but if you don't mind it, you can skip this time-consuming step. In addition to stuffing, a duxelle can be used to flavor soups, sauces, and other mixtures.

Cinnamon-Roasted New Potatoes

Created by Michael Degenhart
Executive Chef, Restaurant Rue Cler
Denver, Colorado

Cinnamon and the complex Moroccan spice blend called *ras el hanout* are the secret to these unique potatoes. Chef Degenhart serves them with Zak's

Grilled Quail with Mustard and Herb Chutney (Chapter 7).

Tools: *Mixing bowl, roasting pan*

Preparation time: *10 minutes*

Cooking time: *40 minutes*

Yield: *4 servings*

1 pound small new potatoes, washed and halved

2 cinnamon sticks

1/4 cup kalamata olives

4 carrots, washed and cut into 1-inch pieces, halved

1 teaspoon ras el hanout

1/2 teaspoon salt

1/2 teaspoon pepper

2 teaspoons olive oil

1/2 teaspoon sugar

1 cup unsalted, fat-free chicken broth

Salt to taste

1. Preheat oven to 400 degrees.
2. Combine all ingredients in a mixing bowl and toss to coat potatoes.
3. Transfer mixture to a roasting pan and cover the pan with aluminum foil.
4. Bake for 40 minutes or until potatoes are tender.
5. Keep warm until ready to serve.

Nutrition at a glance (per serving): *total fat 4g; saturated fat 1g; protein 4g; dietary fiber 5g; carbohydrate 31g; cholesterol 0mg; sodium 318mg; vitamin A (% of Daily Value) 190; vitamin C (% of*

Daily Value) 30; % of calories from fat 22; % of calories from saturated fat 5; calories 167.

***

Meaning "head of the shop," *ras el hanout,* the Moroccan spice blend, can contain up to 50 ingredients. Ingredients can include ginger, anise, cinnamon, nutmeg, peppercorns, cloves, cardamom, turmeric, and mace. You can find ras el hanout in gourmet and specialty stores and some supermarkets.

Chapter 15

Desserts

In This Chapter

- Making delicious low-fat desserts
- Satisfying your sweet tooth without guilt

Recipes in This Chapter

- Phyllo-Crusted Berry Cobbler **(V)**
- Nutty Cran-Apple Crisp **(V)**
- Cranberry Macadamia Nut Biscotti **(V)**
- Peanut Butter Banana Cookies **(V)**
- Poached Pears with Orange Yogurt Sauce **(V)**
- Chilled Strawberry Soup with Champagne **(V)**
- Red Fruits Soup **(V)**
- Chilled Melon Soup with Anise Hyssop **(V)**
- Schaum Torte with Fruit Compote **(V)**
- Caramelized Peach Cake Roll
- Chocolate Meringue Mousse **(V)**
- Dark Fudge Brownies **(V)**

***

A Sweet Way with Fruit

Fruit is a natural for dessert. Served fresh in a compote it makes a delightful end to a meal. But fruit also makes wonderful cobblers, cookies, and many other fancier desserts.

Phyllo-Crusted Berry Cobbler

Created by Carrie Nahabedian
Executive Chef, Four Seasons Hotel, Los Angeles at Beverly Hills
Los Angeles, California

The flaky phyllo pastry crust of this cobbler makes a crispy cobbler that's juicy with the flavor of a combination of berries. It's packed with heart healthy vitamin C, too—one small serving provides more than half the recommended daily value.

Tools: *Ovenproof baking dish, about 6-x-9 inches*

Preparation time: *45 minutes to prepare, 15 minutes to cool before serving*

Cooking time: *30 minutes*

Yield: *4 servings*

2 pints berries (blackberries, raspberries, and blueberries)

2 packets artificial sweetener

1 tablespoon all-purpose flour

1 tablespoon lemon juice

1 tablespoon apple juice concentrate

4 sheets phyllo dough

1 tablespoon light margarine, melted
1 tablespoon granulated sugar

1 Preheat oven to 350 degrees.
2 Toss berries with artificial sweetener, flour, and lemon juice. Place in an adequately sized ovenproof dish about 6-x-9 inches.
3 Brush phyllo dough with melted margarine. Sprinkle with granulated sugar. Layer all 4 sheets of phyllo in this manner. Loosely crumple phyllo and place on top of berry mixture.
4 Bake until golden brown and berries begin to bubble, about 30 minutes.
5 Allow to cool for 15 minutes and then serve.

Nutrition at a glance (per serving): *total fat 3g; saturated fat 1g; protein 3g; dietary fiber 10g; carbohydrate 50g; cholesterol 0mg; sodium 117mg; vitamin C (% of Daily Value) 67; % of calories from fat 12; % of calories from saturated fat 4; calories 225.*

***

Some artificial sweeteners, especially ones made with aspartame, break down when exposed to high heat. A recipe like the one above is best made with a heat-stable artificial sweetener such as acesulfame-K or sucralose, which is the latest food science innovation in calorie and sugar-free sweetening. Look for artificial sweeteners in the baking aisle of your local supermarket.

Nutty Cran-Apple Crisp

Created by Amy Myrdal, M.S., R.D.
Senior Research Dietitian, Rippe Lifestyle Institute
Shrewsbury, Massachusetts

The nuttiness of this dish comes both from the pecans and the wheat germ in the topping, the two ingredients that also contribute significant amounts of vitamin E. Serve this dessert warm with a small spoonful of vanilla ice cream or frozen yogurt. Garnish with mint leaves, if available.

Tools: *8-x-8-x-2-inch baking pan*
Preparation time: *15 minutes*
Cooking time: *35 minutes*
Yield: *6 servings*

3 large (3 1/2-to 4-inch diameter) apples, peeled, cored, quartered and thinly sliced
1/3 cup sweetened dried cranberries
2 tablespoons crushed pineapple, canned in juice
1/4 teaspoon cinnamon
2 tablespoons brown sugar

1 tablespoon unsalted butter, melted
2 tablespoons all-purpose flour
4 tablespoons pecans, chopped
3/4 cup oatmeal
1/4 cup wheat germ
4 tablespoons pineapple juice (use juice from crushed pineapple)
Mint sprigs, for garnish (optional)

1 Peel, core, and slice apples and place in large mixing bowl. Add cranberries, crushed pineapple, and cinnamon and mix well. Spread apple mixture on bottom of 8-x-8-x-2-inch baking pan. Set aside.
2 In the same large mixing bowl, combine brown sugar, melted butter, flour, pecans, oatmeal, and wheat germ. Sprinkle this mixture on top of apple mixture.
3 Drizzle pineapple juice over top.
4 Bake in 350-degree oven for 35 minutes or until top is nicely browned and apples are soft. Allow to cool at least 10 minutes before cutting and serving.

***

You can substitute pears or peaches for the apples in this recipe, too.

Cranberry Macadamia Nut Biscotti

Created by Amy Myrdal, M.S., R.D.
Senior Research Dietitian, Rippe Lifestyle Institute
Shrewsbury, Massachusetts

Biscotti are twice-baked Italian cookies. Many biscotti recipes include added fat, but the fat in this recipe comes only from the egg yolk and macadamia nuts, which provide heart-healthy monounsaturated fat. Some Italians dip their biscotti in wine, whereas most Americans are more used to dipping in coffee or tea. Because these biscotti are very crunchy, dipping in your favorite warm beverage is recommended. Feel free to experiment with this recipe. You can use any type of dried fruit and nuts in this dough to create your own biscotti masterpiece.

Tools: *Parchment or wax paper*
Preparation time: *21/2* hours
Cooking time: *40 minutes*
Yield: *40 servings*
1 1/4 cups sugar
3 eggs
1 teaspoon vanilla extract
Zest of one lemon
1 cup dried cranberries
1 cup unsalted macadamia nuts, toasted and chopped
1 teaspoon baking powder
2 1/2 cups flour

1/8 teaspoon salt

1 Chop macadamia nuts, spread on baking sheet, and toast in 400-degree oven for 3 to 4 minutes or until golden brown.
2 In a large mixing bowl, combine the sugar, eggs, and vanilla. Mix together with a hand mixer or a wooden spoon until creamy. Stir in cranberries, lemon zest, and nuts.
3 In a small bowl, combine the flour, salt, and baking power, stirring to combine. Transfer to the mixing bowl with the wet ingredients and mix until all flour has been incorporated and a dough forms. Gather the dough into a ball.
4 On a lightly floured surface, divide the dough in half. Shape each half into a log, about 10 inches long by 3 inches wide. (The dough may be a bit sticky; you may need to use additional flour when handling the dough.)
5 Place each log on a baking sheet lined with parchment paper or wax paper. Bake logs in 350-degree oven for 25 minutes, until they are dry on top and firm to the touch. Remove from oven and let cool slightly. Reduce oven temperature to 275 degrees.
6 When the logs are still warm, cut each log into 20 slices. Each slice should be about 1/2 inch wide. Place biscotti slices on an unlined, ungreased baking sheet and bake in 275-degree oven for 20 minutes. Turn the slices over and bake for another 20 minutes or until dry and lightly browned.

7 Allow to cool before serving. Biscotti may be stored in an airtight container for up to 2 weeks or frozen for up to 6 months.

***Nutrition at a glance (per serving): total** fat 3g; saturated fat 0.5g; protein 2g; dietary fiber 0.7g; carbohydrate 15g; cholesterol 16mg; sodium 25mg; % of calories from fat 29; % of calories from saturated fat 5; calories 92.*

***

Peanut Butter Banana Cookies

Created by Amy Myrdal, M.S., R.D.
Senior Research Dietitian, Rippe Lifestyle Institute
Shrewsbury, Massachusetts

If you love the combination of peanut butter and bananas, you'll love these cookies. They're crisp on the outside and chewy on the inside, perfect for dipping in milk. Using fresh-ground peanut butter is preferable because no salt, sugar, or hydrogenated oils have been added to it. Many supermarkets provide machines that will grind peanuts for you and produce the fragrant freshly ground peanut butter. You can also buy "natural" peanut butter (the kind with the oil on top). If you buy the natural peanut butter, simply pour off the oil that rests on top. What remains is ground peanuts and usually a little added salt.

***Tools:** Electric mixer, nonstick baking sheet*

Preparation time: *35 minutes*
Cooking time: *12 minutes*
Yield: *36 2-inch cookies*

1 large ripe banana, sliced
1/3 cup peanut butter (freshly ground is preferable)
2 tablespoons full-fat stick margarine, room temperature
1/2 cup granulated sugar
1/2 cup light brown sugar
1 egg
1 1/4 cup all-purpose flour
3/4 teaspoon baking soda
1/4 teaspoon salt
1 tablespoon granulated sugar

1 Preheat the oven to 350 degrees.
2 In a medium mixing bowl, combine the sliced banana, peanut butter, and margarine. Mix until creamy using a handheld or standing mixer.
3 Add the sugars and egg and continue mixing until light and fluffy.
4 In a medium bowl, combine the flour, soda, and salt. Add the dry ingredients to the peanut butter/banana mixture and mix until well combined.
5 Drop by teaspoonfuls onto a nonstick baking sheet.
6 Press a fork into the remaining batter, then dip in sugar and press down lightly on top of each cookie twice to form a crisscross pattern. Be sure to dip the fork into sugar before pressing down each cookie.

7 Bake on the middle rack of the oven for 10 to 12 minutes or until golden brown.
8 Remove from baking sheet and cool on wire racks.

Nutrition at a glance (per serving): *total fat 2g; saturated fat less than 0.5g; protein 1g; dietary fiber 0g; carbohydrate 10g; cholesterol 6mg; sodium 54mg; % of calories from fat 30; % of calories from saturated fat 7; calories 61.*

***

Poached Pears with Orange Yogurt Sauce

Created by Dale R. Gussett, C.E.C.
Executive Chef, L'Antibes Restaurant
Columbus, Ohio

Pears have long been favorite dessert fruits because they come in hundreds of varieties and lend themselves to many different ways of preparation, such as this recipe for poaching. Pears are also one of the few fruits that continue to ripen after being picked. So, at the market, select firm unblemished pears and prepare them for this dish just as they ripen; they should be ripe but still firm, not soft, when you prepare them. You may also enjoy trying several different varieties of pear with this recipe.

Tools: *Large saucepan*

Preparation time: *30 minutes*
Cooking time: *About 25 minutes*
Yield: *6 servings*

For the Poached Pears:

4 cups orange Muscat wine
2 cups orange blossom honey
1 cinnamon stick
10 cardamom seeds
6 ripe pears peeled, halved, and cored

For the Orange Yogurt Sauce:

1 cup low-fat vanilla yogurt
1 orange
2 tablespoons Grand Marnier liqueur
1/2 cup chopped pistachios
6 sprigs of mint

Prepare the Pears:

1 In a large saucepan, combine wine, honey, cinnamon, and cardamom and simmer for 10 minutes.
2 Add the pears and poach until they are tender, about 12 minutes.
3 Place pan in an ice bath to cool pears and poaching liquid.

Prepare the Sauce:

1 Grate the zest off the orange and then juice the orange.
2 Whisk together the yogurt, orange juice, zest, and Grand Marnier.

Presentation:

1 Line 6 plates with yogurt sauce.
2 Drain pears on paper towels, and then place 2 pear halves on each plate.
3 Garnish with chopped pistachios and mint.

Nutrition at a glance (per serving): *total fat 6g; saturated fat 1g; protein 5g; dietary fiber 6g; carbohydrate 51g; cholesterol 2mg; sodium 110mg; vitamin C (% of Daily Value) 31; % of calories from fat 19; % of calories from saturated fat 3; calories 284.*

***

Cardamom is a tropical spice related to ginger that has a spicy-sweet flavor. It is used widely in Indian and Scandinavian cooking. Although it comes ground, get the seed if you can because the ground spice loses flavor quickly.

Muscat wine is made from Muscat grapes, which are grown throughout the world in temperate wine-growing regions. Unlike other wine grapes, Muscat grapes are also eaten fresh and made into raisins. Muscat wine has a characteristic sweet, musky flavor and fragrance.

The flavor of any honey comes from the nectar on which the bees feast. *Orange blossom honey* derives its delicate orange flavor from orange tree blossoms. Orange blossom honey can be found in many supermarkets and specialty foods stores.

Fruit Soups

If you've never tried a fruit soup for dessert, you are missing a treat. *Fruit soups* are a specialty of Scandinavian cuisine. Many varieties are wonderful hot or chilled and make great desserts (or starters). Co-author Amy Myrdal encourages you to try both these recipes, noting that her family "eats Icelandic fruit soup, similar to the Red Fruits Soup, every Christmas Eve. It includes dried fruit, canned Queen Anne cherries, orange rind, and large pearl tapioca. It's so delicious, especially with a splash of cream to cut the sweetness!" You'll find these soups equally delicious.

Chilled Strawberry Soup with Champagne

Created by Hans Bergmann
Executive Chef, Cacharel Restaurant
Arlington, Texas

When dinner calls for an elegant light finale, try this champagne soup. The presentation is as artistic as the flavor is sparkling.

Tools: *Blender*

Preparation time: *20 minutes to prepare, 4 hours to chill*

Cooking time: *1 minute*

Yield: *4 servings*

2 pints strawberries
8 mint leaves
4 mint sprigs for garnish
4 ounces (9 tablespoons) sugar
1/2 cup water
1 cup Champagne (or sparkling cider)
2 tablespoons powdered sugar

1 Boil water with sugar for 1 minute. Set aside to cool.
2 While water is boiling, wash strawberries and cut off stems.
3 Cut 4 strawberries into quarters and set aside for garnish.
4 Place remaining strawberries in a blender with the sugar and the syrup and blend well to get a smooth consistency.
5 Cut mint leaves into thin strips (julienne).
6 Pour soup into a bowl, add mint strips, and refrigerate for 4 hours until the soup is very cold and flavors are blended.
7 When the soup is ready to serve, pour in the Champagne and mix well.

8 Ladle soup into chilled individual serving bowls.
9 In each bowl, arrange four strawberry quarters to form a star and garnish with a mint sprig in the center of the star.
10 Dust with powdered sugar and serve.

Nutrition at a glance (per serving): *total fat 0.5g; saturated fat 0g; protein 1g; dietary fiber 3g; carbohydrate 43g; cholesterol 0mg; sodium 7mg; vitamin C (% of Daily Value) 136; % of calories from fat 2; % of calories from saturated fat 0; calories 208.*

***

Red Fruits Soup

Created by Alvaro Ojeda, Pastry Chef and Laura Maioglio, Owner
Barbetta Restaurant
New York, New York

This cold soup featuring a variety of fruit in a wine base offers a wonderfully complex flavor and a smooth, velvety texture that is rich without being heavy. Though appropriate for many menus, it is a particularly happy ending after a heavier or more elaborate entrée.

Tools: *Medium nonreactive (stainless steel) saucepan*

Preparation time: *10 minutes*

Cooking time: *5 minutes*

Yield: *4 servings*

6 ounces (1 1/4 cup) sour cherries, frozen, thawed

6 ounces (1 1/4 cup) raspberries, fresh or frozen, thawed

6 ounces (1 1/4 cup) strawberries, fresh

1 1/2 cups red wine

Juice from 1 lemon

2 tablespoons sugar

1 teaspoon arrowroot

3 tablespoons cold water

1 Place wine, lemon juice, and sugar in a saucepan and bring to a boil.
2 Add the fruits and bring to a low boil again.
3 In a small bowl, combine water and arrowroot; heat well in a saucepan until arrowroot is dissolved. Pour over fruit, stir, and cook for 1 minute longer.
4 Remove from heat and chill before serving.

Nutrition at a glance (per serving): *total fat 0g; saturated fat 0g; protein 1g; dietary fiber 4g; carbohydrate 22g; cholesterol 0g; sodium 6mg; vitamin C (% of Daily Value) 77; % of calories from fat 0; % of calories from saturated fat 0; calories 144.*

***

> On a cold winter's night, try serving the preceding soup warm.

Chilled Melon Soup with Anise Hyssop

Created by Frank McClelland
Executive Chef/Owner, L'Espalier
Boston, Massachusetts

This recipe is especially appealing for an elegant weekend brunch. It calls for anise hyssop, which is an herb within the mint family that has a bitter, licorice flavor. Fresh anise hyssop may be found at farmers' markets and specialty food shops.

Tools: *Blender, strainer*

Preparation time: *10 minutes to prepare, 30 minutes to chill*

Cooking time: *None*

Yield: *6 servings*

2 ripe cantaloupes
2 cups Champagne
1 tablespoon sugar
1 ounce anise hyssop leaves, for garnish
1 teaspoon salt

1 Peel and seed one of the cantaloupes. Cut into 1-inch chunks and place in blender with the Champagne and sugar. Blend for 1 minute. Strain; chill for 30 minutes.

2 Cut the second melon in half and seed.

3 Take a spoon and shave out the meat of the melon in thin ribbons and place in a chilled bowl. Refrigerate until ready to serve.
4 Ladle the blended chilled soup over the melon ribbons.
5 Wash anise hyssop leaves, cut into thin slices, and sprinkle on soup for garnish.

Nutrition at a glance (per serving): *total fat 0g; saturated fat 0g; protein 2g; dietary fiber 2g; carbohydrate 19g; cholesterol 0mg; sodium 404mg; vitamin A (% of Daily Value) 119; vitamin C (% of Daily Value) 129; % of calories from fat 0; % of calories from saturated fat 0; calories 128.*

***

If you're unable to find anise hyssop, you may wish to try a different fresh mint. A lemon mint would give the recipe a different flavor—less distinctive perhaps—but still interesting and refreshing.

Cakes

For many people *cake* means a rich layer cake covered in icing. These are great for special occasions but are usually so loaded with calories and fat that you don't want to eat them every week. Here are two cake recipes that will give you a tasty opportunity to sample the diversity of cake.

Schaum Torte with Fruit Compote

Created by RoxSand Suarez
Chef/Owner, RoxSand
Phoenix, Arizona

A *torte* is traditionally a cake that uses very little flour and that is composed of many thin layers. Chef Suarez has created a beautifully simple presentation of this classic Austrian torte. The cake is an almond meringue presented in one simple layer and paired with fresh fruit. In addition to monounsaturated fats, almonds offer fiber, calcium, folic acid, and other nutrients.

Tools: *Food processor or electric mixer, baking sheet*

Preparation time: *15 minutes to make, 90 minutes to bake, overnight to dry*

Cooking time: *1 hour, 30 minutes*

Yield: *8 servings*

For the torte:

1 cup egg whites (this will require at least 8 large eggs)

2 cups sugar

1 cup ground almonds

For the fruit compote:

1 pint fresh strawberries

3 fresh peaches or nectarines

2 kiwi fruit

1 cup blueberries

1/4 cup orange juice or pineapple juice

Prepare the torte:

1 Grind almonds in a food processor.

2 Toast the ground almonds on a baking sheet in a 250-degree oven until lightly browned. This can also be done in a large skillet over medium heat until lightly browned and fragrant.

3 Using a standing mixer, a food processor fitted with a whisk, or a handheld electric mixer, whip egg whites until almost stiff.

4 While continuing to whip, slowly add the sugar until whites are shiny and stiff.

5 Fold the toasted almonds into the egg whites and pour mixture into an 8-or 9-inch round nonstick baking pan.

6 Bake at 250 degrees for 1 1/2 hours in the oven. Set aside to dry overnight.

7 Serve with fresh fruit compote.

Prepare the fruit compote:

1 Wash the strawberries and remove the green stems. Cut in half lengthwise.
2 Peel peaches or nectarines, cut in half and remove stones (pits); slice lengthwise, then toss in small bowl with orange juice or pineapple juice to prevent discoloration.
3 Peel and slice kiwi fruit.
4 Wash blueberries.
5 Combine all fruit in a glass, plastic or stainless steel bowl and chill in refrigerator until ready to serve.
6 To serve, remove the torte from the baking pan and with a sharp chef's knife, cut into 8 pieces. Spoon fruit compote over the top of each piece of torte and serve.

Nutrition at a glance (per serving): *total fat 7g; saturated fat 1g; protein 6g; dietary fiber 4g; carbohydrate 65g; cholesterol 0mg; sodium 54mg; vitamin C (% of Daily Value) 78; vitamin E (% of Daily Value) 20; % of calories from fat 19; % of calories from saturated fat 3; calories 330.*

Any number of fresh fruit compotes are possible; the recipe just gives you a sample. You could include pineapple and orange sections in the compote to give it a different flavor. Use whatever fruit is in season. Grapes, raspberries, blackberries, apricots, bananas, melons, and mangos are just a few of the possibilities.

***

Caramelized Peach Cake Roll

Created by Amy Myrdal, M.S., R.D.
Senior Research Dietitian, Rippe Lifestyle Institute
Shrewsbury, Massachusetts'

This recipe is based on a traditional jelly roll recipe, but instead of jelly, caramelized peaches are used for the filling. If fresh peaches aren't available, you can use canned peaches in light syrup, but fresh peaches are preferable. The cognac can be replaced with plain brandy, peach brandy, or apple brandy. Or the cognac can be omitted.

Tools: *10-x-15-x-1-inch jelly roll pan, parchment paper*

Preparation time: *1 hour*
Cooking time: *30 minutes*
Yield: *10 servings*

For the Cake:

4 large eggs, separated
1 cup granulated sugar
1/4 cup fresh orange juice
1 teaspoon vanilla extract
Zest of 1 orange
1 cup flour, sifted
1 1/4 teaspoon baking powder
Powdered sugar

For the Caramelized Peach Filling:

1 teaspoon margarine
5 medium ripe peaches, peeled and sliced
1/4 cup brown sugar (light or dark)
2 tablespoons cognac

Garnishes:

20 tablespoons low-fat non-dairy whipped topping
2 1/2 cups fresh raspberries or strawberries
10 sprigs of fresh mint

Prepare the Filling:

1 In a large frying pan or skillet, melt the margarine over medium heat. Add the peaches and brown sugar and cook for 8 to 10 minutes, gently stirring occasionally.
2 When the peaches have released their juice and the sauce in the pan has caramelized and thickened, remove the pan from the burner and add the cognac. Return the pan to the heat and cook for another 2 to 3 minutes to allow the alcohol to

burn off. You'll be able to smell the alcohol in the air above the pan.

3 Remove from the heat; transfer to a glass or plastic bowl, and place in the refrigerator to cool.
4 When cool, transfer to a blender or food processor to puree.
5 Set aside the pureed peach mixture until you're ready to fill the cake.

Prepare the Cake:

1 Preheat oven to 350 degrees.
2 Line the bottom and sides of the jelly roll pan with parchment paper and spray with nonstick cooking spray.
3 In a medium mixing bowl, beat the egg whites until stiff and add the sugar. Continue beating until the mixture is glossy.
4 In another medium mixing bowl, beat egg yolks, orange juice, and vanilla.
5 Add the egg yolk mixture to the egg white mixture. Use a spoon or rubber scraper to gently combine the two mixtures. Add the orange zest and gently stir again.
6 In a small bowl combine the flour and baking powder stirring well to evenly distribute baking powder. Then add the flour and baking powder all at once and fold in gently.
7 Pour batter onto baking pan and spread to evenly distribute batter around the pan.
8 Bake for 20 minutes or until lightly browned and set in the center.

9 Cool for 2 to 3 minutes and then tip over onto a large sheet of parchment paper that has been sprinkled with powdered sugar. While the cake is still warm, peel off the top layer of parchment paper.

10 Evenly spread the peach filling over the surface of the cake, then, using both hands, carefully roll the cake lengthwise into a tight log.

1 1 Remove the parchment paper and transfer the cake to a serving platter. Slice to serve immediately or wrap in plastic wrap and store in the refrigerator until ready to serve.

12 Cut the roll into 10 slices. Top each slice with 1/4 cup fresh berries, 2 tablespoons of whipped topping, and a sprig of mint. Or serve plain.

Nutrition at a glance (per serving), including 2 tablespoons whipped topping and *1/4 cup fresh berries per serving: total fat 4g; saturated fat 1.7g; protein 5g; dietary fiber 3g; carbohydrate 48g; cholesterol 85mg; sodium 99mg; vitamin C (% of Daily Value) 22; % of calories from fat 14; % of calories from saturated fat 6; calories 248.*

***

Chocolate Treats

When only chocolate will do for dessert, indulge in either the Chocolate Mousse or the Brownies. Your yen for chocolate will be satisfied, and your conscience will rejoice in the fact the treats are low-fat.

Chocolate Meringue Mousse

Created by Angela Kirkpatrick, R.D.
Research Dietitian, Rippe Lifestyle Institute
Shrewsbury, Massachusetts

Did you know that *mousse* means "foam" or "froth"? This dessert is an airy chocolate confection that really melts in your mouth. The meringue for this mousse is made by cooking sugar and water to a softball stage and combining it with egg whites. Don't be concerned about the use of egg whites; the hot sugar-water mixture adequately yet delicately cooks the egg whites. The mousse will keep for a few days in the refrigerator, but cover tightly with plastic wrap so that it doesn't pick up flavors of other foods.

Tools: *Electric mixer*

Preparation time: *3 to 24 hours (chilling time)*

Cooking time: *10 minutes*

Yield: *4 servings*

For the Meringue:

3 egg whites
1/2 cup granulated sugar
3 tablespoons water

For the Chocolate Mousse:

1/3 cup cocoa powder
1/2 cup strong, espresso-strength coffee
1 tablespoon granulated gelatin (equivalent to 1 package)

For Garnish:

8 to 12 fresh raspberries
4 sprigs of fresh mint

Prepare the Meringue:

1 Place the egg whites in the mixing bowl of a standing mixer with a whisk attachment. This can also be done by placing egg whites in a large bowl and whipping with a handheld mixer.

2 Place the sugar and water in a small stainless steel saucepan and gently combine. Cover the pan, and without stirring, bring mixture to a boil. Then remove the pan lid and cook the mixture over medium to high heat for 3 to 3 1/2 minutes, or until it registers 235 to 240 degrees (softball stage) on a candy thermometer and becomes a syrup. To test if the syrup has reached soft ball stage without a thermometer, drop a teaspoonful of syrup into a small bowl of ice water. If it forms a soft ball, it has reached the correct temperature.

3 While the sugar mixture cooks, beat the egg whites at medium to high. When they are firm and glossy, but not grainy, pour the syrup from the pan in a steady thin, thread-like stream

into the middle of the bowl (avoiding the whisk). Continue beating the whites for about 2 minutes longer at medium to high speed. The mixture should be glossy and elastic. Set it aside to cool to room temperature.

Prepare the Chocolate Mousse:

1 In a small saucepan over medium heat combine the coffee, cocoa powder, and gelatin. Warm just until the gelatin dissolves, 1 to 2 minutes. Cool for 1 minute, then fold into the meringue.

2 Pour the mousse into a serving bowl (you should have about 2 1/2 cups). Cover the bowl with plastic wrap and refrigerate it for at least three hours or overnight.

3 To serve the mousse, scoop it into individual bowls. Garnish with a raspberry or two and a sprig of fresh mint.

Nutrition at a glance (per serving): *total fat 2g; saturated fat 0g; protein 5g; dietary fiber 0g; carbohydrate 28g; cholesterol 0mg; sodium 52mg; % of calories from fat 13; % of calories from saturated fat 0; calories 144.*

***

Dark Fudge Brownies

Created by Amy Myrdal, M.S., R.D.
Senior Research Dietitian, Rippe Lifestyle Institute

Shrewsbury, Massachusetts

The secret to these rich and decadent yet low-fat brownies is black beans. Wait, wait, wait! Before you flip the page, give these brownies a chance. You'll be surprised and delighted by the rich chocolate flavor and fudge-like texture of these good-for-you brownies.

Tools: *Food processor*

Preparation time: *45 minutes*

Cooking time: *40 minutes*

Yield: *24 servings*

1 15-ounce can black beans, unseasoned, rinsed well, and drained

1 cup pureed prunes (or prune filling or prune-based oil substitute)

6 egg whites

3/4 cup unsweetened cocoa powder

3 tablespoons canola oil

1 tablespoon stick margarine

1 1/2 cups granulated sugar

1/4 cup all-purpose flour

1 teaspoon pure vanilla extract

1/2 cup walnuts, chopped

Nonstick cooking spray

1 Preheat oven to 350 degrees. Coat 9-x-13-inch baking pan with cooking spray.

2 Blend drained beans and pureed prunes in a food processor until very smooth. Add the egg whites, blend again, and set aside. If you don't have a

food processor, use a blender to blend beans, prunes, and egg whites until very smooth.

3 Melt margarine in a small saucepan on the stove or in the microwave. Stir in cocoa and canola oil until well blended.
4 Combine bean mixture, sugar, flour, and egg whites in a mixing bowl and stir until well combined. Add the cocoa mixture and stir again.
5 Pour mixture into the baking pan and sprinkle the top with walnuts.
6 Bake for 35 to 40 minutes. Cool completely before cutting into 24 squares.
7 Store brownies in an airtight container in the refrigerator for up to 1 week.

Nutrition at a glance (per serving): *total fat 4g; saturated fat 0.5g; protein 4g; dietary fiber 3g; carbohydrate 24g; cholesterol 0mg; sodium 21mg; % of calories from fat 28; % of calories from saturated fat 4; calories 137.*

***

Part IV

The Part of Tens

Image 4.1

In this part...

What would a *For Dummies* book be without The Part of Tens? In this part, you'll find chapters providing great information in a quick-and-easy, waste-no-time format. We cover everything from the tools you need when you're cooking heart-healthy to how to eat well when you're on the road. If you have children or grandchildren, you'll take interest in the chapter we devote to introducing heart-healthy eating habits to kids. Don't have much time? Check out one of the chapters in this part for information to go.

Chapter 16

Ten Tips for Eating on the Road and on the Run

In This Chapter

- Getting a heart-healthy breakfast on the go
- Finding a heart-healthy lunch and dinner anywhere
- Traveling by car or plane and eating healthy along the way

Go, go, go! Eating on the run and on the road have become a part of daily life for many of us. We juggle family, work, school, business travel, community activities, and a thousand other duties. Do you associate eating on the go with junk food and fast food? It doesn't have to be that way. These ten tips can help you continue your heart-healthy eating habits when you leave your kitchen behind.

Brown-Bag Your Breakfast

If you can eat breakfast at home, you're probably better off. Starting your day with a bowl of cereal with low-fat milk and fresh fruit or fruit juice is less expensive and more nutritious than grabbing on the go. However, bagels, cereal bars, yogurt cups, and fresh fruit travel well. So if you have to dash before you dine in the morning, grab a few of these travel buddies to keep you company during the morning commute. Just don't try to eat the yogurt cup while you drive!

Choose Healthier Fast-Food Breakfast Items

When you find your car pulling into the drive-thru at dawn, you can make healthy food choices. I admit it's not easy, but you do have a few good options:

- **Bagel with peanut butter or jelly.** Skip the cream cheese (loaded with saturated fat). If you can get low-fat cream cheese, use it sparingly.
- **English muffin sandwiches without the sausage or cheese.** An egg is okay on the sandwich, if you skip the sausage and cheese, which are full of sodium and saturated fat.
- **Low-fat muffins.** Be aware that large, low-fat muffins usually contain as many calories as their full-fat counterparts.

- **Cereal with 1 percent or skim milk.**

Lighten Your Coffee with Skim Milk

Are you among the millions who fuel their days with coffee? When you drink it black, with no cream or sugar, coffee is a fat-free, almost calorie-free pick-me-up. But if you add milk, cream, sugar, or flavor syrups, the calories and fat grams add up quickly. Besides that, if you let the barrista at your local coffee shop add the extras, you may have a hard time telling how much you're getting. For example, at one popular New England doughnut shop chain, a small (10-ounce) coffee with light cream and sugar contains *at least* 110 calories and 5 grams of fat, if it's prepared exactly as directed by the company procedure manual. So, ask for your coffee—plain or fancy—with *skim milk.*

Beat a Snack Attack by Planning Ahead

There you are at your desk, attacking your work like the next Employee of the Year, when suddenly a snack attack hits you. Your concentration staggers, your stomach growls, your feet propel you down the hall to the vending machine. To avoid the damage 75 cents can do, either pack a snack each day or keep a few healthful snacks at work. Dried fruit, pretzels, whole grain crackers, and cereal keep well in an office drawer, and you can store low-fat or nonfat yogurt in an office refrigerator. Many offices now also have kitchens or break rooms. Consider going together with your coworkers to stock the common area with healthy snacks. Some companies will even contribute fruit and healthy snacks as a perk.

Go Grilled or Do the Deli for Lunch

When you can't pack your lunch, pick a place to dine where you can choose a more healthful lunch. Many fast-food and service restaurants offer baked, broiled, and grilled items; choose these over deep-fat-fried foods. Also avoid "super-sizing" your meal. Leave the extra calories and fat behind the counter. At any deli, you can build a healthy sandwich starting by choosing a lean sandwich filling (no egg, tuna, or chicken salad) and whole grain bread. Then emphasize veggie fillings—lettuce, tomato, onion, peppers—and dress with mustard, ketchup, vinegar, and only a little low-fat dressing or a tiny bit of oil. If the deli serves sandwiches as big as a small country, share with a friend. (A 6-inch sub with the standard 2 ounces of lean meat is okay.)

Use Convenient Whole Foods for Brown-Bag Lunches

Sometimes a whole food (yeah!) and processed convenience (boo!) can join forces to help you pack lunch creatively and healthfully (hooray!). Here are several examples.

Pack frozen vegetables in a plastic container. Then, for lunch, heat the container in a microwave on high for about 2 minutes. How's that for a change from carrot sticks or the insanely popular baby carrots?

Use single-serving dehydrated bean soups, such as those from Nile Valley and Fantastic Foods. Add boiling water, give it two stirs, and 4 minutes later, you've got a very low-fat, fiber-filled lunch. Yes, these soups do contain a lot of sodium, but their fiber and minimal fat content make them smart choices.

Take advantage of leftovers (your own convenience food) to create great lunches. A leftover grilled chicken breast, for example, can turn into a chicken fajita when sliced and placed in a warm flour tortilla with peppers, onions, reduced-fat cheese, and salsa. Leftover chili morphs into a taco salad with baked tortilla chips, lettuce, and tomatoes, with salsa for dressing.

Pick Up a Healthy Pizza for Dinner

After battling traffic home, making dinner sounds like too much of a hassle. So what do you do? Call for pizza. Pizza is the most popular delivery food in the United States. Nutritionally, pizza can be a fabulous choice because it can cover three to four food groups in one meal. The crust counts for grain-based food; the sauce count for vegetables; and cheese counts for dairy. Add some lean meat and additional vegetables and you've got a complete meal. However, pizza can also be a healthy eater's worst nightmare, especially if you order a deep-dish pie loaded with meat and cheese. So stick with the thin crust and lots of vegetable toppings. For meat toppings, choose lean meats such as Canadian bacon, ham, or 90 to 95 percent lean ground beef instead of high-fat meat toppings like pepperoni or sausage.

Choose a Restaurant That Works for Your Goals

Dining out should always be a pleasure. Whether you are at home or on the road, always consider all of your dining options. In my experience, the most interesting menus and the widest variety of heart-healthy options are usually available at independent restaurants operating under the guiding influence of chefs such as those featured in this book. You don't have to choose expensive, upscale eateries, either. I've had satisfying, healthful, and memorable meals in very modest restaurants—some ethnic and some standard American. What makes these restaurants different from most chains? Usually fresher food prepared with more care and attention by the chef. Also, try to pick a menu or cuisine that has more choices for eating heart-healthy. For example, selecting a low-fat, heart-healthy meal is usually much easier at a Japanese restaurant that has lots of low-fat sushi and noodle dishes than at a fried seafood emporium or a barbecued rib shack.

Pack a Flight Survival Kit When You Fly

The basic rule of airline travel is "Expect the unexpected." If you always carry a simple survival kit, you'll be ready to face every adversity, from stuffy air-plane cabins, to flights with no meal service, to delayed or canceled flights. Pack the following three items in your carry-on bag. Because tests show that the air on planes can be drier than the Sahara desert, drinking at least 8 fluid ounces of water every hour before and during a flight may help alleviate the dehydration that is an inevitable part of flying. Because you may be unable to get bottled water on the plane, it's smart to pack a few bottles of your own. Dried fruit and nuts make the perfect "emergency rations" for flying, because fruits provide fat-free, high-carbohydrate energy and nuts provide protein, carbohydrates, and some healthful monounsaturated fat.

Stuff a Cooler with Healthy Snacks for a Road Trip

If a long-distance car trip is in the works for you and your family, packing healthful foods and drinks in a cooler is a smart trick for making a long ride pleasant, enjoyable, and endurable for everyone. Pack that cooler with raw vegetables (pepper strips, baby carrots, jicama sticks, cucumber sticks, broccoli florets), fresh fruit (apples, melon balls, grapes, apricots, orange sections, pears), yogurt, fat-free or low-fat milk, 100 percent juice boxes, bottled water (at least 1 bottle per person), and string cheese. To conveniently keep the cooler safely cold, use ice packs and frozen juice boxes (kids love slushy, half thawed juice).

For crunchy snacks that don't need refrigeration, try rice cakes, low-fat cereal or granola bars, dry cereal, pretzels, and air-popped popcorn packed in plastic bags.

Most of the eating we tend to do during a car trip is motivated by boredom, not hunger. To satisfy the desire to "do something," pack snacks that provide crunch and munch satisfaction while also providing essential nutrients. Also, bring along books, tapes, CDs, and games to stave off boredom and focus your mind on something other than food.

Chapter 17

Ten Simple Steps to Make Your Diet Healthier

In This Chapter
- Choosing foods with more nutrient value
- Snacking the heart-healthy way

A healthy diet is your best defense against seven of the top ten leading causes of death in the United States, including heart disease, the nation's number one killer. These ten simple steps help you prevent or control heart disease while also helping to ward off other diet-related diseases such as cancer and osteoporosis.

Start Your Day with Breakfast

Eating breakfast is one of the most important eating habits you can adopt. But too often patients tell me they don't have time for breakfast. Believe me, I understand lack of time. But making and eating a simple, nutritious breakfast does not take much time. Pouring a bowl of cereal, chopping up a banana, and topping it all off with low-fat milk takes less than a minute. Eating it takes less than five minutes. Just six minutes is a small price for such a big payoff.

Don't believe me? Check out the following proven benefits of eating breakfast:

• **People who eat breakfast (particularly if it includes a fortified cereal) are more likely to get more essential vitamins and minerals in their diets compared to people who never or rarely eat breakfast.**

• **Some studies have shown an association between breakfast consumption and lower cholesterol levels.**

• **Breakfast enhances your performance at work, school, or whatever activities fill your day.** Breakfast gives your brain and body the quick fuel they need after an 8 to 12 hour overnight fast. If your brain and body have to wait for energy, you're left with a sluggish body and sluggish thoughts. So commit to breakfast and reap the rewards of better performance.

• **Eating breakfast can help you lose weight.** Yes, that's right. The body's *metabolic rate* (the rate at which it burns calories) slows down over night and doesn't speed up again until some food is consumed. If you skip breakfast, your metabolic rate stays slower for a longer period of time.

Eat at Least Five Servings of Fruits and Vegetables Every Day

Eating at least five servings of fruits and vegetables helps you get many of the essential vitamins and minerals you need. In addition, fruits and vegetables contain thousands of beneficial phytochemicals, non-essential nutrients that help prevent many diseases including heart disease. In many cases, a fruit or vegetable is the only source of a certain vitamin or mineral. Take vitamin K, for example, a vitamin necessary for normal blood clotting. The best food sources of vitamin K are green leafy vegetables like kale, spinach, broccoli, and some types of lettuce. People who eat few vegetables could go days or weeks without getting enough vitamin K. The heart-healthy recipes in this book feature a wealth of very tasty and innovative ways to use fruits and vegetables in entrées, side dishes, desserts, and more.

Eat More Whole-Grain Foods

In July 1999, based on reams of scientific proof, the U.S. Food and Drug Administration (FDA) approved the following health claim: "Diets rich in whole-grain foods and other plant foods and low in total fat, saturated fat, and cholesterol may help reduce the risk of heart disease and certain cancers."

Of the 6 to 11 servings of grain foods recommended for each day, try to get *at least* three of your grain servings from whole-grain foods. The most significant difference between whole-grain foods and refined-grain foods is that whole-grain foods contain the whole seed kernel, including the fiber-rich outer bran and the nutrient-rich germ. Refined grain foods usually contain only the heart of the kernel, and therefore often contain less fiber and fewer nutrients than whole grain foods. Government regulations require replacing some of the nutrients (such as iron and the B-vitamins thiamin, niacin, and riboflavin) lost in milling or processing. This process is called *enrichment.* But other essential nutrients such as vitamin E and fiber don't have to be added back.

Eat Fish at Least Two to Three Times Each Week

Greenland Eskimos eat a very high-fat diet but have a very low rate of heart disease. What's their secret? It may be their incredibly high intake of fish.

Researchers have been investigating the health benefits of fish for many years and have uncovered some powerful reasons to regularly include fish in your diet.

Cold water fish that grow in natural environments (rather than fish farms) contain high concentrations of polyunsaturated omega-3 fatty acids. Research shows these polyunsaturated fatty acids help reduce cholesterol levels, blood pressure, and the stickiness of platelets, which reduces the likelihood of blood clots that could lead to a heart attack or stroke.

Eat Nuts, Seeds, and Legumes at Least Five Times Each Week

Nuts, seeds, and legumes are fiber-rich, nutrient-rich foods that, when included as part of an overall healthful diet, can help reduce blood pressure (a major risk factor for heart disease), stroke, and kidney disease. Regularly including nuts, seeds, and legumes in your diet may also help you lower your cholesterol because of their high fiber and monounsaturated and polyunsaturated fat content.

Nuts and seeds you can identify. But just what is a *legume?* The term legume refers to any type of plant whose seed pod splits along both sides when ripe. Think *beans* and *peas:* kidney beans, lima beans, soybeans, chick peas, green peas, field peas (all sorts), lentils, and so on. (Even the peanut is technically a legume, but because of its high fat content, treat it like a nut.)

Choose Intensely Colored Fruits and Vegetables

When it comes to fruits and vegetables, bright color equals big benefits. That's because in many fruits and vegetables phytochemical content and color are closely associated. Phytochemicals, as I discuss in Chapter 2, are compounds produced by plants that help protect the plants from fungi, bacteria, insects, and viruses and may also help protect humans from a number of diseases, including heart disease.

The color of the skin or flesh of a fruit or vegetable often gives a strong indication of the *type* of phytochemicals it contains. Plus, the richer the color, the *more* nutrients and phytochemicals it has. For example, beta-carotene, a powerful antioxidant, gives carrots their characteristic orange color. Apricots, papayas, sweet potatoes, mangoes, pumpkins, and squash are rich in beta-carotene as well. So, after you've mastered getting at least five servings of fruits and vegetables each day, go for those with the most intense color. For example, instead of iceberg lettuce choose red leaf. Instead of a white potato choose a sweet potato. Instead of zucchini squash go for butternut squash.

Eat Fortified Breakfast Cereals

Of all the recommendations in this chapter, this is by far the simplest. All you have to do is make sure you're buying breakfast cereals with *added* vitamins and minerals. I call this "getting more nutrition bang for your buck." National surveys show that the average adult American does not meet his or her daily need for many essential vitamins and minerals. Some fortified cereals contain as much as 50 percent or even 100 percent of the recommended daily value of various important vitamins and minerals. Cereals such as *Total* and *Product 19,* for example, contain 100 percent of the recommended daily allowance for at least ten essential vitamins and minerals. Eating a super-fortified cereal like these is similar to taking a multivitamin/mineral supplement. Keep in mind, however, that many of the vitamins and minerals added to cereals are sprayed onto the cereal after it has baked and can easily wash off in milk. So do as your mother told you and drink all your milk! (You have my permission to drink straight from the bowl.)

Snack on Nutrient-Rich Foods

When I ask patients about their favorite snack foods, many sheepishly admit, "Chips, ice cream, and cookies," and a few reply proudly, "pretzels and rice cakes." Whether high-fat or nonfat, *none* of these popular snack foods is rich in important nutrients such as calcium, fiber, antioxidants, or other essential nutrients. I encourage you to choose snacks that provide more than just "empty calories" from fat, sugar, and refined grains. Here are a few suggestions: fresh fruit and dried fruit, yogurt, ready-to-eat cereals, and air-popped popcorn.

Drink Tea

Substitute tea for coffee. It's not that coffee is harmful to your heart, but tea may offer some specific heart-healthy benefits. Black, green, and oolong teas—but not herbal teas—contain a number of powerful antioxidant compounds, called *flavonoids,* which may help reduce the risk of heart disease and some cancers. Studies indicate that these natural antioxidant compounds reduce the risk of heart disease and stroke by improving the health of the body's circulatory system and by reducing the risk of a blood clot.

Emerging research shows the flavonoids in tea may also help inhibit blood platelets from sticking together, thereby providing protection against heart attack or stroke caused by blocked arteries. However, regularly drinking tea does not appear to decrease blood pressure or blood cholesterol levels.

Choose Whole Foods

Whole foods are those that are in their natural state rather than processed. Whole foods, in general, often offer more nutrients than processed foods do. Although some food processing techniques such as fortification *add* nutrients, most techniques *deplete* nutrients. For example, a 4-ounce apple contains 3 grams of dietary fiber whereas 4 ounces of applesauce contains only 1 gram of fiber (because the applesauce is missing the very healthy apple peel). Just as important for heart health, whole foods don't contain hydrogenated fat (trans fatty acids), added sodium, and some other substances common in processed foods that you want to limit in a heart-healthy way of eating. ***Remember:*** Reducing trans-fat intake is just as important as reducing saturated fat intake if you want to reduce your cholesterol level.

Chapter 18

Ten Easy Recipe Modifications for a Heart-Healthy Diet

In This Chapter

- Cutting fat without cutting taste
- Reducing your cholesterol with simple recipe changes

Recipes in This Chapter

- Low-Fat Creamy White Sauce **(V)**

***

You may be surprised to discover that becoming a healthy-heart cook who plans and prepares meals that work for your health and not against it usually doesn't require radical changes. I guarantee that if you put these ten easy—and tasty—recipe modifications and cooking techniques to work in your kitchen, you will take a big step toward your goals of limiting saturated fat and total overall fat and of getting more healthful nutrients in what you eat.

Use Cooking Spray instead of Oil

Using cooking sprays in place of oil can help you significantly reduce your total fat intake. In fact, using cooking spray to coat the pan when you sauté can decrease your total oil use by 15 times. That's a great reason to keep in mind the following sautéing tips:

- **Experiment with different prepared cooking sprays to see which works best for you.** Major brands such as Pam produce sprays in several varieties, including olive oil, butter flavor, or regular vegetable oil. Try several until you find one or two you like.
- **If you prefer the all-natural approach (and no aerosol sprays), add your own olive oil or other vegetable oil to a pump oil sprayer.** You can find these sprayers, such as one called Misto, at kitchen supply stores, home goods stores, and some discount department stores. You can also pour oil directly onto a paper towel, and then, before placing the pan on a heat source, rub the pan with the paper towel to coat it slightly as an alternative.

• **If the pan becomes too hot or food starts sticking as you cook, add a little liquid to the pan.** Be sure to just add a little, though, because too much liquid can change the texture of the food. Depending on the dish you're making, try wines, vinegars, juices, canned low-sodium stock, or just water for this purpose.

Use Egg Whites instead of Whole Eggs

In baked goodies such as cakes, quick breads, cookies, brownies, and muffins, and in other dishes such as vegetable casseroles, you can substitute 2 egg whites for 1 whole egg with very little difference in texture. What you gain by using this simple substitution is less cholesterol and fat in the finished product—about 215 fewer milligrams of cholesterol and 5 fewer grams of fat per egg.

If you're preparing a dish in which the egg stars—an omelet or scrambled eggs, for example—you can still substitute 2 egg whites for 1 whole egg.

You may also want to try one of the very good egg substitutes on the market. Egg substitutes aren't full of chemicals either—99 percent of the substitute comes from real eggs.

Use Oil instead of Butter or Margarine

You can reduce the amount of saturated fat and cholesterol in many muffins, quick breads, brownies, and bar cookies by replacing solid fats, including butter, margarine, and shortening, with a liquid vegetable oil, such as canola oil, safflower oil, or peanut oil. (***Note:*** This substitution does not work for pastries like pie crusts.) The general guideline is to use about 75 percent of the oil that the recipe calls for in solid fat. The reason for using less oil than solid fat is because the solid fats contain some water whereas the oil is all fat. To make the conversion, simply multiply the original amount times 0.75. Many times, the math conversions are easier to make if you switch to tablespoons:

- If a recipe calls for 1 cup solid fat (16 tablespoons), use 3/4 cup oil (12 tablespoons).
- If a recipe calls for 3/4 cup solid fat (12 tablespoons), use 9 tablespoons oil (which is equal to 1/2 cup+1 tablespoon oil).
- If a recipe calls for 1/2 cup solid fat (8 tablespoons), use 6 tablespoons oil.

Use Applesauce or Other Fruit Purees instead of Oil or Solid Fats

One way to reduce all types of fat, including oil, when you're baking brownies, muffins, or other baked goods is to replace the fat with a fruit puree or yogurt.

If the recipe calls for a certain amount of butter, margarine, or shortening substitute half as much applesauce, prune puree or other fruit puree, or nonfat plain yogurt. For example, instead of 1 cup of butter or margarine in muffins, you would use 1/2 cup of prune puree or applesauce.

If the recipe calls for oil, substituting an equal amount of the fruit puree or yogurt usually works. Specific recipes may require a little experimentation to get just the right balance. For instance, to keep the recipe from being too moist and chewy you may need to cut back on the puree a tablespoon or two, or add an extra egg white.

To see for yourself if these modifications and substitutions really result in great tasting baked goods, try the Peanut Butter Banana Cookies recipe (see Chapter 15), which uses mashed banana in place of butter. Also try the Dark Fudge Brownies recipe (see Chapter 15), which uses prune puree and pureed black beans in place of butter.

Use Lower-Fat, Homemade Dressings instead of Higher-Fat, Store-Bought Ones

Salads loaded with colorful fresh vegetables taste great and offer lots of benefits for your heart and waistline—until you drench them with a high-fat dressing. Of course, you can find many varieties of bottled low-fat dressings on the market, but 90 percent of them don't come close to achieving the taste and style you want. So here are some easy low-fat modifications to dress your salads with zest:

- **Make your own low-fat "house" vinaigrette.** Mix 1 part olive oil (a heart-healthy monounsaturated fat) with 3 to 4 parts balsamic vinegar. If you like, add a touch of Dijon or dry mustard, onion and/or garlic powder, and herbs for seasoning. If you're busy throughout the week (and who isn't?), mix about a week's supply in a cruet or covered container and keep in the refrigerator. Making a week's supply rather than a month's ensures you'll have fresh dressing, which is important for taste.
- **Try a squeeze of fresh lemon and lime juice or a tomato or fruit salsa as a salad dressing.**
- **Make a unique dressing by pureeing frozen berries or fruit, such as mangos and pa-**

payas, in a blender with fresh herbs and a little sugar (if you like your dressing sweet) or balsamic and red wine vinegar (if you like it savory).

Whether you are making salad for one or six, you can make a small amount of dressing go a long way by tossing the salad in a bowl before serving it on individual plates. How much is enough? About 2 teaspoons per serving is usually just right.

Select Lean Meats instead of Higher-Fat Ones

Which portion of meat has less fat and cholesterol: 3 ounces of eye-of-round beef steak or 3 ounces of 90 percent lean ground turkey? Most folks would say the ground turkey. In fact the eye-of-round steak has less fat and cholesterol than the ground turkey.

Identifying which meats are high in fat is a challenge for most people, which this example illustrates. Supermarkets usually sell meat by price per pound, not by nutrient content. And words like *lean* or *extra-lean* and percentages of fat content can be misleading. So you need to know which cuts of meat are the leanest, and then enjoy all protein sources within moderation. Check out the introduction to Chapter 7 for a handy checklist.

Use Beans, Tofu, Tempeh, and Lentils instead of Meat

One way to cut back on cholesterol and fat is to enjoy meatless meals or to use less meat in some favorite recipes. One-dish meals such as stews, casseroles, chilies, and soups offer a great place to make some hearty, tasty modifications. Try a meatless chili made with three or four different kinds of beans and your favorite one-or three-alarm seasonings. If a little meat is a must, use a little 97 percent lean ground turkey or thin strips of round steak in addition to the beans. The same approach works for stews and casseroles. Tofu and tempeh, another soy product, adapt well in vegetable soups or in pasta dishes such as vegetable lasagna. And of course, try the tempting vegetarian entrées and sides contributed to this book by our chefs.

Use Low-Fat or Nonfat Yogurt, Sour Cream, or Cream Cheese instead of Their Full-Fat Counterparts

Do you always take your special curried sour cream and crab dip to parties? Do you love pasta with creamy sauces? Well, you may be able to keep your favorite dish and just modify the dairy fat that it uses. In many recipes that call for sour cream or cream cheese, the nonfat version works well. And if it doesn't, the reduced fat version almost always does. In many recipes calling for sour cream, you may also substitute nonfat yogurt. For example, in a dish such as beef stroganoff (made with a lean beef), yogurt makes a tangy sauce.

Are you tired of always pairing your noodles with marinara sauce? Here's a creamy delicious white sauce that you can combine with low-fat cheese, canned clams, steamed shrimp, steamed vegetables, or fresh herbs—wherever your culinary creativity takes you. Then toss it on pasta—and enjoy guilt-free.

Low-Fat Creamy White Sauce

Tools: *Nonstick saucepan, whisk, small bowl*
Preparation time: *5 minutes*
Cooking time: *10 minutes*
Yield: *2 1/4 cups*
2 1/4 cups milk
4 tablespoons instant potato flakes
2 tablespoons flour
1/2 cup low-fat, low-sodium chicken broth
Pinch of minced fresh parsley, dill, or chopped scallions
Salt and pepper to taste

1 Heat 2 cups of the skim milk over medium heat in a nonstick saucepan. When bubbles appear

around the edge of the pan indicating the milk is warm, whisk in the potato flakes.

2 In a small bowl, combine the remaining 1/4 cup milk with the flour, whisking until smooth, and then whisk the milk-flour mixture into the milk-potato flake mixture.

3 Add the chicken broth and spices, and cook an additional 2 minutes or until thickened.

4 Toss in fresh herbs. Add salt and pepper to taste.

5 Pour over pasta, and top with steamed vegetables.

Nutrition at a glance (per 1/2 cup serving): *total fat 0.4g; saturated fat 0.2g; protein 5g; dietary fiber 0g; carbohydrate 11g; cholesterol 2mg; sodium 119mg; percent of calories from fat 5.5; percent of calories from saturated fat 2.6; calories 69*

***

If desired, you can fold in crab, steamed shrimp, or minced clams, or 1/4 cup freshly grated Parmesan or other lower fat cheese to end up with different varieties of this tasty sauce.

Use Homemade Stocks instead of Canned Stocks

Most canned stocks (and cubes or granules) you find in your local supermarket are high in sodium. Although some low-sodium stocks are available, none can have the flavorful intensity of a good homemade stock. Store-bought low-sodium stock has little variety, either—in my market you can have any flavor you like as long as it's chicken. So get in the habit of making your own stock whenever you can; you'll really enjoy the contribution a good stock can make to sauces, soups, and other dishes. If you've never made a stock, consult any basic cookbook for a recipe. We recommend *Cooking For Dummies,* 2nd Edition.

Use Buttermilk, Condensed Skim Milk, or Soy Milk instead of Cream or Half-and-Half

For a rich, creamy flavor and consistency in a soup or sauce, blend your homemade (or store-bought) stock with evaporated skim milk, soy milk, or buttermilk. Buttermilk can really liven up the flavor of a soup's contents. For 1 cup of soup try 1 tablespoon to start. If that's not enough, add another tablespoon. For thick, luscious cream soups, you can puree vegetables such as potatoes, sweet potatoes, pumpkin, or beans in a food processor or blender, then thin them with condensed skim milk or soy milk and/or stock.

Chapter 19

Ten Simple Strategies for Lowering Your Cholesterol

In This Chapter

- Breaking the dietary fat and cholesterol connection
- Eating the right fats in the right amounts
- Tapping the power of mind-body connections

Cholesterol is a naturally occurring waxy substance present in human beings and all other animals. As I discuss in Chapter 2, cholesterol is important for life, but having too much in your bloodstream increases your risk of developing heart disease. The more elevated your cholesterol levels, the greater your risk. So you want to work to keep your overall cholesterol level as low as possible (under 200mg/dl is optimal) and keep your good HDLs *high* and your bad LDLs *low* This chapter shares ten strategies that can help you achieve those goals.

Reduce the Amount of Saturated Fat You Consume

Reducing the amount of saturated fat you consume is the most important dietary change you can make to help reduce your cholesterol level and reduce your risk of heart disease. Saturated fat is found in animal products and in some vegetable products, such as coconut oil, palm kernel oil, and palm oil. Many packaged cookies and crackers contain these harmful tropical oils. You can think *s* for *saturated* and *solid,* because saturated fat is usually found in solid form at room temperature (butter, chocolate, and cheese are all examples of foods high in saturated fat). The more saturated fat in your diet, the more bad cholesterol (LDL) your body makes. To reduce the amount of saturated fat in your diet, switch to lower-fat dairy products, use margarine instead of butter, and choose leaner meats (for example, 93 percent lean ground beef instead of 85 percent lean ground beef). Following the eating plan illustrated by the Food Guide Pyramid will enable you to achieve the recommended goal of consuming less than 10 percent of total calories from saturated fat. All the recipes in this book (with the exception of several in Chapter 10) also contain less than 10 percent saturated fat.

Limit Your Intake of Cholesterol

Because our bodies make all the cholesterol we need, any cholesterol coming from our diet is extra. The American Heart Association and other nutrition groups recommend that you not exceed a daily amount of 300 milligrams. Good ways to achieve this goal include limiting your total intake of meat to 6 ounces a day and choosing lower-fat dairy products. And what about eggs—a well known source of cholesterol with 215 milligrams per yolk? Does this mean one egg per day is the limit? Not necessarily. The American Heart Association recommends limiting egg yolk intake to 4 per week. Egg whites and egg substitutes are cholesterol-free, so if you love egg dishes, use these in place of whole eggs. Two egg whites or 1/4 cup egg substitute are equal to one large egg.

Reduce the Amount of Calories in Your Diet That Come from Fat

Total fat, along with saturated fat and cholesterol, is part of the heart disease puzzle. That's because too much total fat may raise blood pressure and lead to weight gain and obesity, both risk factors for heart disease. ***Remember:*** A fat gram has twice as many calories as a protein or carbohydrate gram (9 calories in 1 gram of fat, compared to 4 calories in 1 gram of protein or carbohydrate).

So your goal is to consume no more than 30 percent of your daily calorie needs as fat. How many fat grams is that?

Because different people can consume different amounts of fat grams depending on the number of calories required to meet their daily energy needs, figure yours this way. Determine your daily calorie needs using the formula I give you in Chapter 2. Multiply that number by 0.3 (30 percent), then divide by 9 (the calories in a fat gram) to determine your daily maximum total fat grams. If you need 2,000 calories daily, for example, 30 percent of 2,000 calories (0.3X2,000) is 600 calories or approximately 65 to 66 fat grams (600/9=66).

Select Most of Your Fat Intake from Monounsaturated Fats

What do olive oil, canola oil, nuts, seeds, and avocado have in common? They are all wonderful sources of monounsaturated fats. Numerous studies have indicated that monounsaturated fats increase the HDL cholesterol—the good cholesterol that helps get rid of the slow, sludgy LDL cholesterol particles that collect inside your arteries. Selecting monounsaturated or polyunsaturated fats while watching out for saturated fats will surely help protect against heart disease as well as improve cholesterol levels.

Use New Types of Margarine to Lower Your Cholesterol

Does this tip sound too good to be true after everything we've said about lowering your fat intake? Thanks to two new products, Benecol Spread and Take Control Spread, using margarine as part of your daily diet may help lower your cholesterol level. Benecol Spread contains a substance derived from pine trees that inhibits the absorption of cholesterol in the gut. Take Control Spread contains a substance from soybeans that also inhibits cholesterol absorption. To reap the benefits of these margarines, you need to eat three servings each day. You can also find these cholesterol-lowering substances in salad dressings and other products (such as yogurt) in your local supermarket. For more information on these spreads and other products that contain them, visit their Web sites at www.benecol.com and www.takecontrol.com.

Exercise Every Day

A sedentary lifestyle is a strong and established risk factor for coronary artery disease. The good news is that increased physical activity not only will lower your overall risk for coronary artery disease, but it will also help control your cholesterol level. Regular aerobic activity of 30 to 60 minutes daily has been shown to increase HDL cholesterol, which, in turn, is associated with decreased risk of heart disease. Even moderately intense physical activity, such as brisk walking, can raise HDL cholesterol.

If you are short on ideas of how to begin or what to do, consult the companion book to this one, *The Healthy Heart For Dummies* (published by IDG Books and written by yours truly). In it, I show you how to evaluate your current level of fitness and create a personal plan for more activity. I even provide a flexible walking program in the book. Of course, if you have been very sedentary or already have established coronary artery disease, checking with your physician before starting a program of increased physical activity is essential.

Eat at Least Five Servings of Fruits and Vegetables Every Day

Am I beginning to sound like a broken record? Maybe so, but I can't say enough good things about fruits and vegetables. They provide so many different vitamins and minerals that the body needs. They are also full of phytochemicals that fight the free radicals that may help damage artery cell walls, enabling the buildup of cholesterol deposits in your arteries. Fruits and vegetables are also rich sources of soluble fiber (which also helps control cholesterol) and insoluble fiber (which helps regulate digestion).

Increase Your Intake of Fiber

Numerous studies have shown that eating foods that are high in fiber can greatly decrease the risk of heart attack. Although scientific research has not yet revealed exactly how the process works, *soluble fiber* helps to reduce cholesterol levels. Even though fiber is good for us, the average American consumes only 7 to 10 grams of fiber a day. That's not even close to the 25 to 30 grams recommended every day. Good sources of soluble fiber include whole oat cereals such as Cheerios; oatmeal; whole grain oats; dry beans and peas; barley; citrus fruits; apples; other fresh fruits; and corn.

Avoid Eating Out Daily

If you dine out often, keeping your total fat and saturated fat levels down can be very difficult. Whether you choose a fast-food drive-thru or a sit-down, chic café, you often may have a tough time steering around a meal containing at least 50 percent if not 75 percent of your total fat grams for the day. That puts a real bind on what you eat for the rest of the day if you want to stay in balance. If you must eat out often, because of business appointments or travel, then you may want to emphasize brown bagging lunches and preparing tasty, heart-smart dinners at home when you're not on the run.

Sidestep Stress

Although no studies scientifically prove that stress can directly increase your cholesterol levels, stress *can* trigger an excessive intake of food, especially high-fat, non-nutritive snacks, which in turn affects your cholesterol level. And, as I've said often, high fat, high salt, high calories, and low nutrients set you up for cardiovascular disaster. You can use strategies other than overeating comfort food to help control stress in your life:

- **Modify any lifestyle practices or habits that may contribute to stress.** Cut back on caffeine-containing beverages, such as coffee, tea, and many soft drinks, for example, and make sure to get a good night's sleep.
- **Live in the present.** It may sound simple, but many people spend an inordinate amount of time either regretting the past or fearing the future. Strategies such as biofeedback, visualization, and meditation can help you live in the present and substantially lower stress. Just taking time each day to go for a walk, take a nap, or put your feet up for ten minutes with the phone shut off can help.

Chapter 20

Ten Ways to Teach Your Children Healthy-Heart Habits

In This Chapter

- Involving your children in heart-healthy food selection and preparation
- Choosing the healthiest beverages for your children
- Finding heart-healthy meals for your children at restaurants

The earlier a child develops healthy lifestyle habits, the less likely he or she is to develop heart disease later in life. As a parent, you can help reduce your children's risk of heart disease by teaching them these good habits from the time they are toddlers. The ten strategies in this chapter provide a framework for action—and fun.

Model Healthy-Heart Habits for Your Children

Children start learning the day they are born. Your heart-healthy habits and behaviors encourage your children to pick up the same good habits. On the other hand, if you lounge on the couch munching nachos and chips, letting your arteries harden as you watch TV, your children will probably do the same. So take a few moments to think about the behaviors you're modeling for your kids. Which are good? Which should you target for change to help improve your health *and* the health of your children?

Cook with Your Kids

Bring out the Julia Child in *your* child. Being able to cook is a *very* valuable skill when it comes to eating well and eating a heart-healthy diet. If you can cook, teach your kids what you know. If you're just learning how to cook, learn with your children. That way, your children won't reach adulthood thinking that everyday dinners come from a box (macaroni-and-cheese, hamburger-and-noodle casserole, and so on) and that takeout pizza is haute cuisine. You'll eat better, too. If you want to read more about including your kids in the kitchen, check out *Cooking with Kids For Dummies* by Kate Heyhoe (published by IDG Books Worldwide, Inc.) for some great suggestions.

Spend Quality Time at the Market with Your Children

Great heart-healthy cooking begins with choosing heart-healthy recipes and ingredients at the market. Having your children help with the shopping can spark their interest in healthy foods and cooking and give them a sense of ownership that may encourage them to be more adventurous eaters. Start by letting your children look for healthy recipes in magazines and newspapers (or this book!) that they would like to try. Then help them hunt for the ingredients for "their recipe" in the supermarket. If you're shopping at a farmer's market, encourage your children to ask the growers questions. Interesting information about how foods are grown or cooking tips may further whet your child's appetite for learning ... and for the dish!

Make Mealtime Family Time

Research shows that children (and adults) who eat regular meals and snacks, rather than snacking nonstop, eat more healthful diets. Standard mealtimes with a definite meal pattern give your children a sense of security and help them learn by example how to plan healthy meals. Although it's difficult, try to get your family to sit down together for at least one meal every day (even if it's only breakfast some days). Eating together gives you an opportunity to learn more about what's happening in each other's lives. Create an environment of comfortable, open communication. Really talk with your children. This way your children learn to associate meals with a relaxing environment, interesting conversation, and the enjoyment of good food.

"Cooking coupons"

As part of, or in addition to, an allowance, consider giving your kids "cooking coupons" for kid-friendly recipe books, fun kitchen gadgets (such as pint-size rolling pins), or new ingredients and foods to try (such as exotic fruits or a fish they pick out themselves). The coupons give kids an opportunity to exercise their buying power for useful, healthful items rather than trendy toys that soon lose their appeal.

Encourage Heart-Healthy Snacking

Snacks are very important for children, because they have little bellies that need frequent feeding. Snacks relieve hunger that often develops between meals, and healthy snacks can provide essential nutrients that your growing children need more of, such as calcium and iron. Just be sure to keep snacks small so that they don't take the place of meals, which often provide essential nutrients not found in snacks as well as essential socialization time with the whole family.

To encourage your children to choose healthy snacks, keep on hand a wide variety of fruits, cut-up vegetables, yogurt, whole grain crackers and cereal, and only a few, if any, sodas, cookies, or candies. Research shows that if kids are presented with a wide variety of healthy foods and a limited variety of "junk" food, over time they will be more likely to choose the healthy foods most often.

Rethink That Drink

- **Low-fat milk.** Growing children need the bone-building nutrients in milk. After age 3, children will get more of the nutrients they need from skim or 1 percent milk than from 2 percent or whole milk (skim and 1 percent have more calcium). Skim and 1 percent milk also contain little or no saturated fat and cholesterol, which makes them great heart-healthy beverages. Under 2 years of age, children should drink *whole milk,* because they need the fat for brain development.

• **Juices.** Stick with 100 percent juice products that are rich in essential vitamins, minerals, and heart-healthy antioxidant nutrients. One hundred percent juice products with added vitamin C or calcium are even better choices. Because many children prefer juice to other essential beverages such as milk and water, experts recommend limiting juice intake to 4 to 8 ounces per day, depending on the age of the child.

• **Water.** Most Americans don't drink adequate water for proper hydration. Our bodies may be fueled by food, but whereas you can go a fairly long time without food, water is so vital that only a few days without it is fatal. The more you learn to enjoy water as a child, the more likely you are to continue drinking plenty of water as an adult.

Use Your Sense of Humor to Encourage Healthy Eating

Playing with your food is a time-honored tradition. You can also have some intellectual fun with the serious business of healthy eating. Some parents create stories around healthy eating and physical activity to teach heart-healthy habits. One set of children I know can't resist their mother's challenge of besting "The Germ and His Gang of Health Robbers" by drinking their orange juice and eating their vegetables. They laugh at the silliness, but they get the message and even share it with their friends and cousins.

What about picky eaters? Experts recommend that instead of getting upset with a picky toddler or young child, you should have fun with the situation. Do you remember the *Calvin and Hobbes* comic strip in which Calvin is suspiciously eyeing a new dish? His first response to the mysterious dish (stuffed green peppers) is "Gross, what's that!" "Stuffed monkey heads," says Calvin's father. What a splendidly outrageous dish! Calvin eagerly gobbles up his dinner while excitedly contemplating his incredible luck.

Drop That Kids' Menu!

At most restaurants the children's menus contain few, if any, healthy foods. But that doesn't have to stop your children from getting healthy food in restaurants. If the kids' menu at a family-style restaurant, as typical, features everything fried (corn dog, chicken nuggets, French fries, and so on), go to the regular menu for better choices. Order a more healthful item such as a grilled chicken sandwich or plain spaghetti. Help your child build a healthy, kid-pleasing "monster" salad from the salad bar. Split a healthy adult entrée with your child; the generous portions at most restaurants make this an easy and smart option for everyone.

Make F.I.T. (Fitness Instead of Television) Your Family Motto

How many days have you rented movies when it was an absolutely gorgeous day outside? Or how often have your kids wanted to play video games instead of playing outside? Is your family spending more time watching TV than being physically active? No, don't ditch the TV set. Just engage in more family-oriented physical activities that are fun and good for your heart and soul. Go for family bike rides, hikes, or even just window-shopping to get moving around. Wrestle on the freshly cut grass with your children. Chase the dog around the yard until you all fall on the lawn laughing. It doesn't matter what activity you choose, as long as everyone involved enjoys it

Discourage Dieting

Nutrition experts agree: Dieting is not appropriate for growing children or teenagers. If you think your child may be overweight and you're concerned about the health effects, have a health professional assess your child's weight. Many children gain weight before gaining height and a sudden increase in weight may soon be followed by a spurt in height that balances the weight gain. Limiting the caloric intake of a growing child limits his or her ability to reach full growth potential. Instead of dieting, encourage physical activity, which helps improve coordination and cardiovascular health and provides the best way to combat weight problems at any age.

Chapter 21

Ten Essential Kitchen Tools for Healthy-Heart Cooking

In This Chapter

- Tools for preserving valuable nutrients in vegetables
- Grilling your way to a healthy heart
- Tools for saving prep time in the kitchen

Out of the staggering array of kitchen equipment available to the home O cook, what do you really need? To help you differentiate between essential and excessive, here's a list of ten pieces of equipment that you will find very useful in your kitchen if you're serious about heart-healthy cooking.

Sauté Pan

If you invest in only one piece of heart-healthy kitchen equipment, make it a nonstick sauté pan of at least 10 or 12 inches. Buy a high-quality pan with a commercial-quality, durable, nonstick interior that allows you to cook with little or no added oil. You'll be surprised at how little added oil you'll need to sauté, especially if you've been using a regular stainless-steel-bottom skillet in which food can easily stick without copious amounts of oil.

Blender

Whether you're emulsifying an oil-in-vinegar salad dressing or pureeing potato soup, a blender makes the task fast and easy. A number of companies make blenders in various styles (contemporary versus retro), colors (from white to silver), and speeds (from two to twenty). If you plan to use the blender simply to finish sauces and soups, make smoothies, or emulsify dressings, all you need is a basic machine. More challenging tasks, such as making crushed ice for the bed of a seafood serving platter, require a top-of-the-line, commercial-quality blender.

One other factor to consider is whether to get a blender with a plastic, glass, or stainless steel container. Plastic containers are lighter and easier to handle but are more likely to absorb flavors from their contents. If you plan to use your blender to puree flavorful sauces, prepare marinades, or emulsify garlic dressings, get a blender with a glass or stainless steel container.

Grill

Just how heart-healthy is grilling as a cooking technique? Flip to the front of this book and run your finger down the list of "Recipes at a Glance." You'll see that grilling is a favorite of the chefs who contributed to this book. In fact, grilling gets two thumbs up from both chefs and health professionals because of its versatility and health benefits. Grilling is an especially healthful way to cook meats, because a grated surface allows fat to drip away from the surface of the food instead of being reabsorbed.

If you have a garden or patio appropriate for an outdoor grill, choose a gas grill if you want fast, convenient, and predictable. Gas grills heat up quickly and allow you to control the intensity of the flame by turning a knob. If you want the smoky flavor of authentic barbecue, get a charcoal grill. Even if you own an outdoor grill, I recommend you have a heavy-gauge grill pan. Basically a grill pan looks like a sauté or frying pan except the bottom is ridged instead of flat and costs about the same.

To discover more about grilling and to get more great grill recipes, pick up a copy of *Grilling For*

Dummies by Marie Rama and John Mariani (IDG Books Worldwide, Inc.).

Steamer

Steaming is superior to boiling when it comes to cooking vegetables because water-soluble vitamins and minerals don't leach into the cooking water. You have several options:

- **Steamer basket:** A collapsible steamer basket is a small stainless steel basket with collapsible walls that fits in the bottom of any pan with a cover. Simply place about 1 inch of water in the bottom of your pan, place your vegetables in the basket, cover the pan, and cook over medium to high heat until your vegetables are the desired tenderness. Steamer baskets are very economical, costing only a few dollars.
- **Stockpot with steamer insert:** If you need a stockpot for making soups, stocks, and cooking large quantities of pasta, I'd select this option. But if you already own a number of stockpots, go with the inexpensive steamer basket above.
- **Bamboo steamer:** Some folks swear by their inexpensive bamboo steamers, standbys in Asian cookery. Like a steamer basket, these are set over water in a wok or large sauté pan. Vegetables, dumplings, fish, or other items to be steamed are placed on small plates (or other liner such as a cabbage leaf) and set within the basket. An advantage to the bamboo steamer

is that you can stack baskets to steam more than one dish at a time.

Non-Aerosol Oil Sprayer

Spraying olive or vegetable oil rather than pouring it into the cooking pan saves a lot of calories from fat. One of the criticisms of commercially available cooking sprays is that they are off-flavor. To avoid this perceived problem, buy a non-aerosol oil sprayer that you can fill with any type of oil you choose. Use canola oil when you don't want added flavor and olive oil or herb-infused oils when you want a lot of flavor. Non-aerosol oil sprayers can be found at kitchen supply stores, home stores, and department stores. All brands come with instructions even the novice chef can follow easily.

Mini Food Processor

A mini food processor can perform a number of time-consuming tasks. For instance, if you use a lot of fresh ingredients for flavor such as garlic and fresh herbs, simply drop the ingredients in the mini food processor and seconds later very finely chopped garlic or herbs are ready to drop into a soup or sauce at the last moment. Or, when you're cooking for one or two, you can puree small amounts of sauce without having to perform magic to coax small amounts of sauce out from the bottom of a blender. For a few dollars, you can have a kitchen helper that won't demand a raise in its allowance every time you ask it to help.

Kitchen Scale

A kitchen scale lets you judge the weight on an amount of food very accurately, which can be a great help if you are trying to lose weight or maintain a healthy weight. But the primary reason I recommend a kitchen scale for everyone is for weighing meat portions. Most folks are accustomed to eating far more than the recommended total daily intake of 6 ounces of cooked meat, fish, or poultry, a practice that's important for controlling your intake of dietary cholesterol. For simplicity's sake, I recommend you weigh meat, fish, or poultry portions prior to cooking or marinating. Just remember to practice safe food handling techniques when handling raw meat, fish, or poultry. Wash your hands well with warm, soapy water before handling other foods and wash the scale in warm, soapy water before weighing any other foods as well.

Pepper Grinder

No professional chef worth his or her reputation would ever use stale ground black pepper and neither should you. Ground pepper loses its flavor very quickly when exposed to air. When you see black pepper called for in this cookbook, the chefs intend for you to use *freshly ground* black pepper. A handheld pepper grinder can grind peppercorns for you in seconds. Look for a beautiful yet functional pepper grinder that can go from your stovetop to tabletop so your family and guests can grind to their heart's delight, too! You can find them for a few dollars.

Basket or Platter

If you're trying to include more fruits and vegetables in your diet, consider placing a beautiful platter or basket on your kitchen counter to fill with fresh fruits. When a variety of ripe fruit is in plain view, you're much more likely to grab a piece for a convenient snack than if the fruit is hiding in the produce drawer of your refrigerator. Whether you choose a basic basket or an exquisite hand-painted platter, a beautiful still life of fresh fruit nestled together is a work of art that is good for the heart and soul.

Hot Air Popcorn Popper

For the quickest and best heart-healthy snack at home, place some popcorn in a hot air popper and, in two minutes, out pops a very low-fat, high-fiber snack that satisfies your desire to munch and crunch. Hot air poppers are easy to locate and are relatively inexpensive. If you look at the money you'll save by no longer buying low-fat microwave popcorn, a hot air popper will pay for itself in a couple of months.

Appendix

Resources

Whether you live in the heart of the city or ten miles from your nearest neighbor, if you have a computer wired to the Internet, you have access to a vast amount of information on food, nutrition, and heart health as well as thousands of recipes. With a click of the mouse (or often a toll-free call, if you prefer), you can also find specialty ingredients and equipment that are unlikely to appear in local markets. And don't forget the library and bookstores. There are good print resources, too, to help in your quest for delicious, heart-healthy eating and a healthy lifestyle.

Web Sites

To give you a place to start in selecting from hundreds of online resources, here are some sites that my team and I find useful. When available, we also provide phone numbers, in case you prefer to speak to a customer service representative.

Food and nutrition

For recipes, food facts, and hot topics check out these sites:

- **The American Dietetic Association,** www.eatright.org

Find the "official word" at this site as well as accurate, consumer-friendly information. You can also use the site to find a registered dietitian in your community.

• ***Cooking Light* Magazine,** www.cookinglight.com

If you're looking for mouth-watering recipes and up-to-date information on food and healthy living, click onto this site. Browse through thousands of *Cooking Light* recipes, and use the Clueless Gourmet or Cooking 101 for step-by-step guides to various cooking techniques.

• **Epicurious Food,** www.epicurious.com

Search more than 10,000 recipes and more than 950 beverages, plus see monthly recipes additions from *Gourmet* and *Bon Appetit* magazines. If you don't recall the name of the recipe, simply plug in one or two ingredients and a list will be provided for you. There's also a food and wine dictionary that defines more than 4,200 ingredients, dishes, and phrases as well as the chef finder, a database of 850 restaurants and top chefs.

• **FATFREE: The Low Fat Vegetarian Recipe Archive,** www.fatfree.com

This site offers about 2,500 meatless, low-fat recipes. Because the recipes are contributed by individuals, there's no guarantee that every recipe will work equally well. But you'll find lots of good ideas. A great bonus is that this Web site has an easy-to-use interface with the United States Department of Agriculture's Nutritional Analysis and Food Composition tables.

- **FoodTV,** www.foodtv.com

If you want to catch the latest about your favorite chefs and programs on Food TV, just click online to this site. You can get your very own printout of your favorite recipes and more!

- **Meals For You,** www.mealsforyou.com

Use this site to custom-build meal plans quickly and to look up recipes by name, ingredient, or nutrition information. Recipes automatically adjust for number of servings. Plus, you can find shopping lists that itemize all ingredients for you.

- **Tufts University Nutrition Navigator: A Rating Guide to Nutrition Websites,** www.navigator.tufts.edu

This online rating and review guide is designed to help you sort through the large volume of nutrition information on the Internet and find accurate, useful nutrition information you can trust.

- **The Kitchen Link,** www.kitchenlink.com

The site provides an easy way to link to a number of food sites online. If you've just begun to explore what's out there, here's one place to start browsing.

Specialty ingredients and cooking equipment

So your local supermarket doesn't yet stock truffle oil? When you need a hard-to-find spice or ingredient or a special piece of cooking equipment, one of these sources probably has it. ***Remember:*** When considering the cost of a product, take into account any shipping fees.

- **Dean and Deluca,** www.deandeluca.com

A marketplace for fine culinary edibles and equipment, Dean and Deluca's Web site also offers tips on wine, entertaining, and the latest market trends in gourmet foods, beverages, and supplies. You can also order by phone at 316-838-1255 or (toll-free) at 877-826-9246.

- **Earthy Delights,** www.earthy.com

This online market bills itself as offering "the finest specialty produce for the adventurous home gourmet." Browsing this Web site is interesting and informative, even when you don't need a wild leek, a truffle, or some other specialty ingredient. You can also reach Earthy Delights by phone at 517-668-2402 or (toll-free) at 800-367-4709.

- **Spices Etc.,** www.spicesetc.com

For spices common and uncommon, not to mention 100 percent natural flavorings and such specialty items as dried wild mushrooms or lavender flowers, check out this Web site. Or give them a call (toll free) at 800-827-6373.

- **The Great American Spice Company,** www.americanspice.com

Another source for all kinds of herbs and spices in all sorts of quantities.

- **Flying Noodle,** www.flyingnoodle.com

Check out this site for noodles and sauces—Italian, Asian, gluten-free, whole wheat. A nutrition analysis guide for each product helps you stay within low-fat guidelines. You can order by phone, too, by calling 781-829-6879 or (toll-free) 800-566-0599.

• **Cooks Corner,** www.cookscorner.com

A chain of kitchenware stores, Cooks Corner offers a wide range of equipment in its online market. Order online or by phone (toll-free) at 800-236-2433.

• **Williams and Sonoma,** www.williams-sonoma.com

Here's another source for a wide variety of cookware, tableware, and some specialty ingredients. Order online or by phone (toll-free) at 800-541-2233.

A heart-healthy lifestyle

Heart health is about more than just eating right. The following Web sites offer good information about a wide range of fitness and health issues.

• **The National Heart, Lung, and Blood Institute,** www.nhlbi.nih.gov

Part of the National Institutes of Health, this site provides excellent information on many issues and conditions related to heart health.

•**American Heart Association,** www.americanheart.org

Up-to-date and accurate information about preventing and controlling heart disease and conditions associated with it.

• **Mayo Clinic,** www.mayohealth.org

• **Johns Hopkins Health Information:** www.intellihealth.com

• **MSN Health,** www.health.msn.com

These sites contain information or links to information on a wide range of health concerns: illnesses and conditions, diet and nutrition, fitness, relationships, insurance and legal matters, drug reference, and emotional resources, along with a reference library.

• **Doctor's Guide,** www.docguide.com

This site provides information services to help promote the informed and appropriate use of medicines by health care professionals and organizations as well as by the people to whom they are prescribed.

• **Rippe Lifestyle Institute,** www.rippelifestyle.com

For weekly tips and articles on healthy-heart lifestyle practices and issues and the latest research, visit the Web site of my very own Rippe Lifestyle Institute. We also post additional healthy-heart recipes on a regular basis, so check it out.

Further Reading

Too many good books and too little time, right? But here are just a handful that you may find helpful:

- *Almost Vegetarian: A Primer for Cooks Who Are Eating Vegetarian Most of* the *Time,* Chicken & Fish Some of the Time & Altogether Well All of the Time, by Diana Shaw (published by Crown)

- *The American Dietetic Association's Complete Food and Nutrition Guide,* by Roberta Larson Duyff, M.S., R.D., C.F.C.S. (published by John Wiley & Sons)
- *Being Vegetarian,* by Suzanne Havala (published by John Wiley & Sons)
- *Feeding Your Child for Lifelong Health: Birth through Age 6,* by Susan B. Roberts, Ph.D. and Melvin B. Heyman, M.D., with Lisa Tracy (published by Bantam Doubleday Dell)
- *Fit over Forty: A Revolutionary Plan to Achieve Lifelong Physical and Spiritual Health and Well-Being,* by James M. Rippe, M.D. (published by Quill)
- *Gourmet Cooking For Dummies,* by Charlie Trotter, with Judi Carle and Sarni Zernich (published by IDG Books Worldwide, Inc.)
- *The Healthy Heart For Dummies,* by James M. Rippe, M.D. (published by IDG Books Worldwide, Inc.)
- *Lowfat Cooking For Dummies,* by Lynn Fischer (IDG Books Worldwide, Inc.)
- *The New Food Lover's Companion: Comprehensive Definitions of Over 4,000 Food, Wine, and Culinary Terms,* by Sharon Tyler Herbst (published by Barrons Education Series)
- *Nutrition For Dummies,* by Carol Ann Rinzler (published by IDG Books Worldwide, Inc.)
- *The Tufts University Guide to Total Nutrition,* by Stanley Gershoff, Ph.D., with Catherine Whitney (published by HarperCollins)

Notes

[space left intentionally blank in the original book]

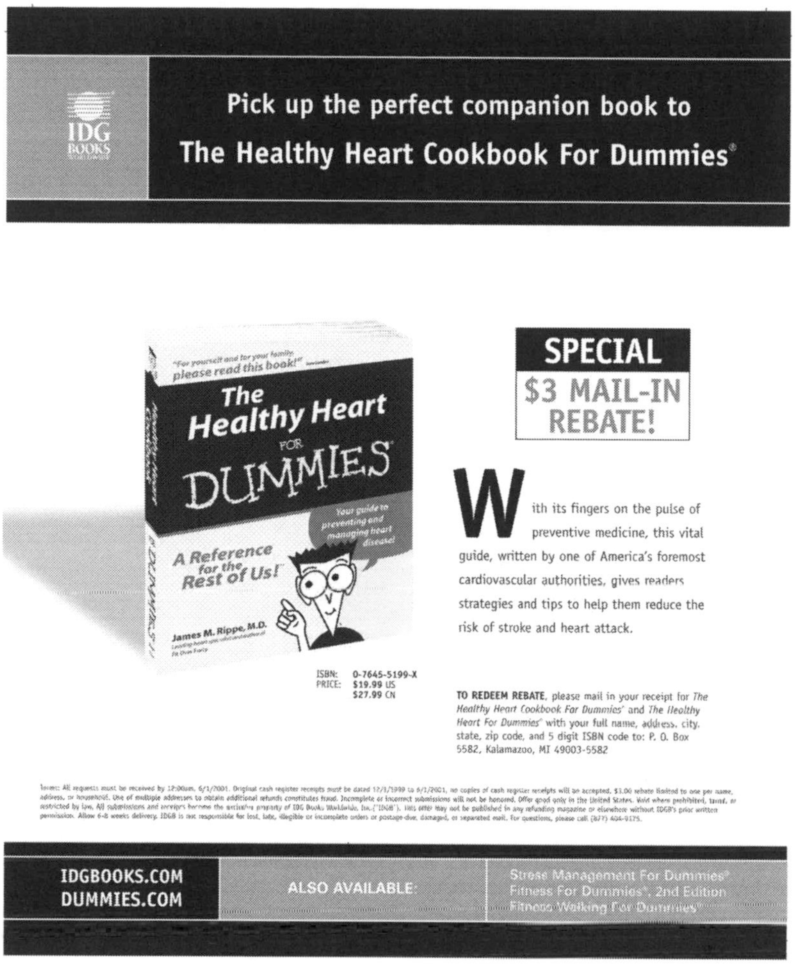
Pick up the perfect companion book to
The Healthy Heart Cookbook For Dummies®
SPECIAL
$3 MAIL-IN REBATE!
The Healthy Heart For Dummies
A Reference for the Rest of Us!
James M. Rippe, M.D.
With its fingers on the pulse of preventive medicine, this vital guide, written by one of America's foremost cardiovascular authorities, gives readers strategies and tips to help them reduce the risk of stroke and heart attack.
ISBN: 0-7645-5199-X
PRICE: $19.99 US
$27.99 CN
TO REDEEM REBATE, please mail in your receipt for The Healthy Heart Cookbook For Dummies® and The Healthy Heart For Dummies® with your full name, address, city, state, zip code, and 5 digit ISBN code to: P. O. Box 5582, Kalamazoo, MI 49003-5582
Terms: All requests must be received by 12:00am, 6/1/2001. Original cash register receipts must be dated 12/1/1999 to 6/1/2001, no copies of cash register receipts will be accepted. $3.00 rebate limited to one per name, address, or household. Use of multiple addresses to obtain additional refunds constitutes fraud. Incomplete or incorrect submissions will not be honored. Offer good only in the United States. Void where prohibited, taxed, or restricted by law. All submissions and receipts become the exclusive property of IDG Books Worldwide, Inc. ("IDGB"). This offer may not be published in any refunding magazine or elsewhere without IDGB's prior written permission. Allow 6-8 weeks delivery. IDGB is not responsible for lost, late, illegible or incomplete orders or postage-due, damaged, or separated mail. For questions, please call (877) 404-9175.
IDGBOOKS.COM
DUMMIES.COM
ALSO AVAILABLE:
Stress Management For Dummies®
Fitness For Dummies®, 2nd Edition
Fitness Walking For Dummies®

Image I

Image II

Discover Dummies Online!

The Dummies Web Site is your fun and friendly online resource for the latest information about *For Dummies*® books and your favorite topics. The Web site is the place to communicate with us, exchange ideas with other For Dummies readers, chat with authors, and have fun!

Ten Fun and Useful Things You Can Do atwww.dummies.com

1. Win free For Dummies books and more!
2. Register your book and be entered in a prize drawing.
3. Meet your favorite authors through the IDG Books Worldwide Author Chat Series.
4. Exchange helpful information with other For Dummies readers.
5. Discover other great For Dummies books you must have!
6. Purchase Dummieswear® exclusively from our Web site.
7. Buy For Dummies books online.
8. Talk to us. Make comments, ask questions, get answers!
9. Download free software.

10. Find additional useful resources from authors

Image III: For other technology titles from IDG Books Worldwide, go to www.idgbooks.com

Link directly to these ten fun and useful things at http://www.dummies.com/10useful

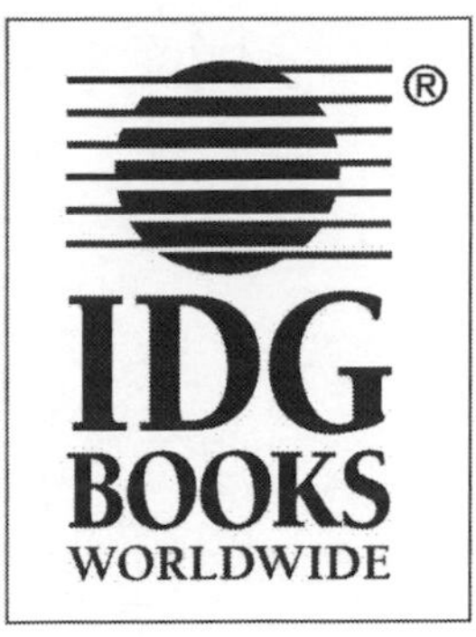

Image IV

IDG BOOKS WORLDWIDE BOOKS REGISTRATION

10475 Crosspoint Blvd.
Indianapolis, IN 46256

Image V

C

D

F

G

H

M

N

O

P

Q

R

S

T

U

V

W

Y

Z

Books For ALL Kinds of Readers

At ReadHowYouWant we understand that one size does not fit all types of readers. Our innovative, patent pending technology allows us to design new formats to make reading easier and more enjoyable for you. This helps improve your speed of reading and your comprehension. Our EasyRead printed books have been optimized to improve word recognition, ease eye tracking by adjusting word and line spacing as well as minimizing hyphenation. Our EasyRead SuperLarge editions have been developed to make reading easier and more accessible for vision-impaired readers. We offer Braille and DAISY formats of our books and all popular E-Book formats.

We are continually introducing new formats based upon research and reader preferences. Visit our web-site to see all of our formats and learn how you can Personalize our books for yourself or as gifts. Sign up to Become A RHYW Registered Reader.

www.readhowyouwant.com

Made in the USA
Lexington, KY
07 October 2011